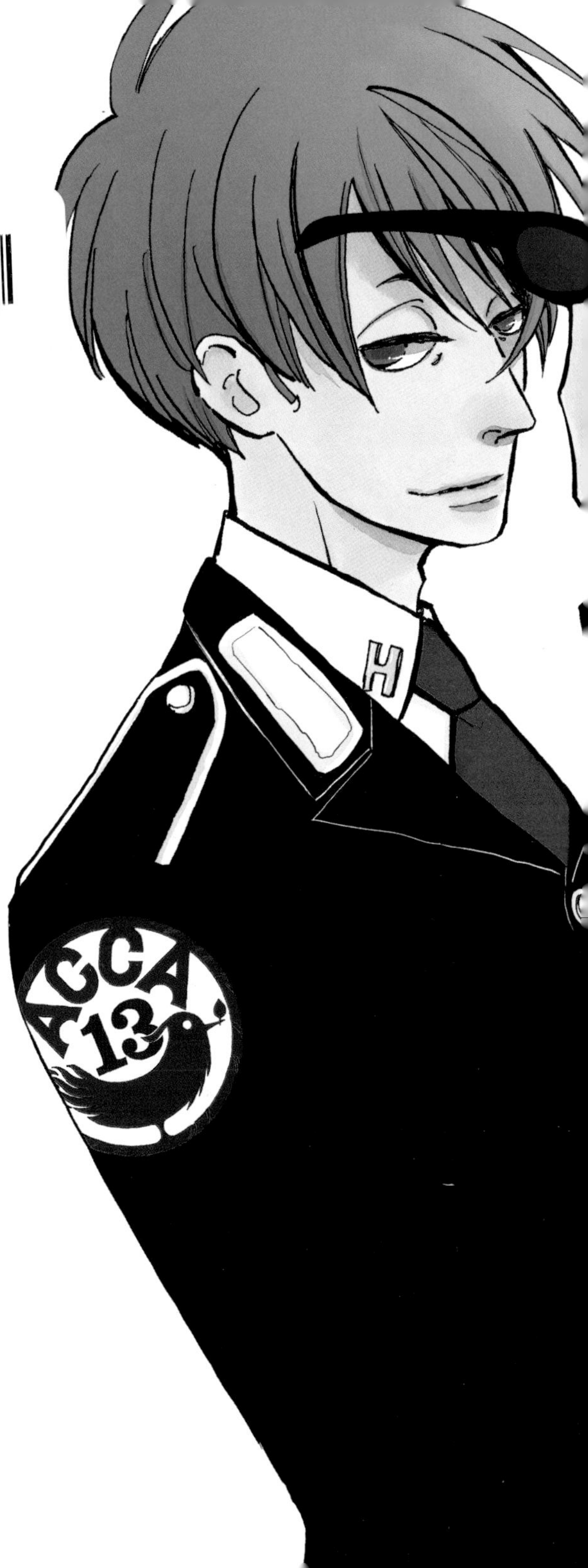
ACCA
13

ACCA 13

TERRITORY INSPECTION DEPARTMENT

NATSUME ONO

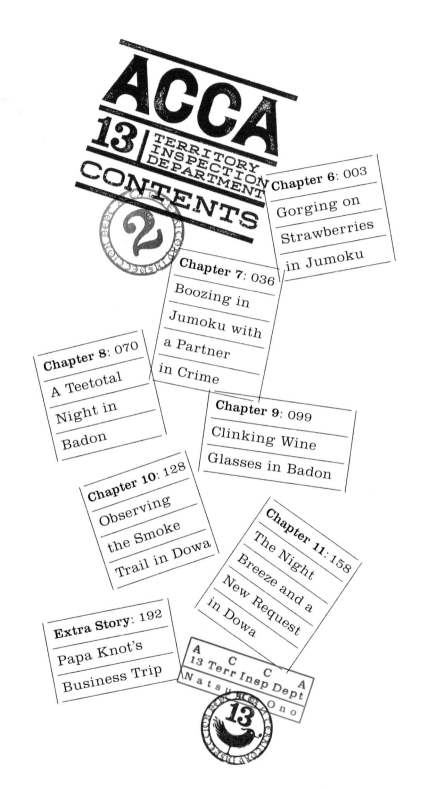

ACCA 13 TERRITORY INSPECTION DEPARTMENT

CONTENTS 2

A C C A
13 Terr Insp Dept
Natsume Ono

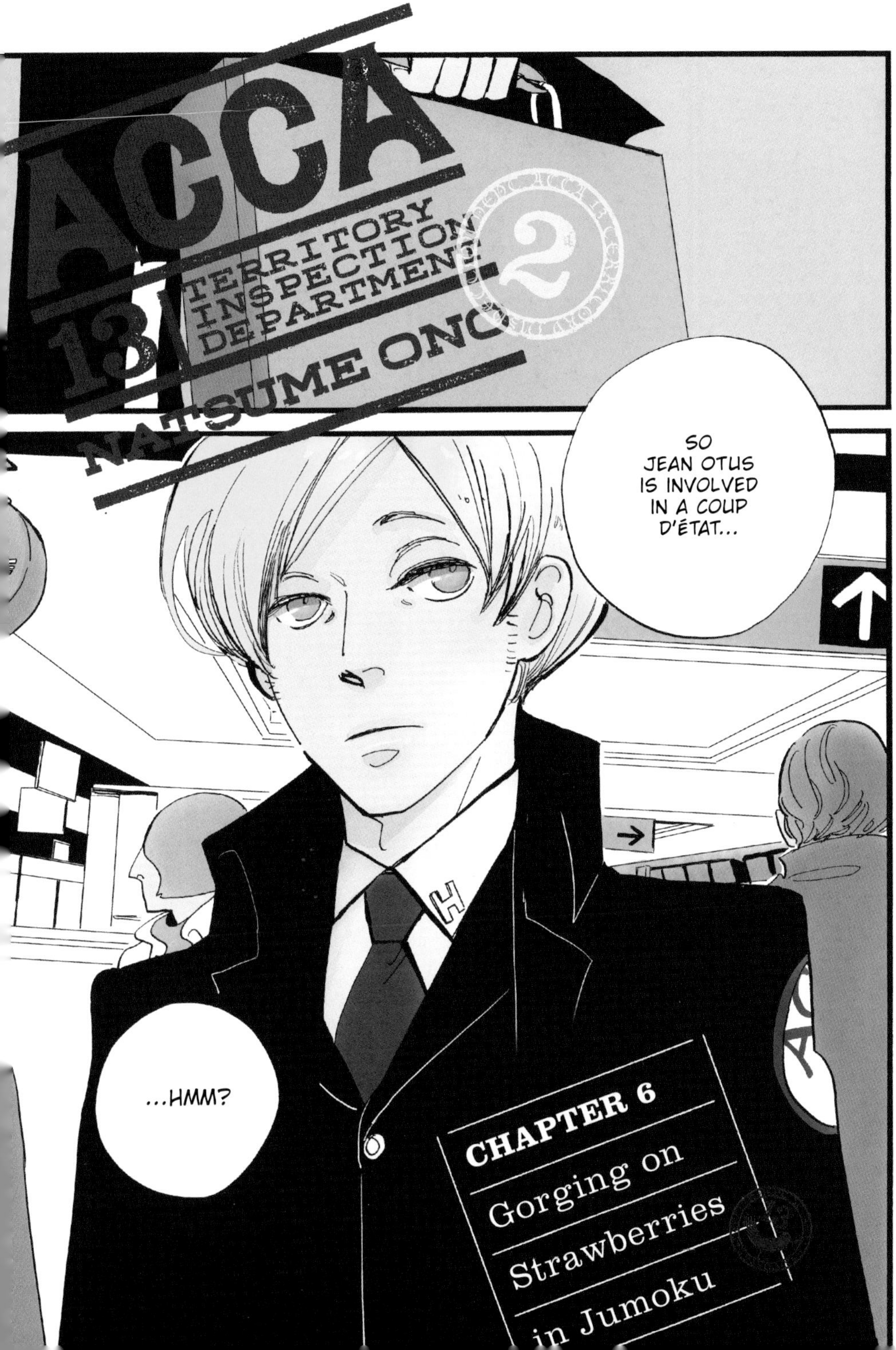
ACCA
13
TERRITORY
INSPECTION
DEPARTMENT
2
NATSUME ONO
SO JEAN OTUS IS INVOLVED IN A COUP D'ÉTAT...
...HMM?
CHAPTER 6
Gorging on Strawberries in Jumoku

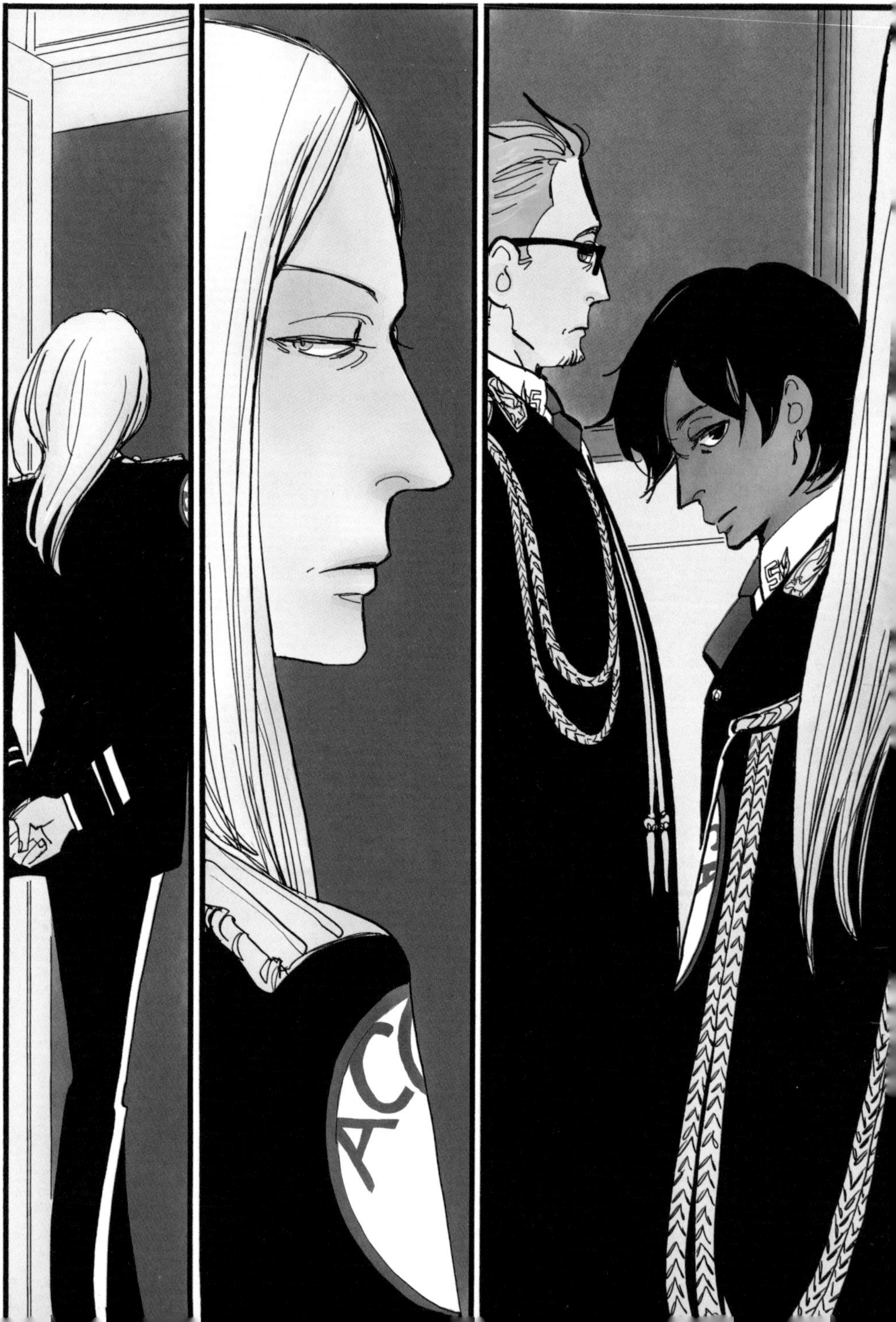

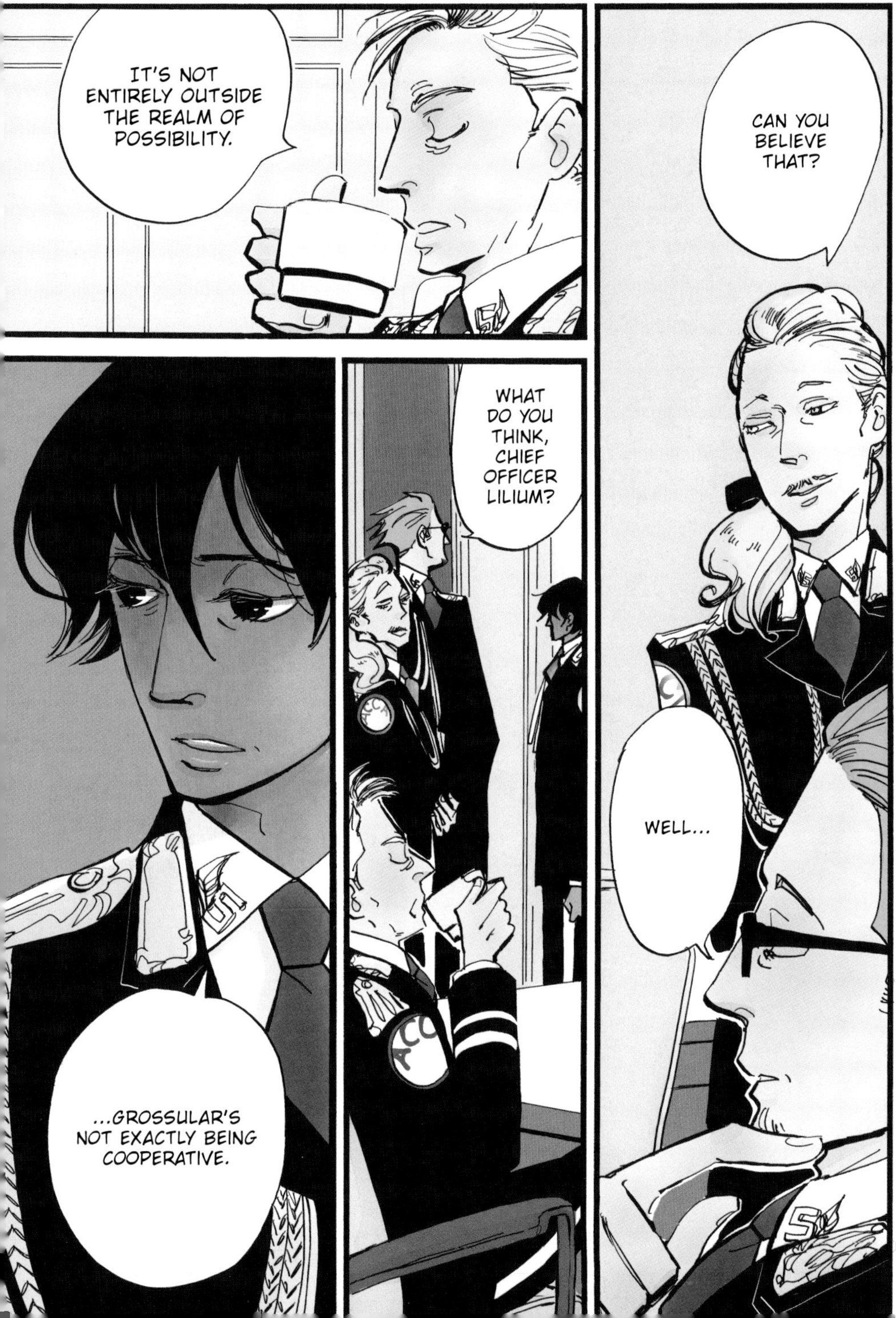
CAN YOU BELIEVE THAT?
WELL...
IT'S NOT ENTIRELY OUTSIDE THE REALM OF POSSIBILITY.
WHAT DO YOU THINK, CHIEF OFFICER LILIUM?
...GROSSULAR'S NOT EXACTLY BEING COOPERATIVE.

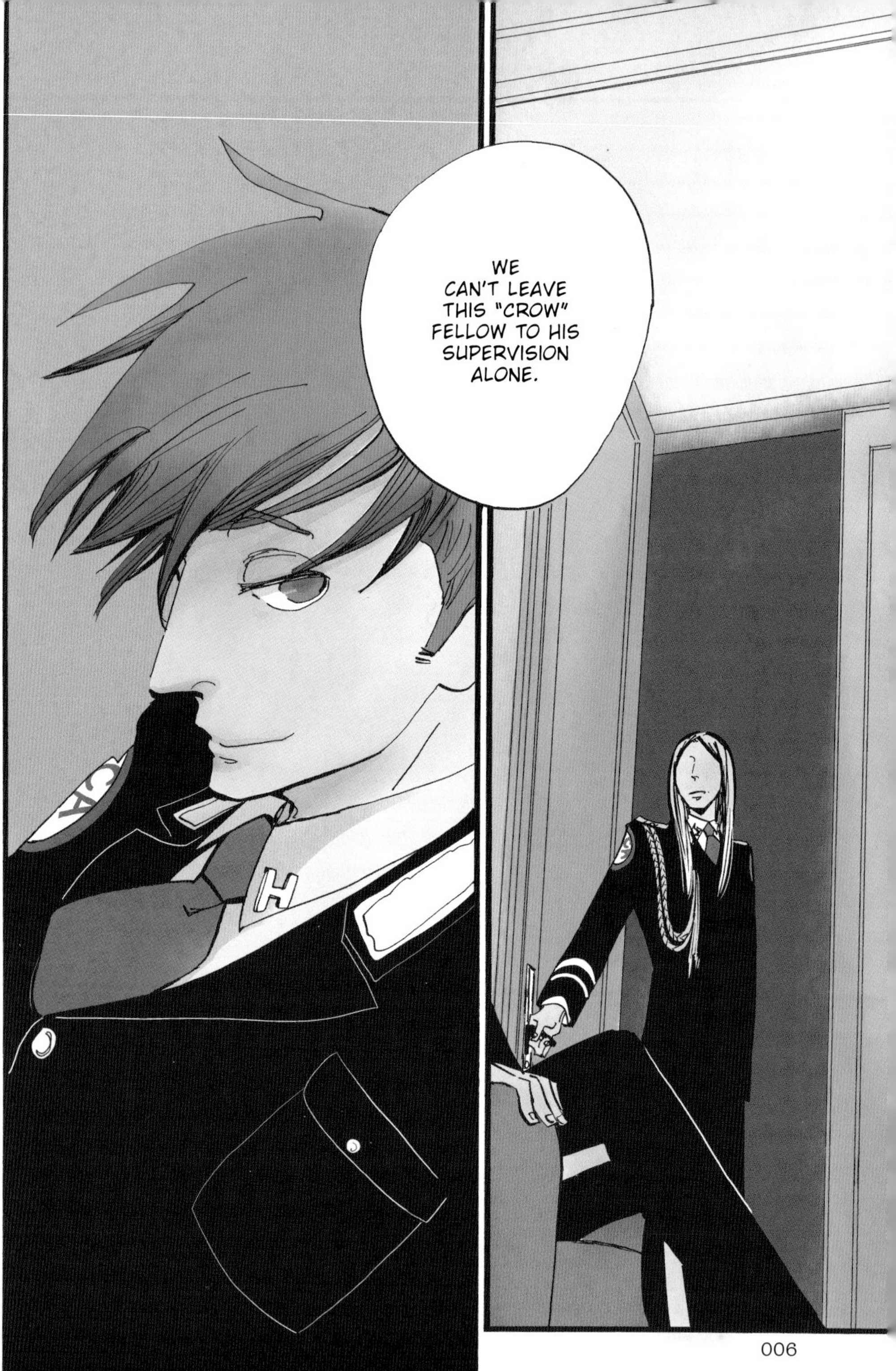
WE CAN'T LEAVE THIS "CROW" FELLOW TO HIS SUPERVISION ALONE.

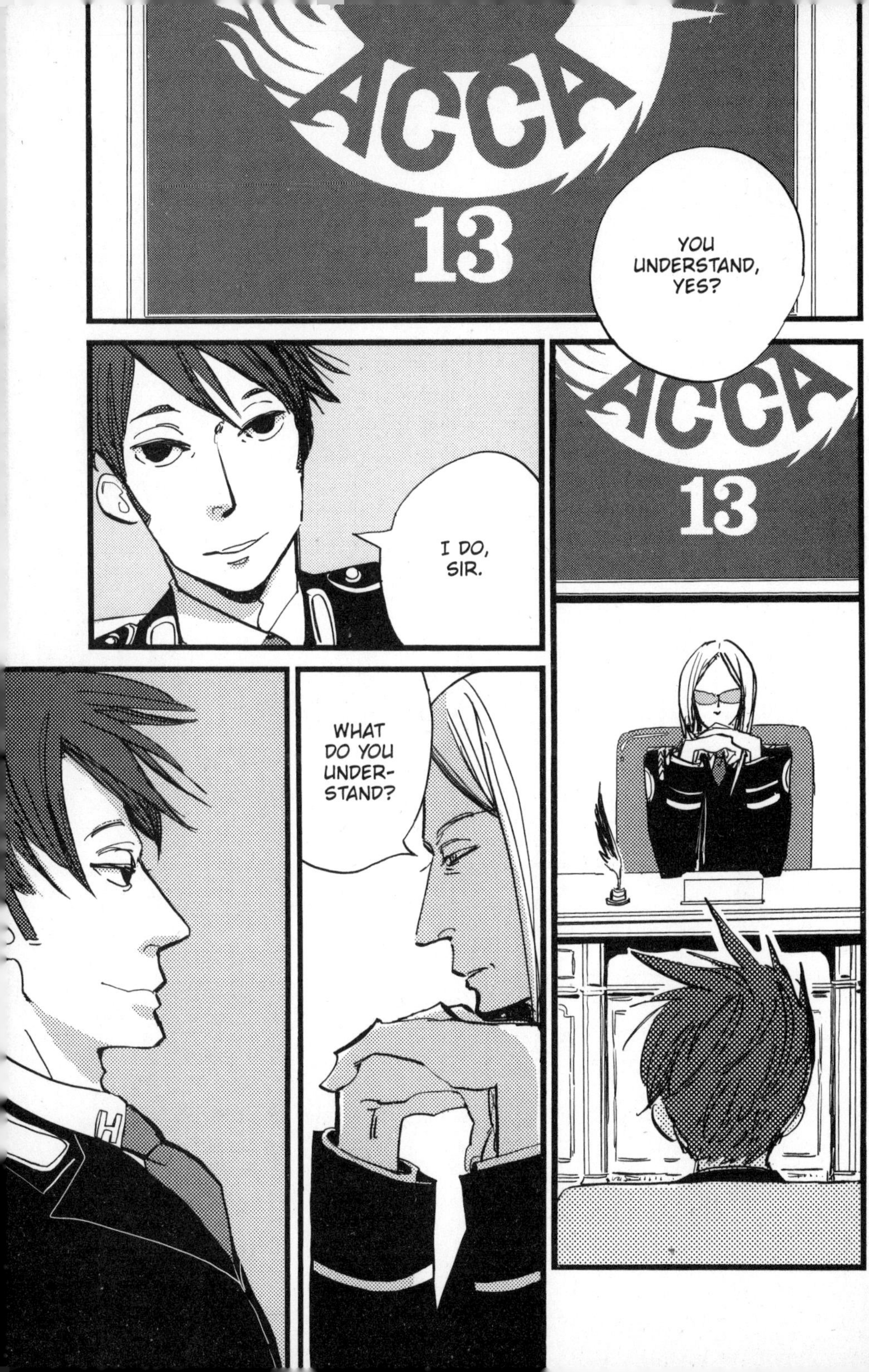
ACCA
13
YOU UNDERSTAND, YES?
ACCA
13
I DO, SIR.
WHAT DO YOU UNDER-STAND?

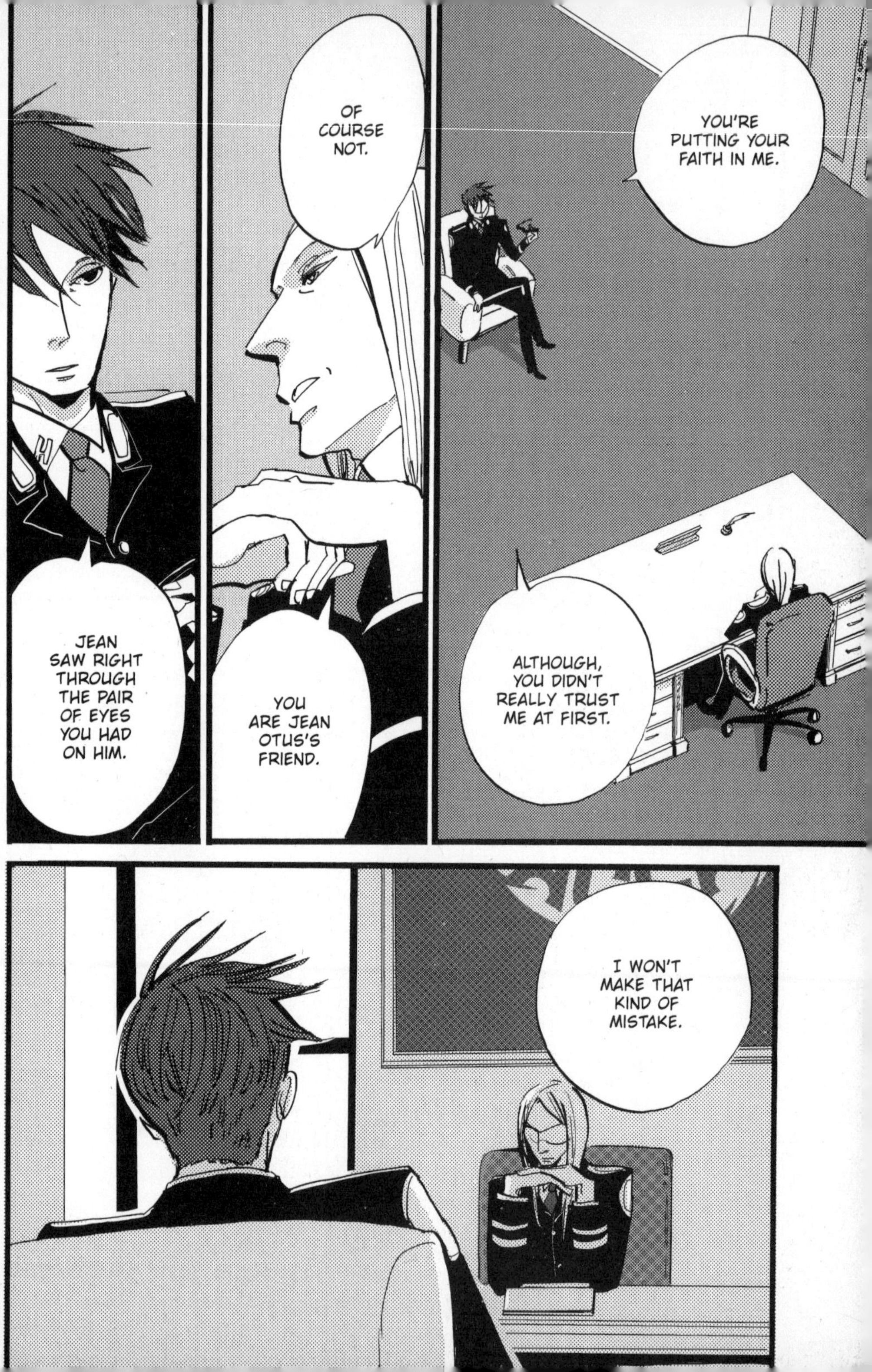
YOU'RE PUTTING YOUR FAITH IN ME.
ALTHOUGH, YOU DIDN'T REALLY TRUST ME AT FIRST.
OF COURSE NOT.
YOU ARE JEAN OTUS'S FRIEND.
JEAN SAW RIGHT THROUGH THE PAIR OF EYES YOU HAD ON HIM.
I WON'T MAKE THAT KIND OF MISTAKE.

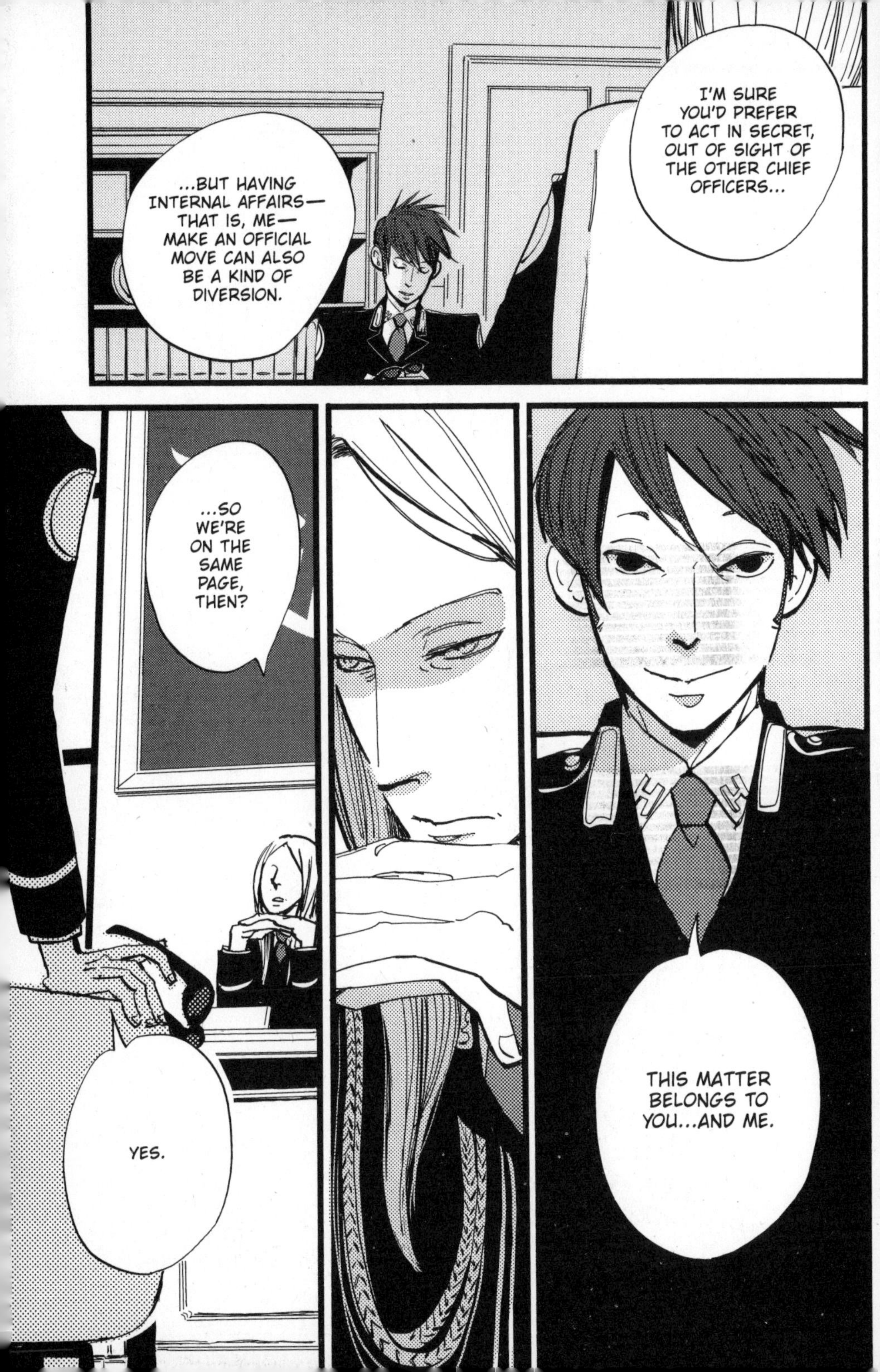
I'M SURE YOU'D PREFER TO ACT IN SECRET, OUT OF SIGHT OF THE OTHER CHIEF OFFICERS...
...BUT HAVING INTERNAL AFFAIRS—THAT IS, ME—MAKE AN OFFICIAL MOVE CAN ALSO BE A KIND OF DIVERSION.
THIS MATTER BELONGS TO YOU...AND ME.
...SO WE'RE ON THE SAME PAGE, THEN?
YES.

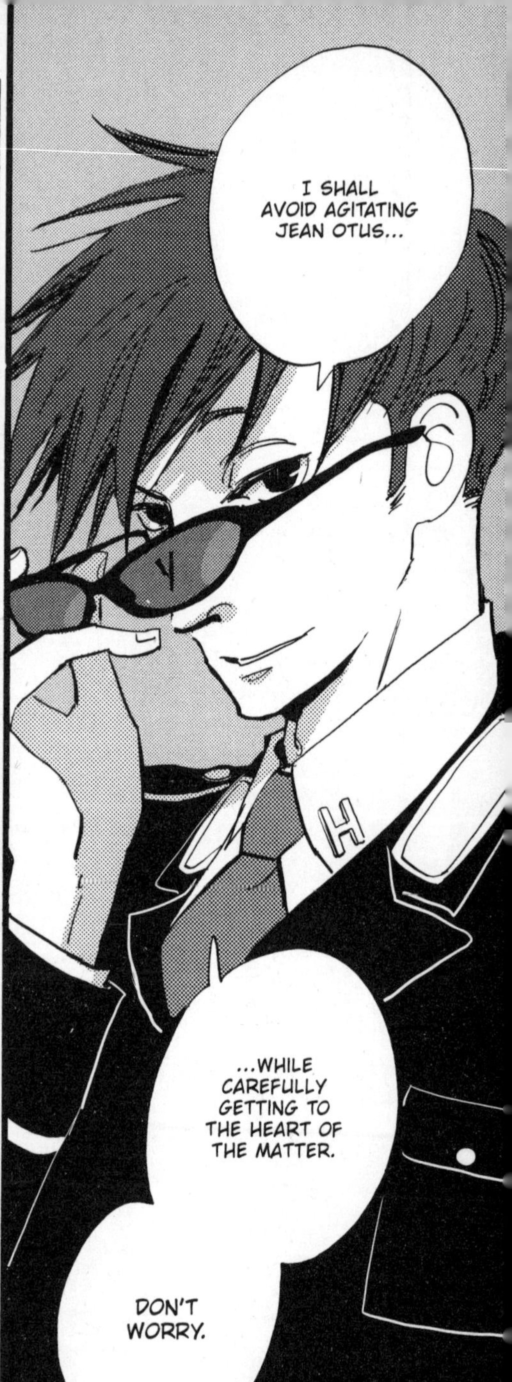
I SHALL AVOID AGITATING JEAN OTUS...
...WHILE CAREFULLY GETTING TO THE HEART OF THE MATTER.
DON'T WORRY.

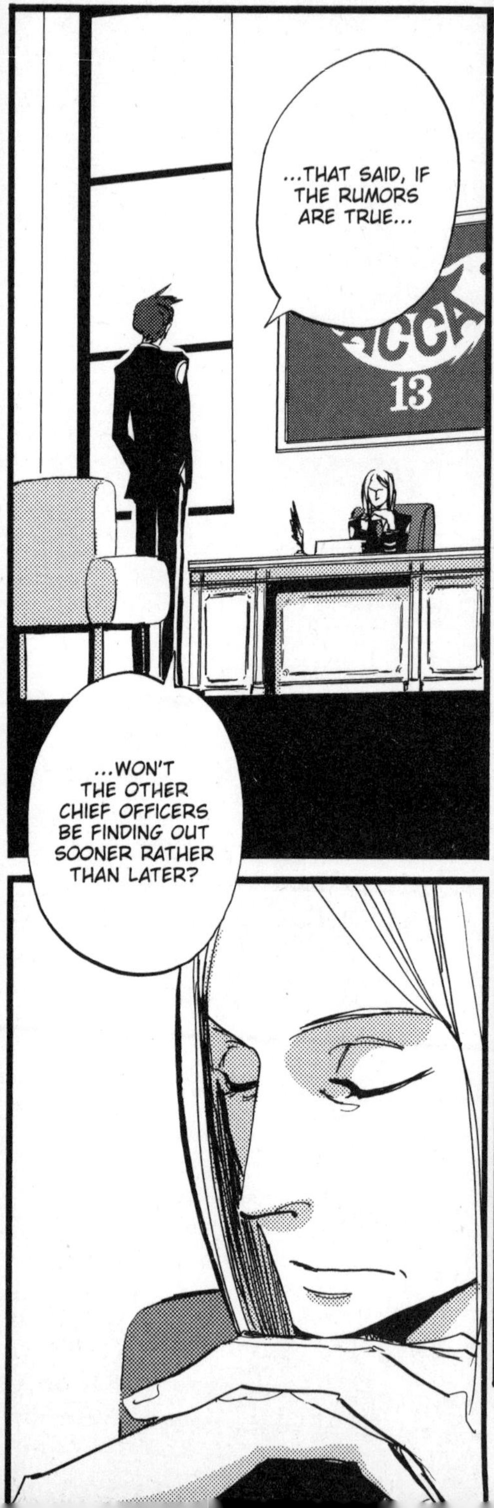
...THAT SAID, IF THE RUMORS ARE TRUE...
ICCA
13
...WON'T THE OTHER CHIEF OFFICERS BE FINDING OUT SOONER RATHER THAN LATER?

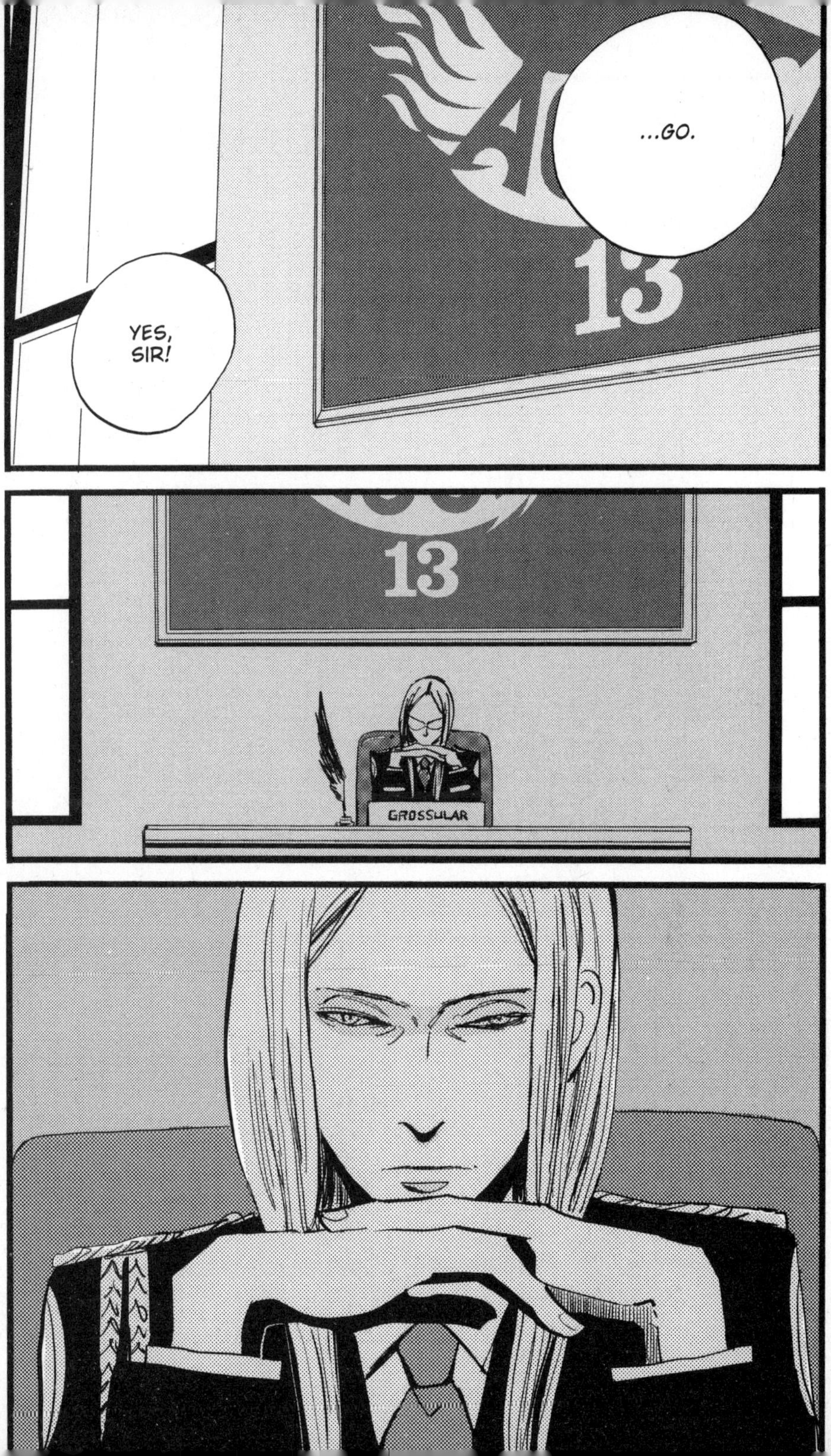
...GO.
YES, SIR!
GROSSULAR

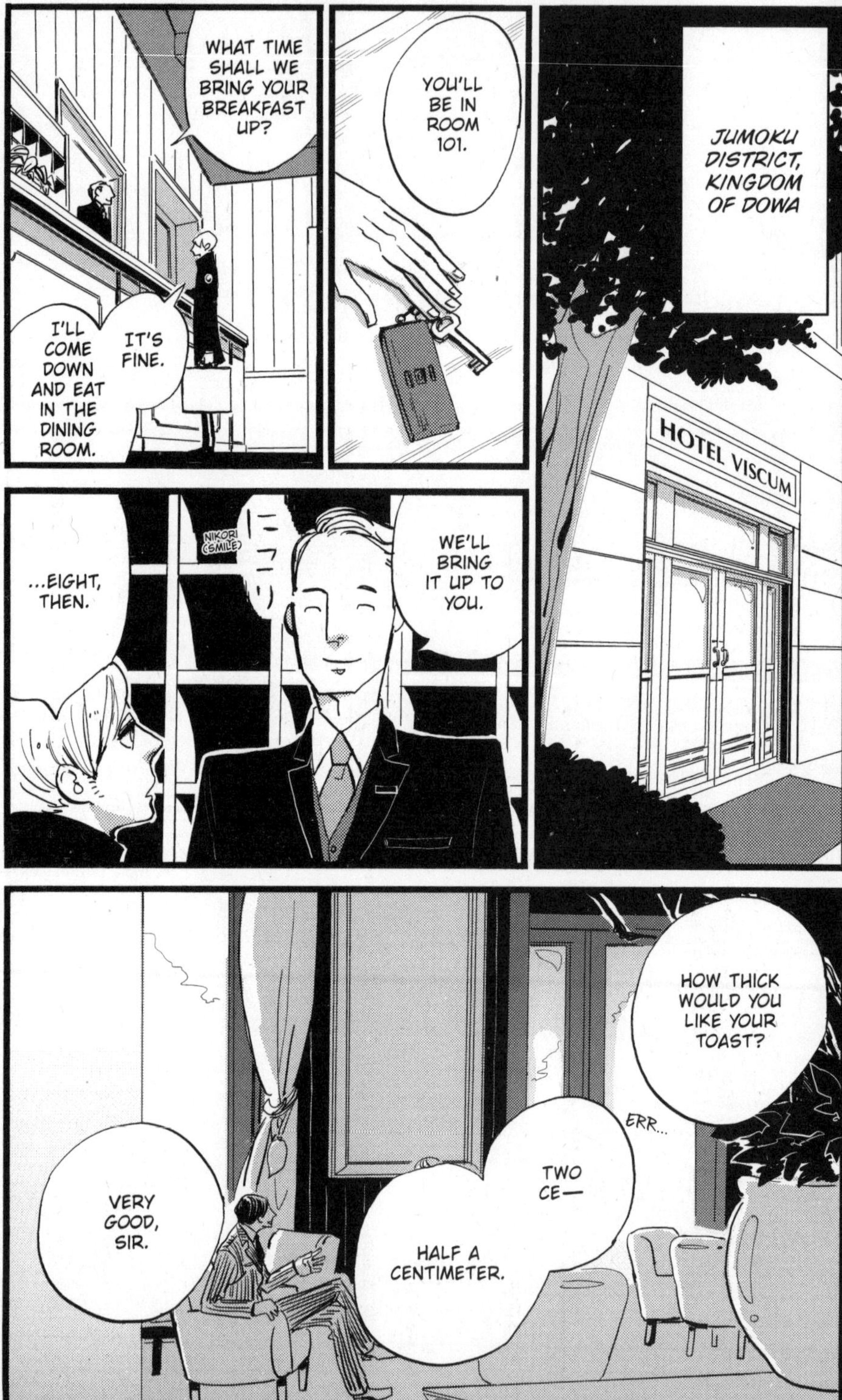
JUMOKU DISTRICT, KINGDOM OF DOWA
HOTEL VISCUM
YOU'LL BE IN ROOM 101.
101
WHAT TIME SHALL WE BRING YOUR BREAKFAST UP?
IT'S FINE.
I'LL COME DOWN AND EAT IN THE DINING ROOM.
WE'LL BRING IT UP TO YOU.
NIKORI (SMILE)
...EIGHT, THEN.
HOW THICK WOULD YOU LIKE YOUR TOAST?
ERR...
TWO CE—
HALF A CENTIMETER.
VERY GOOD, SIR.

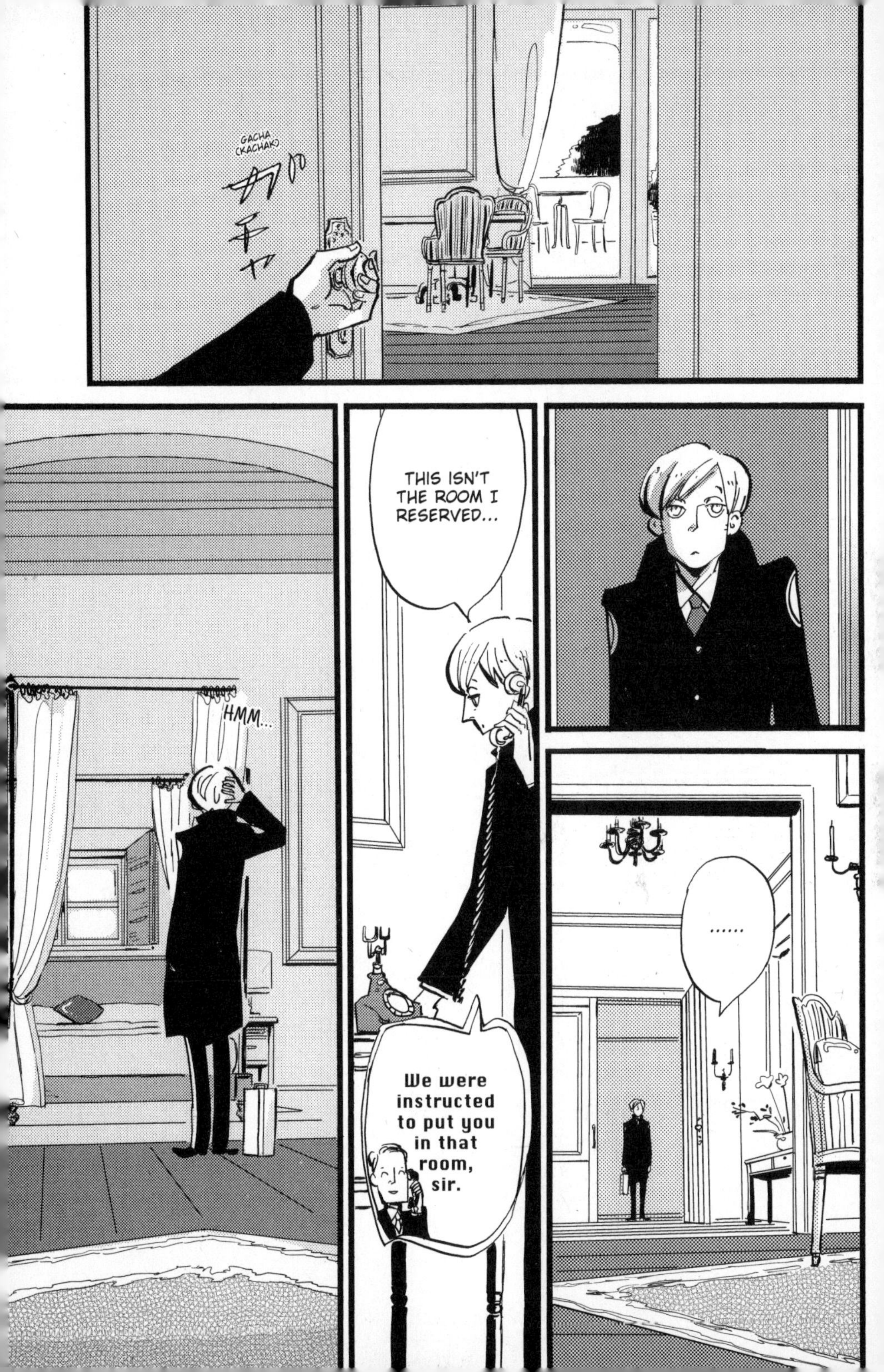
GACHA
(KACHAK)
カチャ
......
THIS ISN'T THE ROOM I RESERVED...
We were instructed to put you in that room, sir.
HMM...

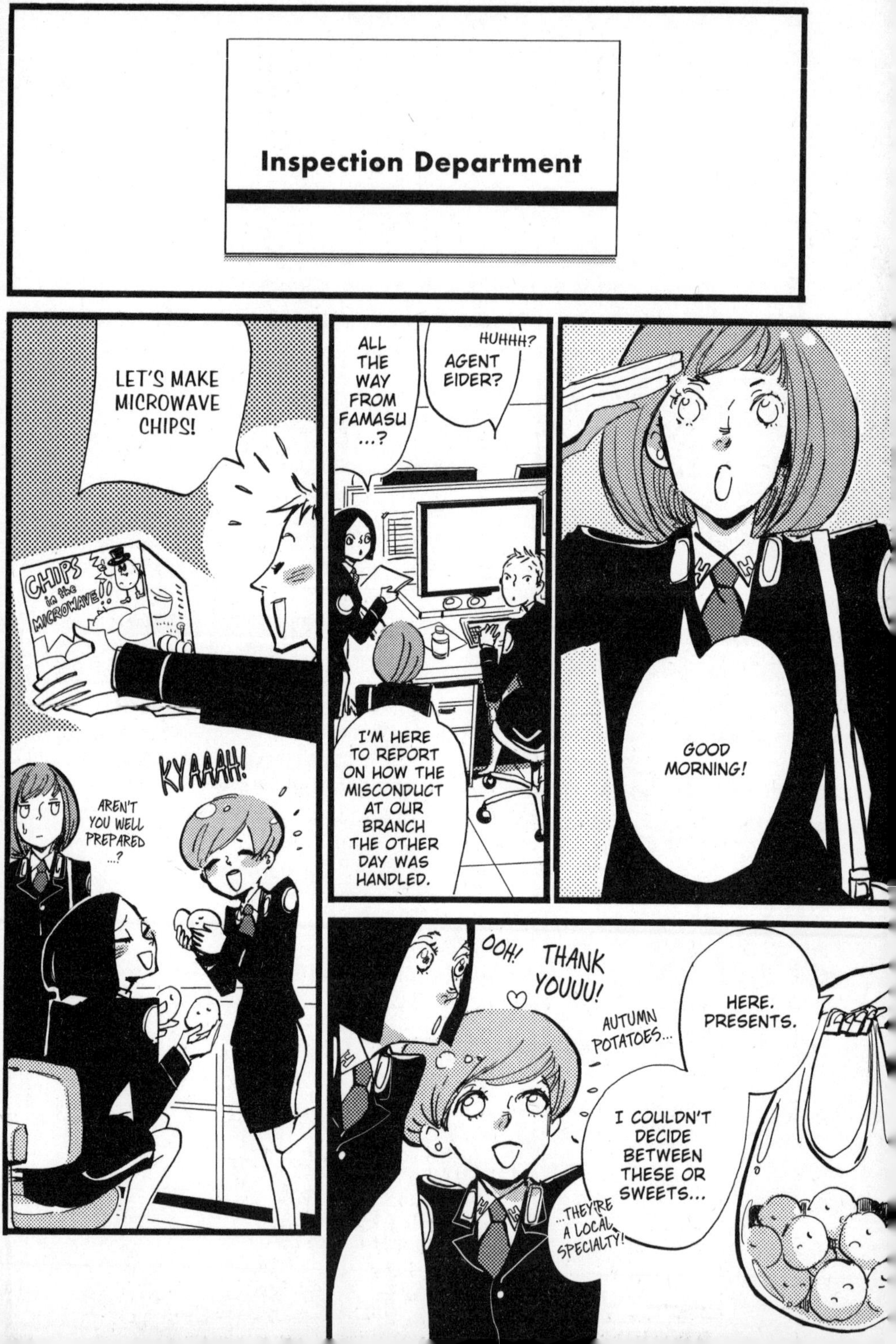
Inspection Department
GOOD MORNING!
HUHHH? AGENT EIDER?
ALL THE WAY FROM FAMASU ...?
I'M HERE TO REPORT ON HOW THE MISCONDUCT AT OUR BRANCH THE OTHER DAY WAS HANDLED.
HERE. PRESENTS.
I COULDN'T DECIDE BETWEEN THESE OR SWEETS...
...THEY'RE A LOCAL SPECIALTY!
AUTUMN POTATOES...
OOH! THANK YOUUU!
LET'S MAKE MICROWAVE CHIPS!
CHIPS in the MICROWAVE!!
KYAAAH!
AREN'T YOU WELL PREPARED ...?

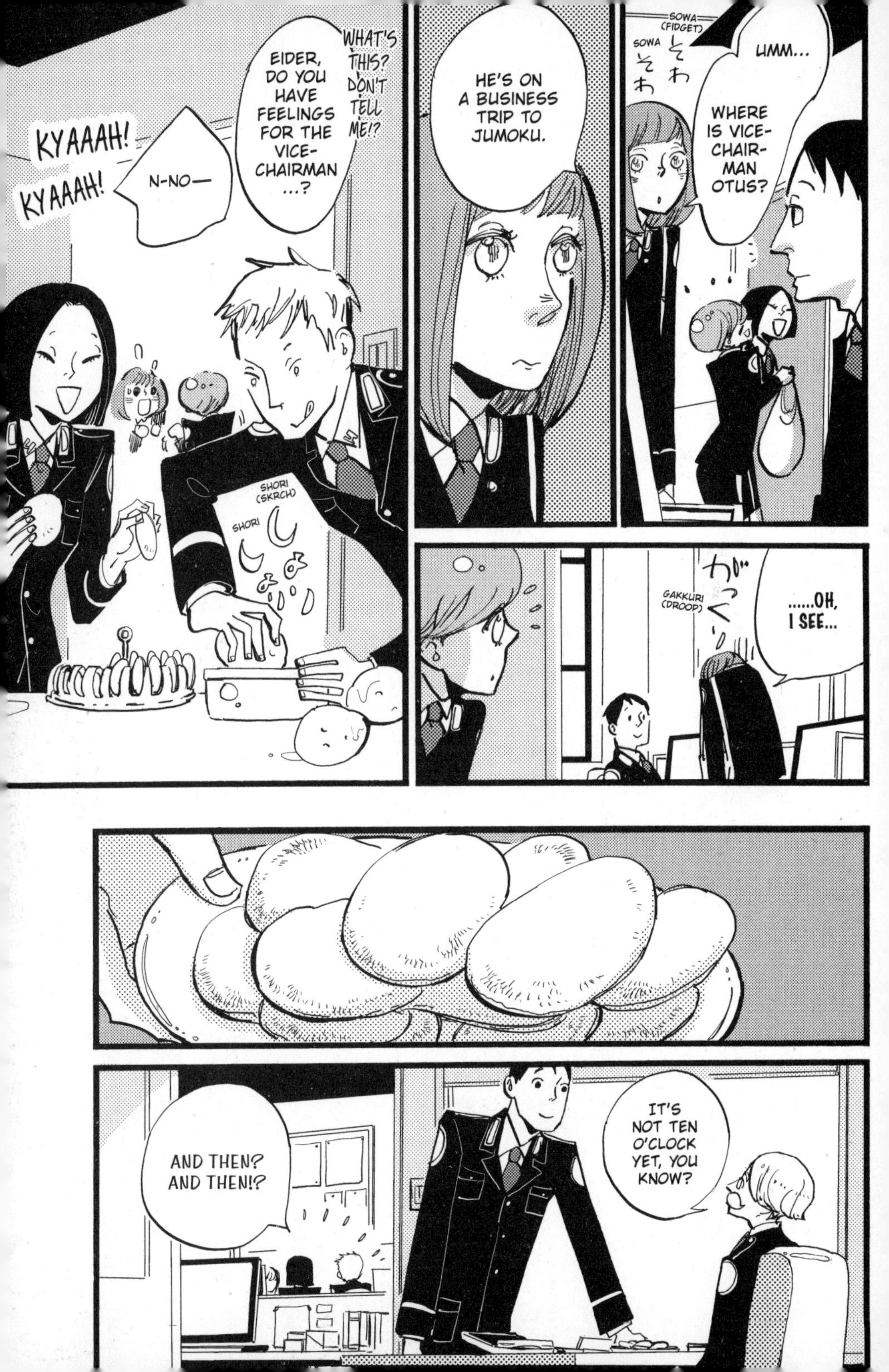

SOWA (FIDGET)
SOWA
UMM...
WHERE IS VICE-CHAIRMAN OTUS?
HE'S ON A BUSINESS TRIP TO JUMOKU.
GAKKURI (DROOP)
......OH, I SEE...
WHAT'S THIS? DON'T TELL ME!?
EIDER, DO YOU HAVE FEELINGS FOR THE VICE-CHAIRMAN ...?
N-NO—
KYAAAH!
KYAAAH!
SHORI (SKRCH)
SHORI
IT'S NOT TEN O'CLOCK YET, YOU KNOW?
AND THEN? AND THEN!?

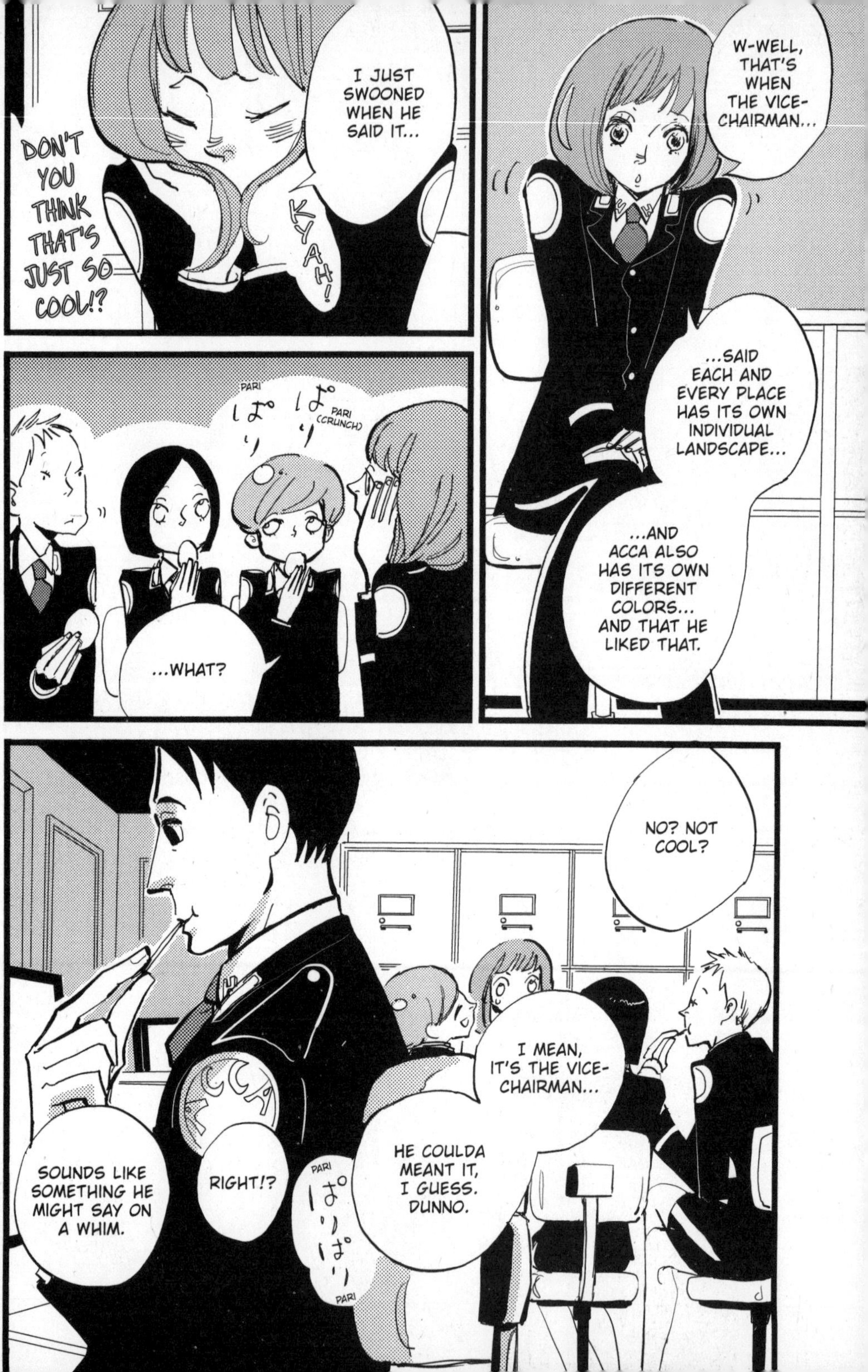
W-WELL, THAT'S WHEN THE VICE-CHAIRMAN...
...SAID EACH AND EVERY PLACE HAS ITS OWN INDIVIDUAL LANDSCAPE...
...AND ACCA ALSO HAS ITS OWN DIFFERENT COLORS... AND THAT HE LIKED THAT.
I JUST SWOONED WHEN HE SAID IT...
KYAH!
DON'T YOU THINK THAT'S JUST SO COOL!?
ぱり PARI (CRUNCH)
ぱり PARI
...WHAT?
NO? NOT COOL?
I MEAN, IT'S THE VICE-CHAIRMAN...
HE COULDA MEANT IT, I GUESS. DUNNO.
ぱり PARI
ぱり PARI
RIGHT!?
SOUNDS LIKE SOMETHING HE MIGHT SAY ON A WHIM.

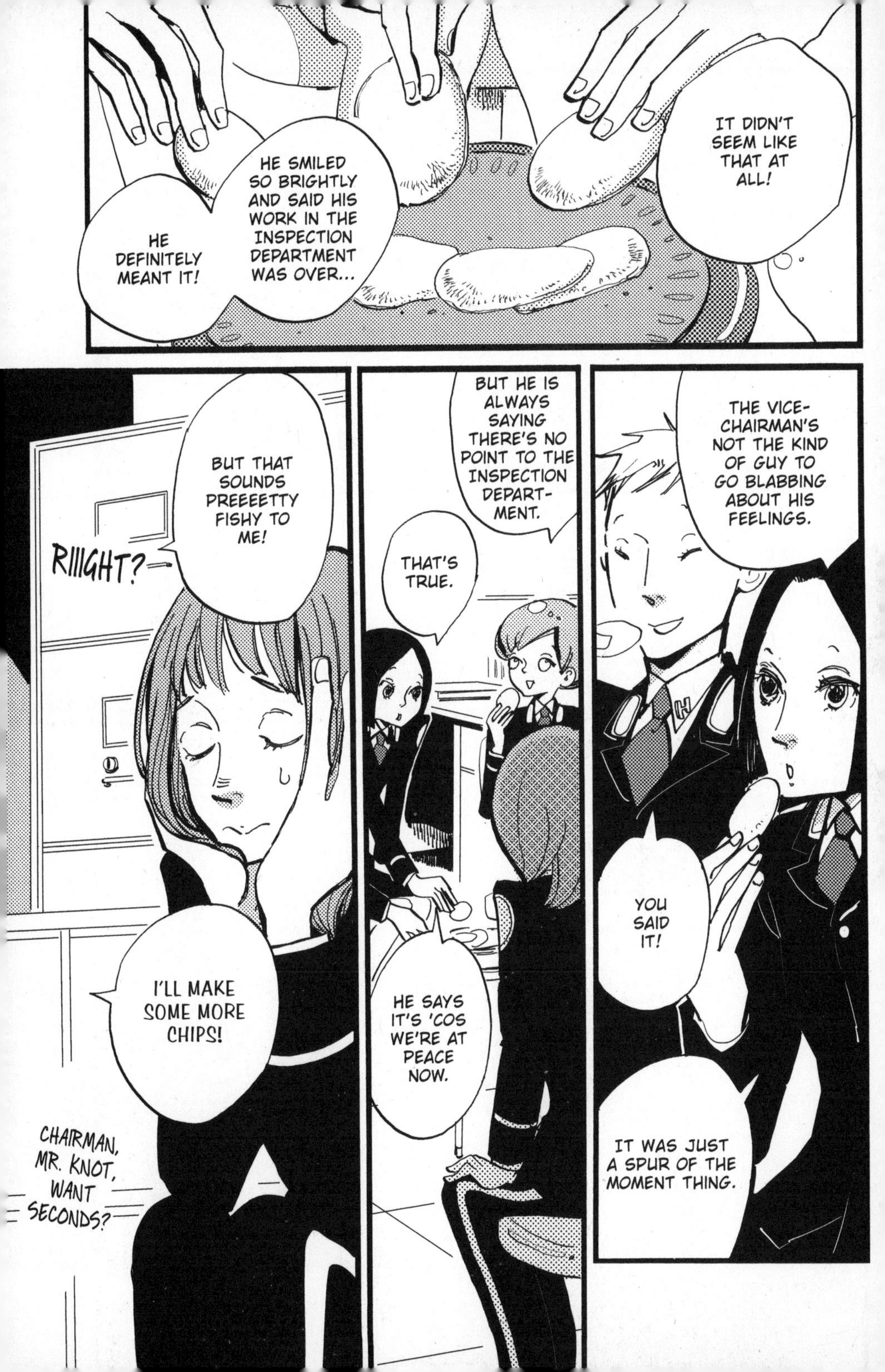
IT DIDN'T SEEM LIKE THAT AT ALL!
HE SMILED SO BRIGHTLY AND SAID HIS WORK IN THE INSPECTION DEPARTMENT WAS OVER...
HE DEFINITELY MEANT IT!
THE VICE-CHAIRMAN'S NOT THE KIND OF GUY TO GO BLABBING ABOUT HIS FEELINGS.
YOU SAID IT!
IT WAS JUST A SPUR OF THE MOMENT THING.
BUT HE IS ALWAYS SAYING THERE'S NO POINT TO THE INSPECTION DEPART-MENT.
THAT'S TRUE.
HE SAYS IT'S 'COS WE'RE AT PEACE NOW.
BUT THAT SOUNDS PREEEETTY FISHY TO ME!
RIIIGHT?
I'LL MAKE SOME MORE CHIPS!
CHAIRMAN, MR. KNOT, WANT SECONDS?

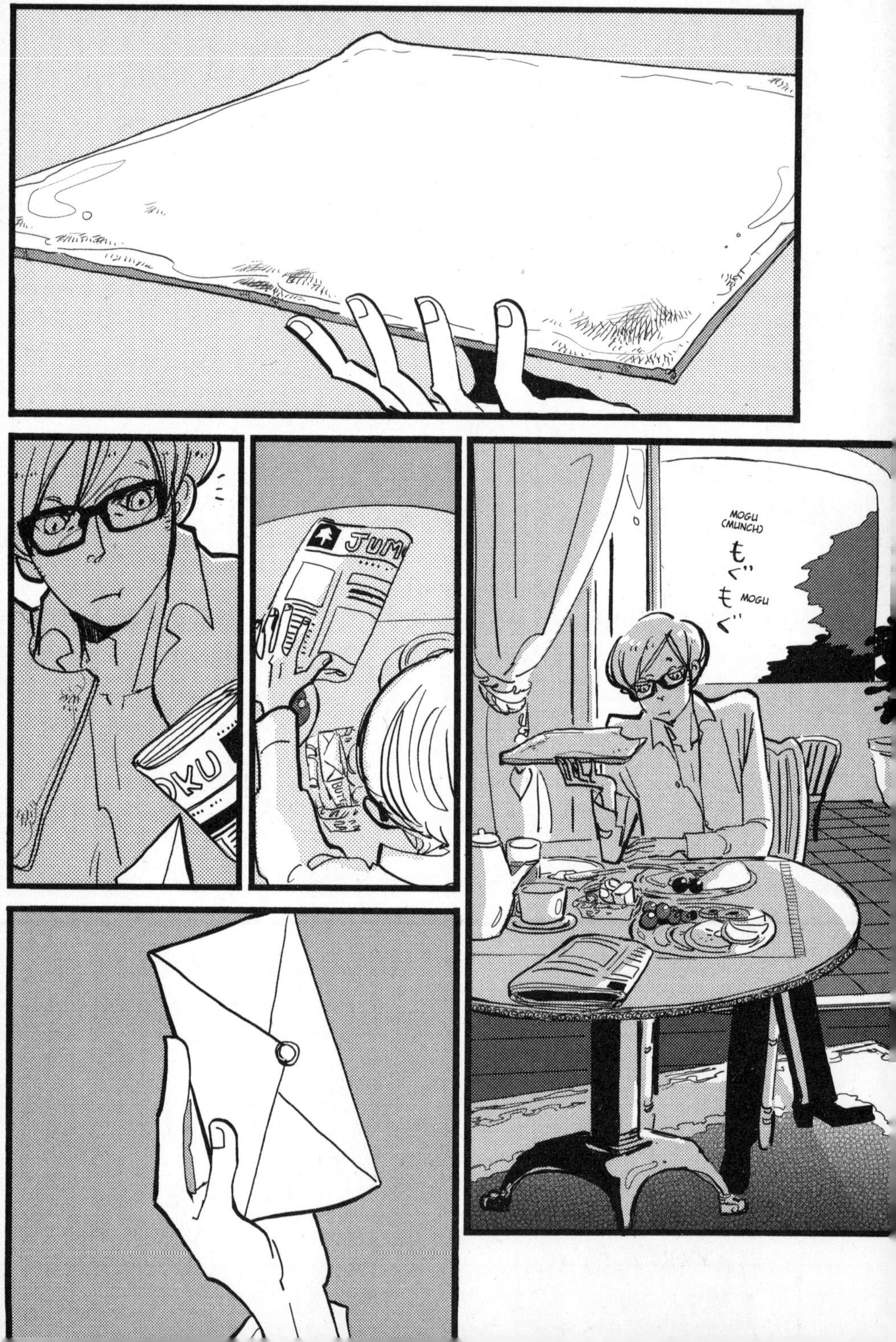
MOGU (MUNCH)
もぐもぐ
MOGU

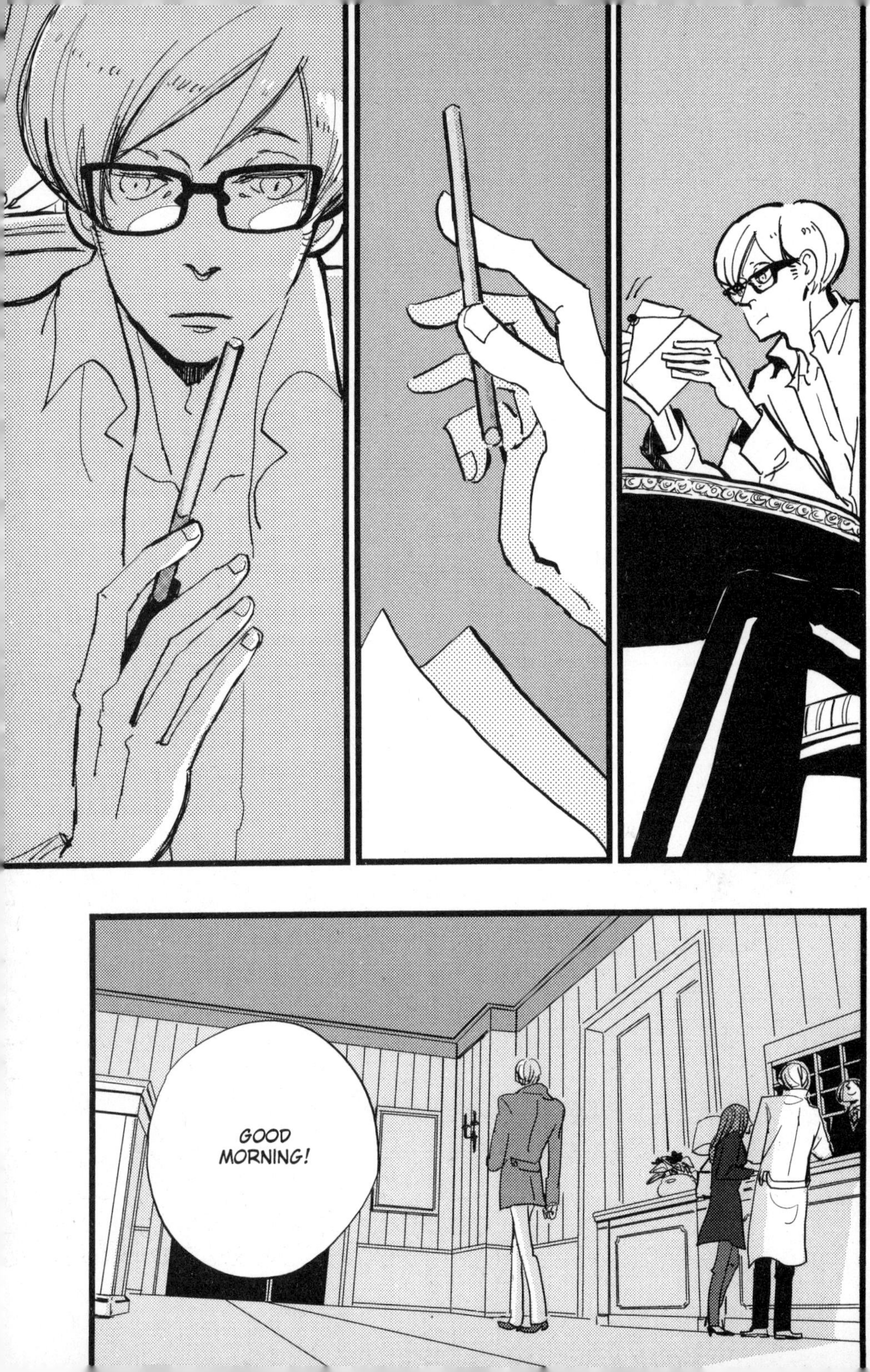
GOOD MORNING!

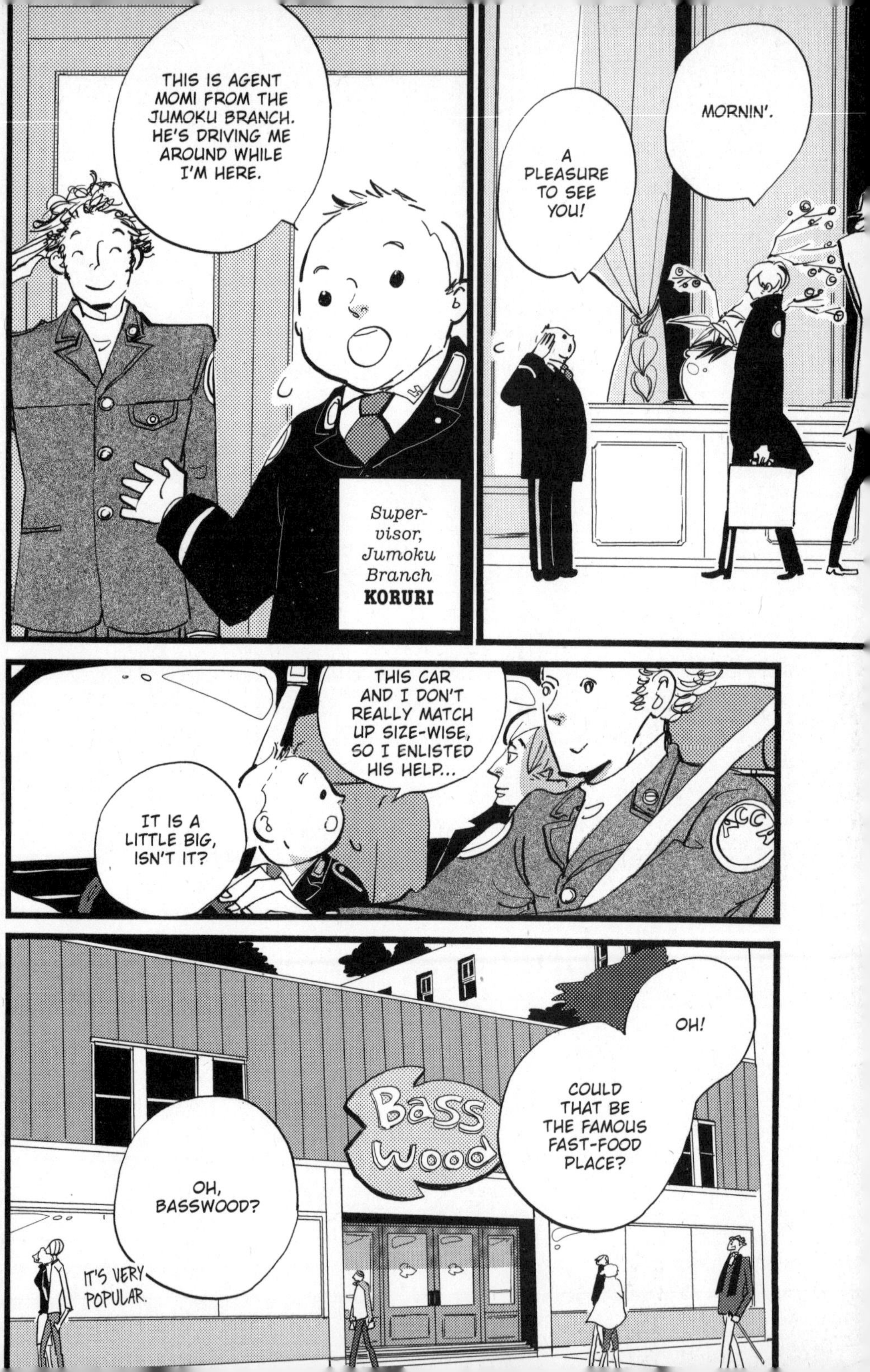
MORNIN'.
A PLEASURE TO SEE YOU!
THIS IS AGENT MOMI FROM THE JUMOKU BRANCH. HE'S DRIVING ME AROUND WHILE I'M HERE.
Supervisor, Jumoku Branch KORURI
THIS CAR AND I DON'T REALLY MATCH UP SIZE-WISE, SO I ENLISTED HIS HELP...
IT IS A LITTLE BIG, ISN'T IT?
OH!
COULD THAT BE THE FAMOUS FAST-FOOD PLACE?
Bass Wood
OH, BASSWOOD?
IT'S VERY POPULAR.

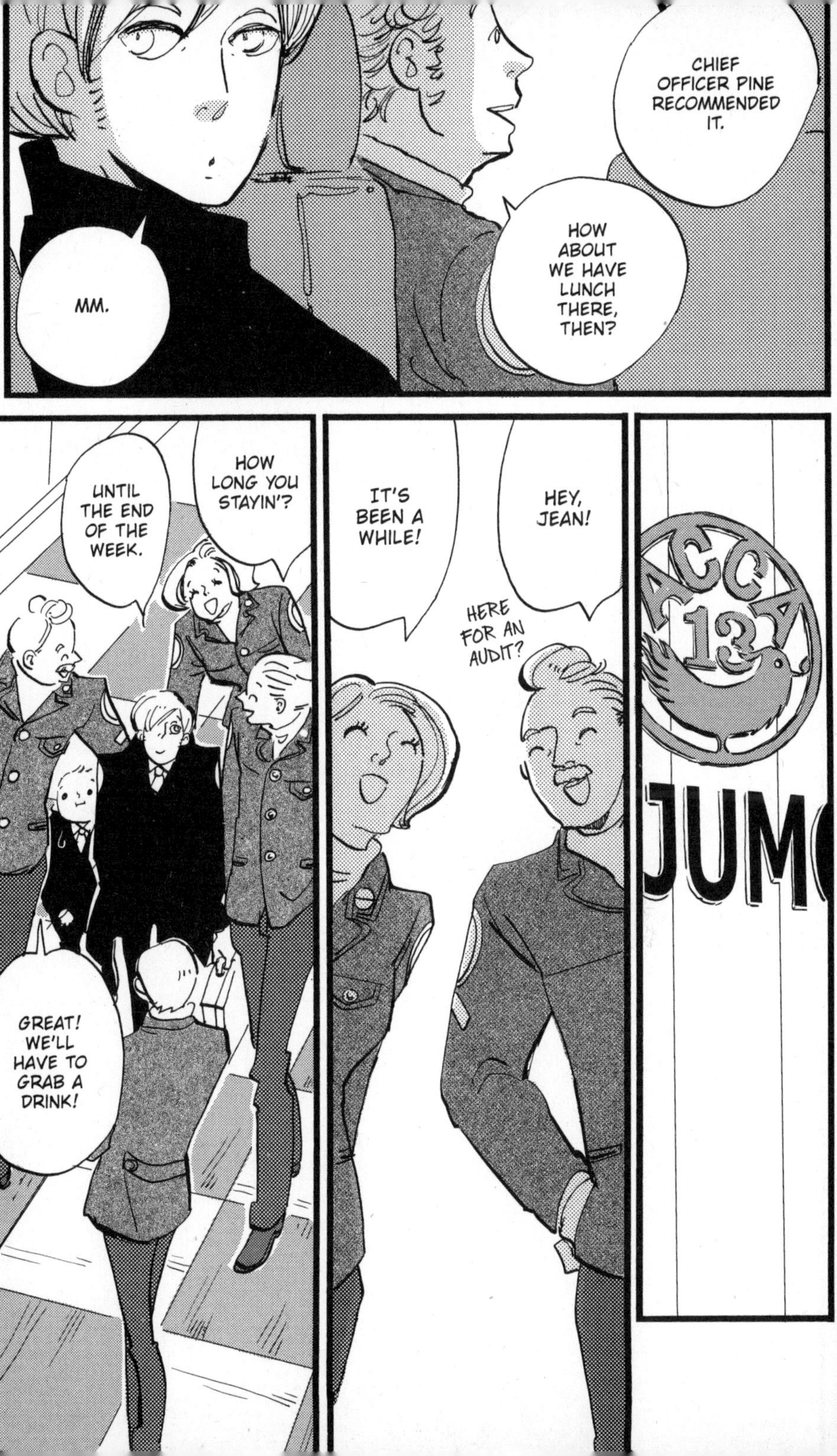
CHIEF OFFICER PINE RECOMMENDED IT.
HOW ABOUT WE HAVE LUNCH THERE, THEN?
MM.
ACCA 13
HEY, JEAN!
IT'S BEEN A WHILE!
HERE FOR AN AUDIT?
HOW LONG YOU STAYIN'?
UNTIL THE END OF THE WEEK.
GREAT! WE'LL HAVE TO GRAB A DRINK!

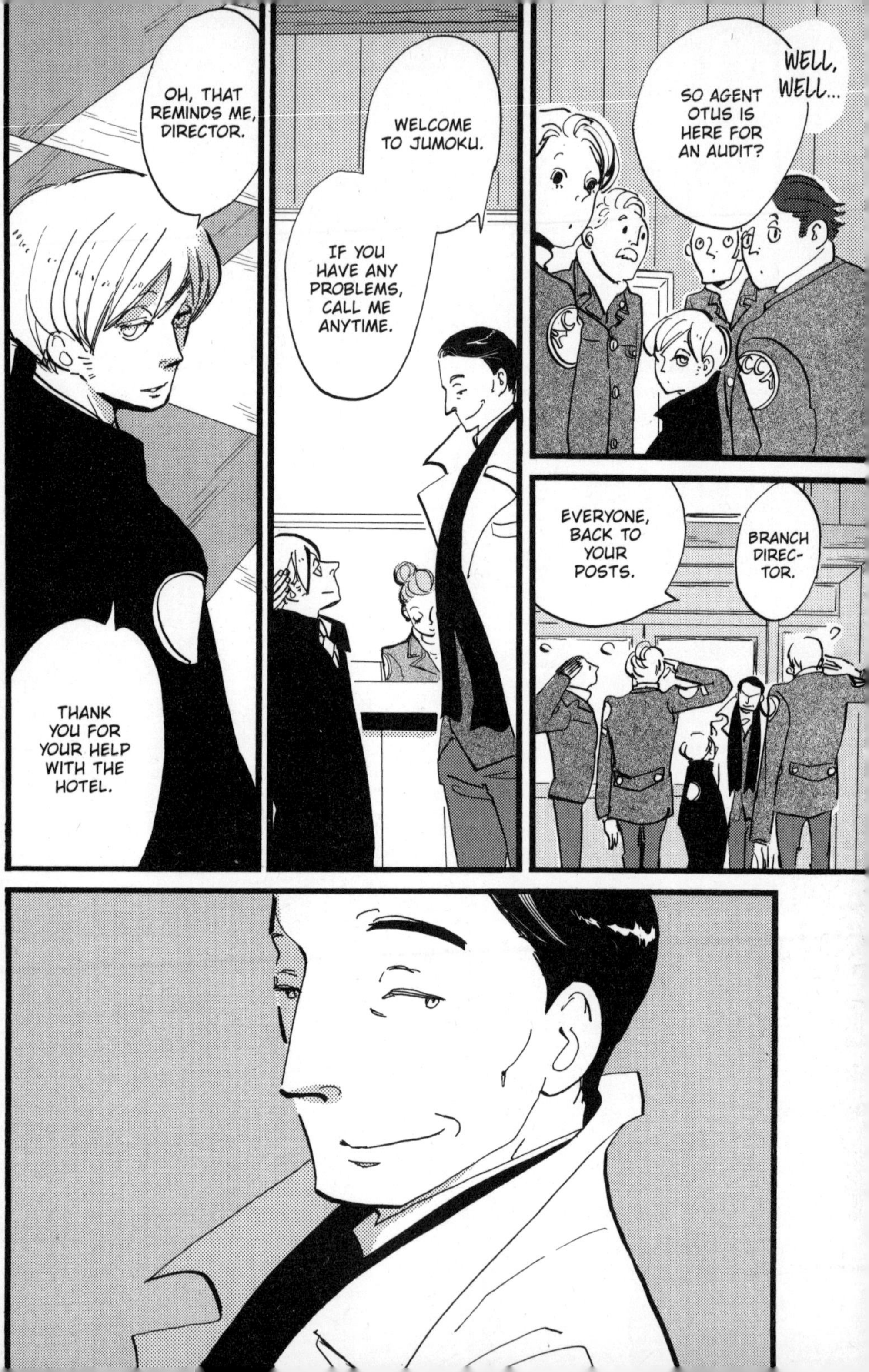
WELL, WELL...
SO AGENT OTUS IS HERE FOR AN AUDIT?
BRANCH DIRECTOR.
EVERYONE, BACK TO YOUR POSTS.
WELCOME TO JUMOKU.
IF YOU HAVE ANY PROBLEMS, CALL ME ANYTIME.
OH, THAT REMINDS ME, DIRECTOR.
THANK YOU FOR YOUR HELP WITH THE HOTEL.

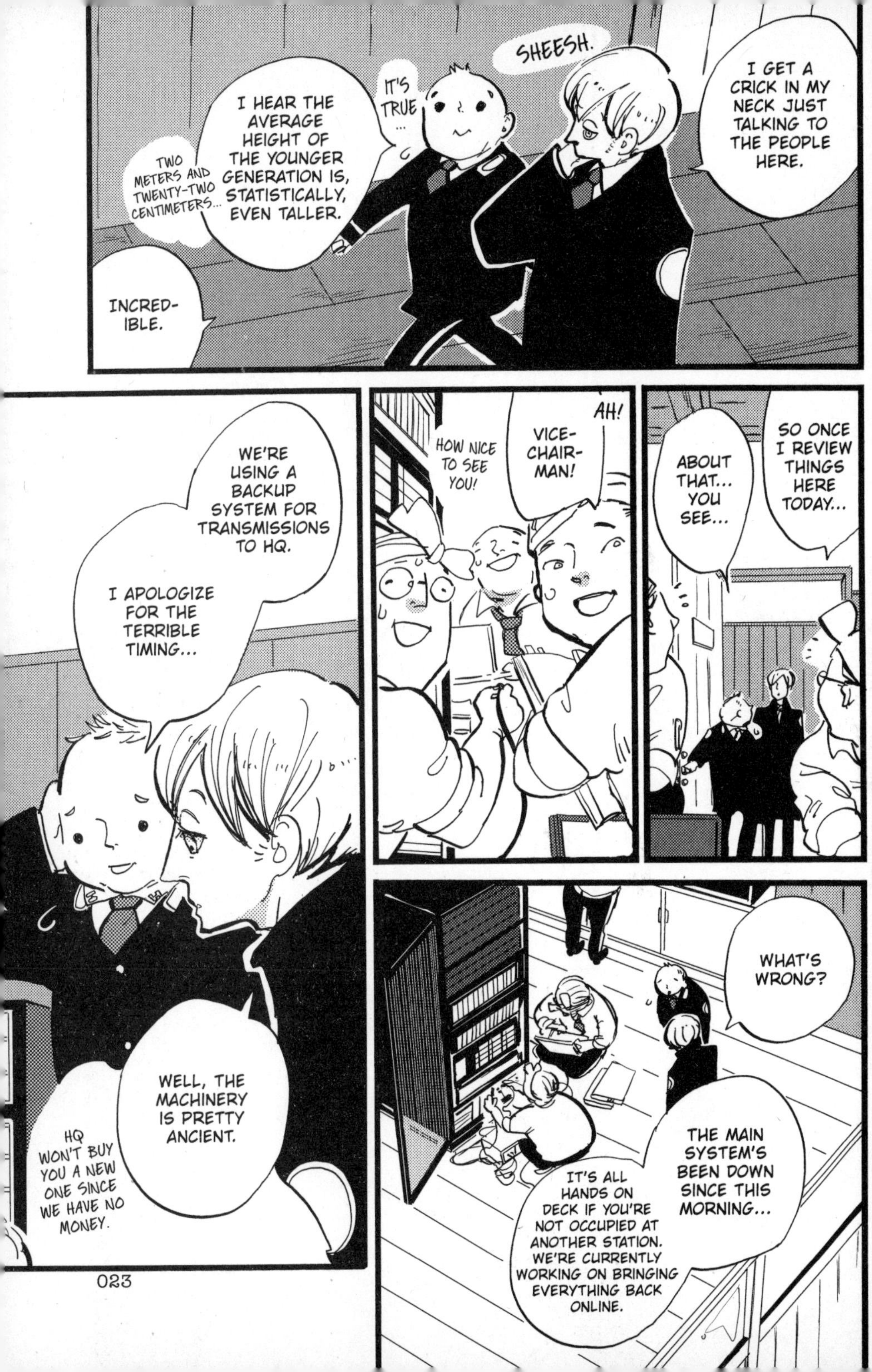
I GET A CRICK IN MY NECK JUST TALKING TO THE PEOPLE HERE.
SHEESH.
IT'S TRUE...
I HEAR THE AVERAGE HEIGHT OF THE YOUNGER GENERATION IS, STATISTICALLY, EVEN TALLER.
TWO METERS AND TWENTY-TWO CENTIMETERS...
INCRED-IBLE.
SO ONCE I REVIEW THINGS HERE TODAY...
ABOUT THAT... YOU SEE...
AH!
VICE-CHAIR-MAN!
HOW NICE TO SEE YOU!
WHAT'S WRONG?
THE MAIN SYSTEM'S BEEN DOWN SINCE THIS MORNING...
IT'S ALL HANDS ON DECK IF YOU'RE NOT OCCUPIED AT ANOTHER STATION. WE'RE CURRENTLY WORKING ON BRINGING EVERYTHING BACK ONLINE.
WE'RE USING A BACKUP SYSTEM FOR TRANSMISSIONS TO HQ.
I APOLOGIZE FOR THE TERRIBLE TIMING...
WELL, THE MACHINERY IS PRETTY ANCIENT.
HQ WON'T BUY YOU A NEW ONE SINCE WE HAVE NO MONEY.

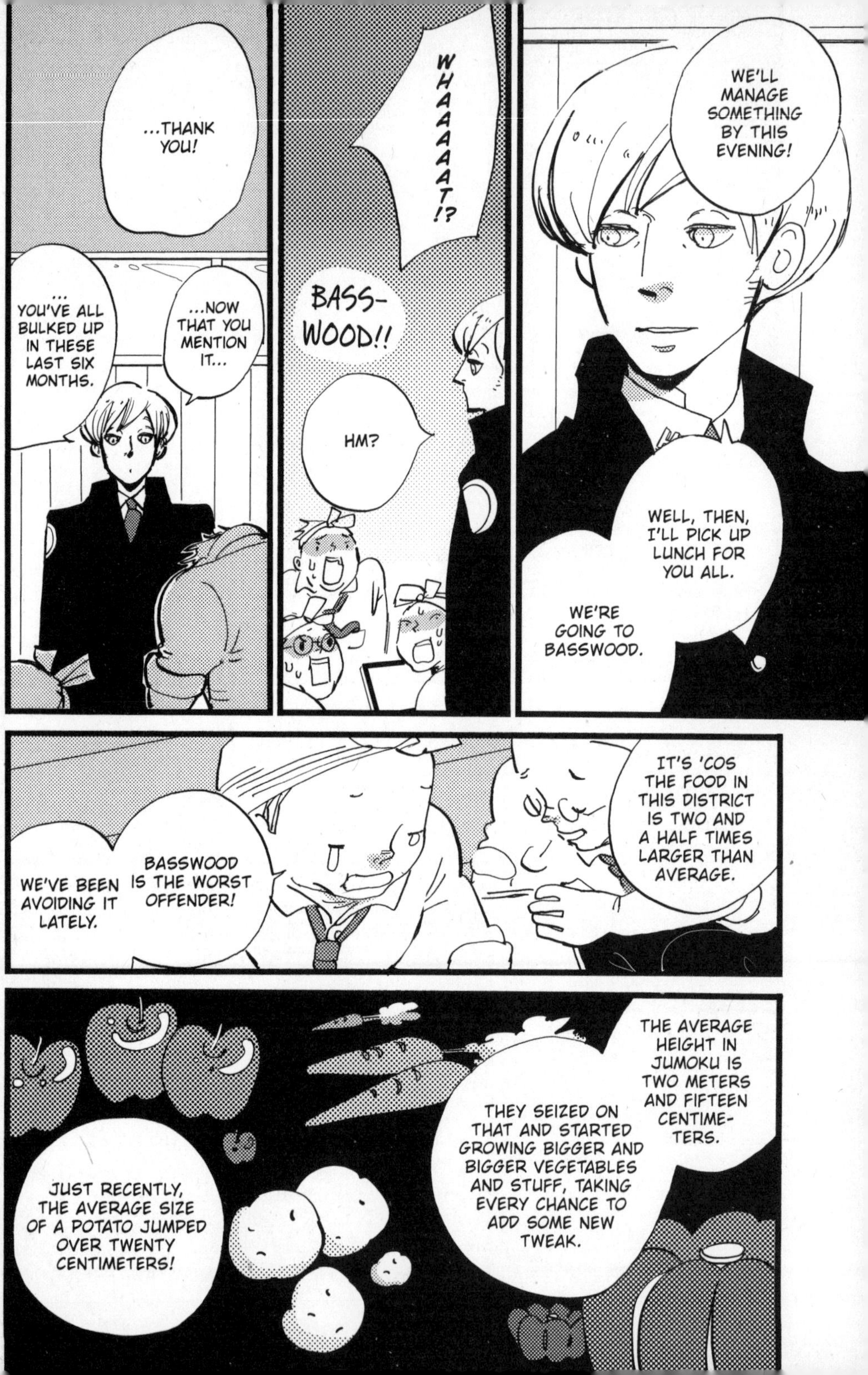
WE'LL MANAGE SOMETHING BY THIS EVENING!
WELL, THEN, I'LL PICK UP LUNCH FOR YOU ALL.
WE'RE GOING TO BASSWOOD.
WHAAAAAAT!?
BASS-WOOD!!
HM?
...THANK YOU!
...NOW THAT YOU MENTION IT...
... YOU'VE ALL BULKED UP IN THESE LAST SIX MONTHS.
IT'S 'COS THE FOOD IN THIS DISTRICT IS TWO AND A HALF TIMES LARGER THAN AVERAGE.
BASSWOOD IS THE WORST OFFENDER!
WE'VE BEEN AVOIDING IT LATELY.
THE AVERAGE HEIGHT IN JUMOKU IS TWO METERS AND FIFTEEN CENTIME-TERS.
THEY SEIZED ON THAT AND STARTED GROWING BIGGER AND BIGGER VEGETABLES AND STUFF, TAKING EVERY CHANCE TO ADD SOME NEW TWEAK.
JUST RECENTLY, THE AVERAGE SIZE OF A POTATO JUMPED OVER TWENTY CENTIMETERS!

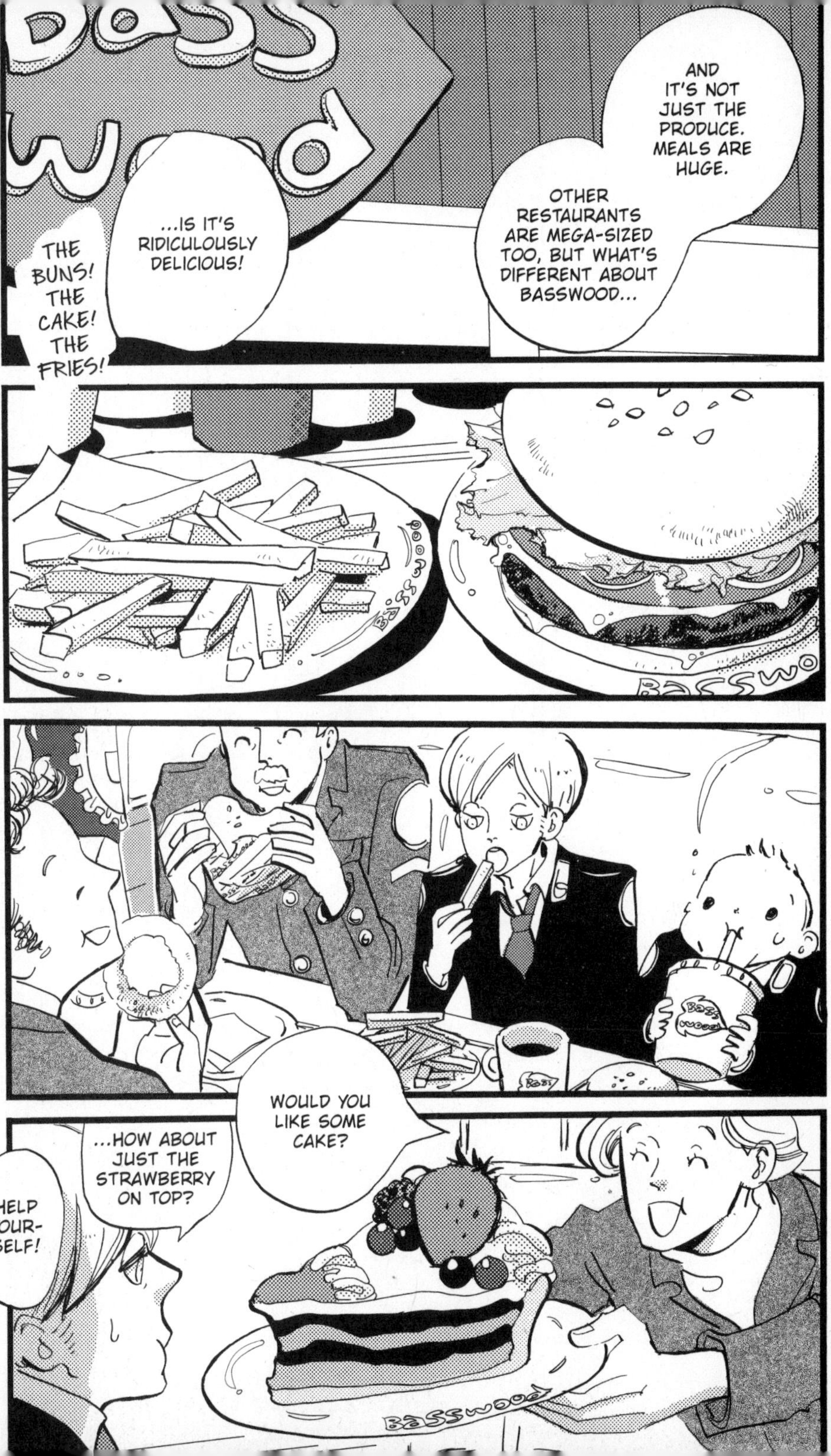
AND IT'S NOT JUST THE PRODUCE. MEALS ARE HUGE.
OTHER RESTAURANTS ARE MEGA-SIZED TOO, BUT WHAT'S DIFFERENT ABOUT BASSWOOD...
...IS IT'S RIDICULOUSLY DELICIOUS!
THE BUNS! THE CAKE! THE FRIES!
WOULD YOU LIKE SOME CAKE?
...HOW ABOUT JUST THE STRAWBERRY ON TOP?
HELP YOURSELF!
BASSWOOD

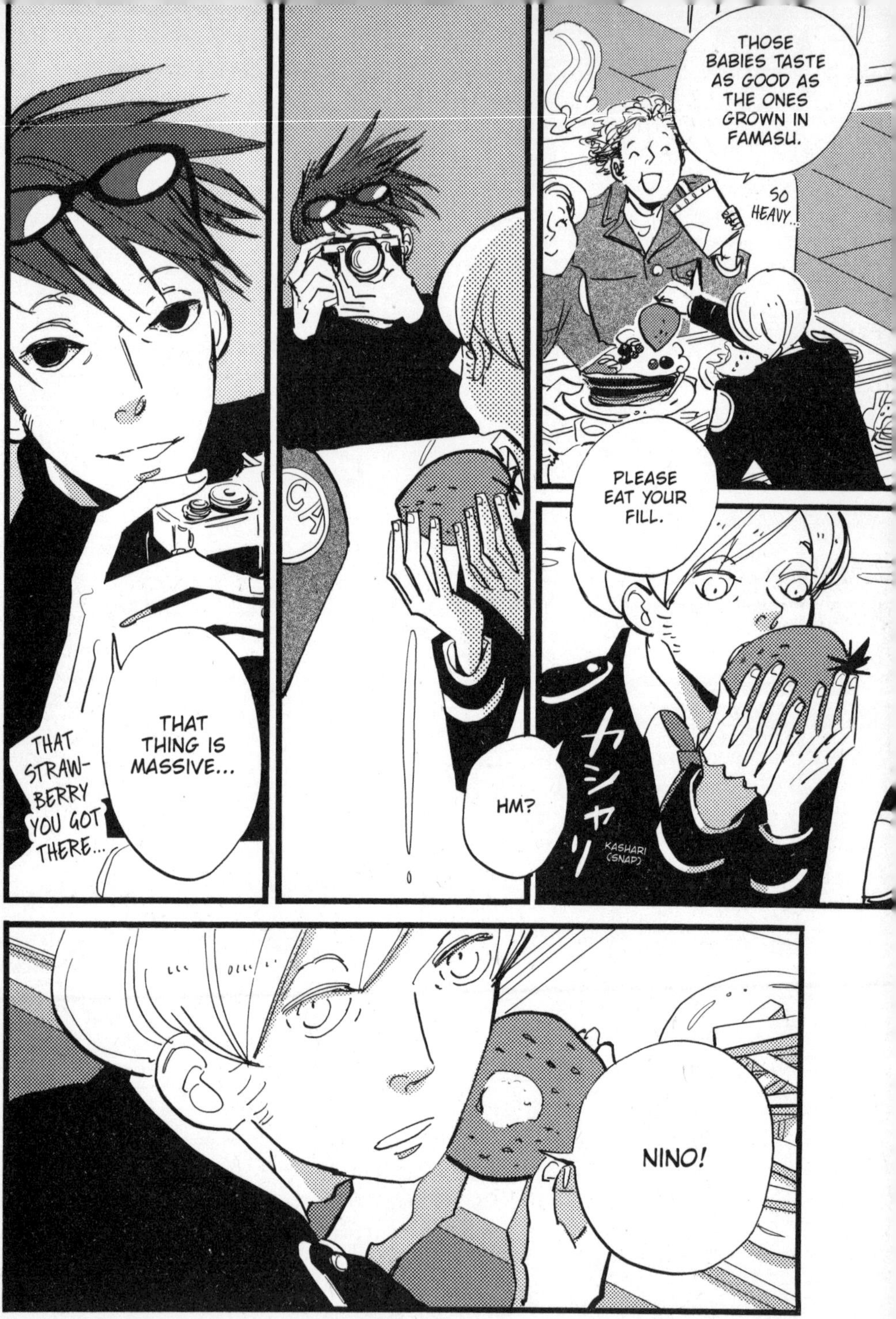
THOSE BABIES TASTE AS GOOD AS THE ONES GROWN IN FAMASU.
SO HEAVY...
PLEASE EAT YOUR FILL.
HM?
カシャリ
KASHARI (SNAP)
THAT THING IS MASSIVE...
THAT STRAW-BERRY YOU GOT THERE...
NINO!

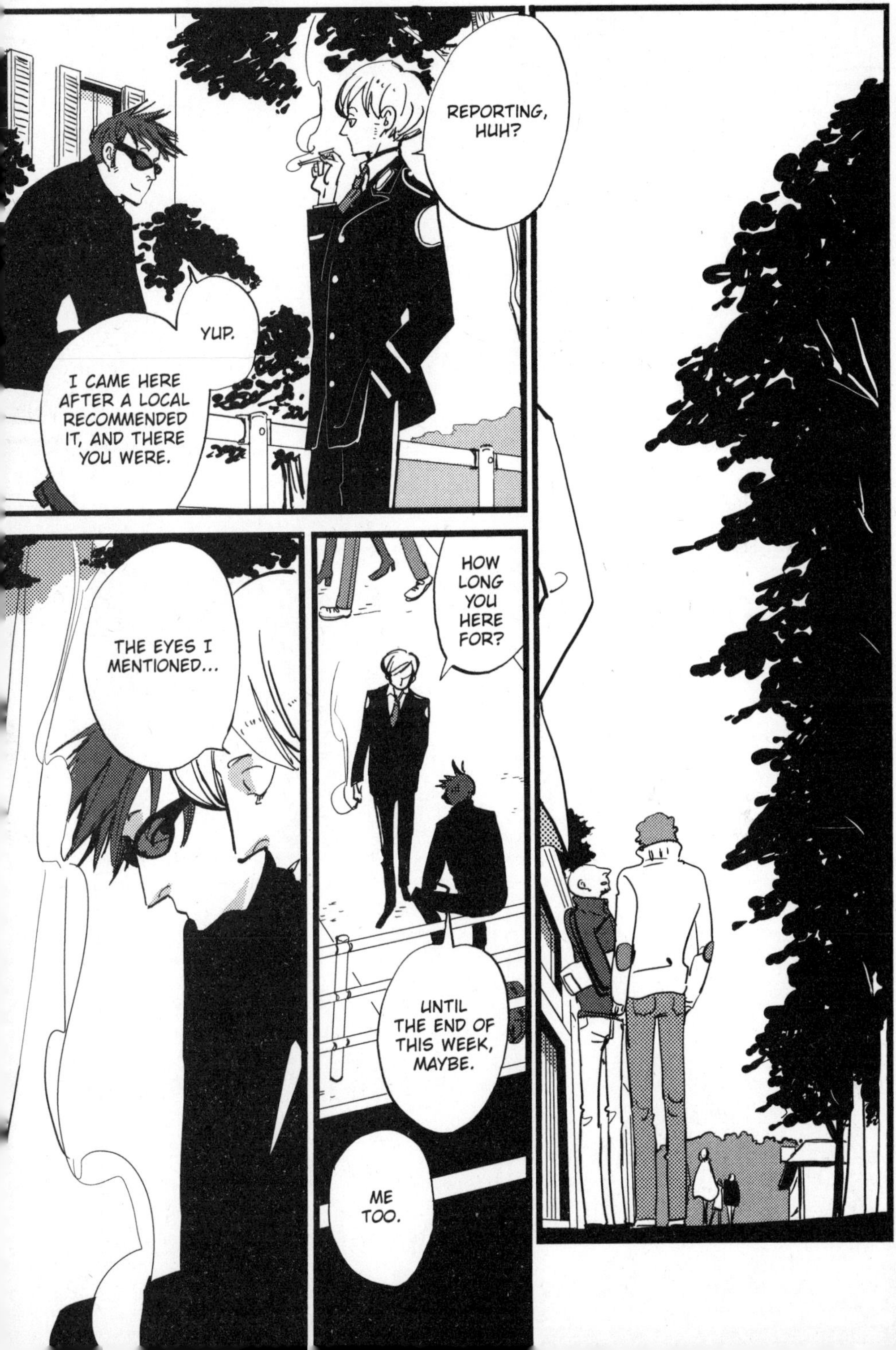
REPORTING, HUH?
YUP.
I CAME HERE AFTER A LOCAL RECOMMENDED IT, AND THERE YOU WERE.
HOW LONG YOU HERE FOR?
UNTIL THE END OF THIS WEEK, MAYBE.
ME TOO.
THE EYES I MENTIONED...

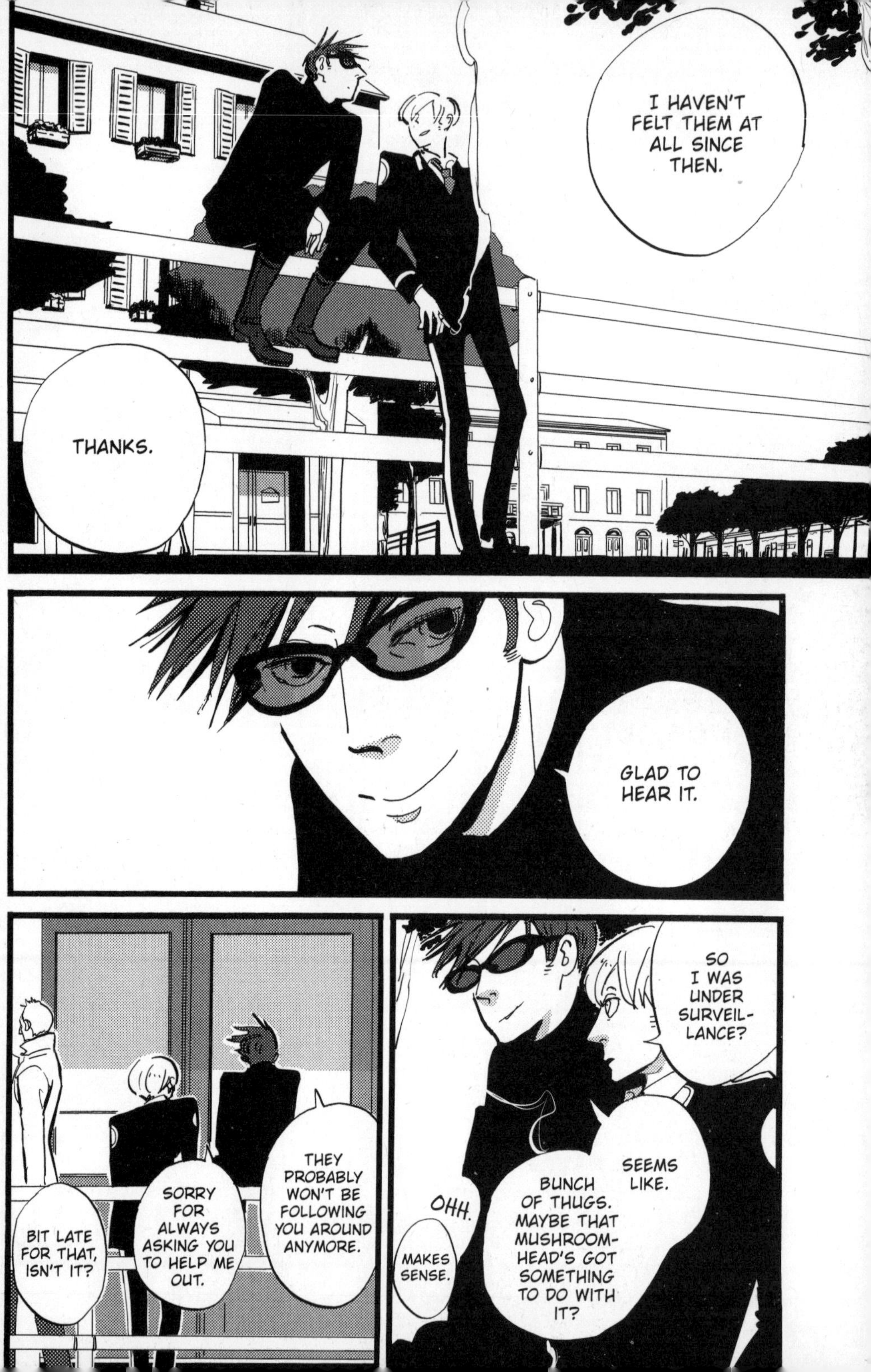
I HAVEN'T FELT THEM AT ALL SINCE THEN.
THANKS.
GLAD TO HEAR IT.
SO I WAS UNDER SURVEIL-LANCE?
SEEMS LIKE.
BUNCH OF THUGS. MAYBE THAT MUSHROOM-HEAD'S GOT SOMETHING TO DO WITH IT?
OHH.
MAKES SENSE.
THEY PROBABLY WON'T BE FOLLOWING YOU AROUND ANYMORE.
SORRY FOR ALWAYS ASKING YOU TO HELP ME OUT.
BIT LATE FOR THAT, ISN'T IT?

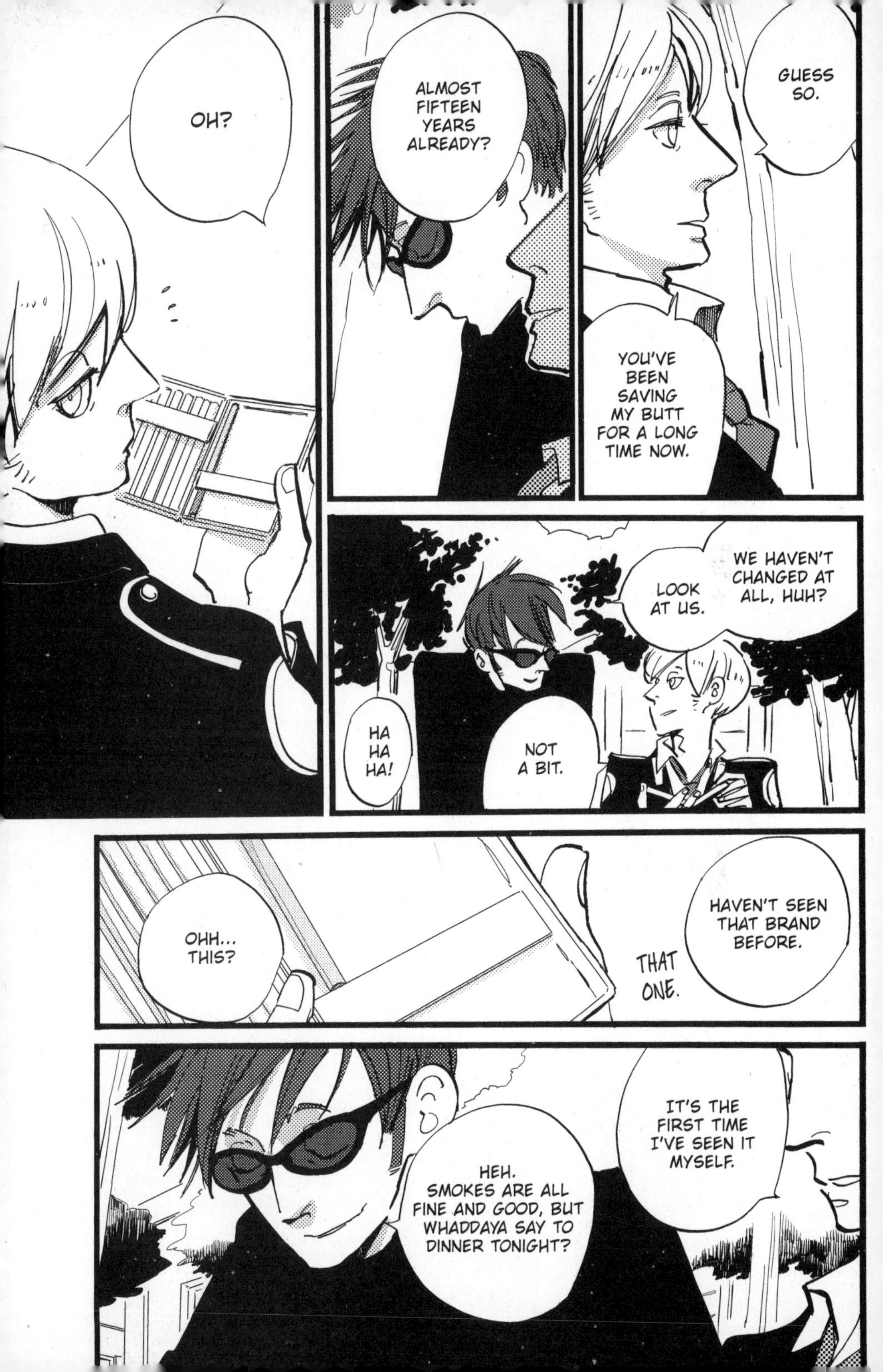
GUESS SO.
YOU'VE BEEN SAVING MY BUTT FOR A LONG TIME NOW.
ALMOST FIFTEEN YEARS ALREADY?
WE HAVEN'T CHANGED AT ALL, HUH?
LOOK AT US.
NOT A BIT.
HA HA HA!
OH?
HAVEN'T SEEN THAT BRAND BEFORE.
THAT ONE.
OHH... THIS?
IT'S THE FIRST TIME I'VE SEEN IT MYSELF.
HEH. SMOKES ARE ALL FINE AND GOOD, BUT WHADDAYA SAY TO DINNER TONIGHT?

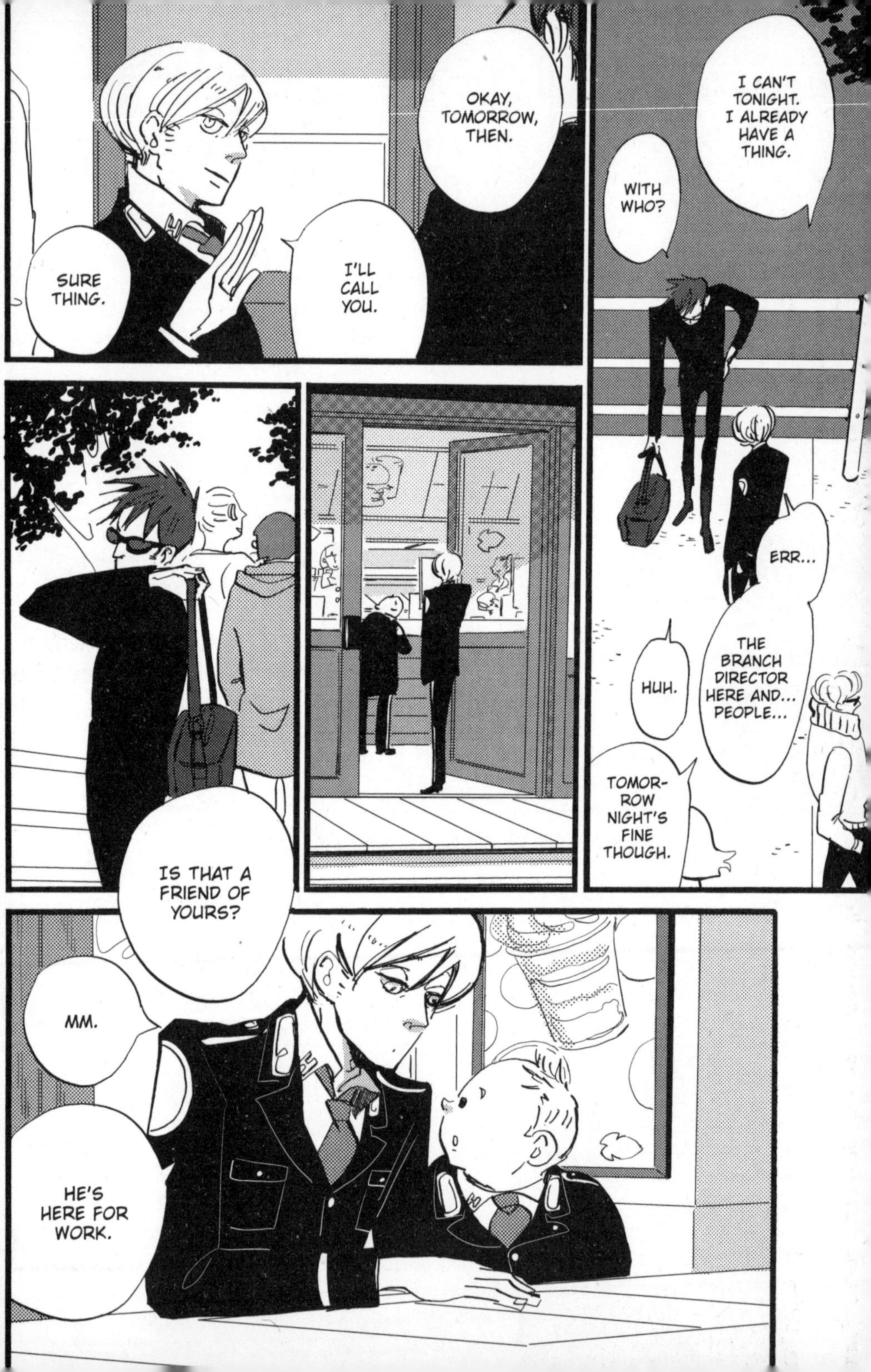
I CAN'T TONIGHT. I ALREADY HAVE A THING.
WITH WHO?
ERR...
THE BRANCH DIRECTOR HERE AND... PEOPLE...
HUH.
TOMOR-ROW NIGHT'S FINE THOUGH.
OKAY, TOMORROW, THEN.
I'LL CALL YOU.
SURE THING.
IS THAT A FRIEND OF YOURS?
MM.
HE'S HERE FOR WORK.

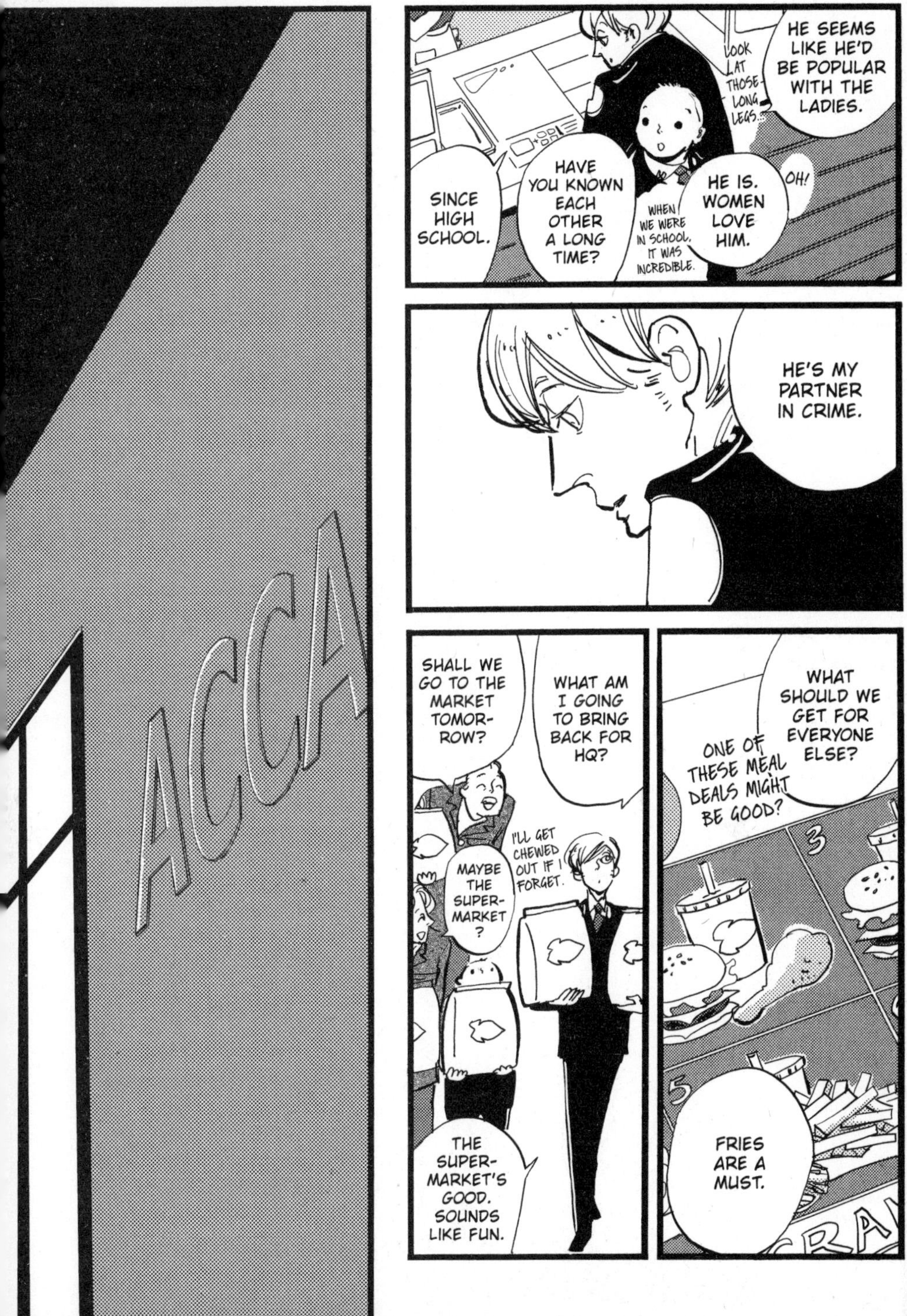
HE SEEMS LIKE HE'D BE POPULAR WITH THE LADIES.
LOOK AT THOSE LONG LEGS...
OH!
HE IS. WOMEN LOVE HIM.
WHEN WE WERE IN SCHOOL, IT WAS INCREDIBLE.
HAVE YOU KNOWN EACH OTHER A LONG TIME?
SINCE HIGH SCHOOL.
HE'S MY PARTNER IN CRIME.
WHAT SHOULD WE GET FOR EVERYONE ELSE?
ONE OF THESE MEAL DEALS MIGHT BE GOOD?
FRIES ARE A MUST.
WHAT AM I GOING TO BRING BACK FOR HQ?
SHALL WE GO TO THE MARKET TOMORROW?
I'LL GET CHEWED OUT IF I FORGET.
MAYBE THE SUPERMARKET?
THE SUPERMARKET'S GOOD. SOUNDS LIKE FUN.
ACCA

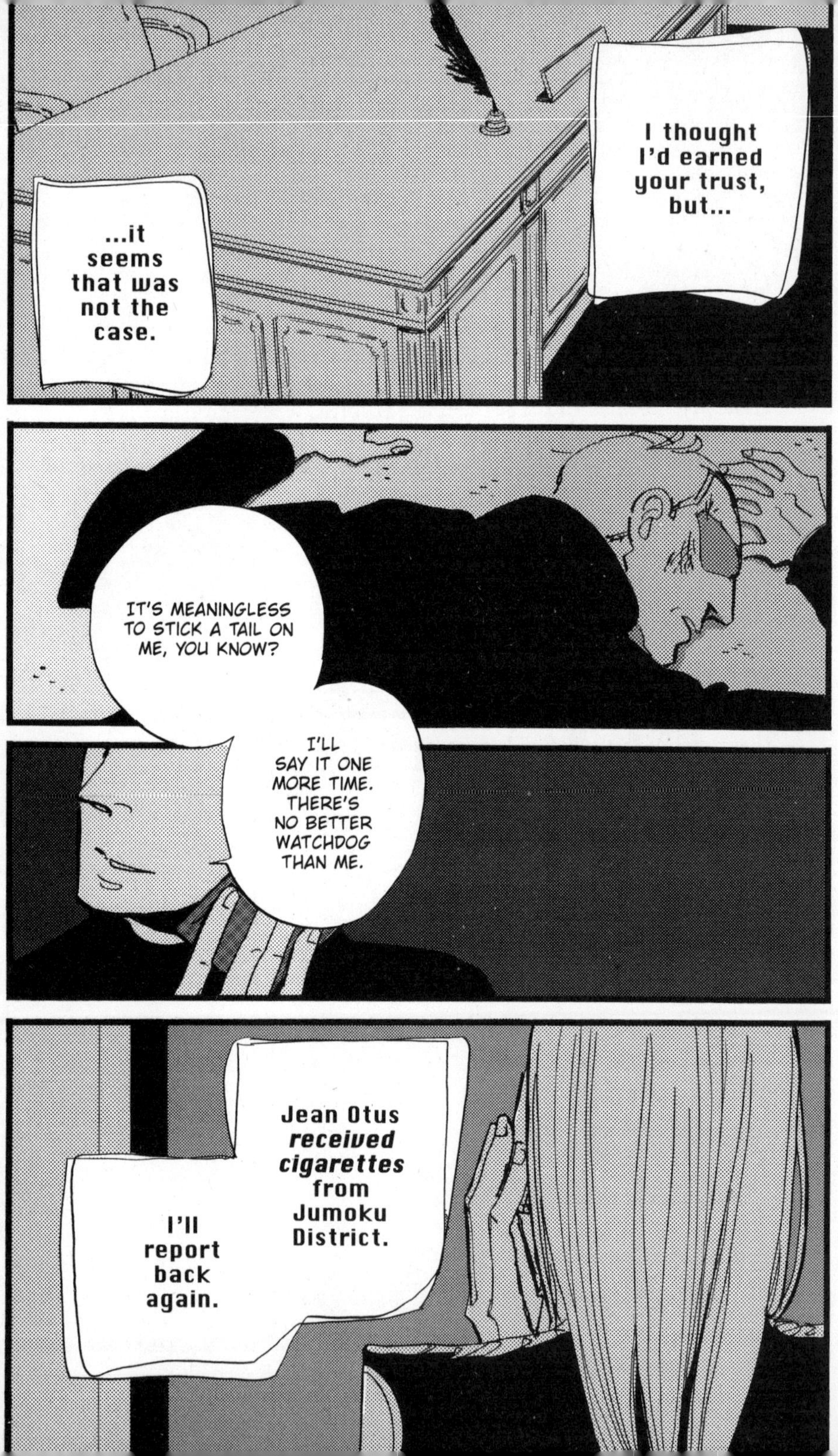
I thought I'd earned your trust, but...
...it seems that was not the case.
IT'S MEANINGLESS TO STICK A TAIL ON ME, YOU KNOW?
I'LL SAY IT ONE MORE TIME. THERE'S NO BETTER WATCHDOG THAN ME.
Jean Otus *received cigarettes* from Jumoku District.
I'll report back again.

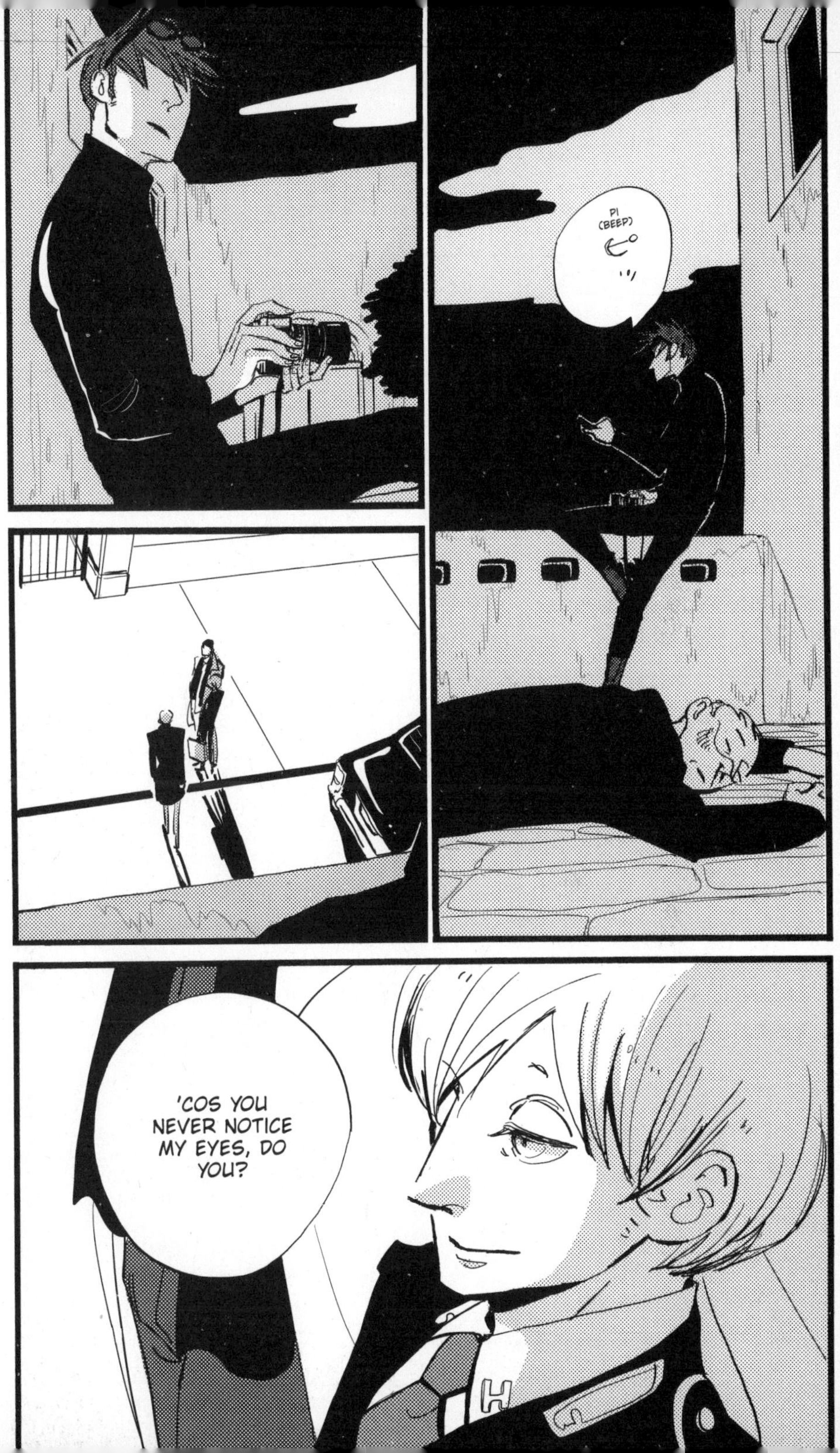
PI (BEEP)
'COS YOU NEVER NOTICE MY EYES, DO YOU?

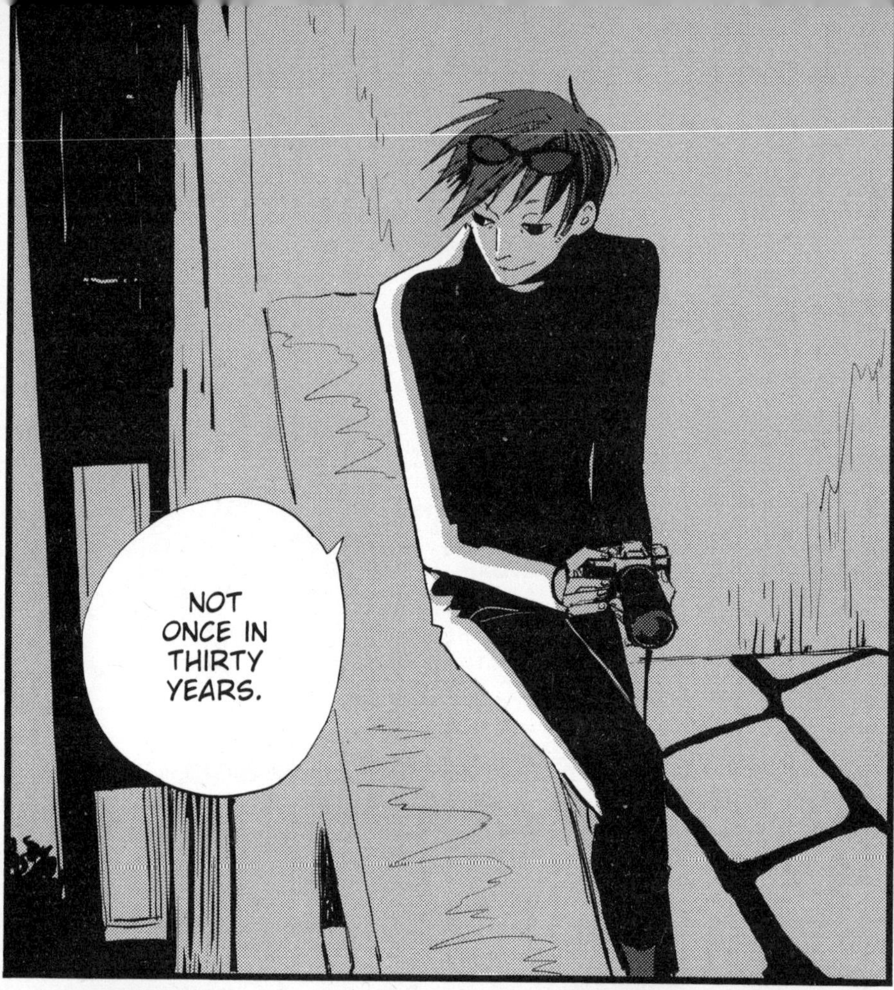
NOT ONCE IN THIRTY YEARS.
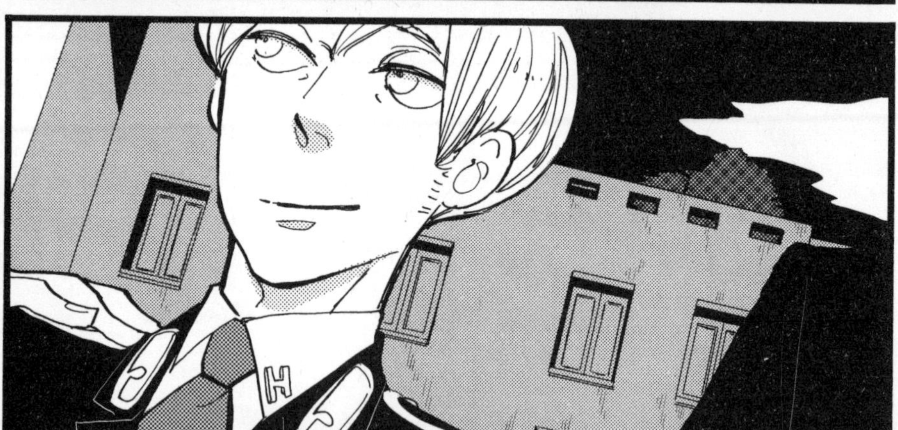

ACCA Branch Uniforms | 3

Jumoku District

With the average height being 2.15 m, everything is bigger in Jumoku, including agricul-tural products. The color of the knit shirt under the jacket is different at each office.

CHAPTER 6

Gorging on Strawberries in Jumoku

PASS

ACCA 13 TERRITORY INSPECTION DEPT

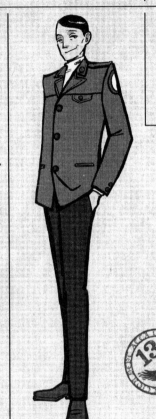

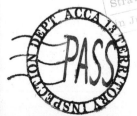

CHAPTER 7

Boozing in Jumoku with a Partner in Crime

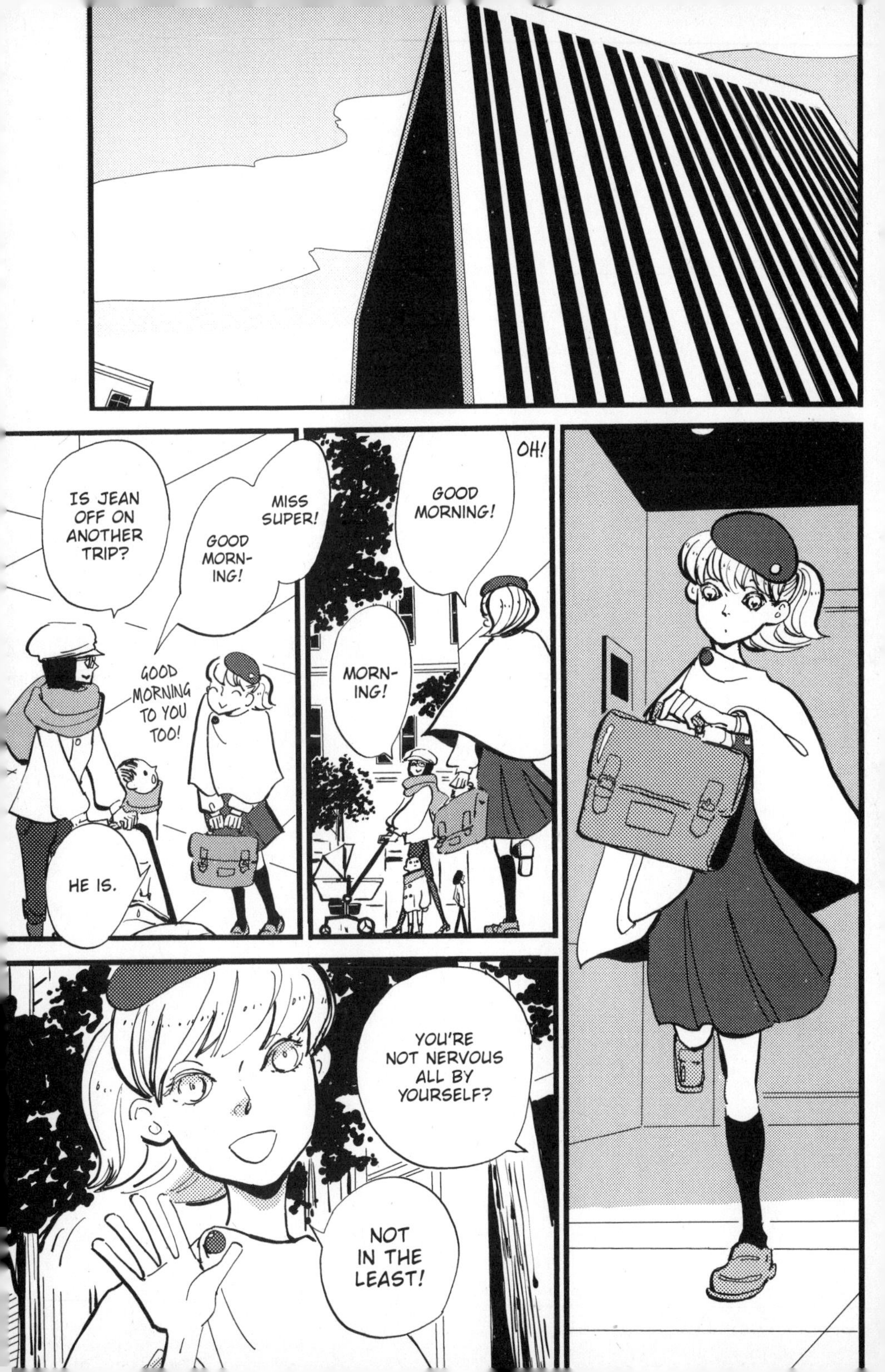
OH!
GOOD MORNING!
MORNING!
GOOD MORNING! MISS SUPER!
IS JEAN OFF ON ANOTHER TRIP?
GOOD MORNING TO YOU TOO!
HE IS.
YOU'RE NOT NERVOUS ALL BY YOURSELF?
NOT IN THE LEAST!

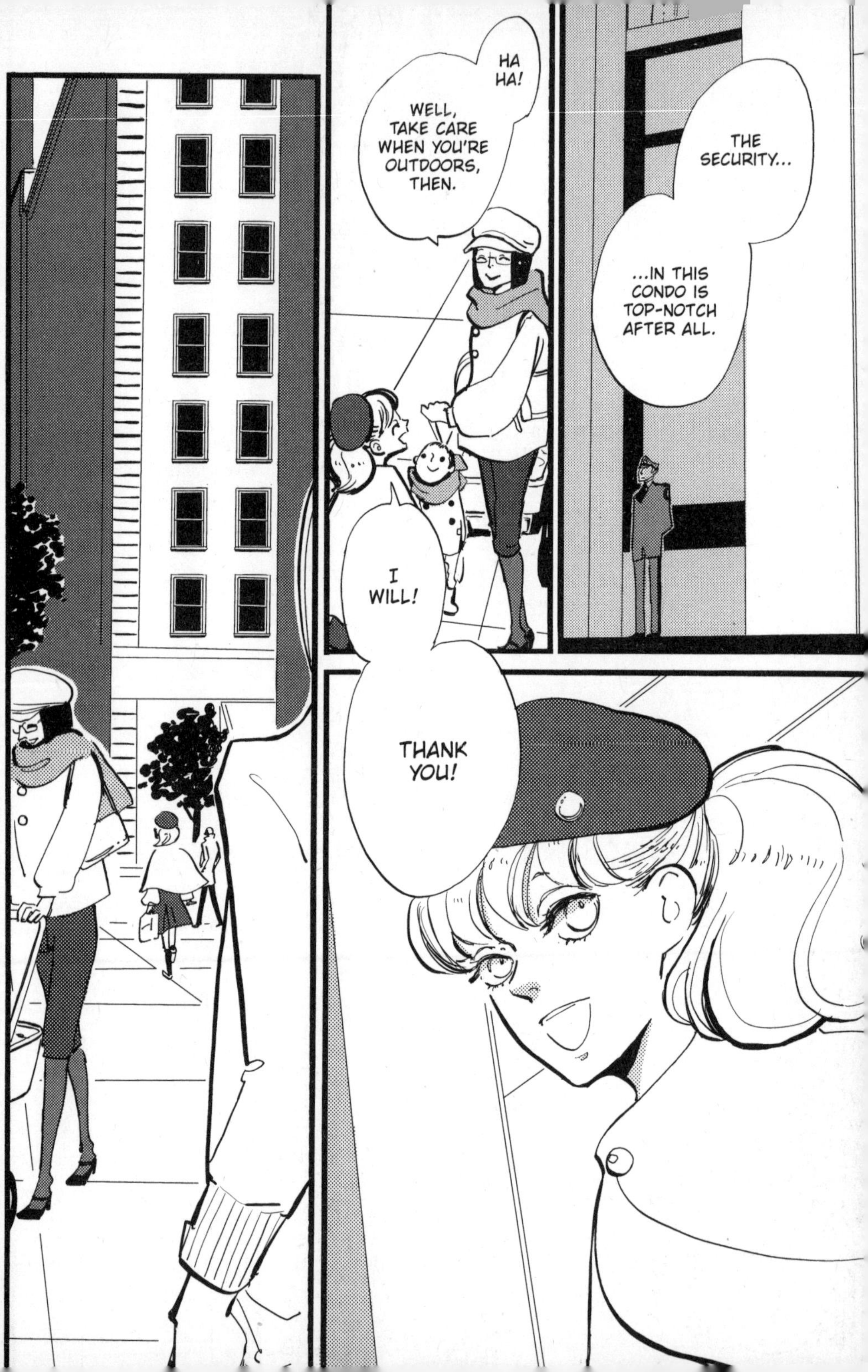
THE SECURITY...
...IN THIS CONDO IS TOP-NOTCH AFTER ALL.
HA HA!
WELL, TAKE CARE WHEN YOU'RE OUTDOORS, THEN.
I WILL!
THANK YOU!

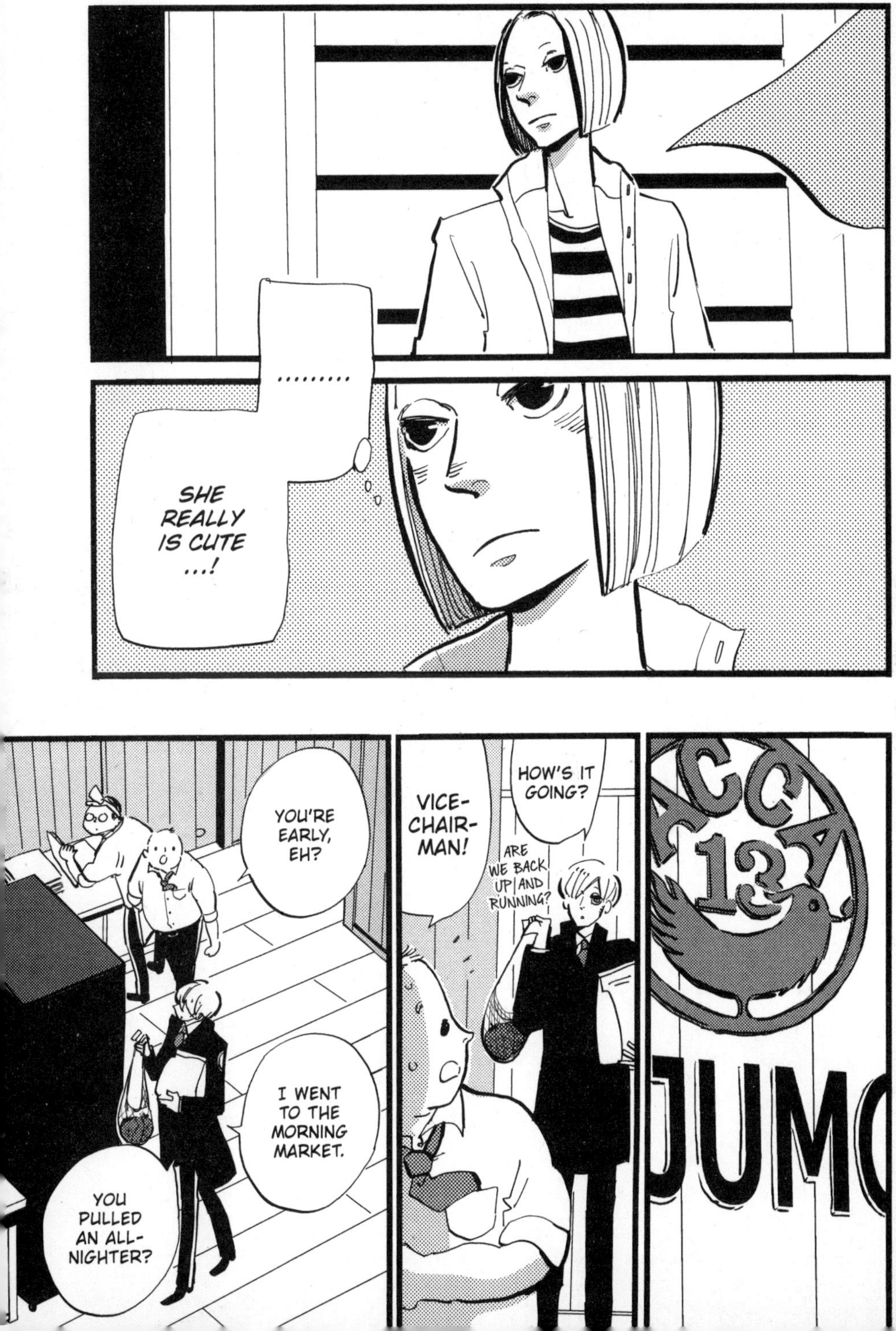
....
SHE REALLY IS CUTE ...!
ACCA 13
JUMO
HOW'S IT GOING?
VICE-CHAIRMAN!
ARE WE BACK UP AND RUNNING?
YOU'RE EARLY, EH?
I WENT TO THE MORNING MARKET.
YOU PULLED AN ALL-NIGHTER?

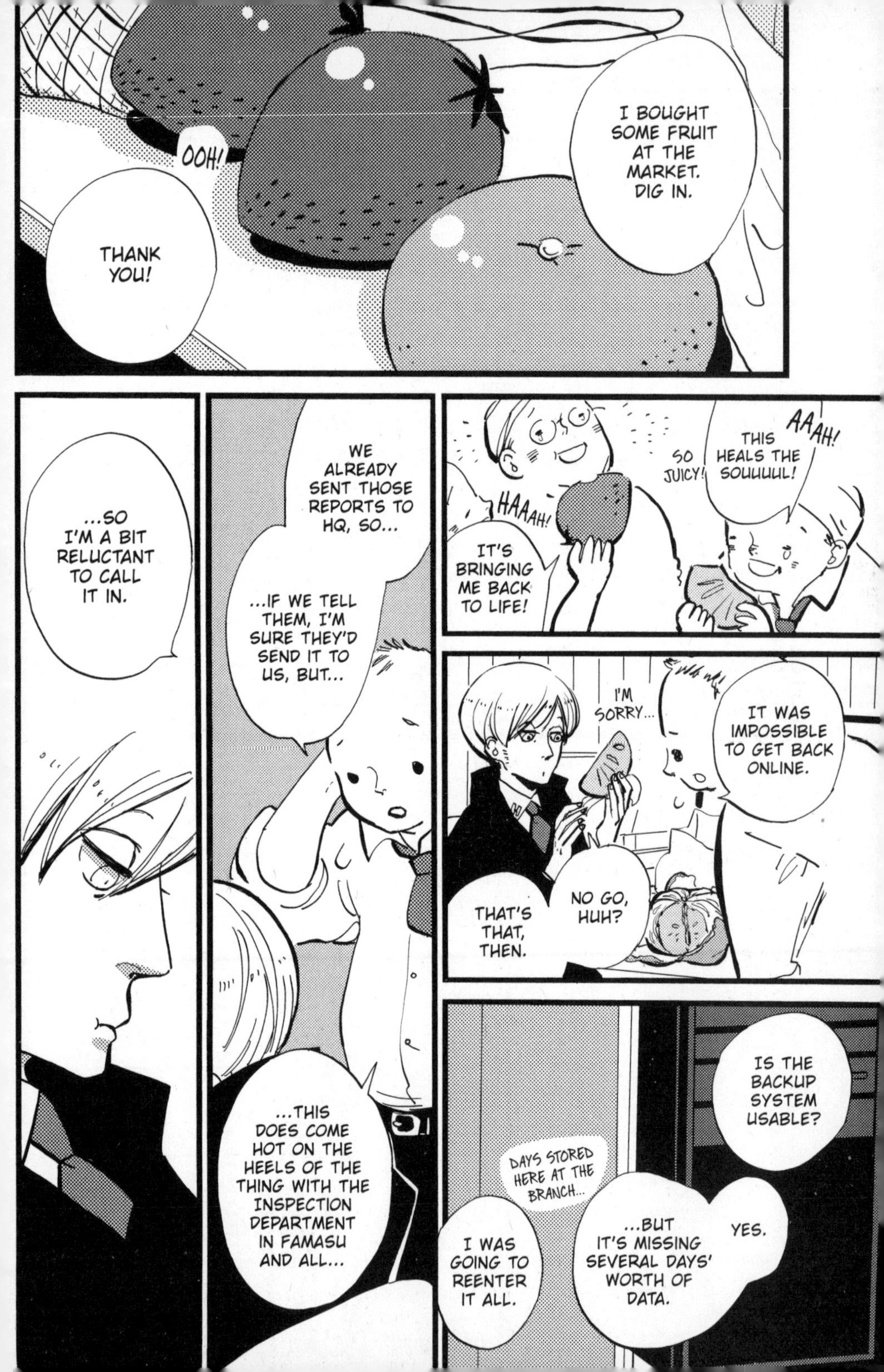
I BOUGHT SOME FRUIT AT THE MARKET. DIG IN.
OOH!
THANK YOU!
AAAAH!
THIS HEALS THE SOUUUUL!
SO JUICY!
HAAAAH!
IT'S BRINGING ME BACK TO LIFE!
IT WAS IMPOSSIBLE TO GET BACK ONLINE.
I'M SORRY...
NO GO, HUH?
THAT'S THAT, THEN.
IS THE BACKUP SYSTEM USABLE?
YES.
...BUT IT'S MISSING SEVERAL DAYS' WORTH OF DATA.
DAYS STORED HERE AT THE BRANCH...
I WAS GOING TO REENTER IT ALL.
WE ALREADY SENT THOSE REPORTS TO HQ, SO...
...IF WE TELL THEM, I'M SURE THEY'D SEND IT TO US, BUT...
...THIS DOES COME HOT ON THE HEELS OF THE THING WITH THE INSPECTION DEPARTMENT IN FAMASU AND ALL...
...SO I'M A BIT RELUCTANT TO CALL IT IN.

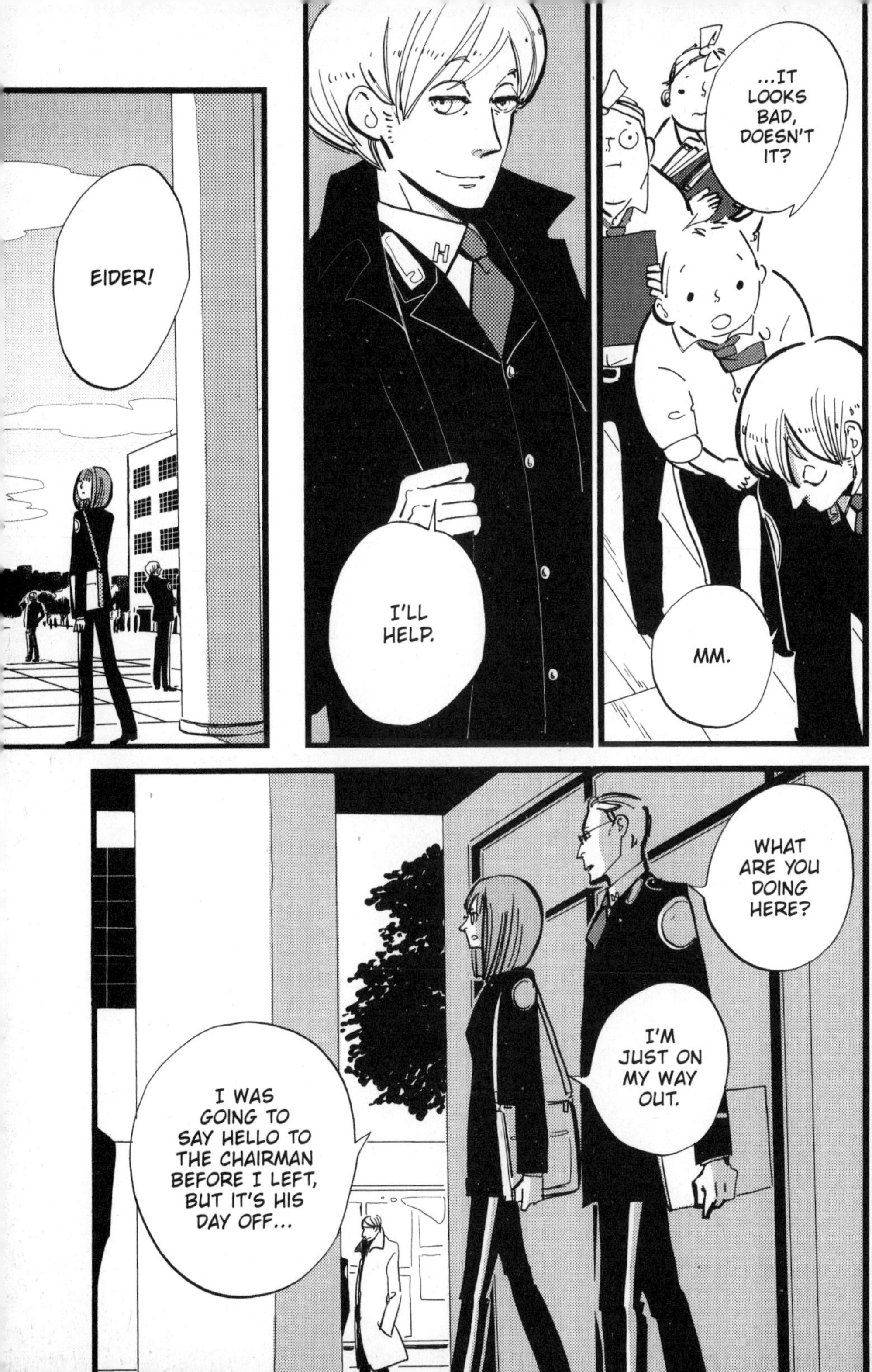
...IT LOOKS BAD, DOESN'T IT?
MM.
I'LL HELP.
EIDER!
WHAT ARE YOU DOING HERE?
I'M JUST ON MY WAY OUT.
I WAS GOING TO SAY HELLO TO THE CHAIRMAN BEFORE I LEFT, BUT IT'S HIS DAY OFF...

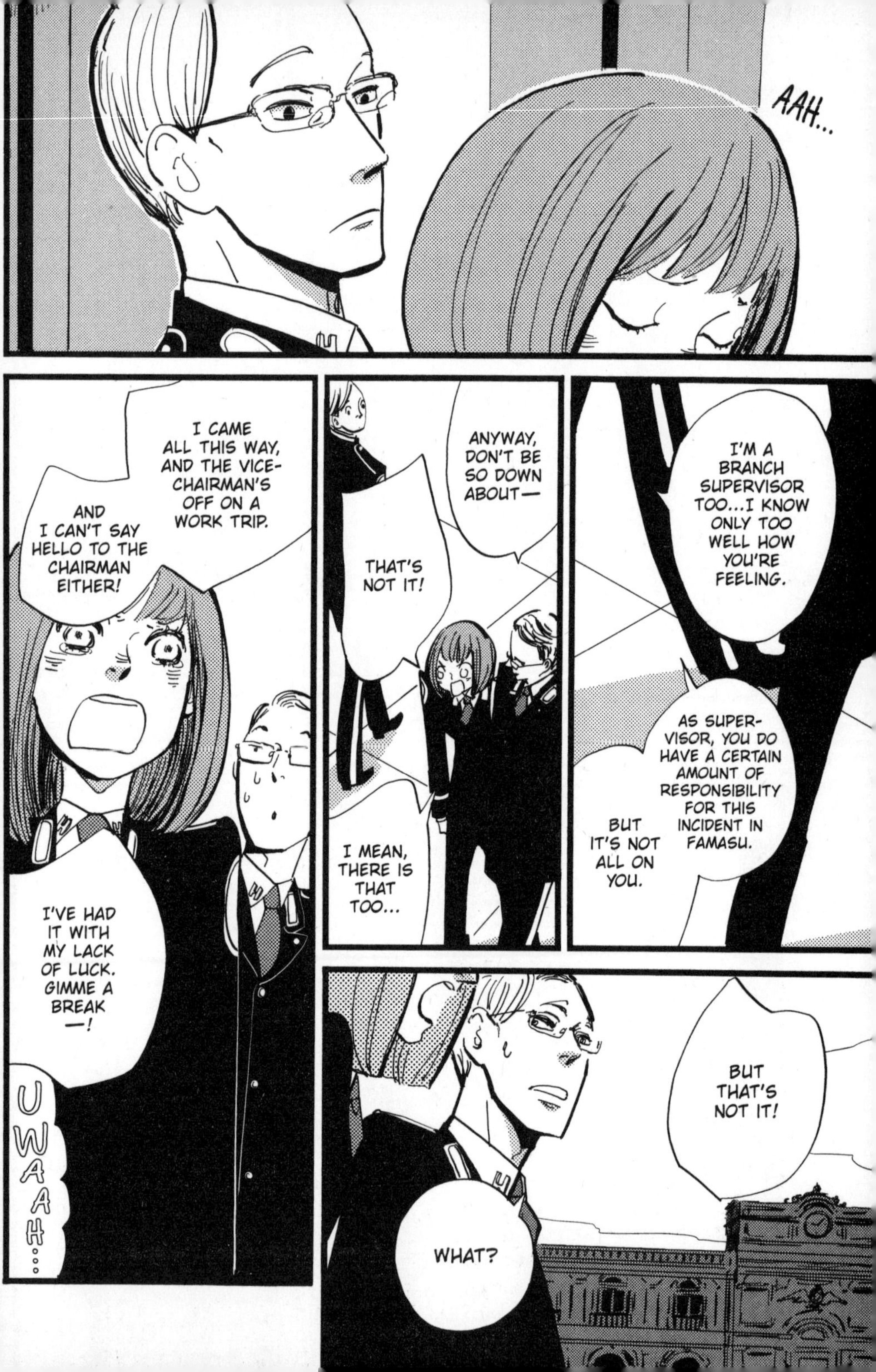
AAH...
I'M A BRANCH SUPERVISOR TOO...I KNOW ONLY TOO WELL HOW YOU'RE FEELING.
AS SUPER-VISOR, YOU DO HAVE A CERTAIN AMOUNT OF RESPONSIBILITY FOR THIS INCIDENT IN FAMASU.
BUT IT'S NOT ALL ON YOU.
ANYWAY, DON'T BE SO DOWN ABOUT—
THAT'S NOT IT!
I MEAN, THERE IS THAT TOO...
BUT THAT'S NOT IT!
WHAT?
I CAME ALL THIS WAY, AND THE VICE-CHAIRMAN'S OFF ON A WORK TRIP.
AND I CAN'T SAY HELLO TO THE CHAIRMAN EITHER!
I'VE HAD IT WITH MY LACK OF LUCK. GIMME A BREAK—!
UWAAAH...

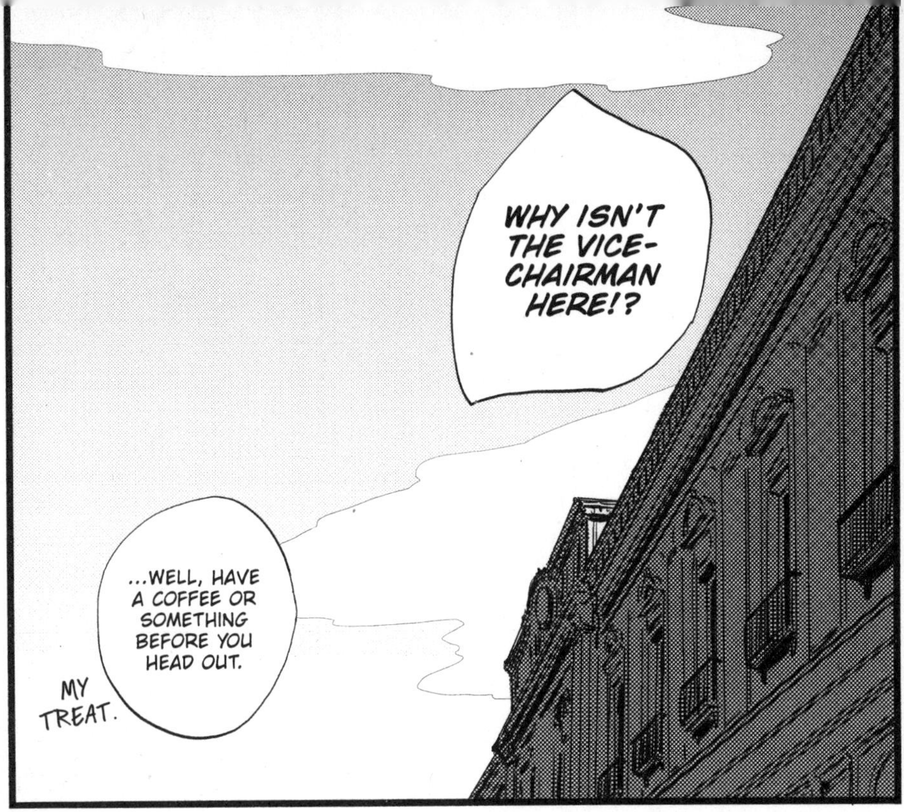
WHY ISN'T THE VICE-CHAIRMAN HERE!?
...WELL, HAVE A COFFEE OR SOMETHING BEFORE YOU HEAD OUT.
MY TREAT.
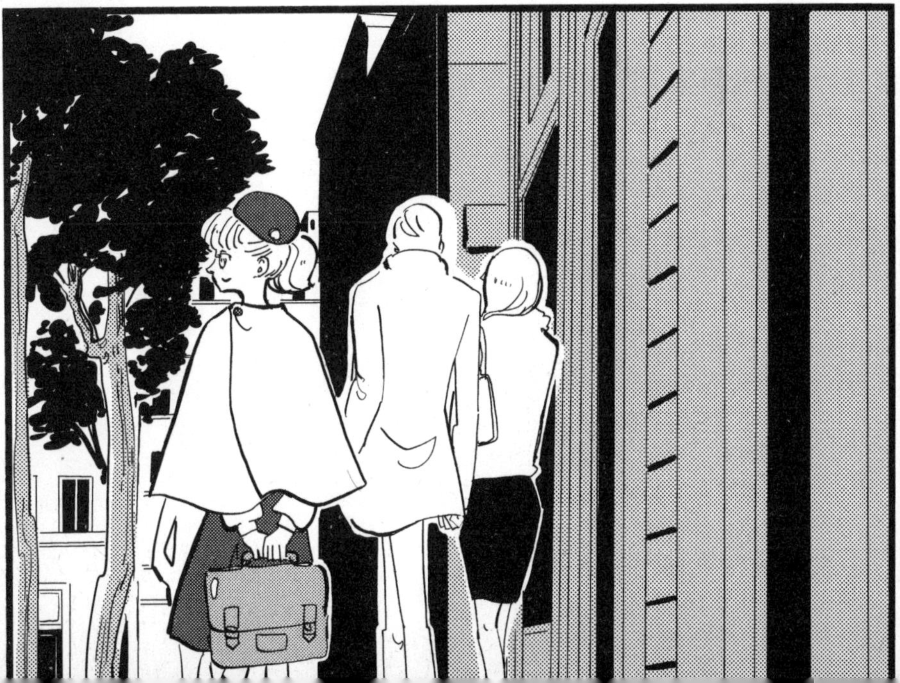

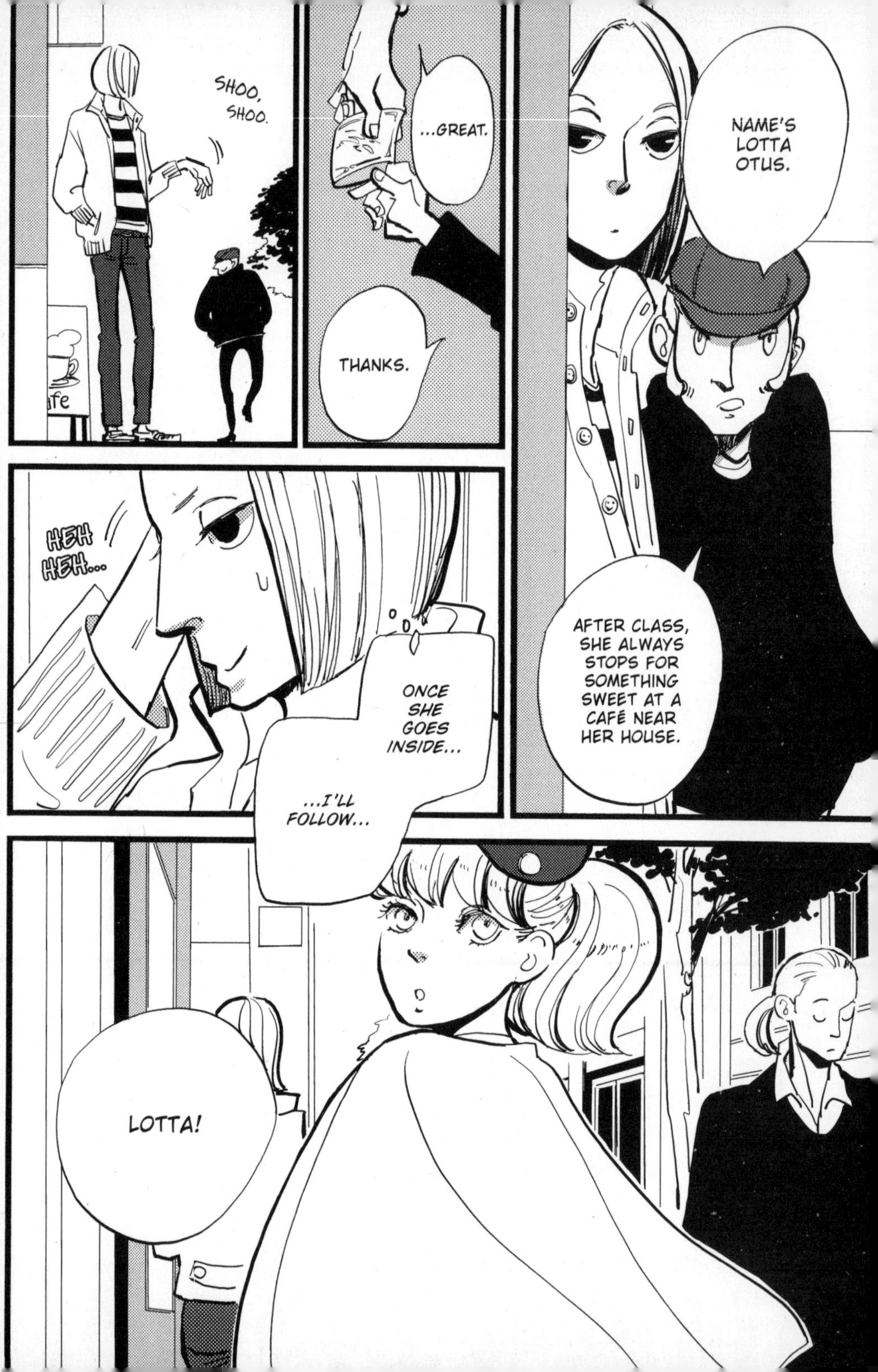
NAME'S LOTTA OTUS.
AFTER CLASS, SHE ALWAYS STOPS FOR SOMETHING SWEET AT A CAFÉ NEAR HER HOUSE.
...GREAT.
THANKS.
SHOO, SHOO.
HEH HEH...
ONCE SHE GOES INSIDE...
...I'LL FOLLOW...
LOTTA!

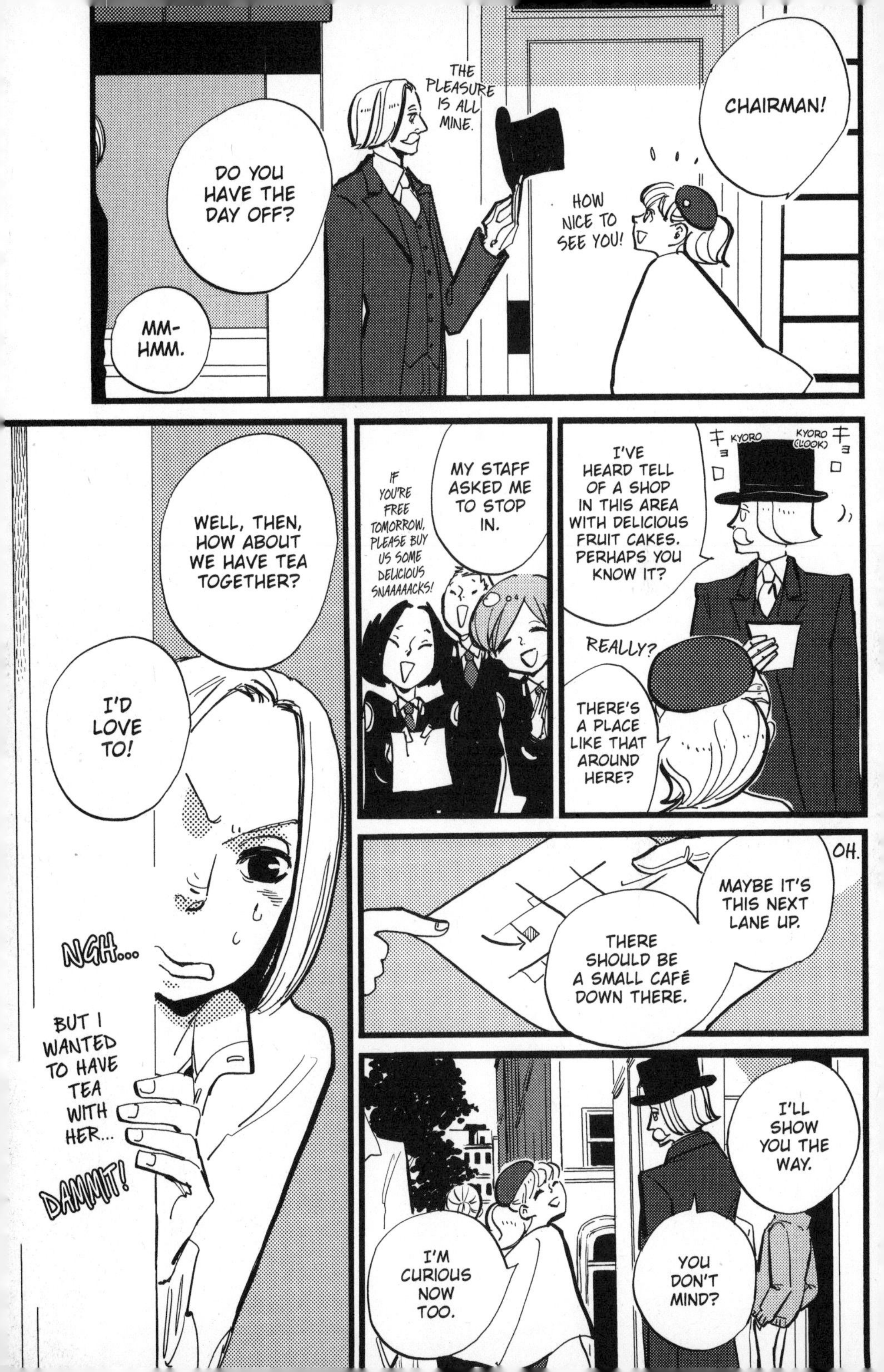
CHAIRMAN!
HOW NICE TO SEE YOU!
THE PLEASURE IS ALL MINE.
DO YOU HAVE THE DAY OFF?
MM-HMM.
KYORO (LOOK)
KYORO
I'VE HEARD TELL OF A SHOP IN THIS AREA WITH DELICIOUS FRUIT CAKES. PERHAPS YOU KNOW IT?
REALLY?
THERE'S A PLACE LIKE THAT AROUND HERE?
MY STAFF ASKED ME TO STOP IN.
IF YOU'RE FREE TOMORROW, PLEASE BUY US SOME DELICIOUS SNAAAAACKS!
OH.
MAYBE IT'S THIS NEXT LANE UP.
THERE SHOULD BE A SMALL CAFÉ DOWN THERE.
I'LL SHOW YOU THE WAY.
YOU DON'T MIND?
I'M CURIOUS NOW TOO.
WELL, THEN, HOW ABOUT WE HAVE TEA TOGETHER?
I'D LOVE TO!
NGH...
BUT I WANTED TO HAVE TEA WITH HER...
DAMMIT!

HOW IS MY BROTHER DOING AT WORK?

QUITE WELL.

HE'S NOT CAUSING ANY PROBLEMS?

NONE AT ALL.

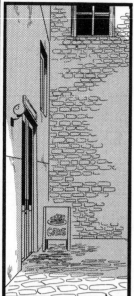

HE BARELY MOVES WHEN HE'S AT HOME.

THIS IS SOOOOO GOOD!

DOWA'S FAMOUS FOR IT.

THIS CAKE.

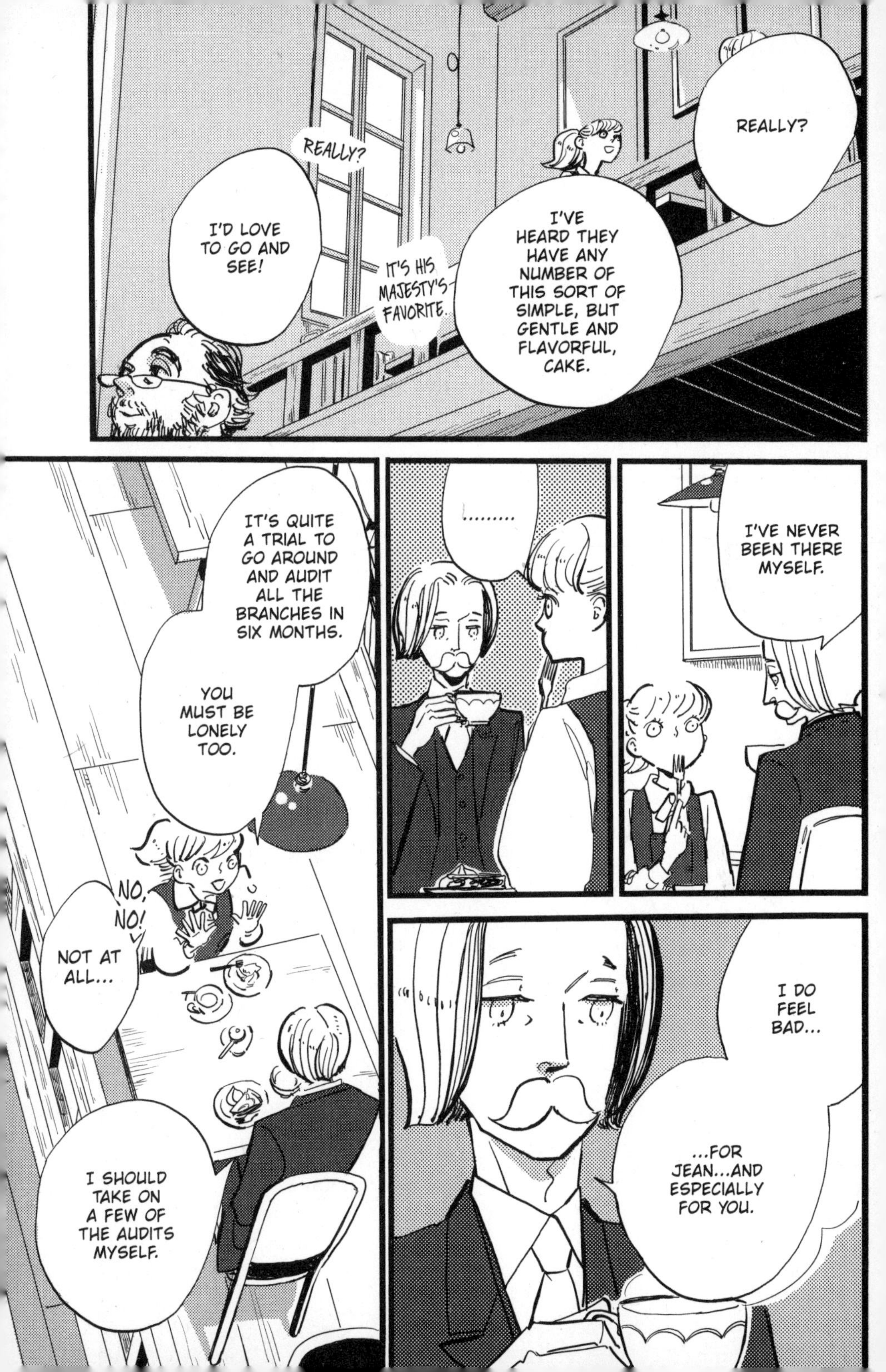
REALLY?
I'VE HEARD THEY HAVE ANY NUMBER OF THIS SORT OF SIMPLE, BUT GENTLE AND FLAVORFUL, CAKE.
IT'S HIS MAJESTY'S FAVORITE.
REALLY?
I'D LOVE TO GO AND SEE!
I'VE NEVER BEEN THERE MYSELF.
....
I DO FEEL BAD...
...FOR JEAN...AND ESPECIALLY FOR YOU.
IT'S QUITE A TRIAL TO GO AROUND AND AUDIT ALL THE BRANCHES IN SIX MONTHS.
YOU MUST BE LONELY TOO.
NO, NO!
NOT AT ALL...
I SHOULD TAKE ON A FEW OF THE AUDITS MYSELF.

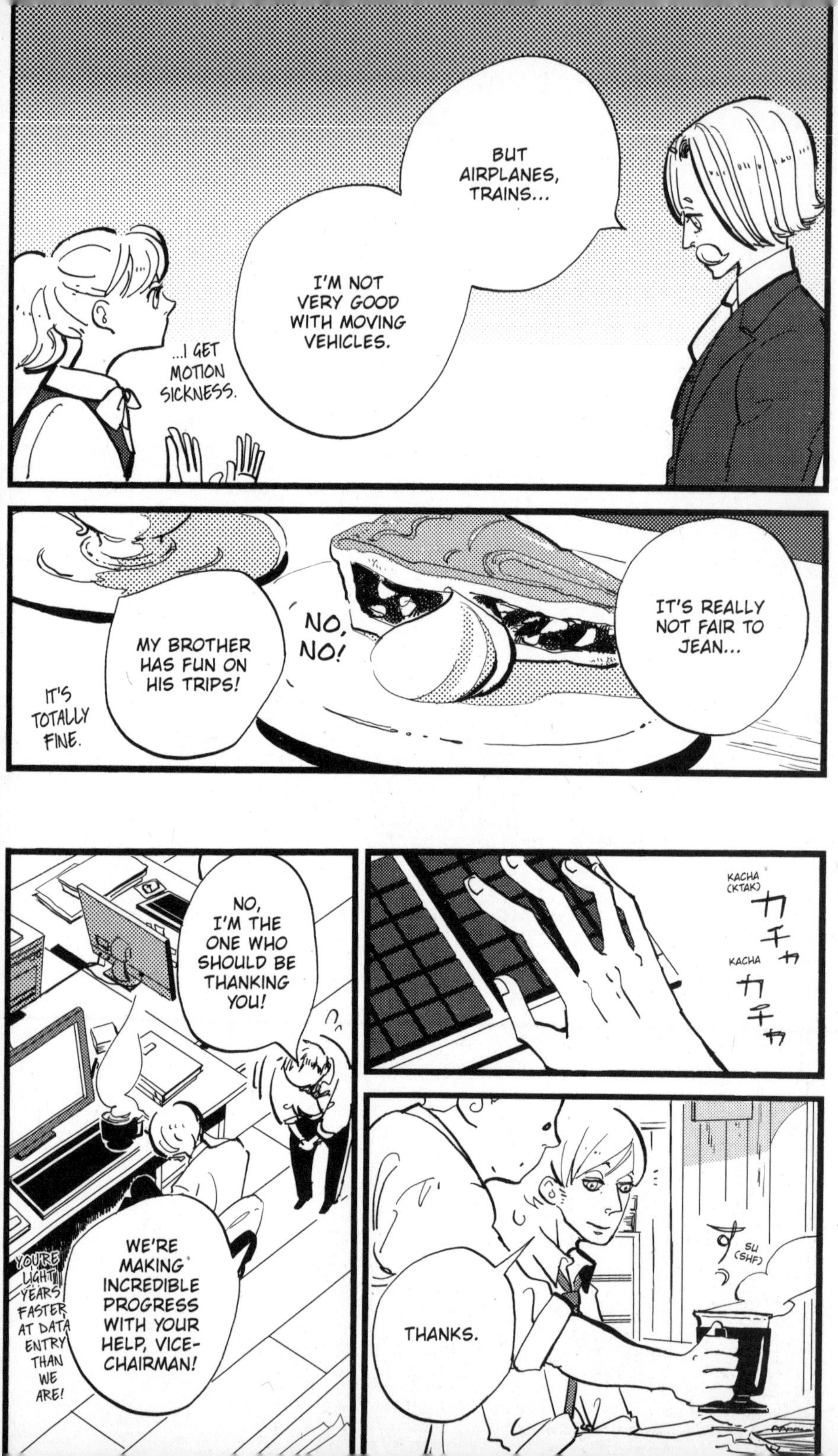
BUT AIRPLANES, TRAINS...
I'M NOT VERY GOOD WITH MOVING VEHICLES.
...I GET MOTION SICKNESS.
IT'S REALLY NOT FAIR TO JEAN...
NO, NO!
MY BROTHER HAS FUN ON HIS TRIPS!
IT'S TOTALLY FINE.
KACHA (KTAK)
カチャ
KACHA
カチャ
SU (SHF)
す
THANKS.
NO, I'M THE ONE WHO SHOULD BE THANKING YOU!
WE'RE MAKING INCREDIBLE PROGRESS WITH YOUR HELP, VICE-CHAIRMAN!
YOU'RE LIGHT YEARS FASTER AT DATA ENTRY THAN WE ARE!

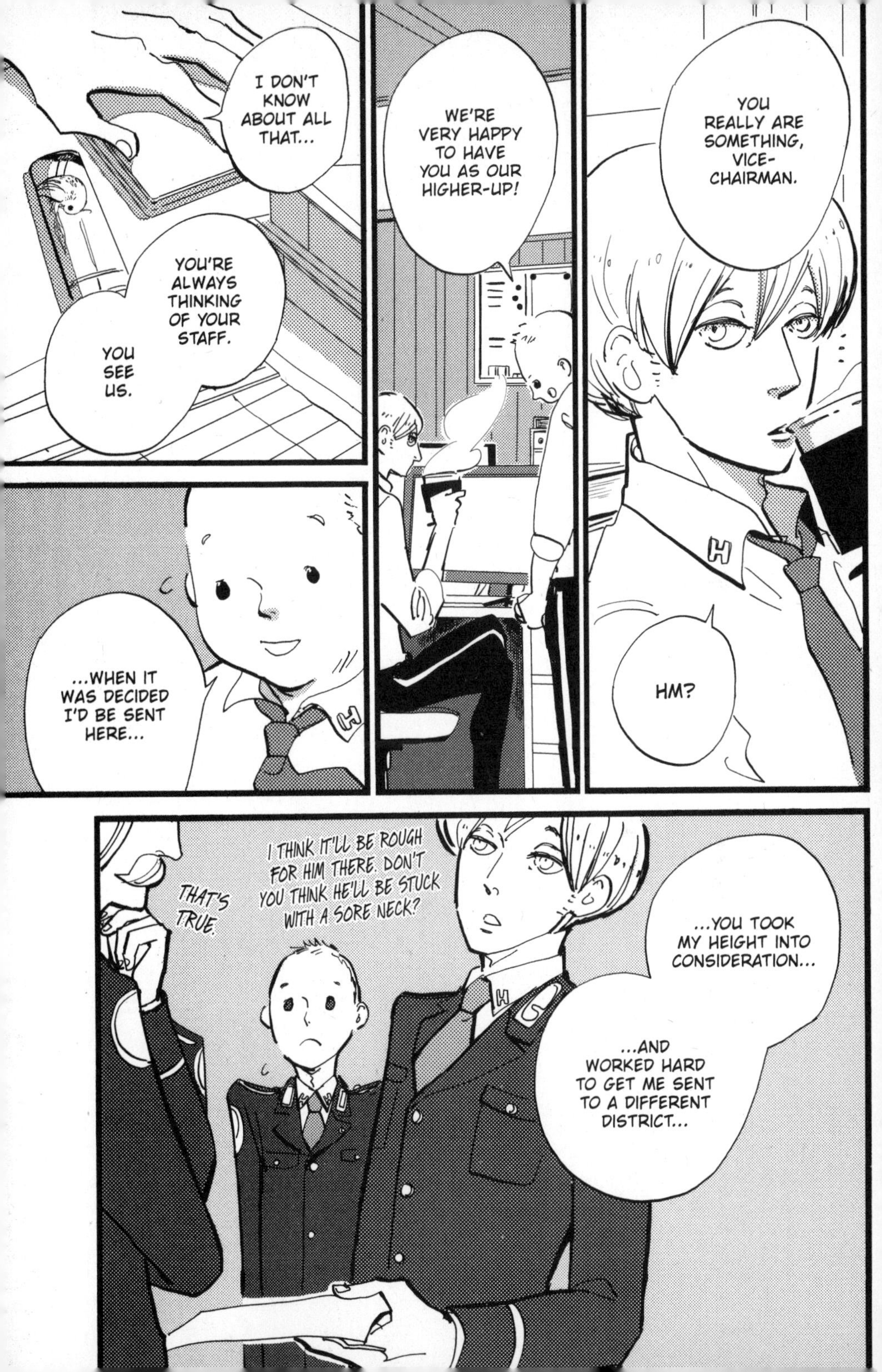
YOU REALLY ARE SOMETHING, VICE-CHAIRMAN.
HM?
WE'RE VERY HAPPY TO HAVE YOU AS OUR HIGHER-UP!
I DON'T KNOW ABOUT ALL THAT...
YOU'RE ALWAYS THINKING OF YOUR STAFF.
YOU SEE US.
...WHEN IT WAS DECIDED I'D BE SENT HERE...
...YOU TOOK MY HEIGHT INTO CONSIDERATION...
...AND WORKED HARD TO GET ME SENT TO A DIFFERENT DISTRICT...
I THINK IT'LL BE ROUGH FOR HIM THERE. DON'T YOU THINK HE'LL BE STUCK WITH A SORE NECK?
THAT'S TRUE.

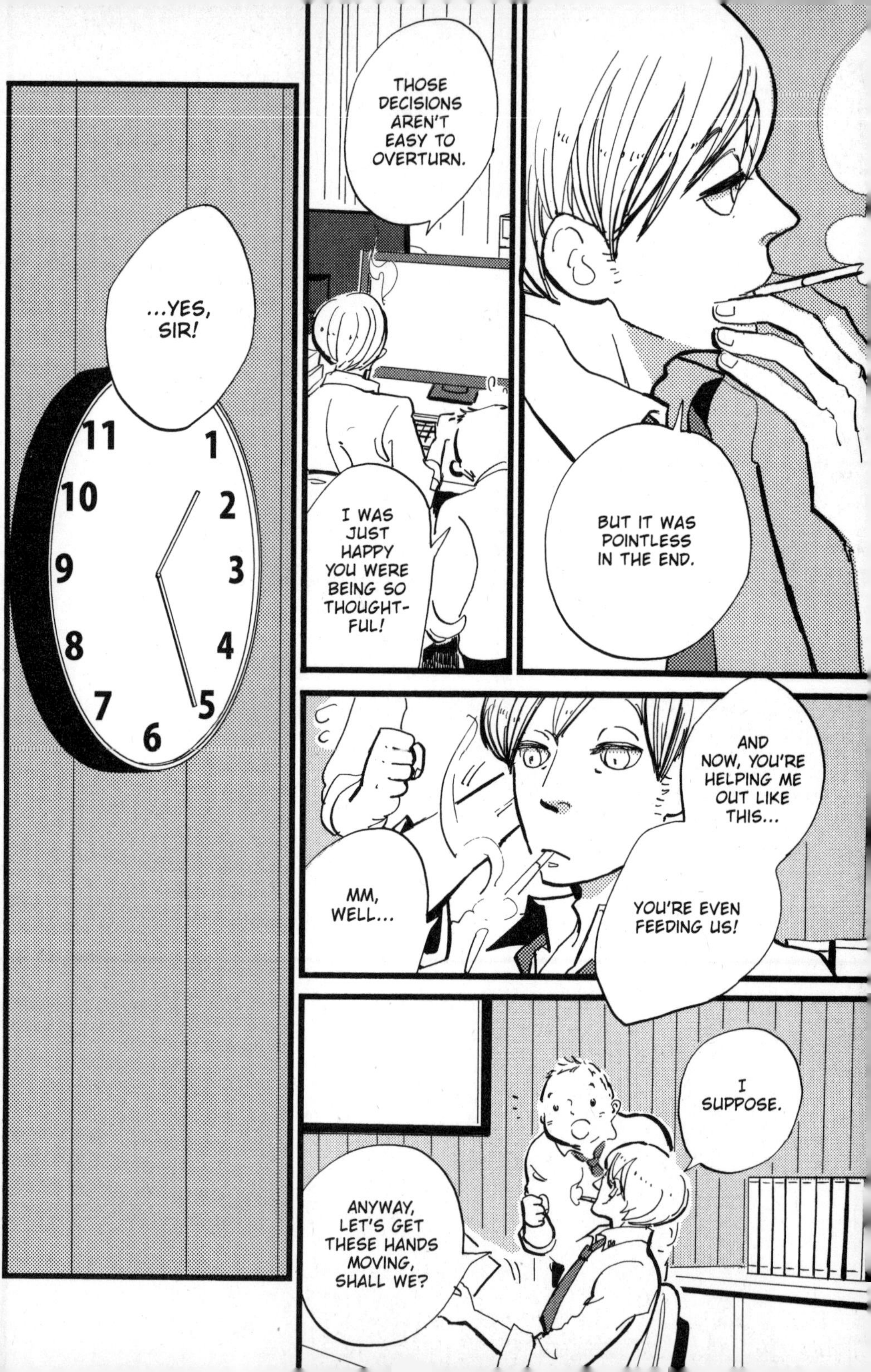
BUT IT WAS POINTLESS IN THE END.
THOSE DECISIONS AREN'T EASY TO OVERTURN.
I WAS JUST HAPPY YOU WERE BEING SO THOUGHT-FUL!
AND NOW, YOU'RE HELPING ME OUT LIKE THIS...
YOU'RE EVEN FEEDING US!
MM, WELL...
I SUPPOSE.
ANYWAY, LET'S GET THESE HANDS MOVING, SHALL WE?
...YES, SIR!

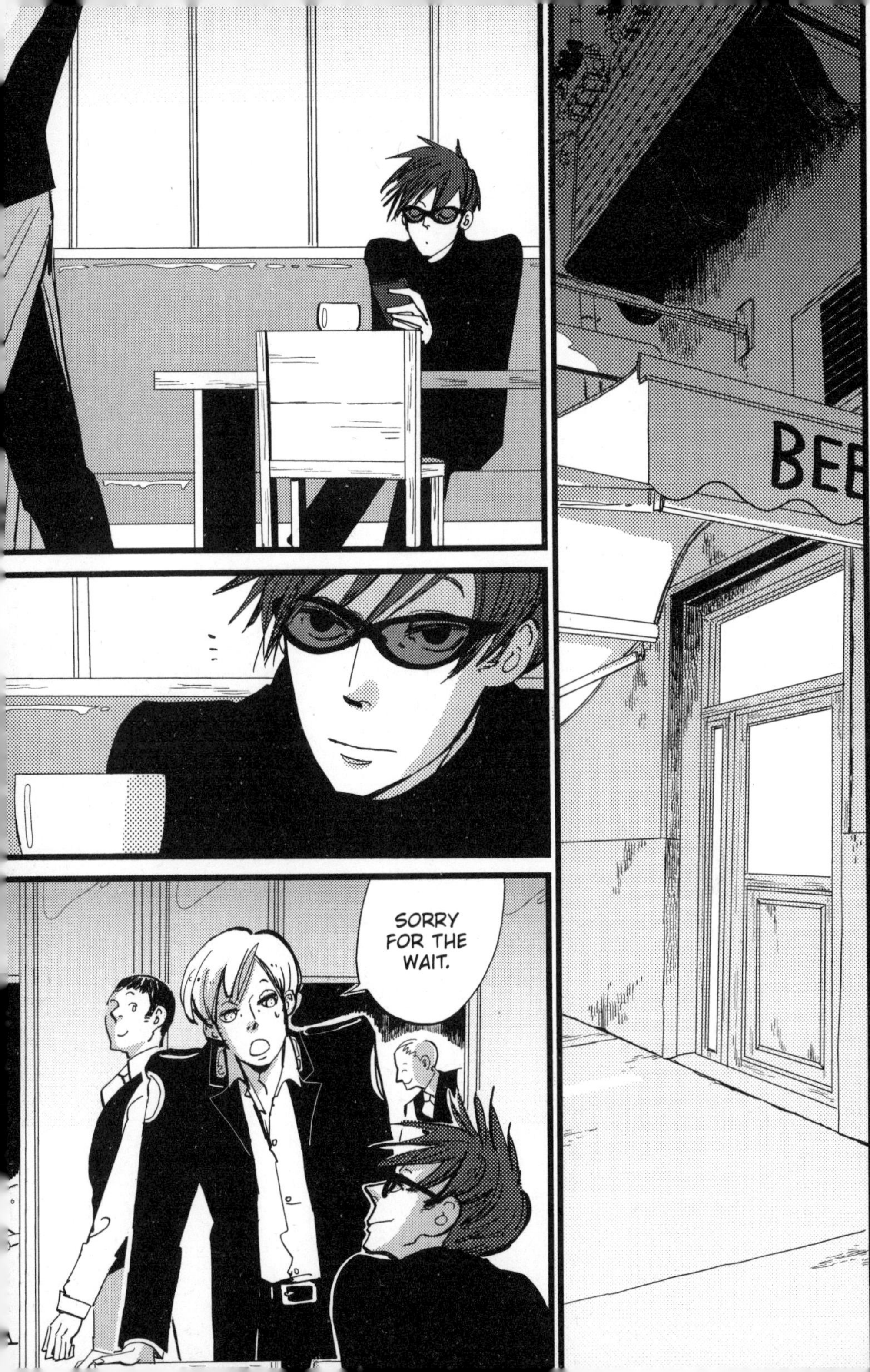
BEE
SORRY FOR THE WAIT.

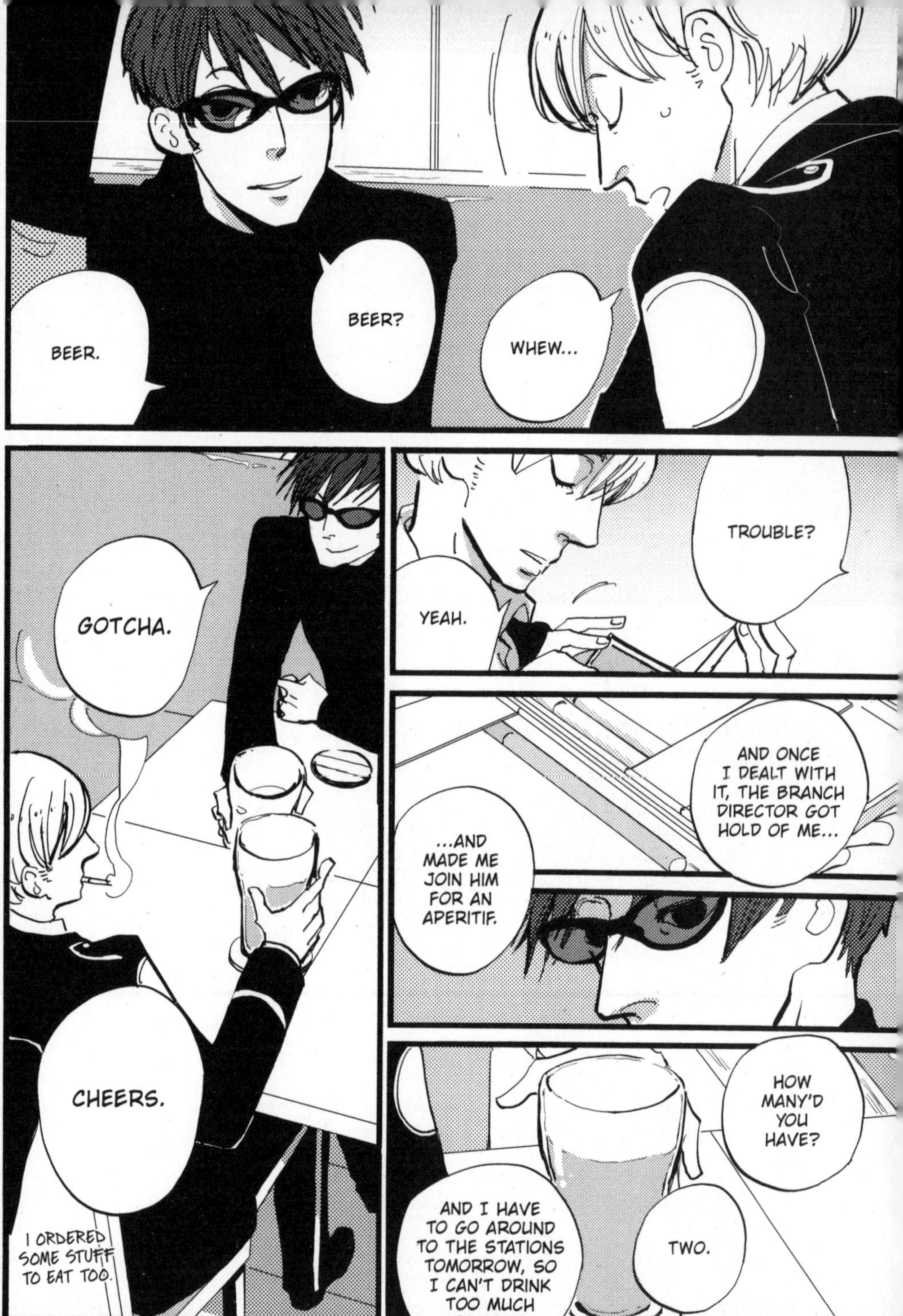
WHEW...
BEER?
BEER.
TROUBLE?
YEAH.
AND ONCE I DEALT WITH IT, THE BRANCH DIRECTOR GOT HOLD OF ME...
...AND MADE ME JOIN HIM FOR AN APERITIF.
HOW MANY'D YOU HAVE?
TWO.
AND I HAVE TO GO AROUND TO THE STATIONS TOMORROW, SO I CAN'T DRINK TOO MUCH TONIGHT.
GOTCHA.
CHEERS.
I ORDERED SOME STUFF TO EAT TOO.

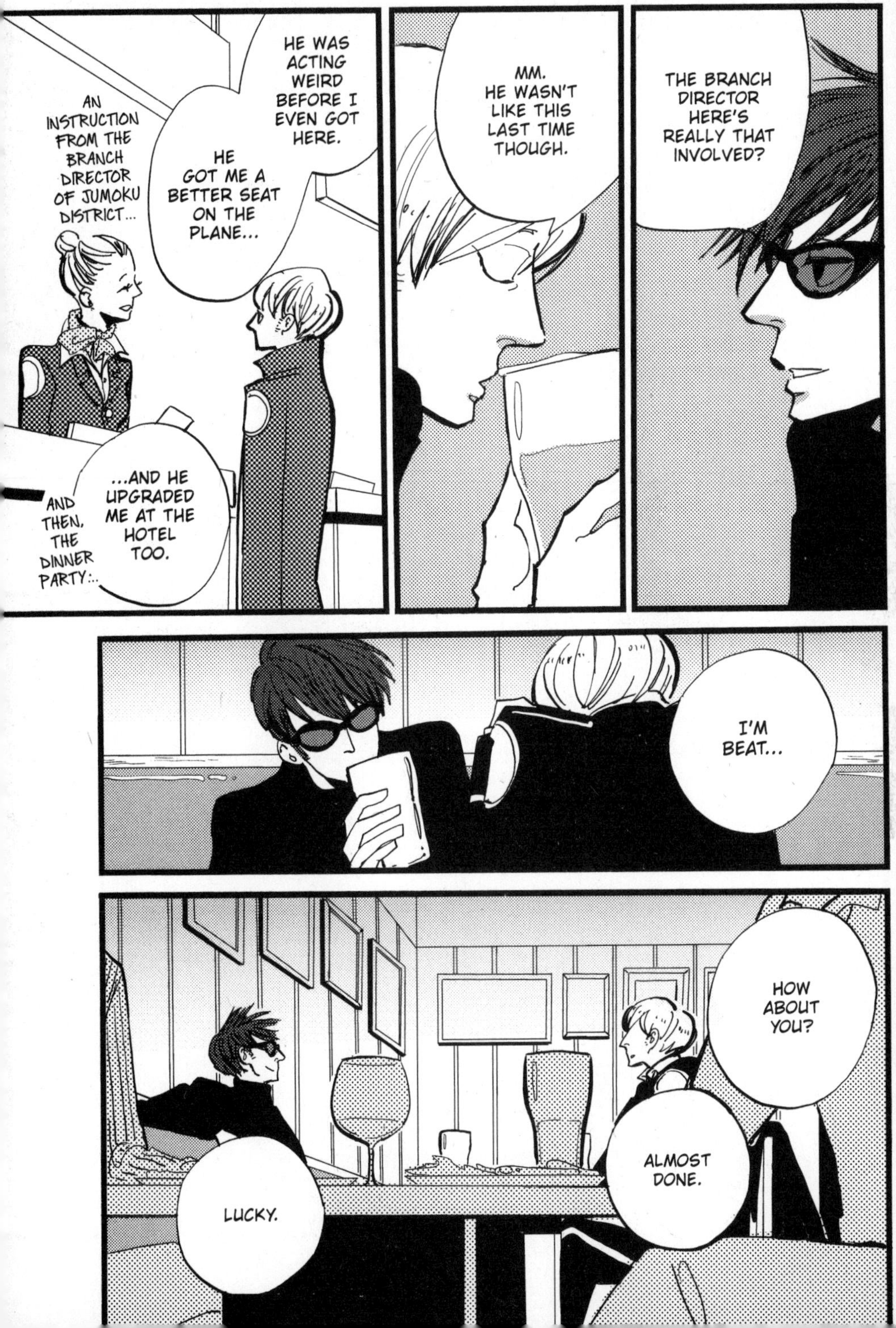
THE BRANCH DIRECTOR HERE'S REALLY THAT INVOLVED?
MM. HE WASN'T LIKE THIS LAST TIME THOUGH.
HE WAS ACTING WEIRD BEFORE I EVEN GOT HERE.
HE GOT ME A BETTER SEAT ON THE PLANE...
AN INSTRUCTION FROM THE BRANCH DIRECTOR OF JUMOKU DISTRICT...
...AND HE UPGRADED ME AT THE HOTEL TOO.
AND THEN, THE DINNER PARTY...
I'M BEAT...
HOW ABOUT YOU?
ALMOST DONE.
LUCKY.

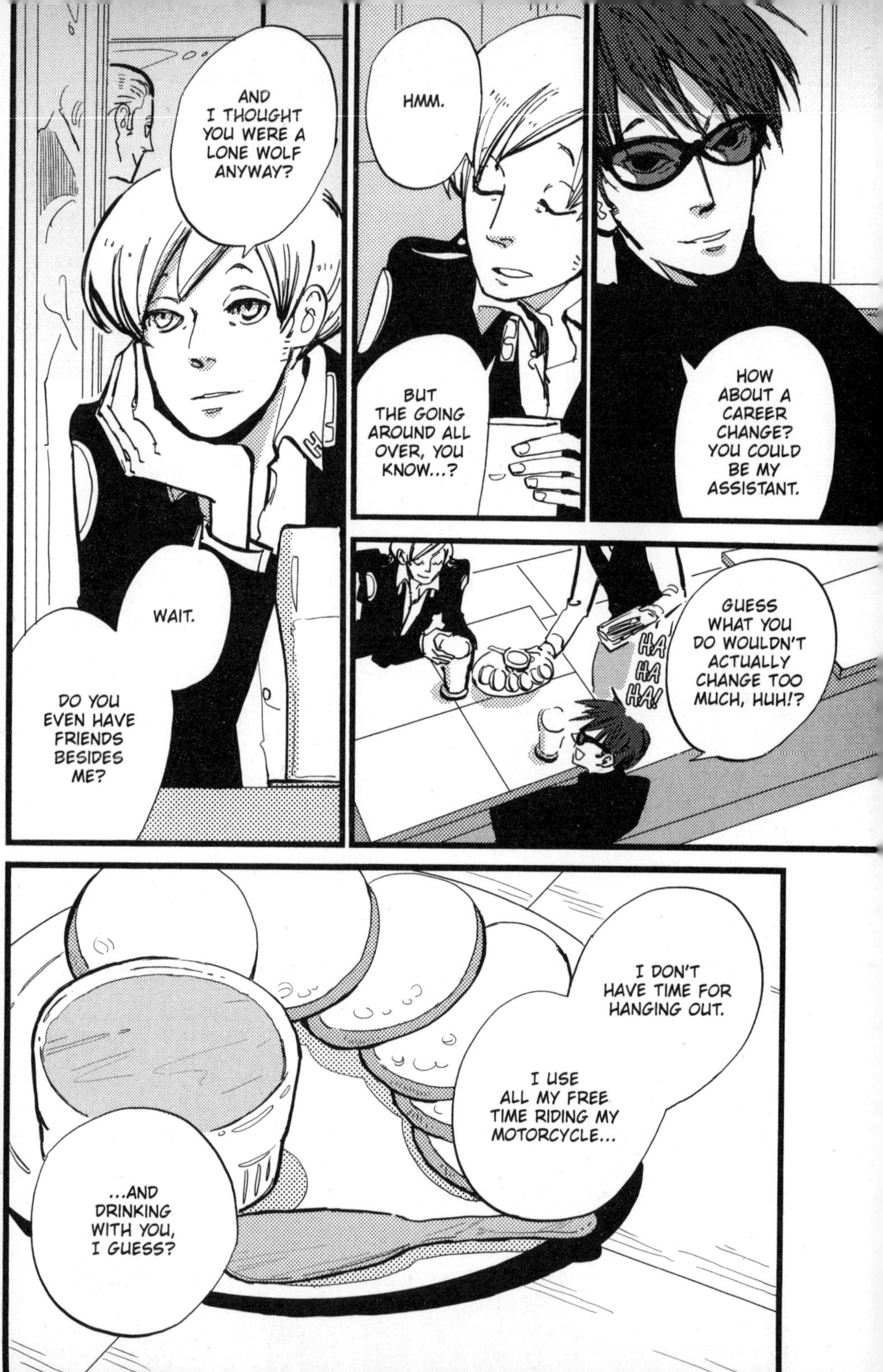
HOW ABOUT A CAREER CHANGE? YOU COULD BE MY ASSISTANT.
HMM.
BUT THE GOING AROUND ALL OVER, YOU KNOW...?
GUESS WHAT YOU DO WOULDN'T ACTUALLY CHANGE TOO MUCH, HUH!?
HA HA HA!
AND I THOUGHT YOU WERE A LONE WOLF ANYWAY?
WAIT.
DO YOU EVEN HAVE FRIENDS BESIDES ME?
I DON'T HAVE TIME FOR HANGING OUT.
I USE ALL MY FREE TIME RIDING MY MOTORCYCLE...
...AND DRINKING WITH YOU, I GUESS?

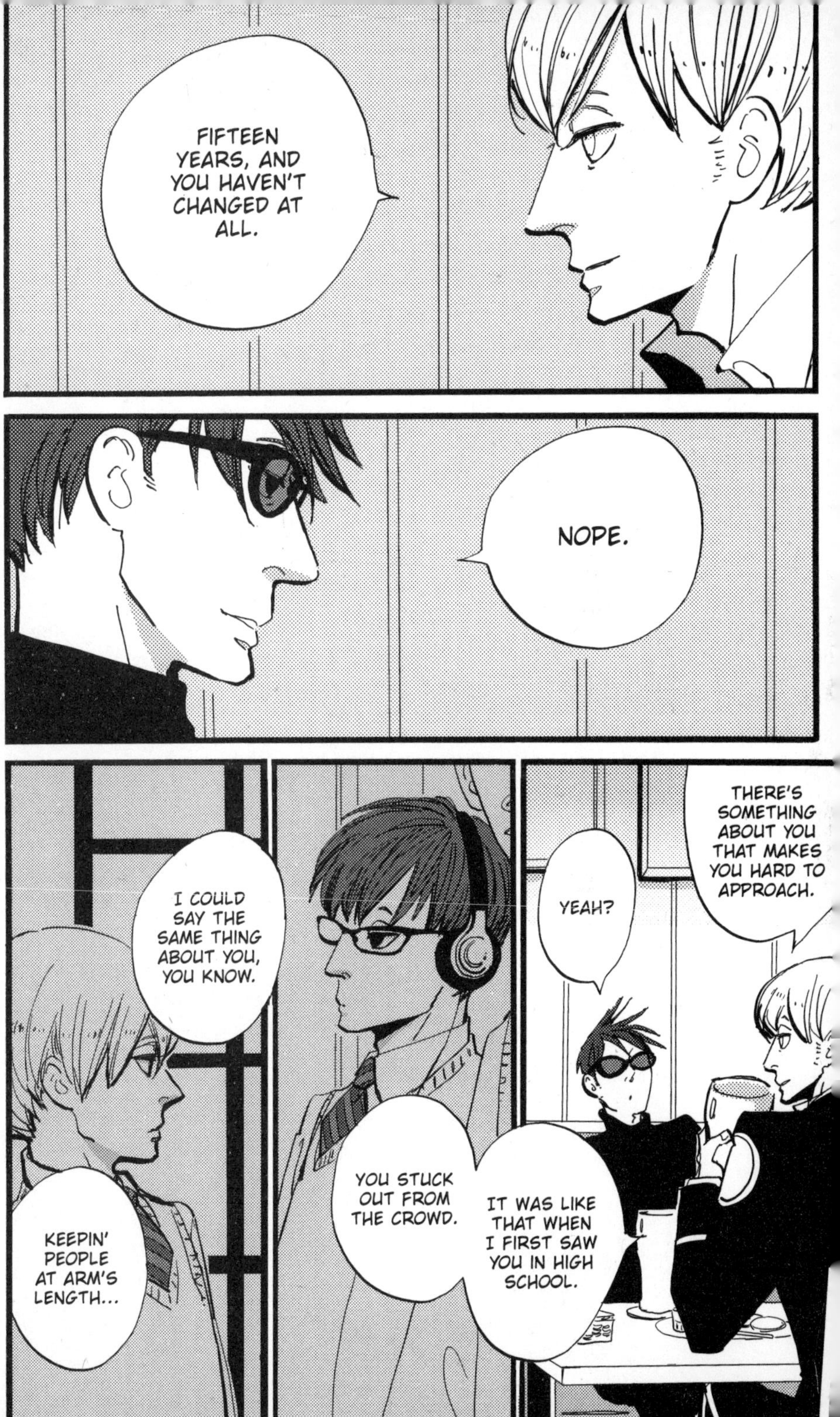
FIFTEEN YEARS, AND YOU HAVEN'T CHANGED AT ALL.
NOPE.
THERE'S SOMETHING ABOUT YOU THAT MAKES YOU HARD TO APPROACH.
YEAH?
IT WAS LIKE THAT WHEN I FIRST SAW YOU IN HIGH SCHOOL.
YOU STUCK OUT FROM THE CROWD.
KEEPIN' PEOPLE AT ARM'S LENGTH...
I COULD SAY THE SAME THING ABOUT YOU, YOU KNOW.

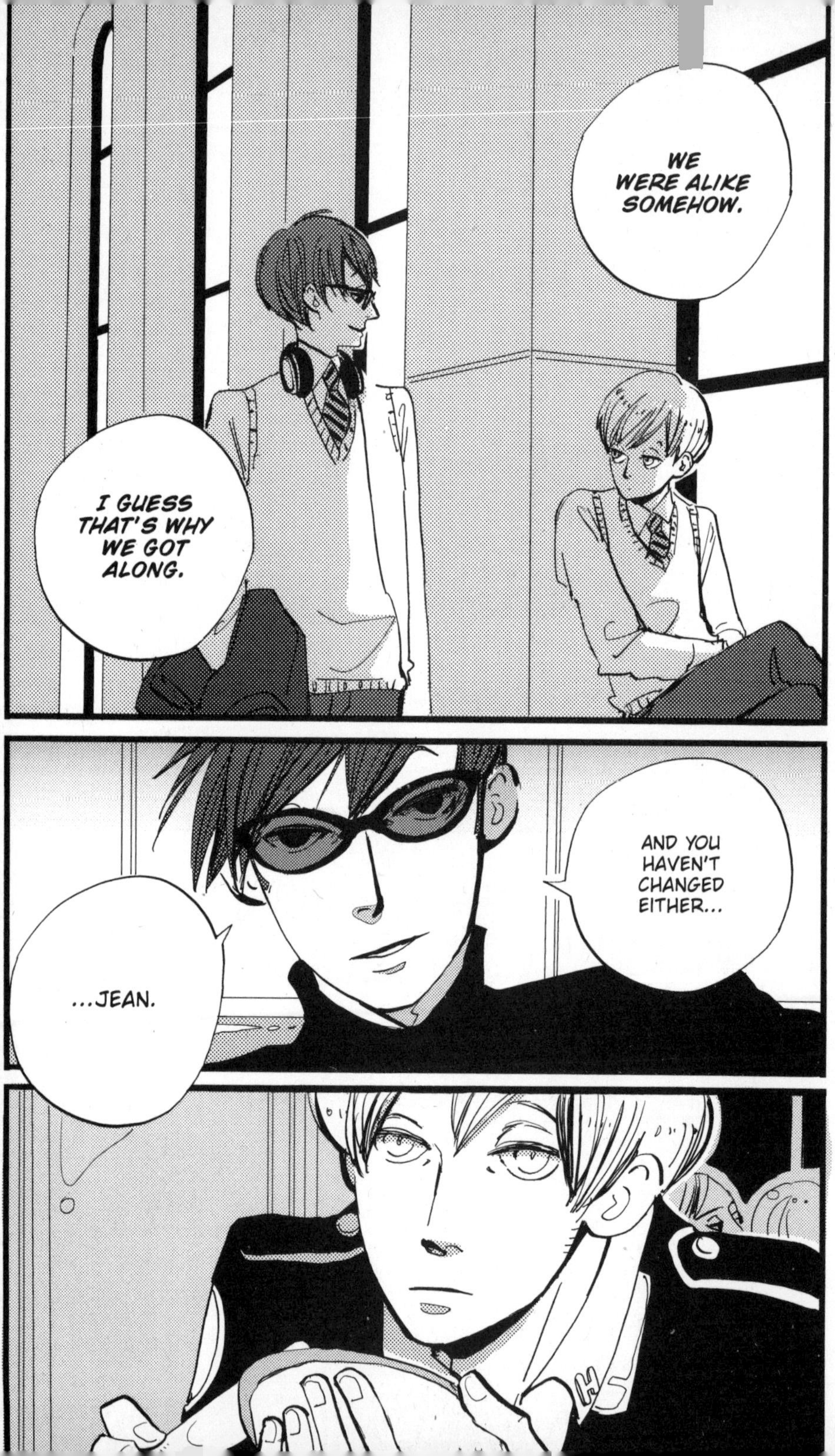
WE WERE ALIKE SOMEHOW.
I GUESS THAT'S WHY WE GOT ALONG.
AND YOU HAVEN'T CHANGED EITHER...
...JEAN.

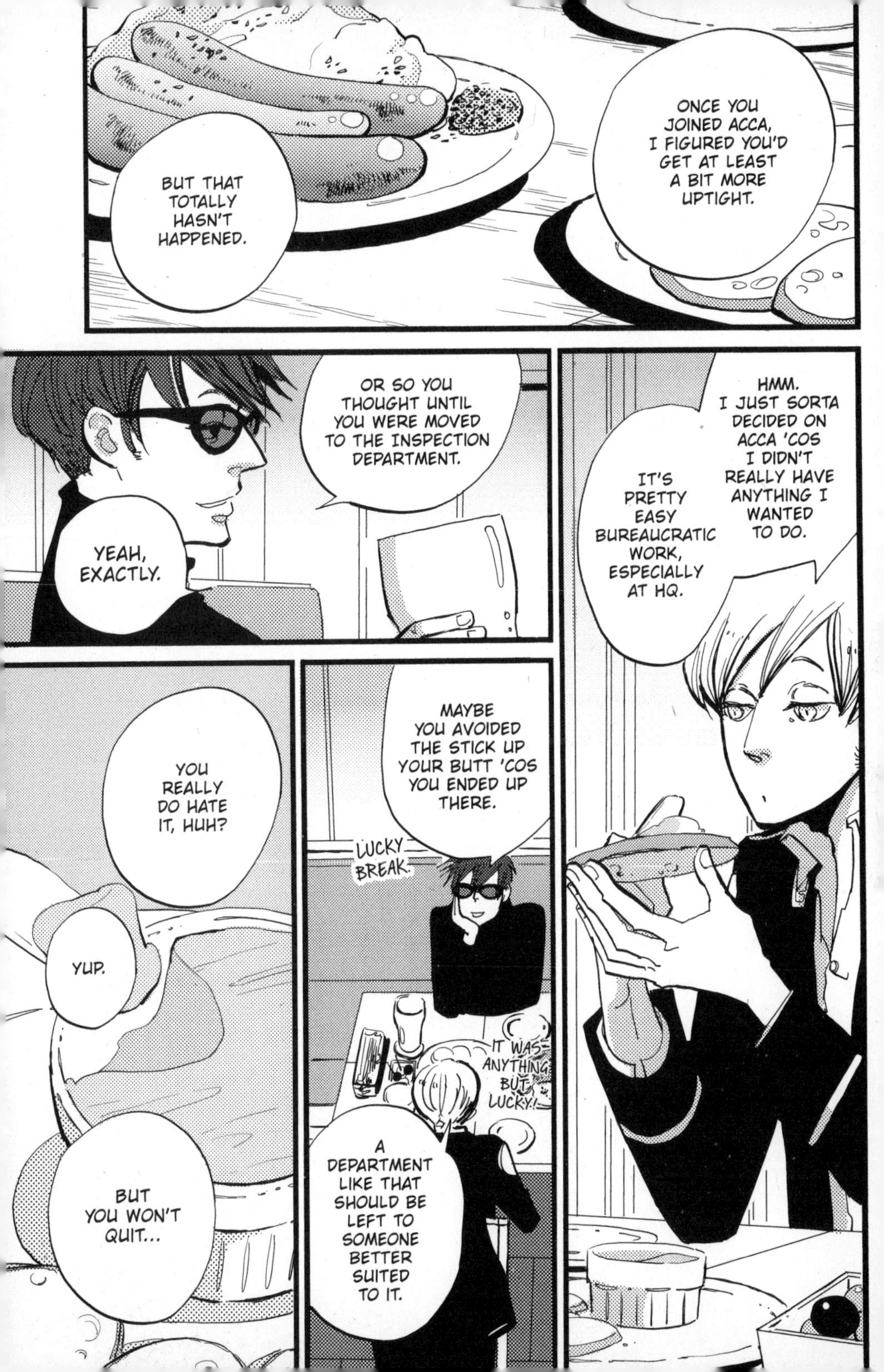
ONCE YOU JOINED ACCA, I FIGURED YOU'D GET AT LEAST A BIT MORE UPTIGHT.
BUT THAT TOTALLY HASN'T HAPPENED.
HMM. I JUST SORTA DECIDED ON ACCA 'COS I DIDN'T REALLY HAVE ANYTHING I WANTED TO DO.
IT'S PRETTY EASY BUREAUCRATIC WORK, ESPECIALLY AT HQ.
OR SO YOU THOUGHT UNTIL YOU WERE MOVED TO THE INSPECTION DEPARTMENT.
YEAH, EXACTLY.
MAYBE YOU AVOIDED THE STICK UP YOUR BUTT 'COS YOU ENDED UP THERE.
LUCKY BREAK.
IT WAS ANYTHING BUT LUCKY!
A DEPARTMENT LIKE THAT SHOULD BE LEFT TO SOMEONE BETTER SUITED TO IT.
YOU REALLY DO HATE IT, HUH?
YUP.
BUT YOU WON'T QUIT...

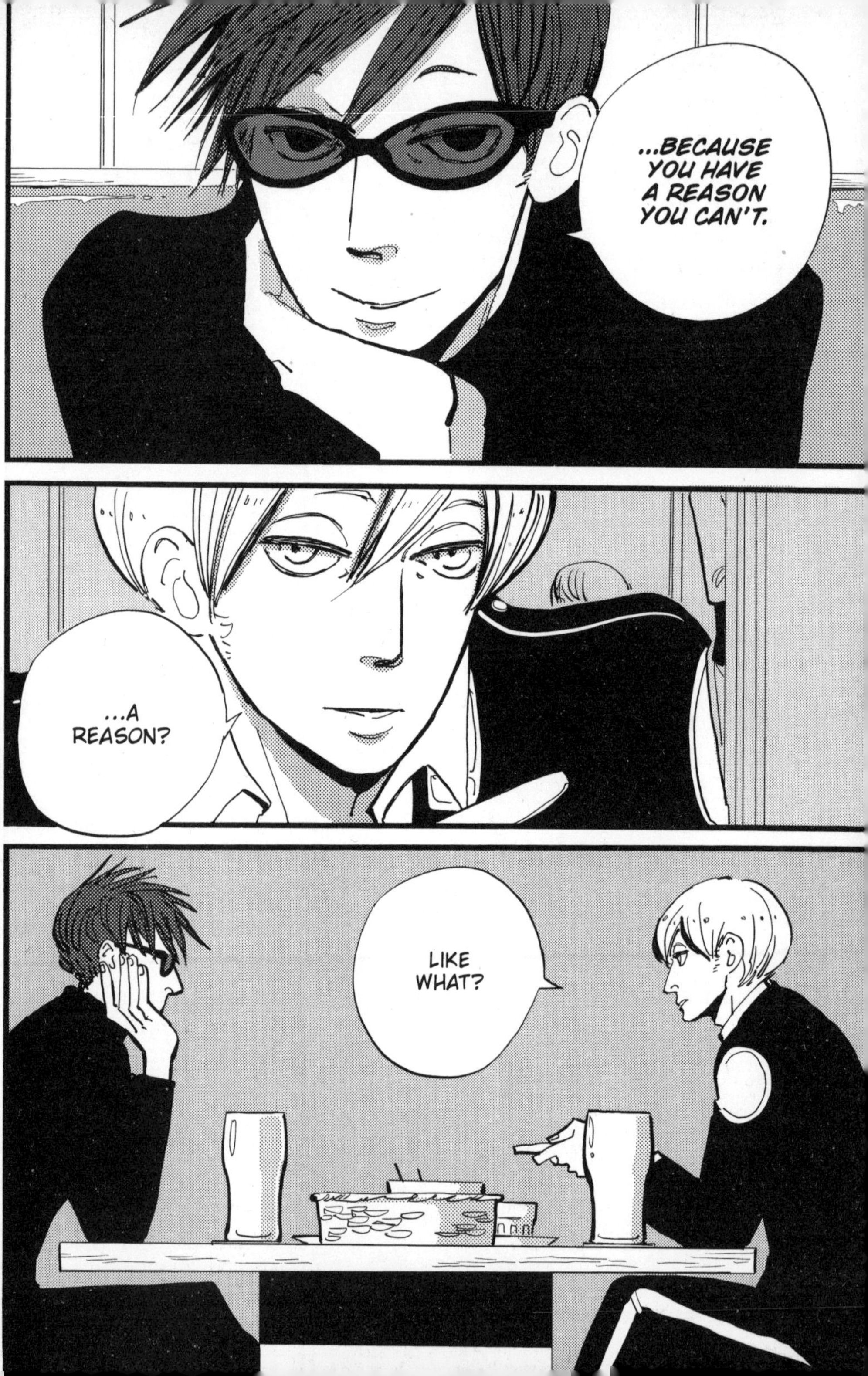
...BECAUSE YOU HAVE A REASON YOU CAN'T.
...A REASON?
LIKE WHAT?

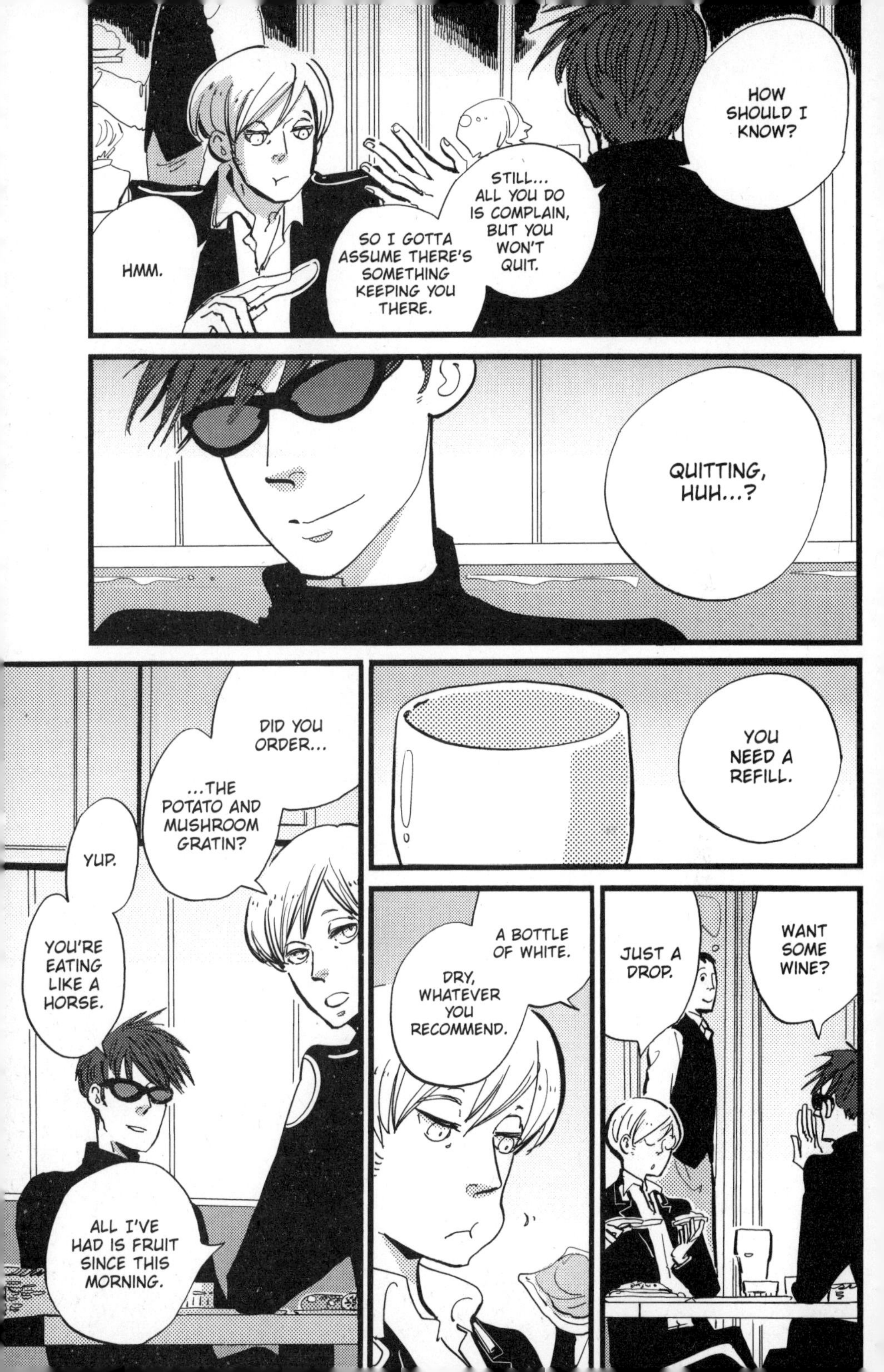
HOW SHOULD I KNOW?
STILL... ALL YOU DO IS COMPLAIN, BUT YOU WON'T QUIT.
SO I GOTTA ASSUME THERE'S SOMETHING KEEPING YOU THERE.
HMM.
QUITTING, HUH...?
YOU NEED A REFILL.
WANT SOME WINE?
JUST A DROP.
A BOTTLE OF WHITE.
DRY, WHATEVER YOU RECOMMEND.
DID YOU ORDER...
...THE POTATO AND MUSHROOM GRATIN?
YUP.
YOU'RE EATING LIKE A HORSE.
ALL I'VE HAD IS FRUIT SINCE THIS MORNING.

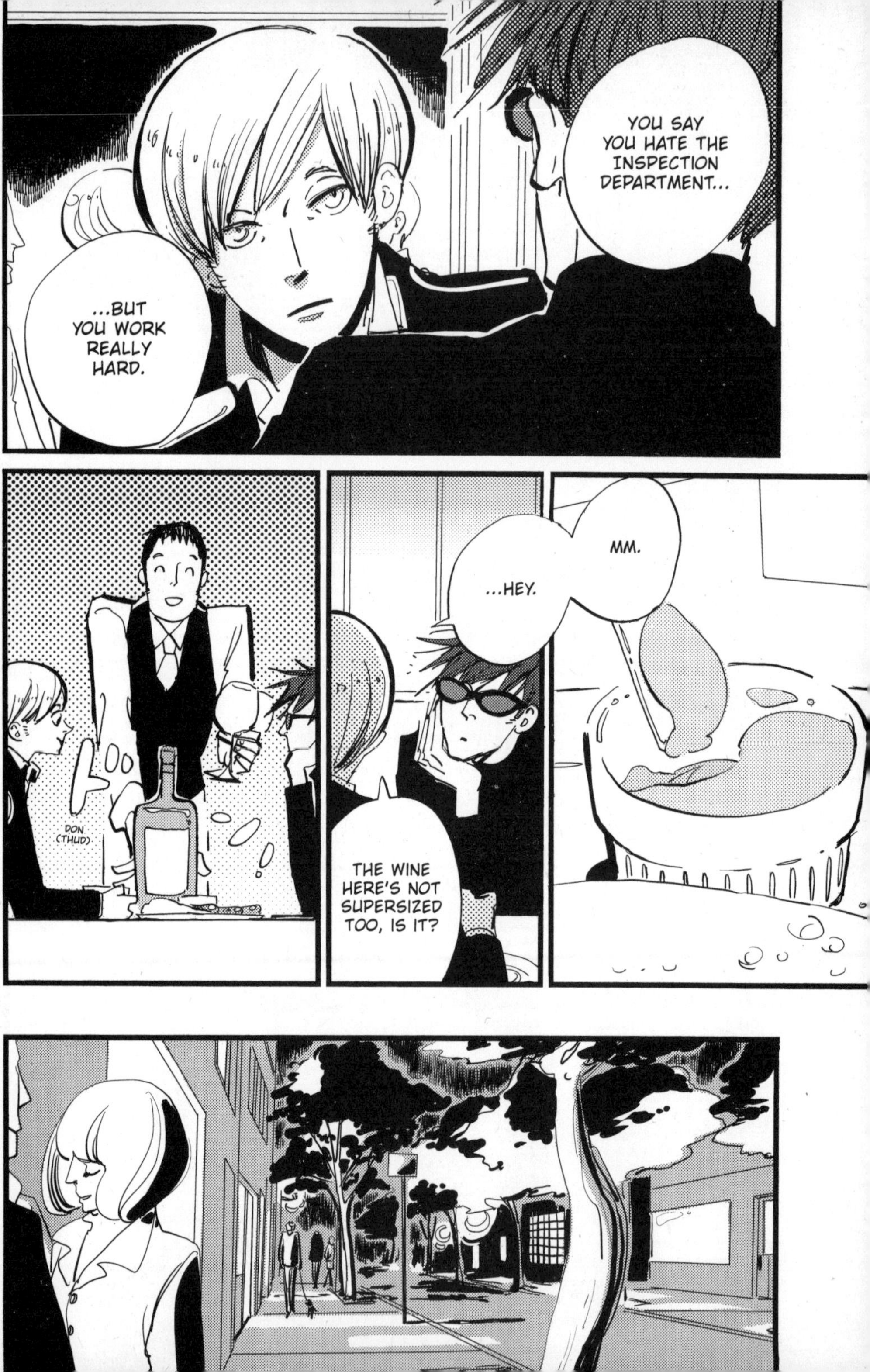
YOU SAY YOU HATE THE INSPECTION DEPARTMENT...
...BUT YOU WORK REALLY HARD.
MM.
...HEY.
THE WINE HERE'S NOT SUPERSIZED TOO, IS IT?
DON (THUD)

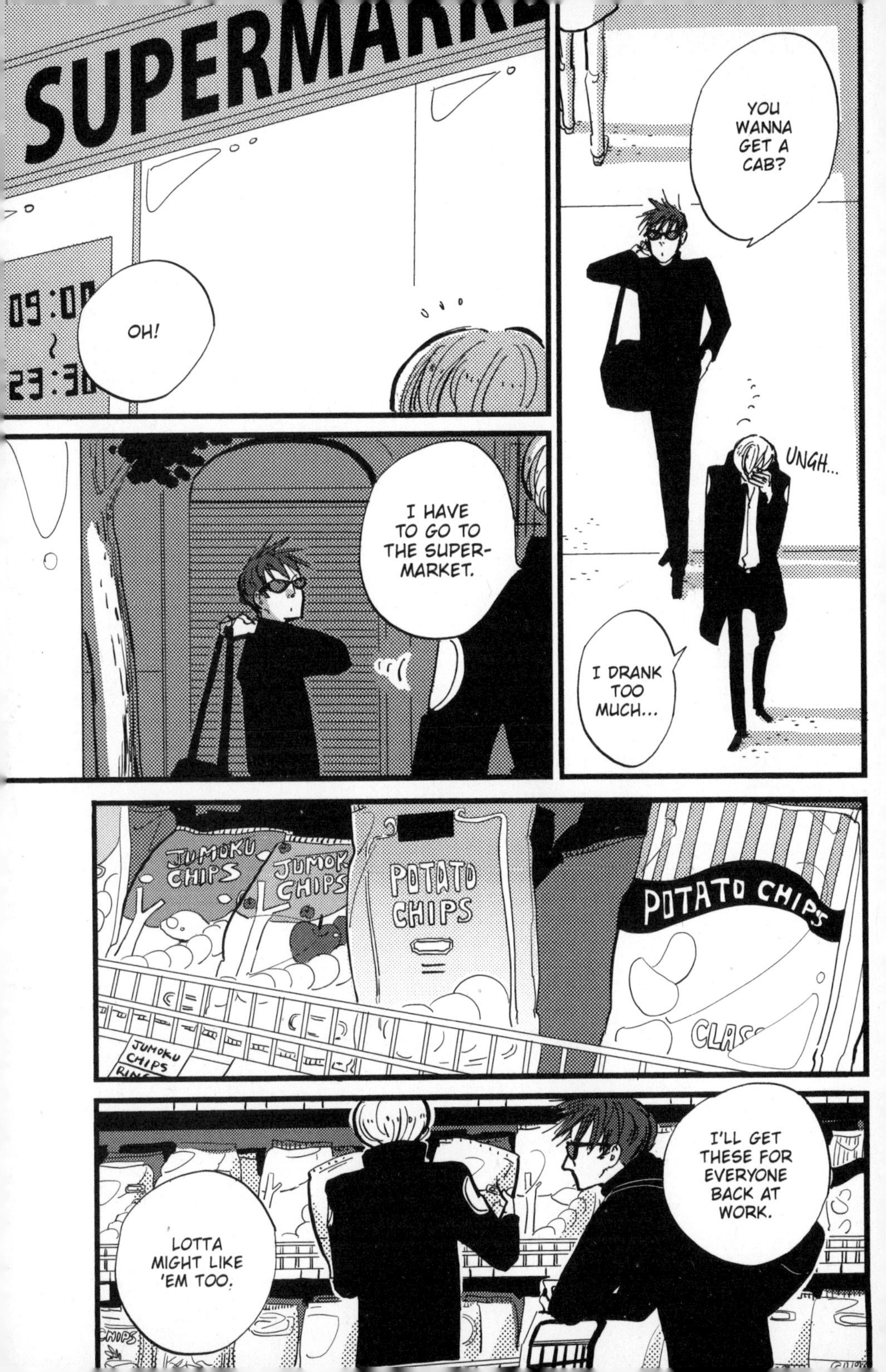
YOU WANNA GET A CAB?
UNGH...
I DRANK TOO MUCH...
09:00 ~ 23:30
OH!
I HAVE TO GO TO THE SUPER-MARKET.
POTATO CHIPS
POTATO CHIPS
CHIPS
JUMOKU CHIPS
JUMOKU CHIPS
I'LL GET THESE FOR EVERYONE BACK AT WORK.
LOTTA MIGHT LIKE 'EM TOO.

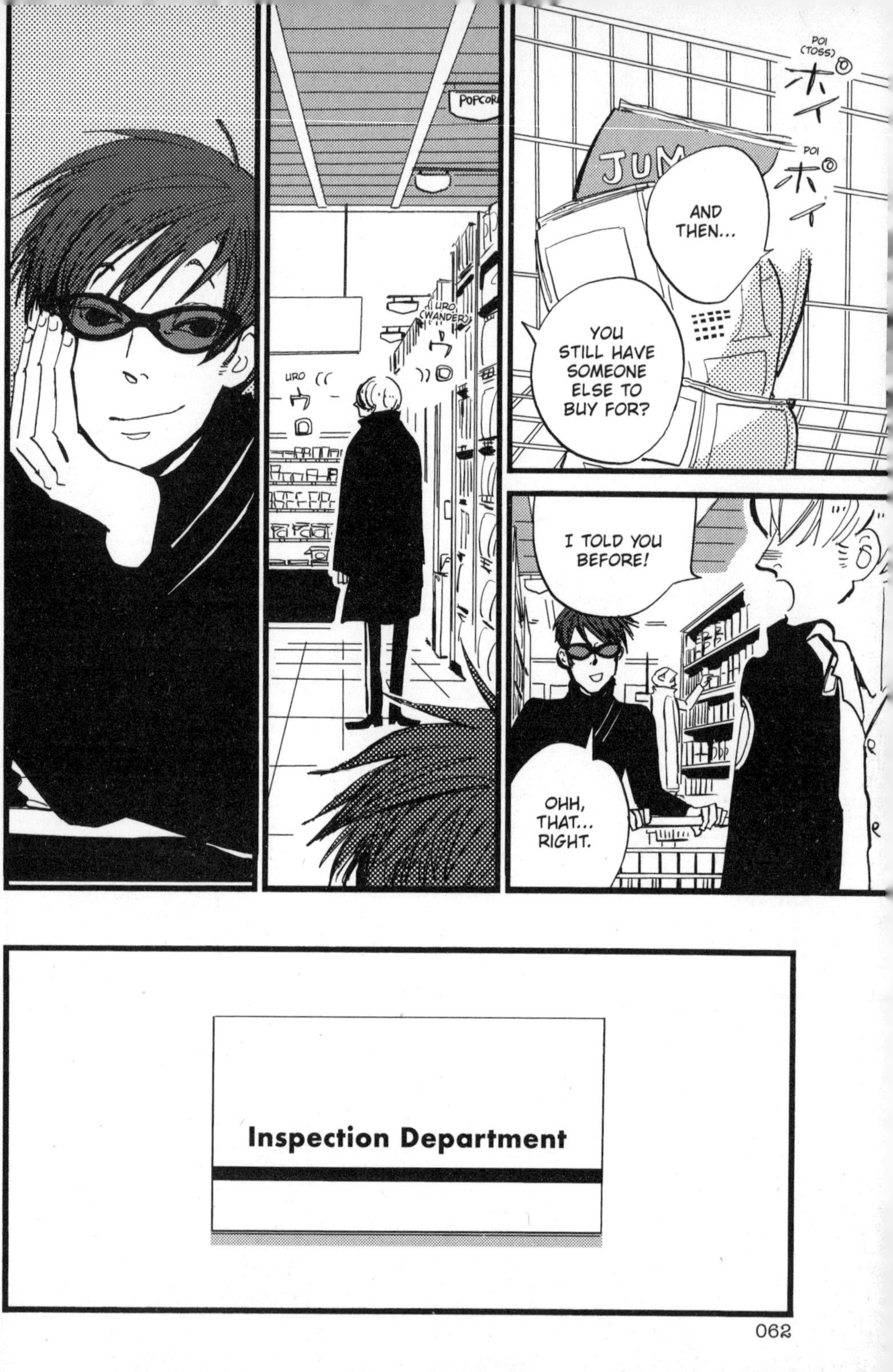
POI (TOSS)
POI
AND THEN...
YOU STILL HAVE SOMEONE ELSE TO BUY FOR?
I TOLD YOU BEFORE!
OHH, THAT... RIGHT.
POPCOR
URO (WANDER)
URO
Inspection Department

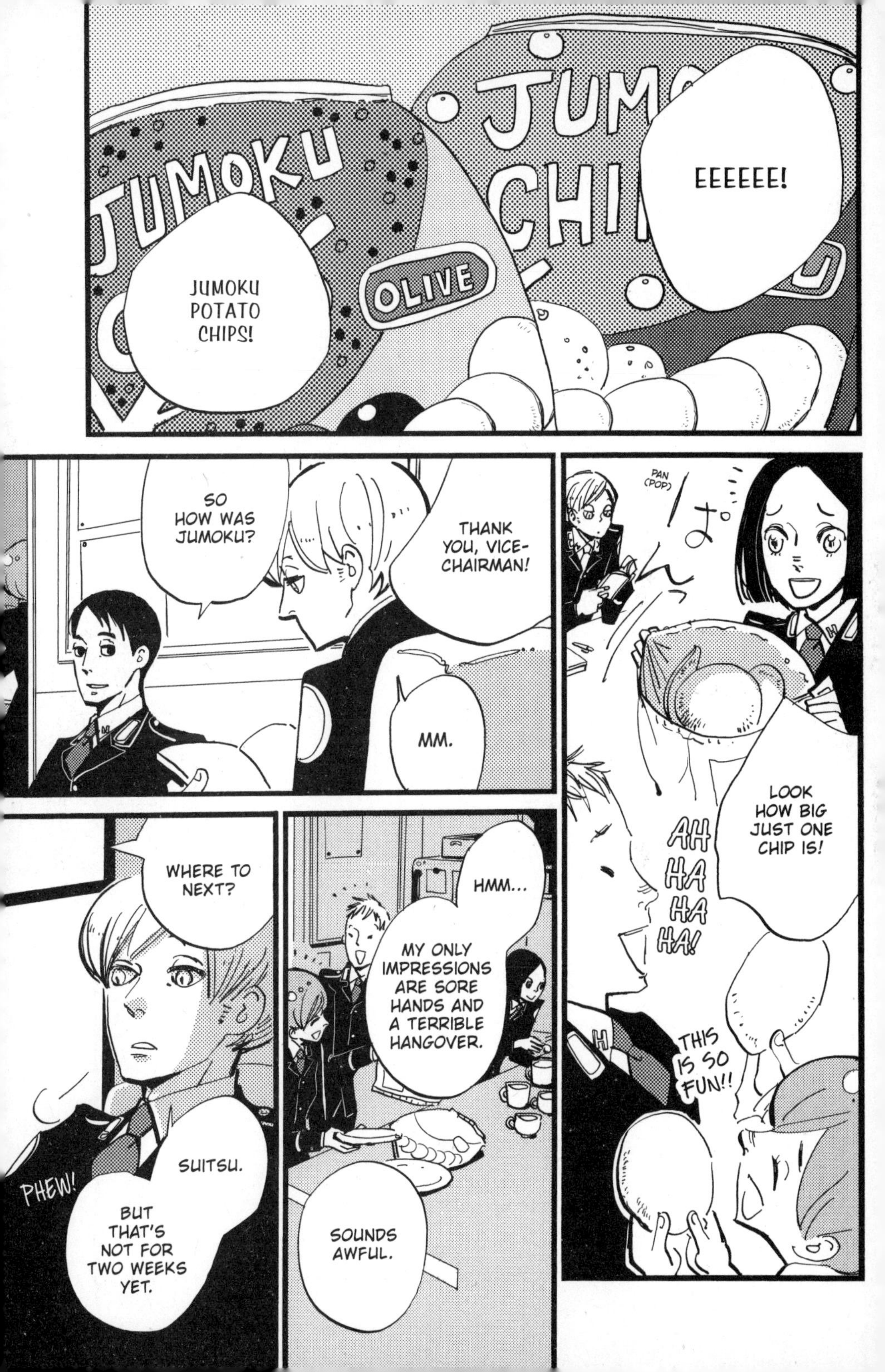
EEEEEE!
JUMOKU POTATO CHIPS!
JUMOKU
OLIVE
PAN (POP)
ぱ
LOOK HOW BIG JUST ONE CHIP IS!
AH HA HA HA HA!
THIS IS SO FUN!!
THANK YOU, VICE-CHAIRMAN!
SO HOW WAS JUMOKU?
MM.
HMM...
MY ONLY IMPRESSIONS ARE SORE HANDS AND A TERRIBLE HANGOVER.
SOUNDS AWFUL.
WHERE TO NEXT?
SUITSU.
BUT THAT'S NOT FOR TWO WEEKS YET.
PHEW!

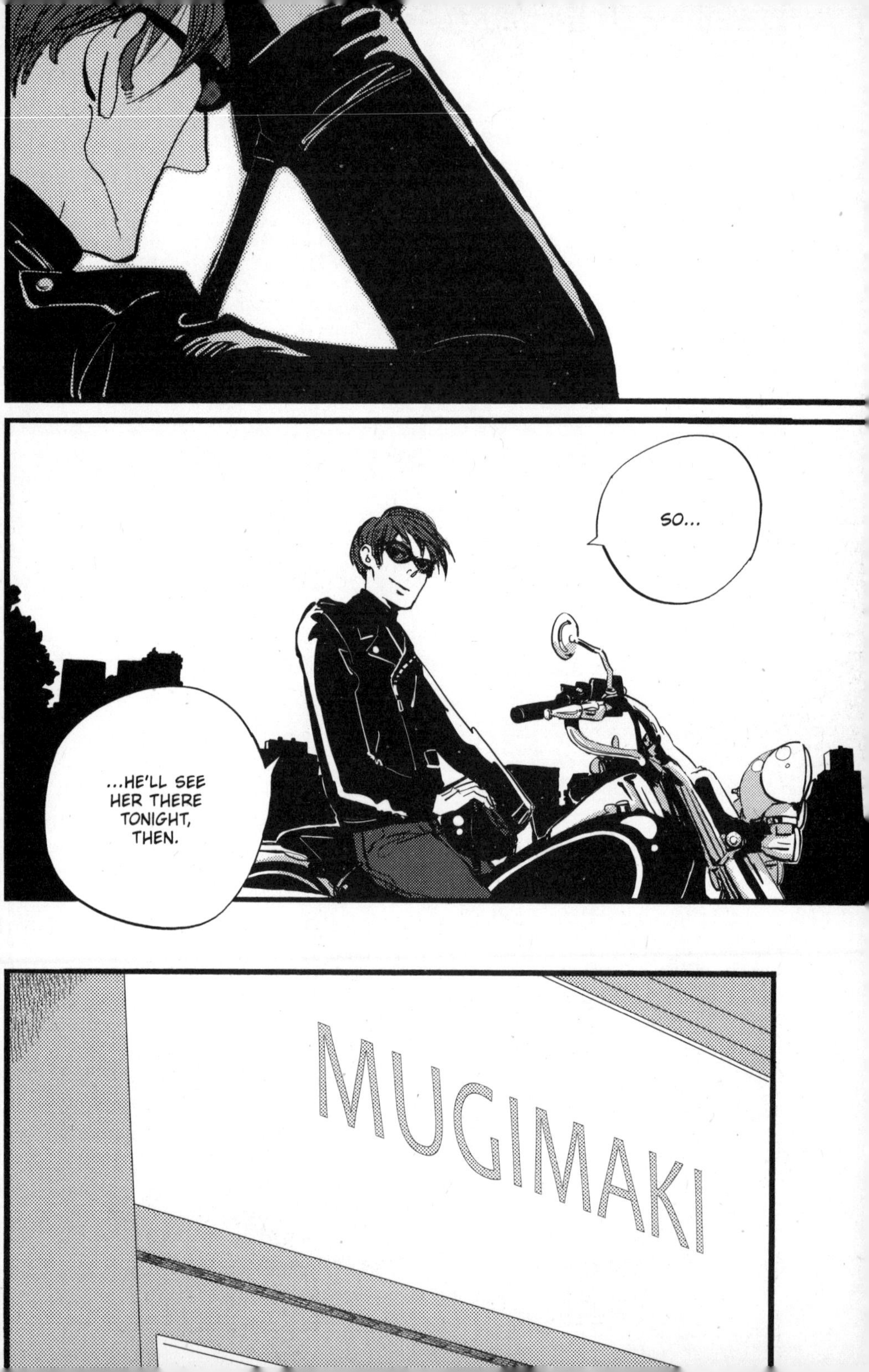
SO...
...HE'LL SEE HER THERE TONIGHT, THEN.
MUGIMAKI

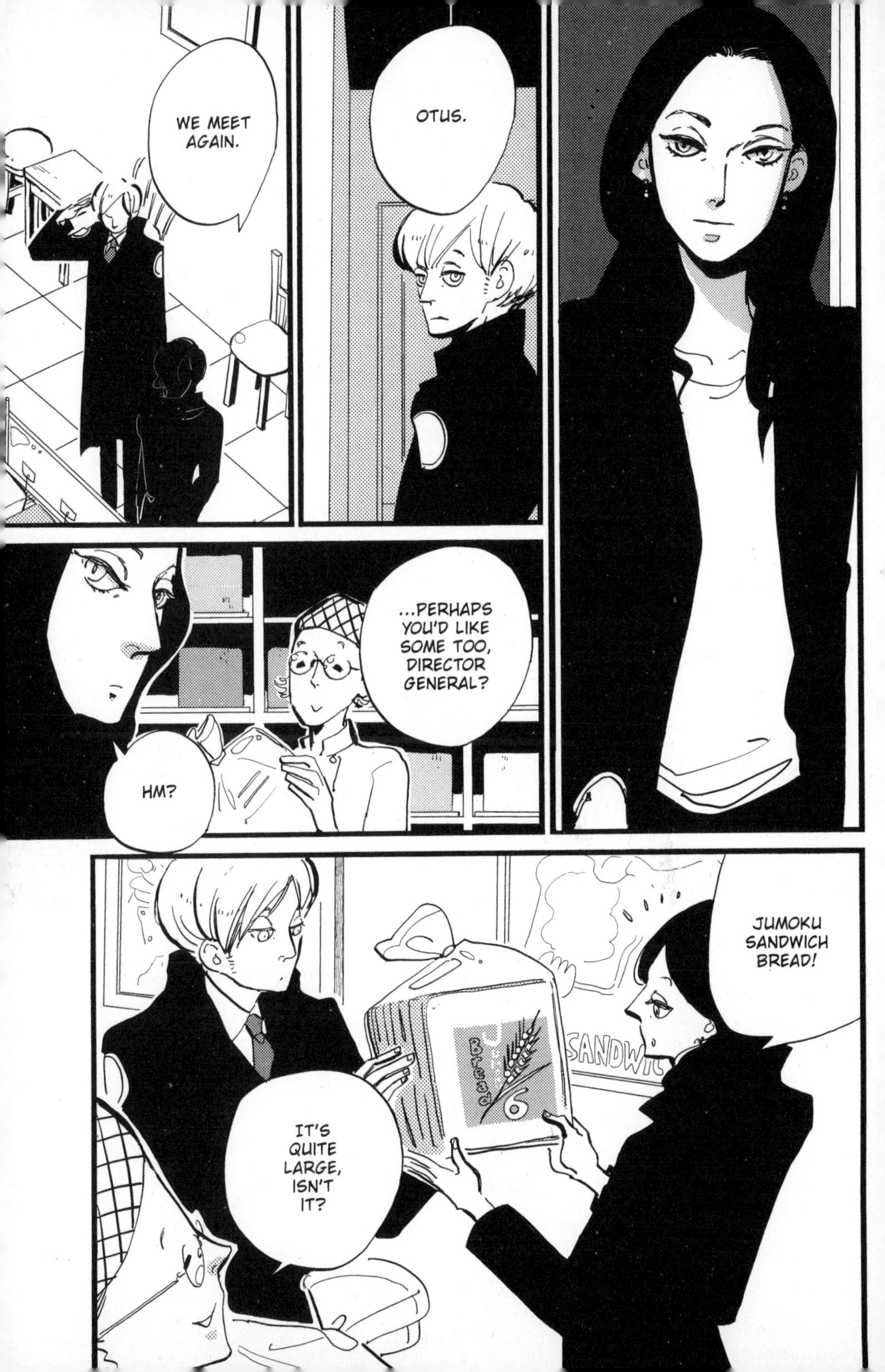
OTUS.
WE MEET AGAIN.
...PERHAPS YOU'D LIKE SOME TOO, DIRECTOR GENERAL?
HM?
JUMOKU SANDWICH BREAD!
IT'S QUITE LARGE, ISN'T IT?

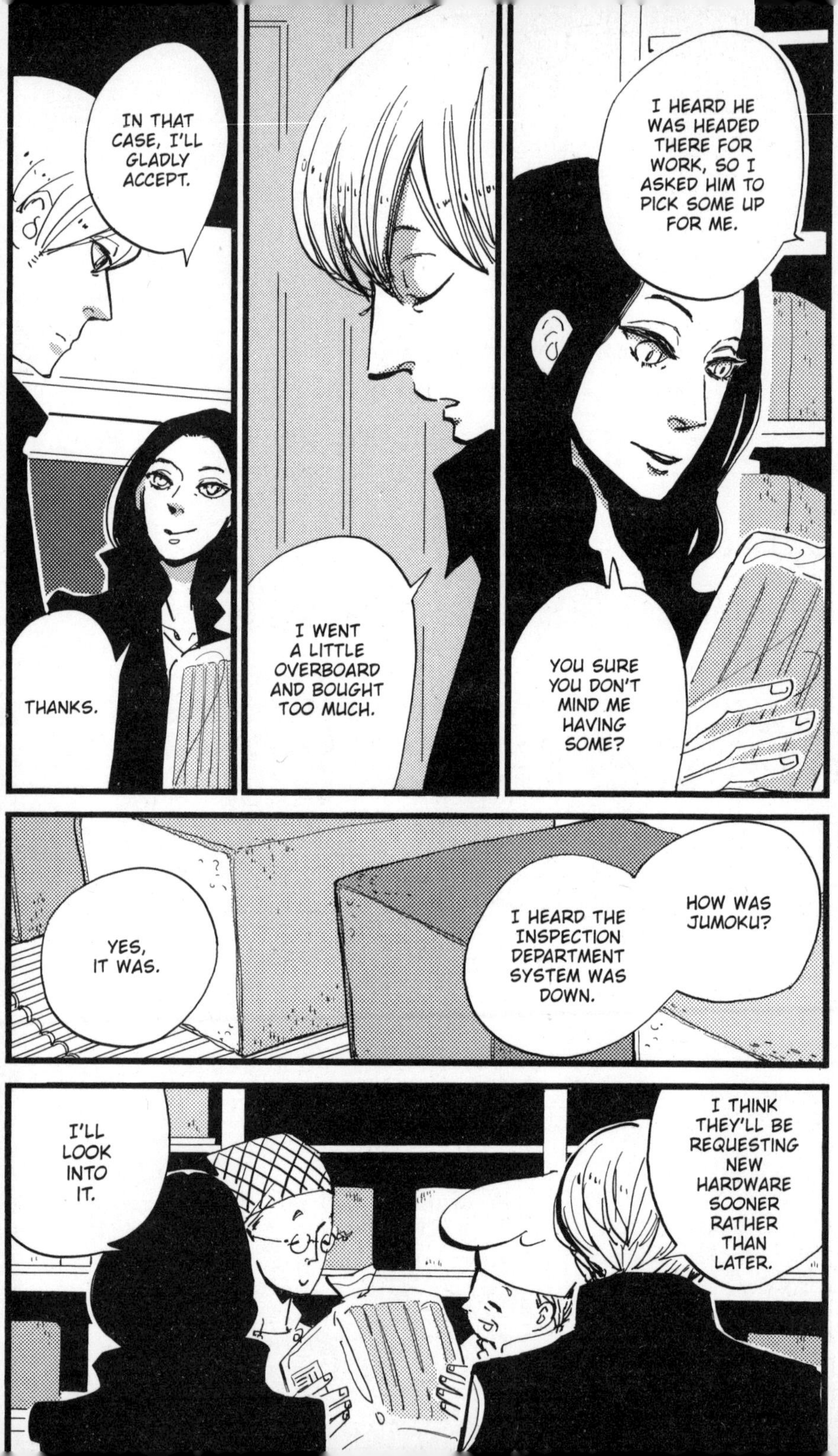
I HEARD HE WAS HEADED THERE FOR WORK, SO I ASKED HIM TO PICK SOME UP FOR ME.
YOU SURE YOU DON'T MIND ME HAVING SOME?
I WENT A LITTLE OVERBOARD AND BOUGHT TOO MUCH.
IN THAT CASE, I'LL GLADLY ACCEPT.
THANKS.
HOW WAS JUMOKU?
I HEARD THE INSPECTION DEPARTMENT SYSTEM WAS DOWN.
YES, IT WAS.
I THINK THEY'LL BE REQUESTING NEW HARDWARE SOONER RATHER THAN LATER.
I'LL LOOK INTO IT.

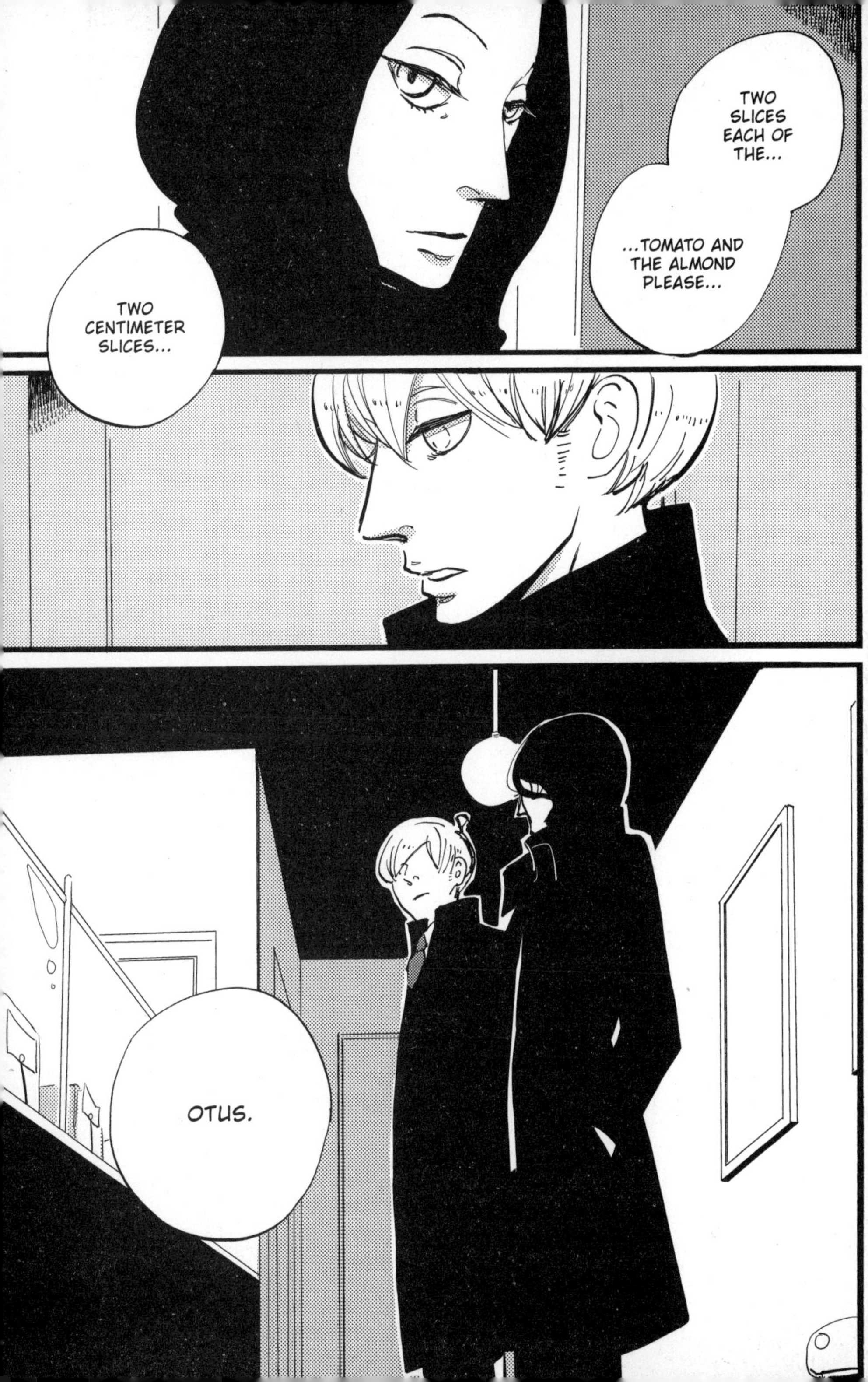
TWO SLICES EACH OF THE...
...TOMATO AND THE ALMOND PLEASE...
TWO CENTIMETER SLICES...
OTUS.

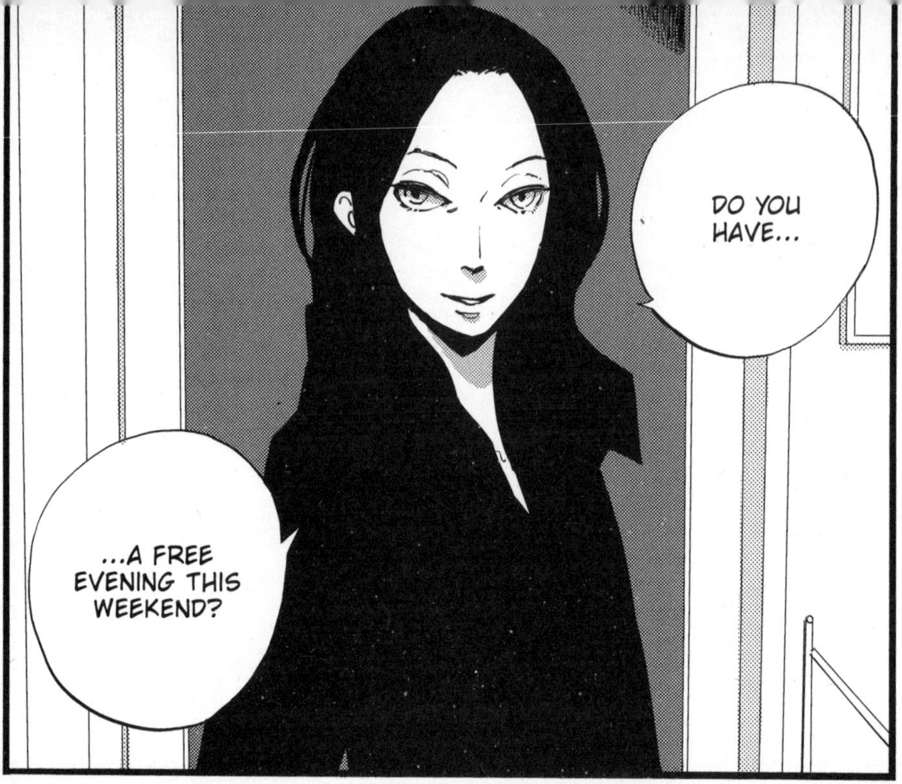
DO YOU HAVE...
...A FREE EVENING THIS WEEKEND?

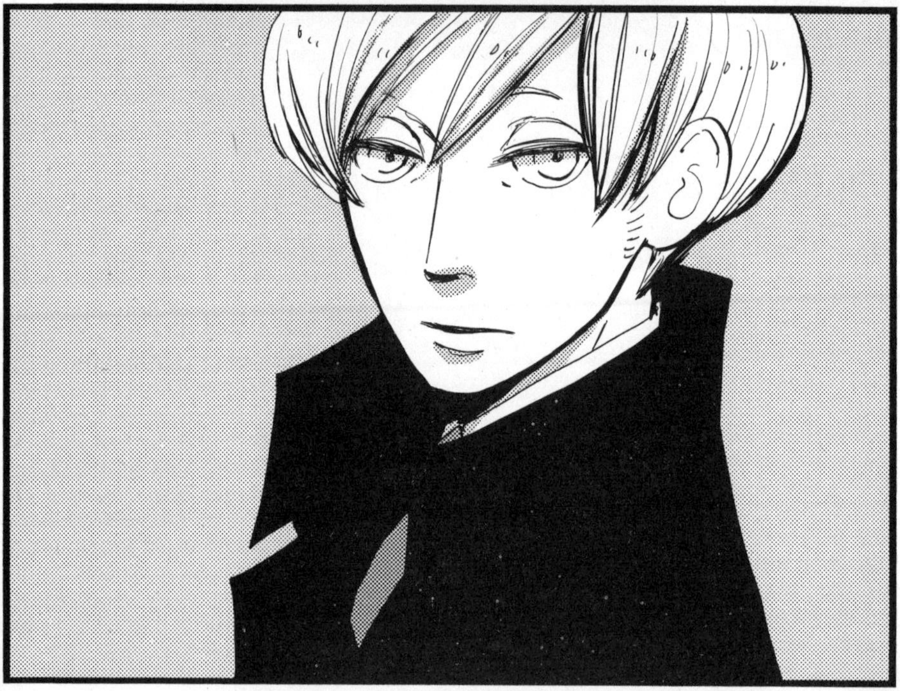

CHAPTER 7

Boozing in

Jumoku with

a Partner

in Crime

CHAPTER 8

A Teetotal Night in Badon

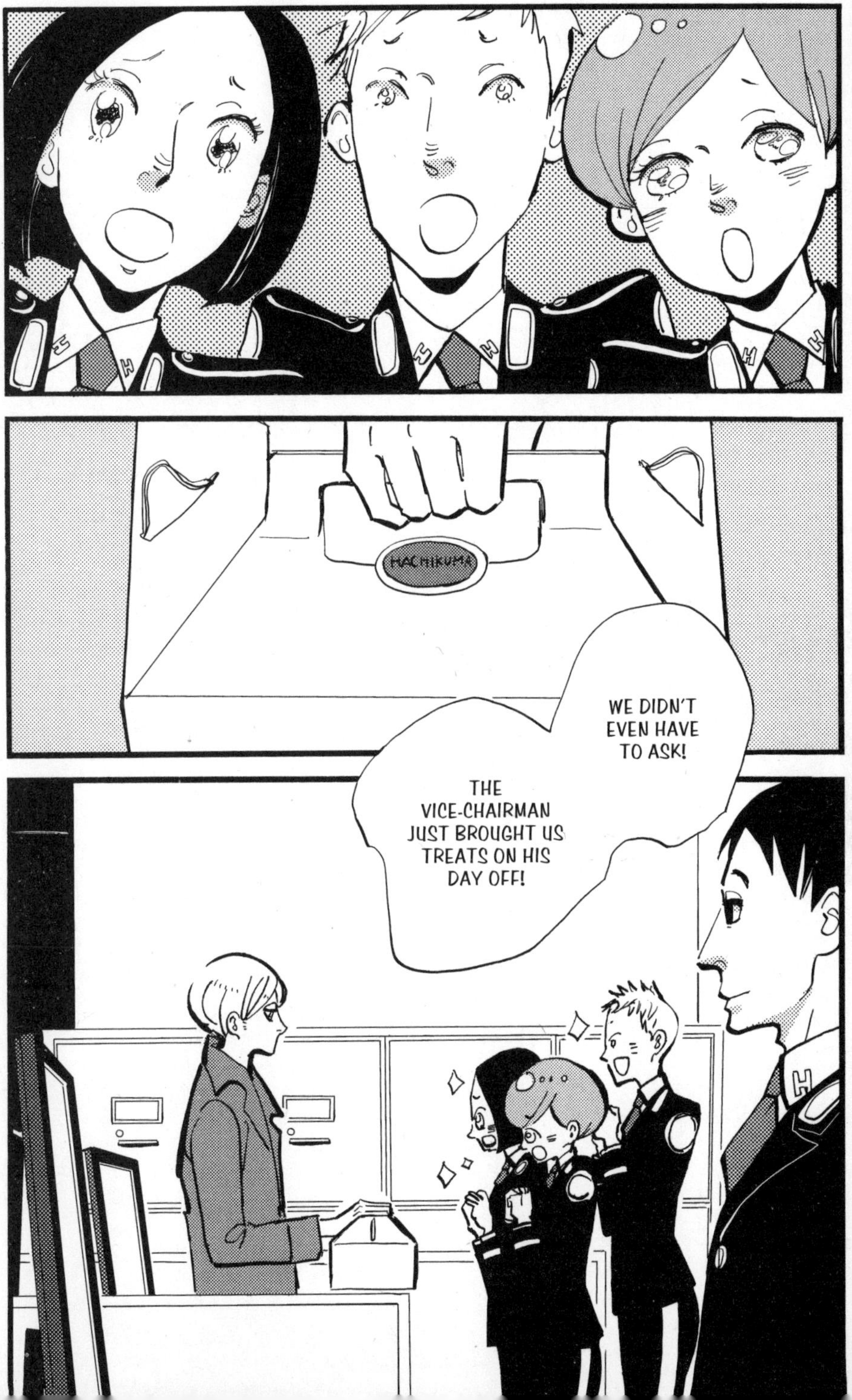
HACHIKUMA
WE DIDN'T EVEN HAVE TO ASK!
THE VICE-CHAIRMAN JUST BROUGHT US TREATS ON HIS DAY OFF!

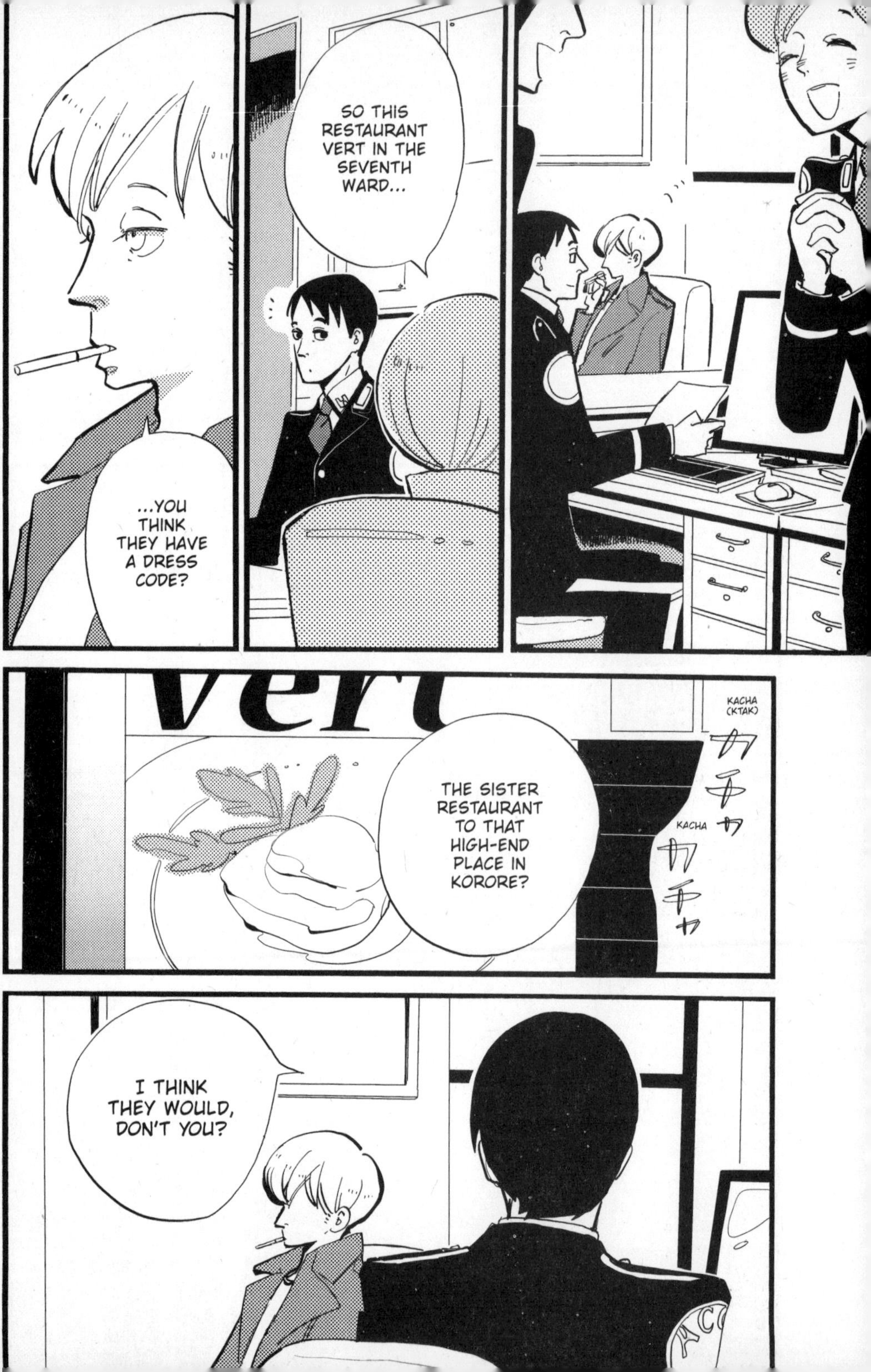
SO THIS RESTAURANT VERT IN THE SEVENTH WARD...
...YOU THINK THEY HAVE A DRESS CODE?
vert
KACHA (KTAK)
KACHA
THE SISTER RESTAURANT TO THAT HIGH-END PLACE IN KORORE?
I THINK THEY WOULD, DON'T YOU?

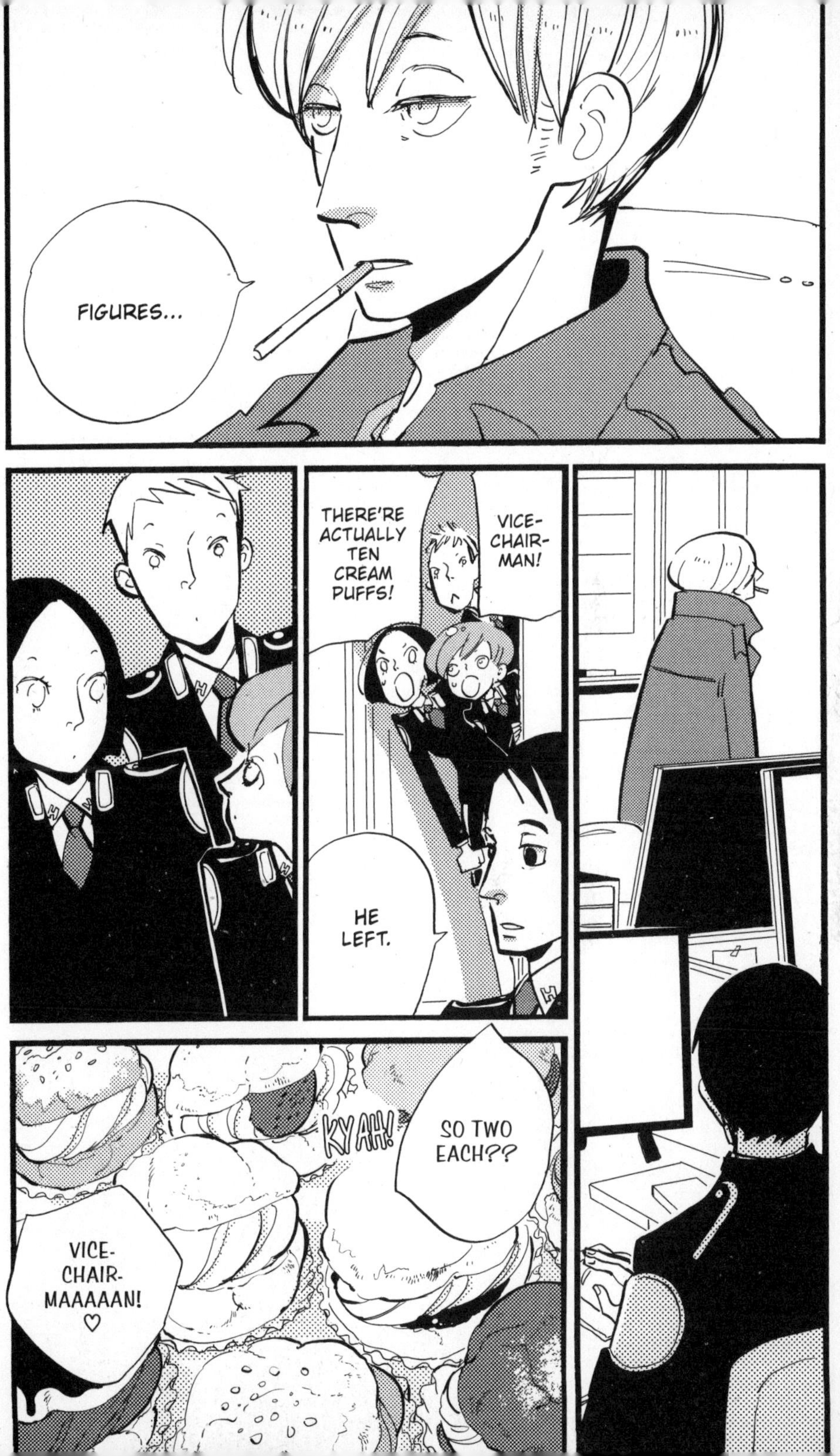
FIGURES...
VICE-CHAIRMAN!
THERE'RE ACTUALLY TEN CREAM PUFFS!
HE LEFT.
SO TWO EACH??
KYAH!
VICE-CHAIRMAAAAAN! ♡

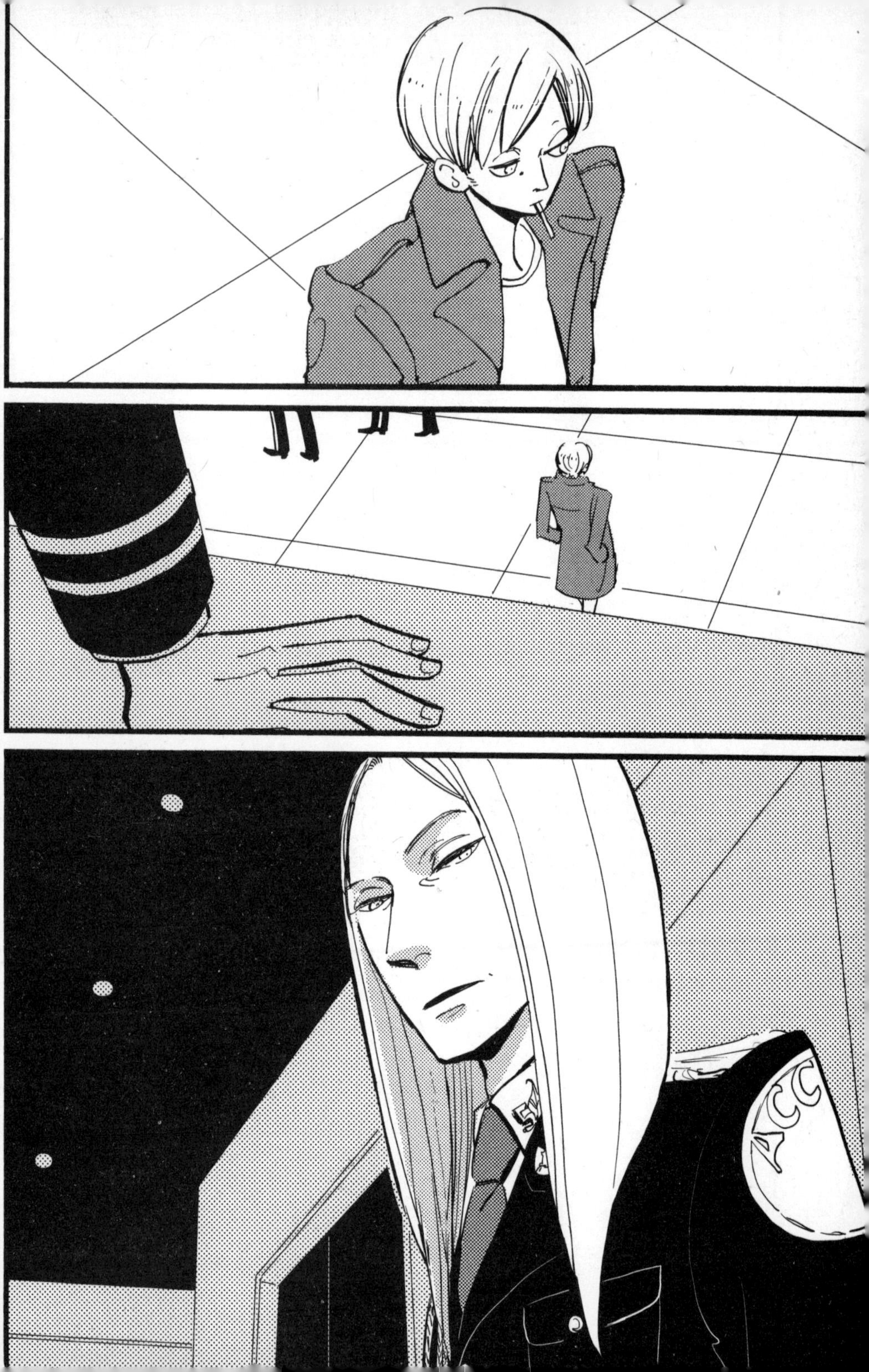
ACC

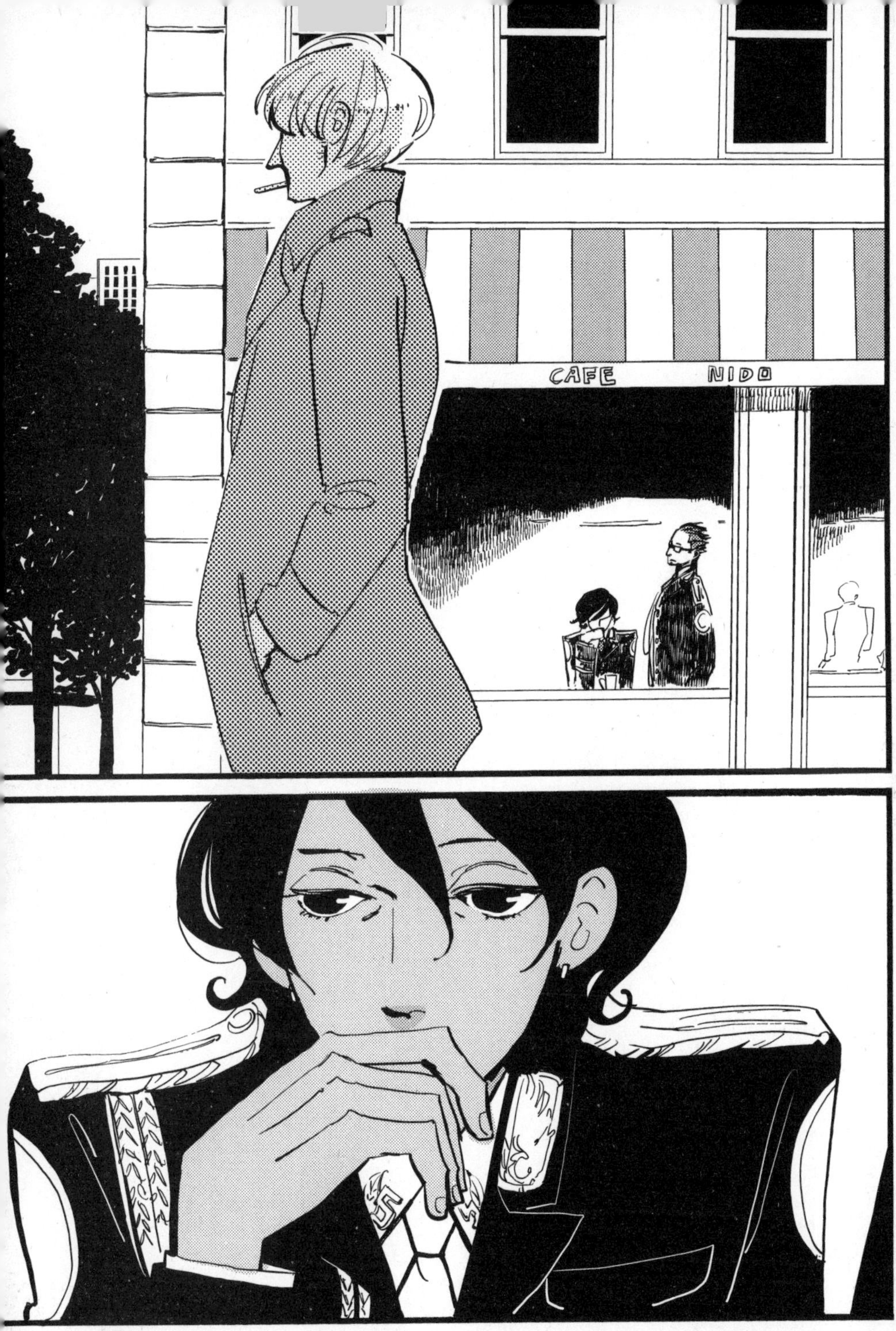
CAFE NIDO

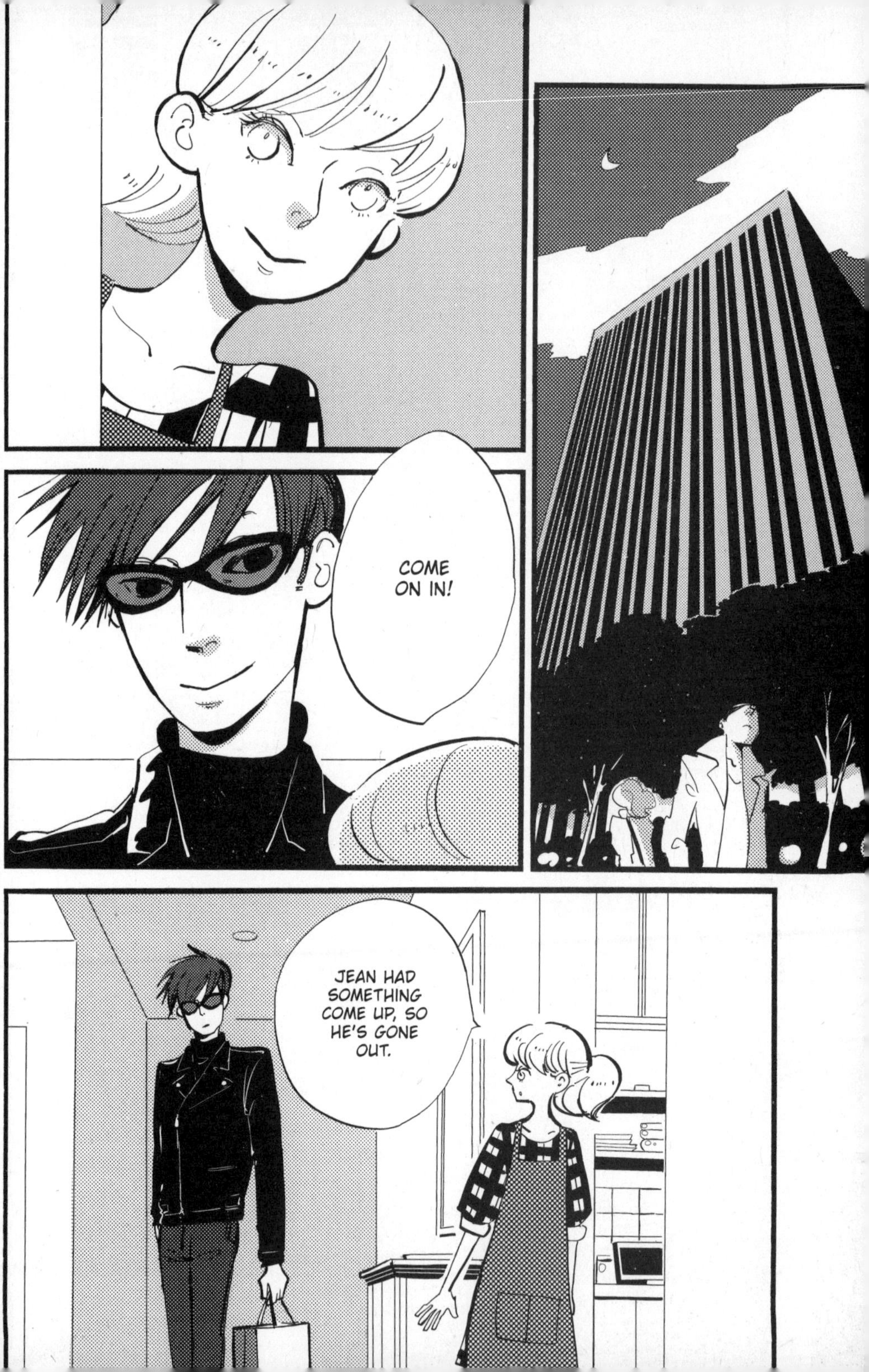
COME ON IN!
JEAN HAD SOMETHING COME UP, SO HE'S GONE OUT.

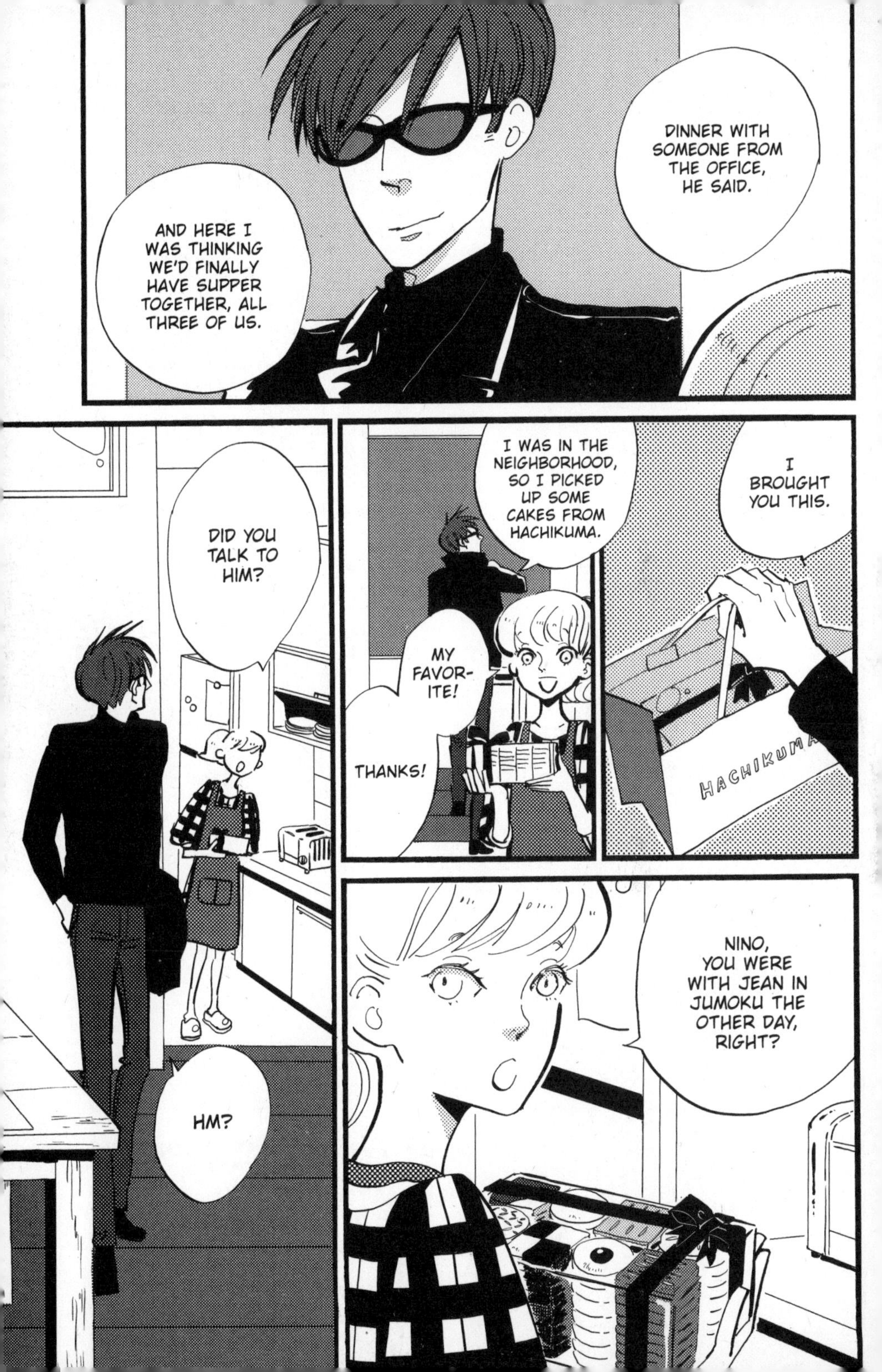
DINNER WITH SOMEONE FROM THE OFFICE, HE SAID.
AND HERE I WAS THINKING WE'D FINALLY HAVE SUPPER TOGETHER, ALL THREE OF US.
I BROUGHT YOU THIS.
HACHIKUMA
I WAS IN THE NEIGHBORHOOD, SO I PICKED UP SOME CAKES FROM HACHIKUMA.
MY FAVOR-ITE!
THANKS!
NINO, YOU WERE WITH JEAN IN JUMOKU THE OTHER DAY, RIGHT?
DID YOU TALK TO HIM?
HM?

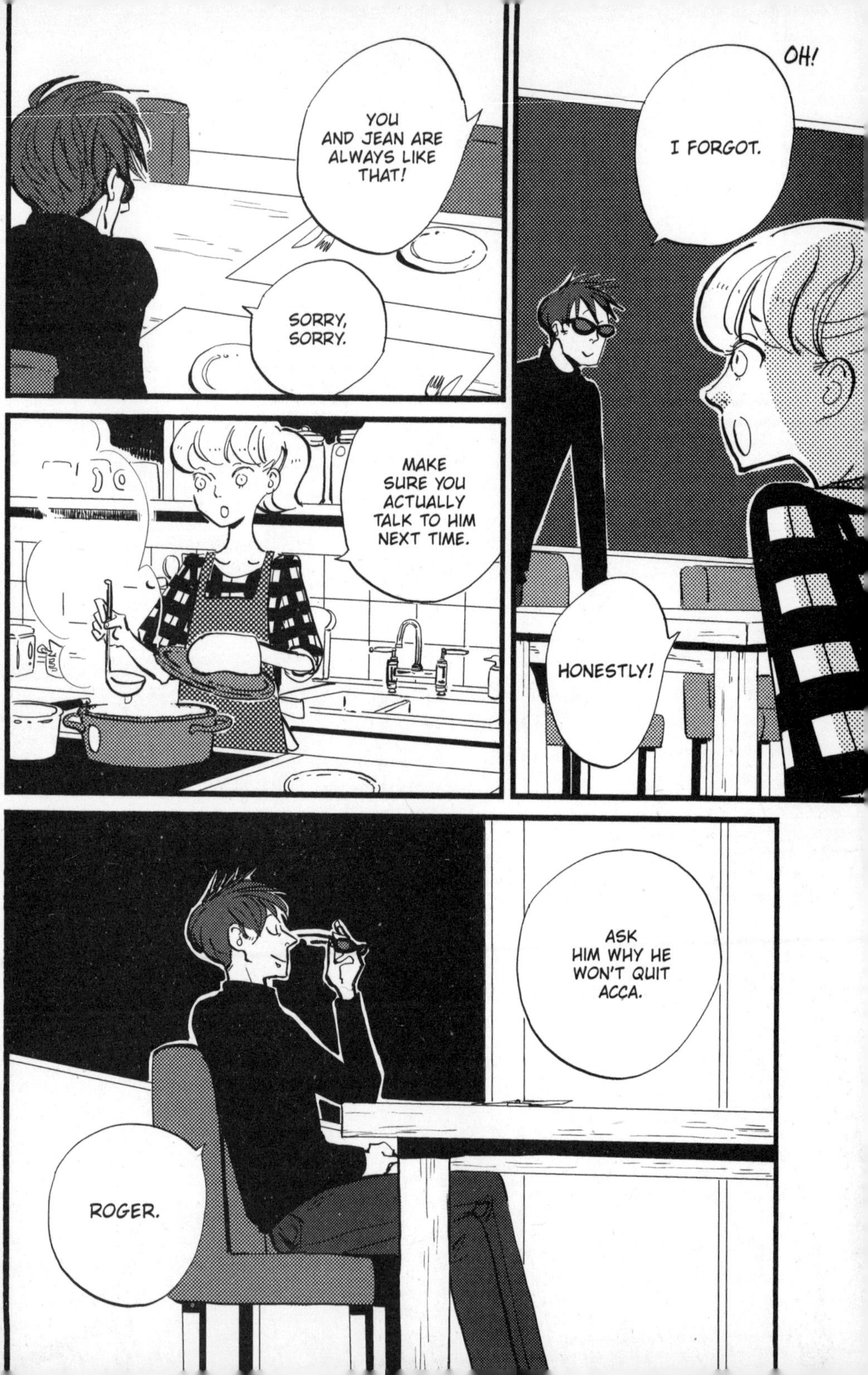
OH!
I FORGOT.
HONESTLY!
YOU AND JEAN ARE ALWAYS LIKE THAT!
SORRY, SORRY.
MAKE SURE YOU ACTUALLY TALK TO HIM NEXT TIME.
ASK HIM WHY HE WON'T QUIT ACCA.
ROGER.

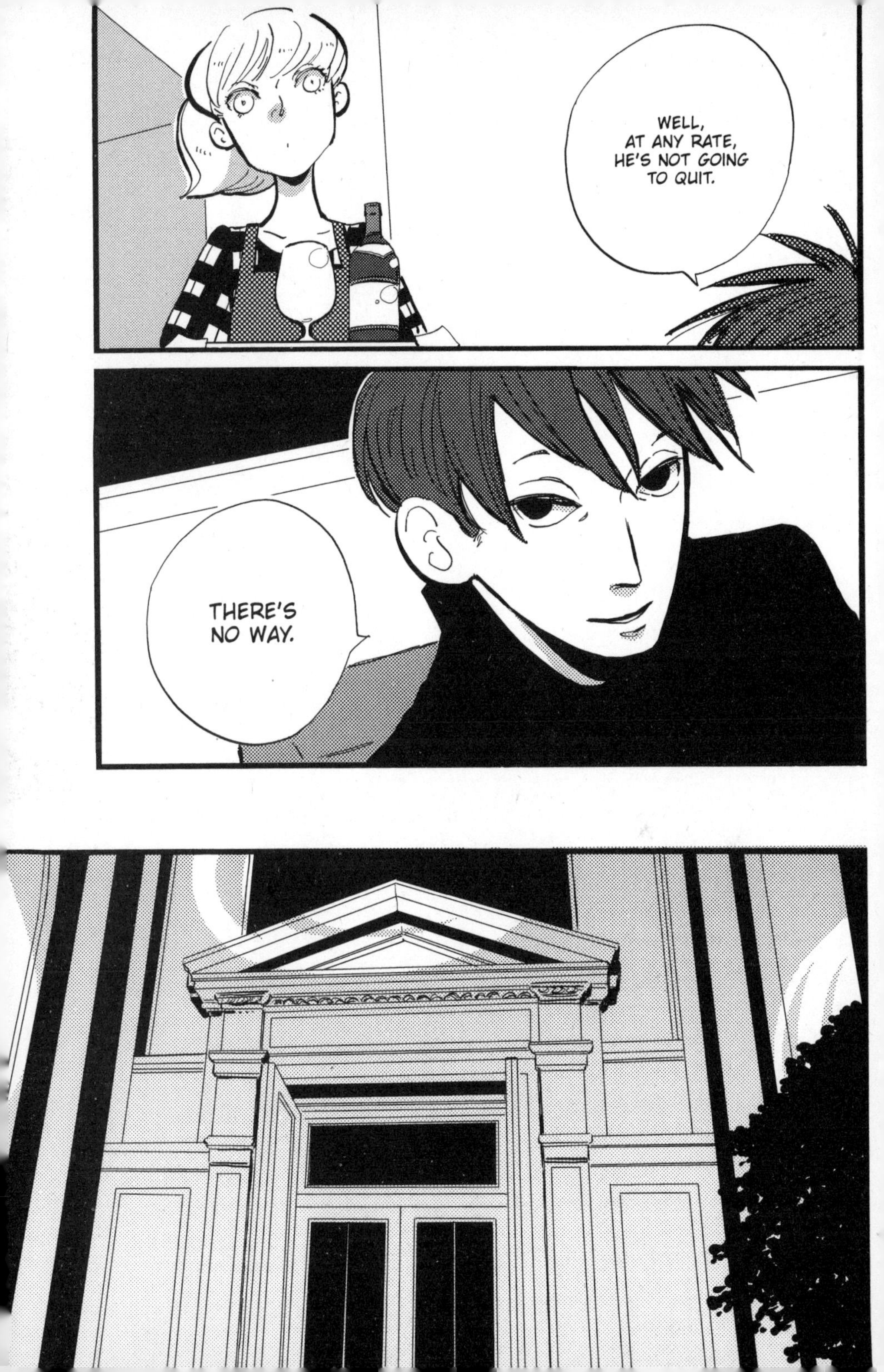
WELL, AT ANY RATE, HE'S NOT GOING TO QUIT.
THERE'S NO WAY.

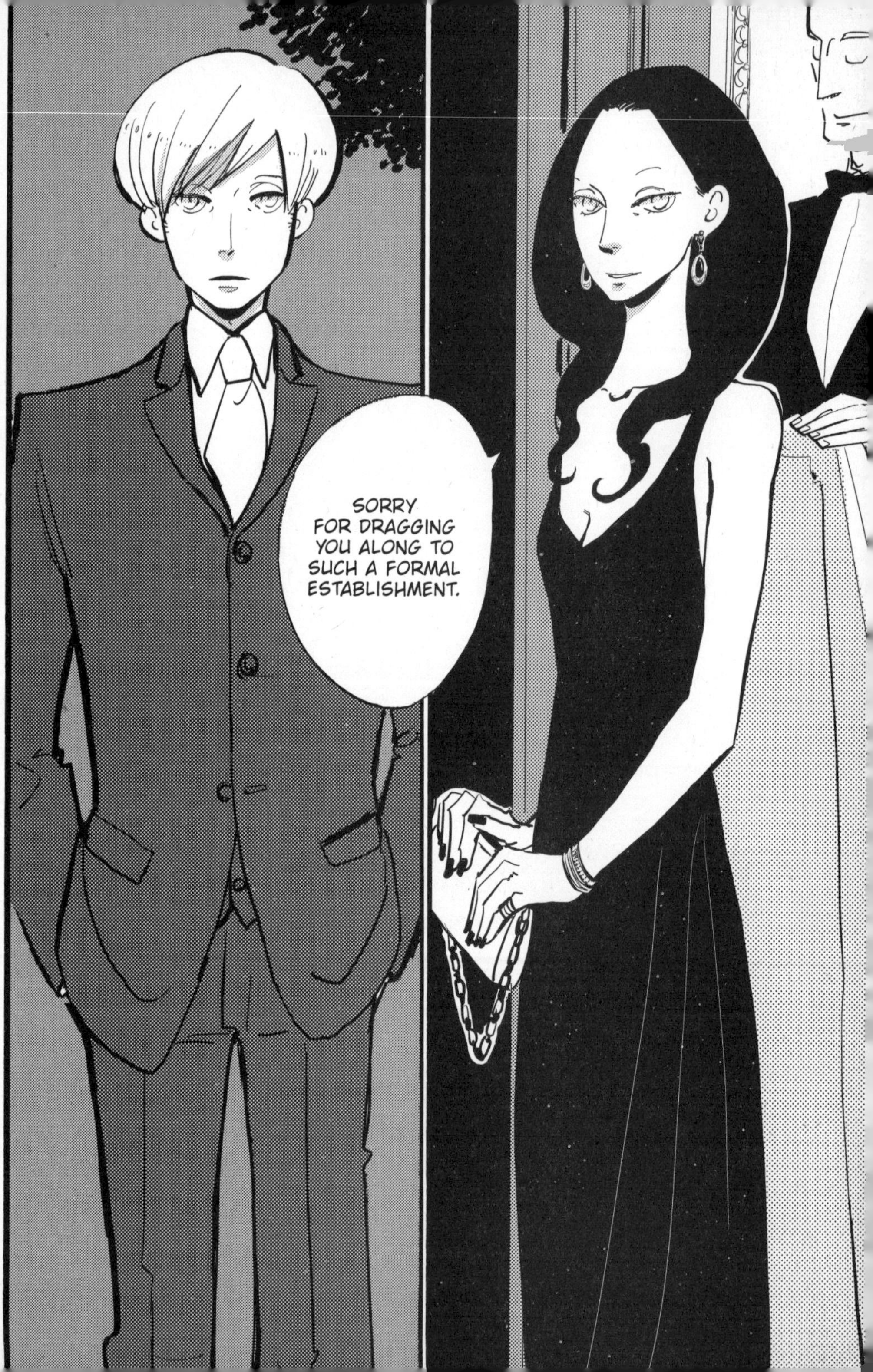
SORRY FOR DRAGGING YOU ALONG TO SUCH A FORMAL ESTABLISHMENT.

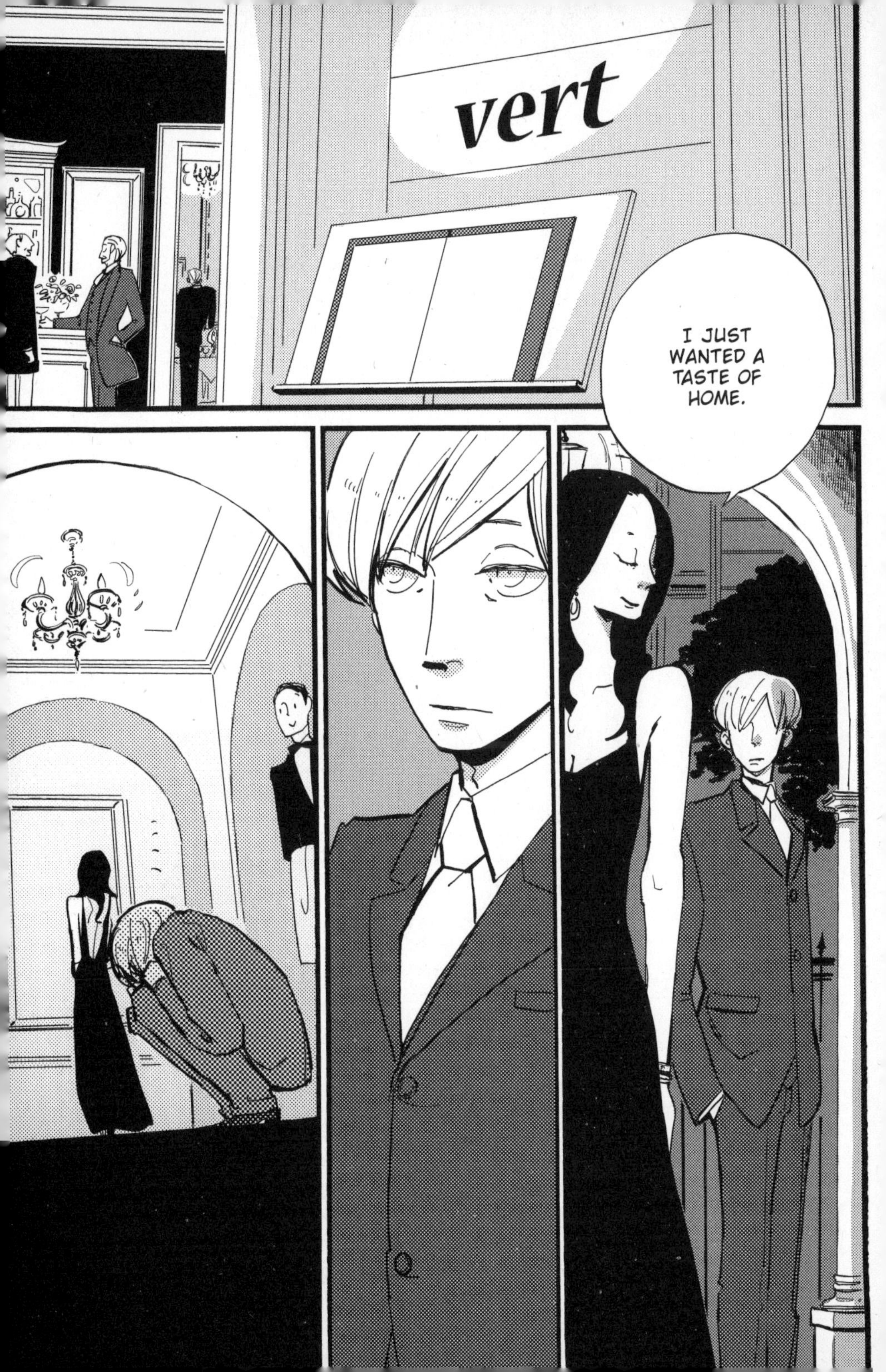
vert
I JUST WANTED A TASTE OF HOME.

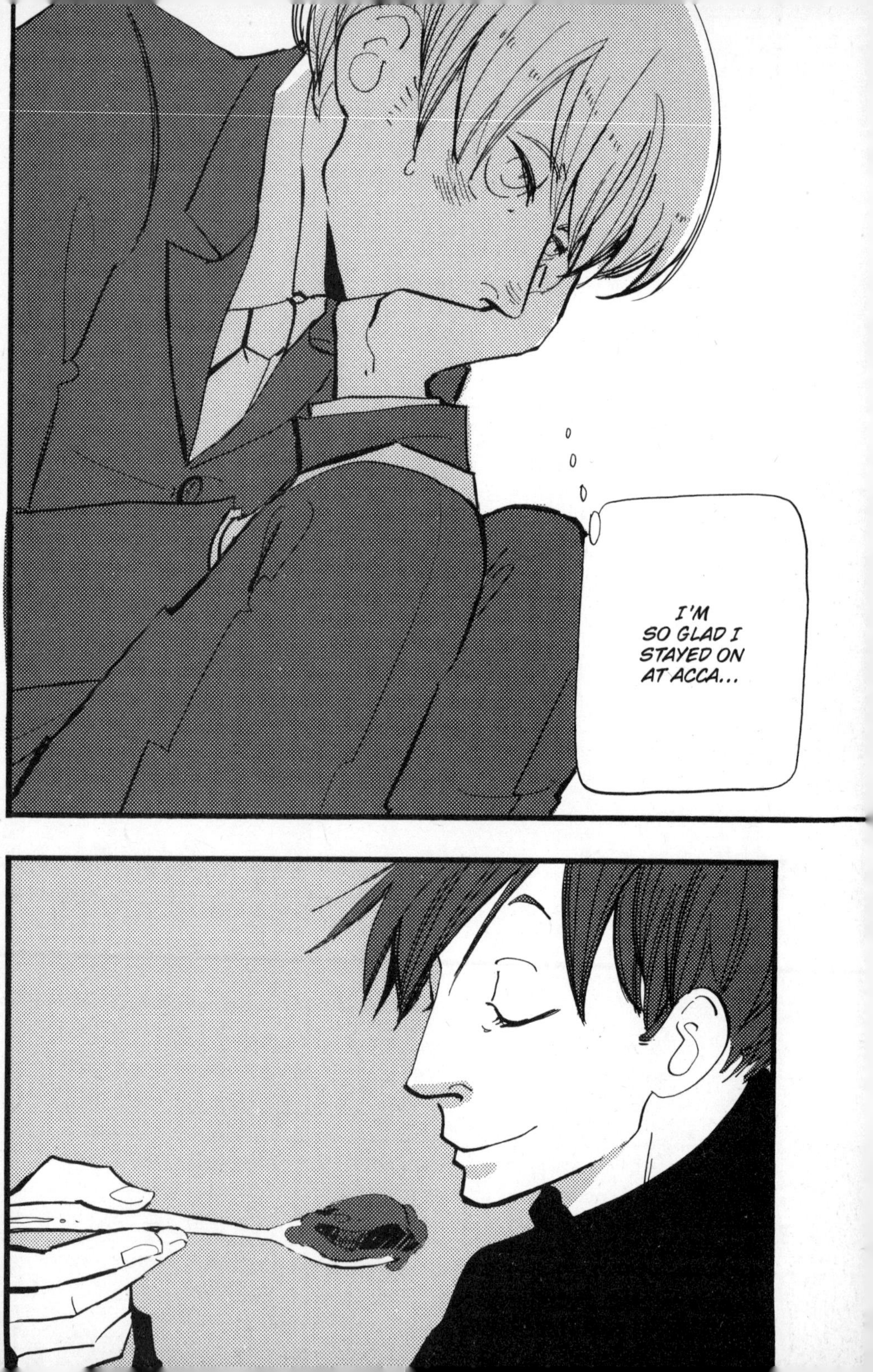
I'M SO GLAD I STAYED ON AT ACCA...

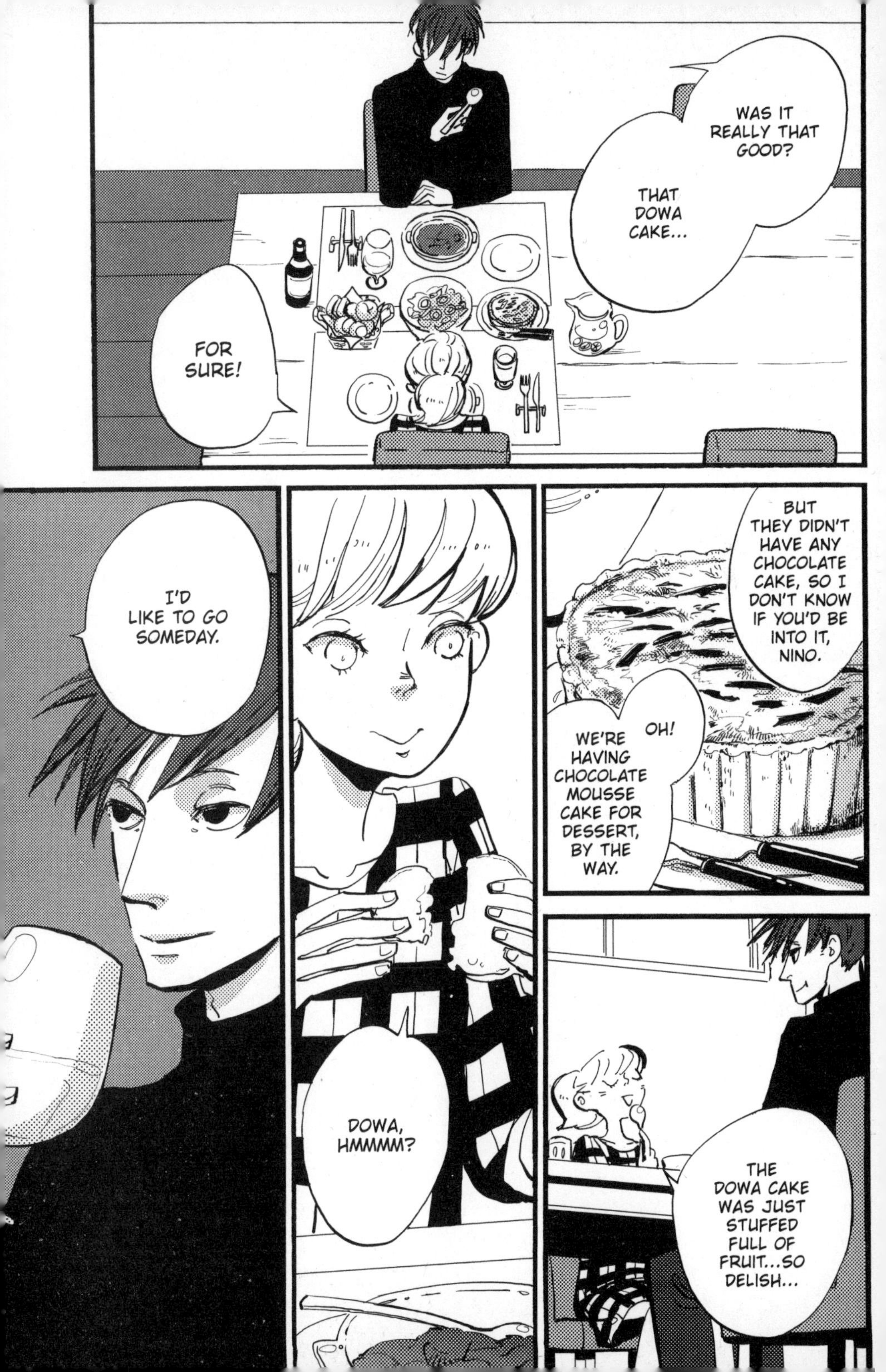
WAS IT REALLY THAT GOOD?
THAT DOWA CAKE...
FOR SURE!
BUT THEY DIDN'T HAVE ANY CHOCOLATE CAKE, SO I DON'T KNOW IF YOU'D BE INTO IT, NINO.
OH!
WE'RE HAVING CHOCOLATE MOUSSE CAKE FOR DESSERT, BY THE WAY.
THE DOWA CAKE WAS JUST STUFFED FULL OF FRUIT...SO DELISH...
DOWA, HMMMM?
I'D LIKE TO GO SOMEDAY.

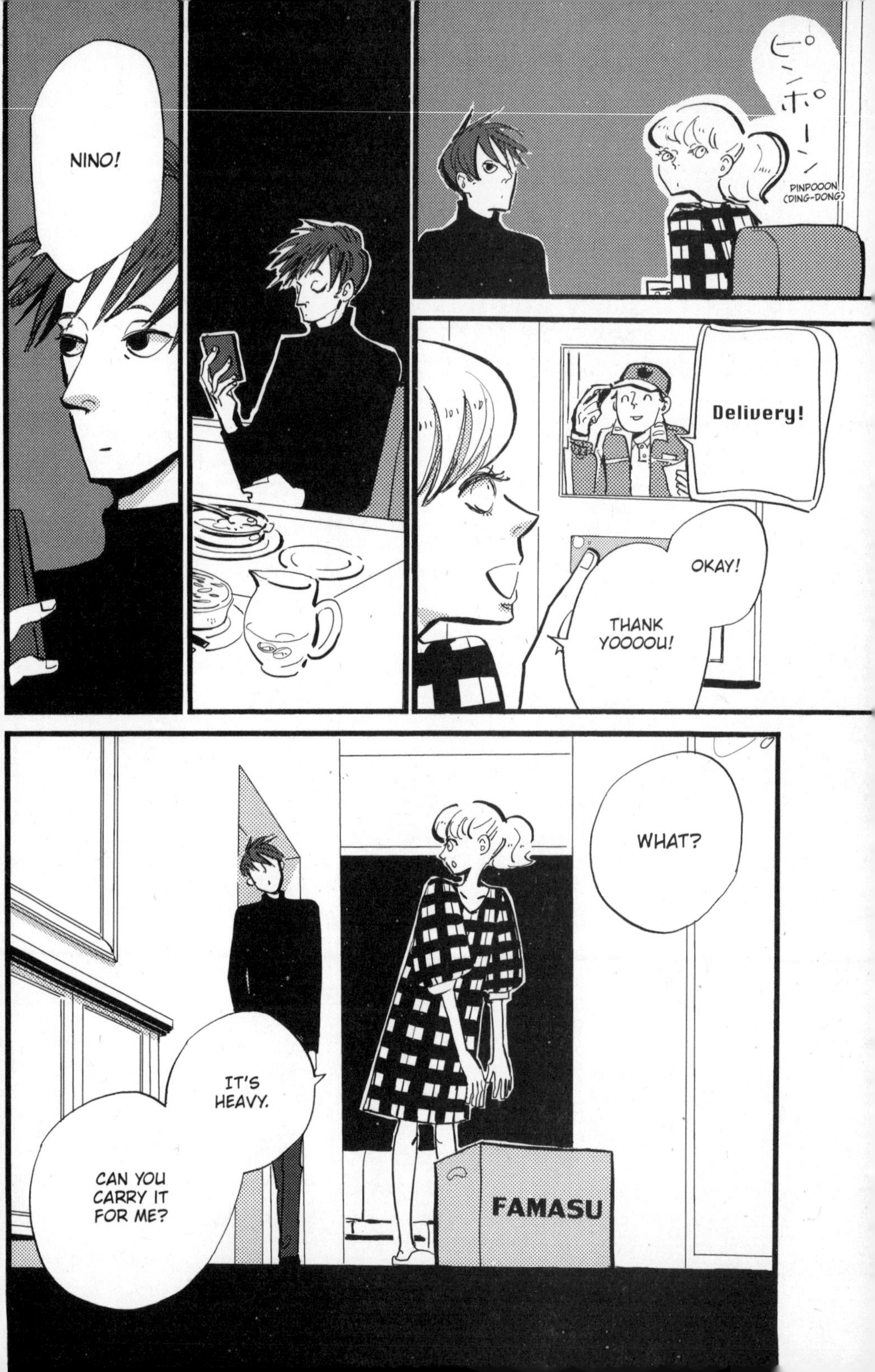
ピンポーン
PINPOOON (DING-DONG)
Delivery!
OKAY!
THANK YOOOOU!
NINO!
WHAT?
IT'S HEAVY.
FAMASU
CAN YOU CARRY IT FOR ME?

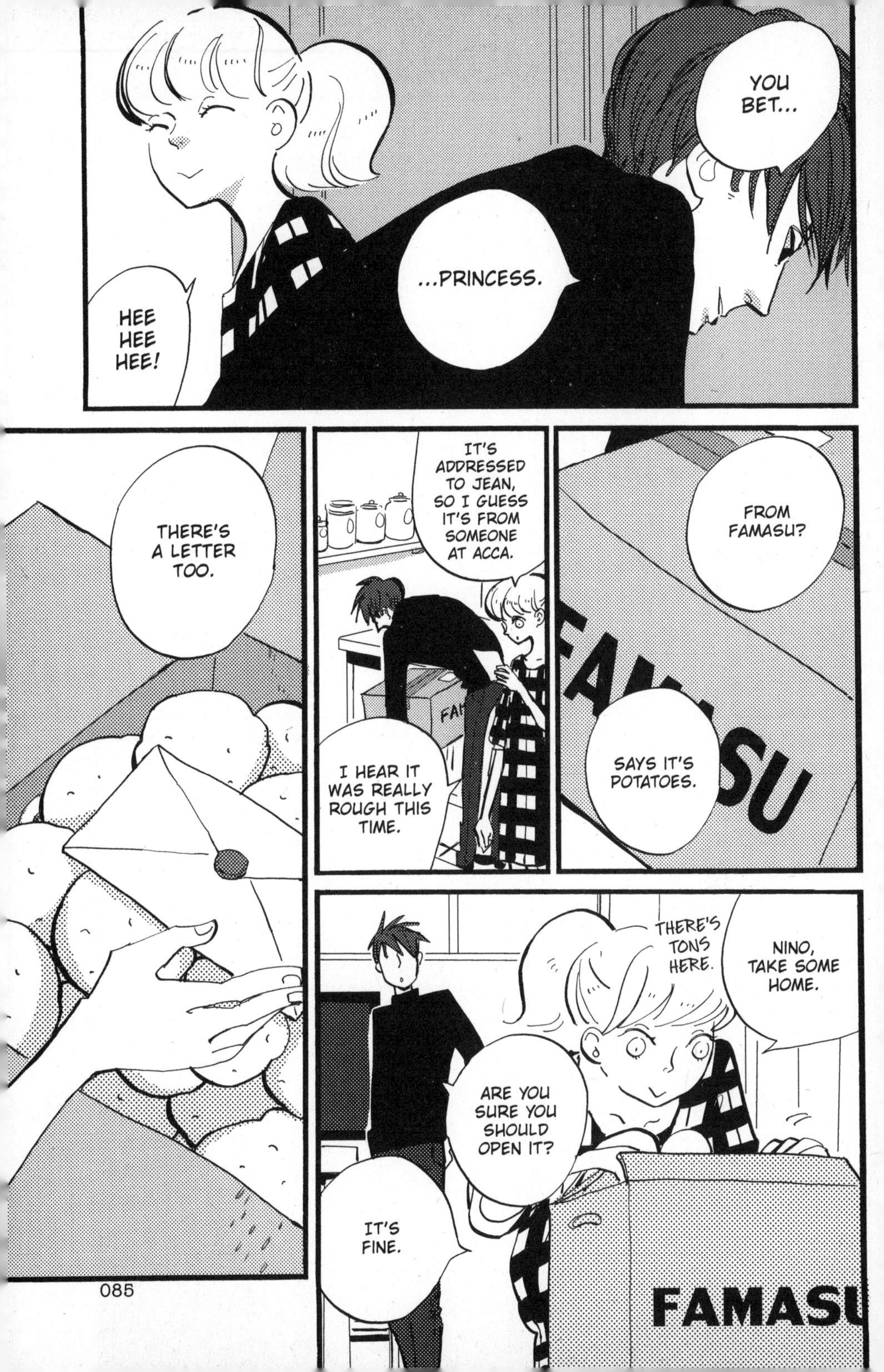
YOU BET...
...PRINCESS.
HEE HEE HEE!
FROM FAMASU?
FAMASU
SAYS IT'S POTATOES.
IT'S ADDRESSED TO JEAN, SO I GUESS IT'S FROM SOMEONE AT ACCA.
I HEAR IT WAS REALLY ROUGH THIS TIME.
NINO, TAKE SOME HOME.
THERE'S TONS HERE.
ARE YOU SURE YOU SHOULD OPEN IT?
IT'S FINE.
FAMASU
THERE'S A LETTER TOO.

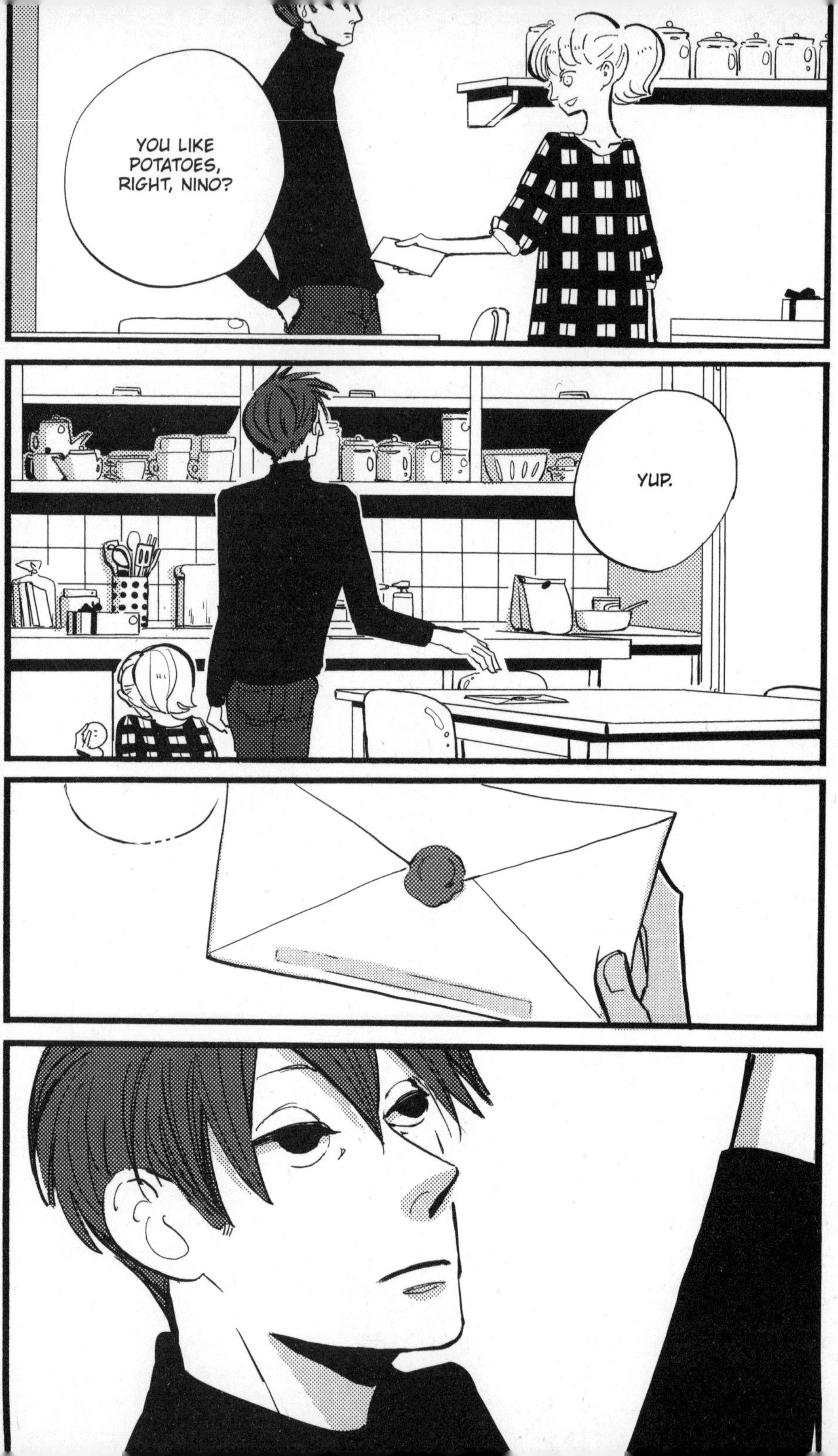
YOU LIKE POTATOES, RIGHT, NINO?
YUP.

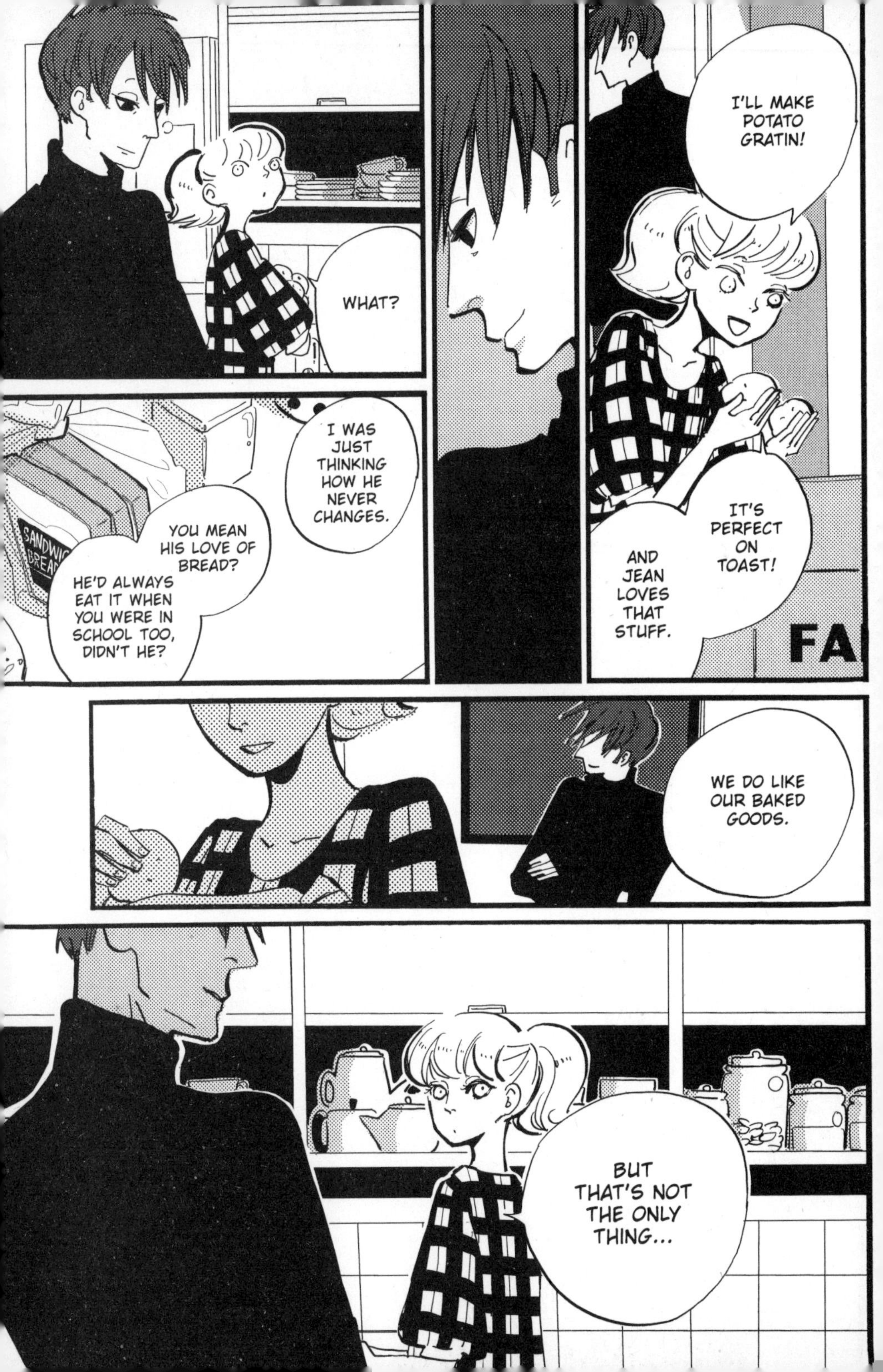
I'LL MAKE POTATO GRATIN!
IT'S PERFECT ON TOAST!
AND JEAN LOVES THAT STUFF.
FA
WHAT?
I WAS JUST THINKING HOW HE NEVER CHANGES.
YOU MEAN HIS LOVE OF BREAD?
HE'D ALWAYS EAT IT WHEN YOU WERE IN SCHOOL TOO, DIDN'T HE?
SANDWICH BREAD
WE DO LIKE OUR BAKED GOODS.
BUT THAT'S NOT THE ONLY THING...

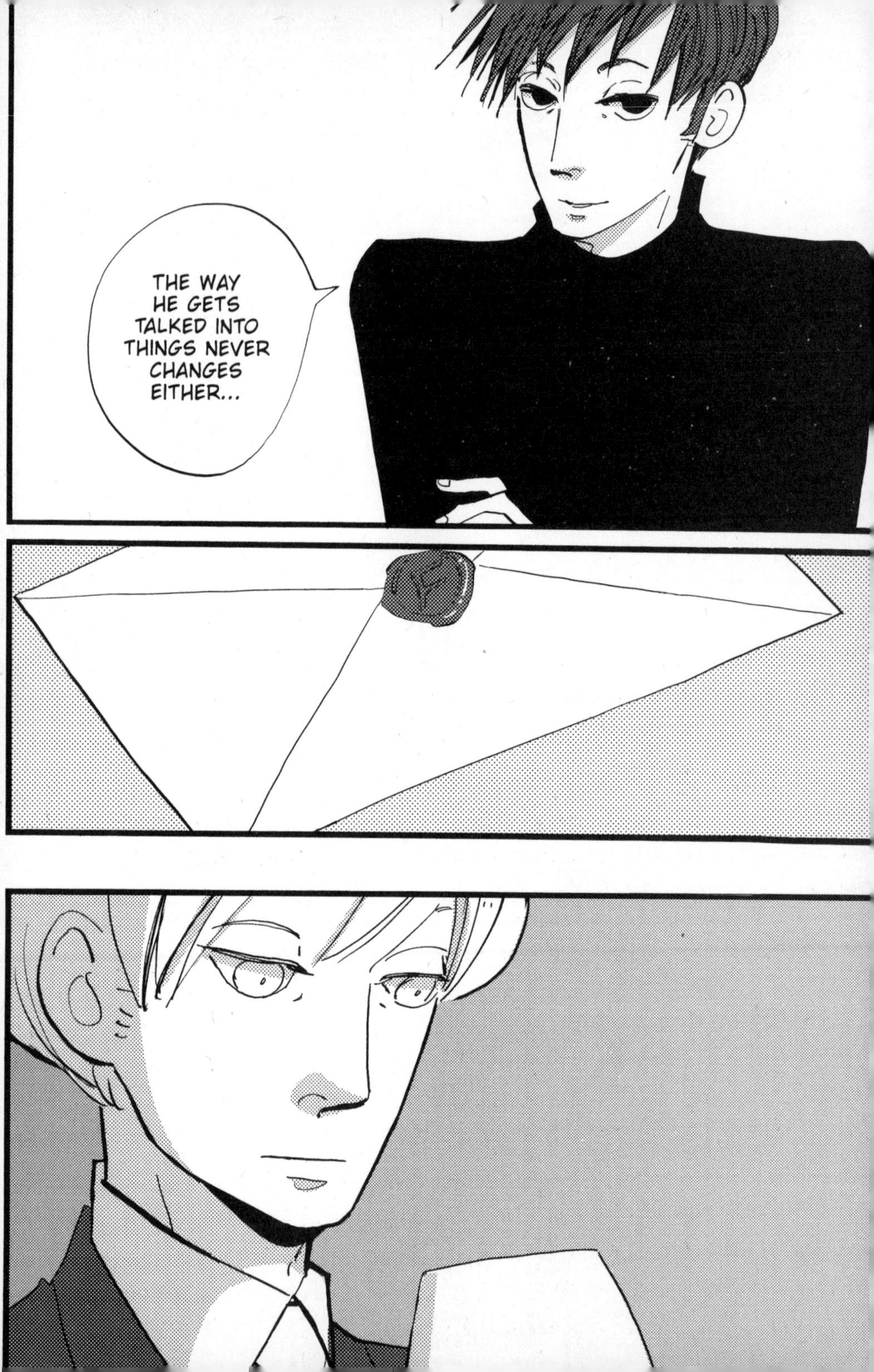
THE WAY HE GETS TALKED INTO THINGS NEVER CHANGES EITHER...

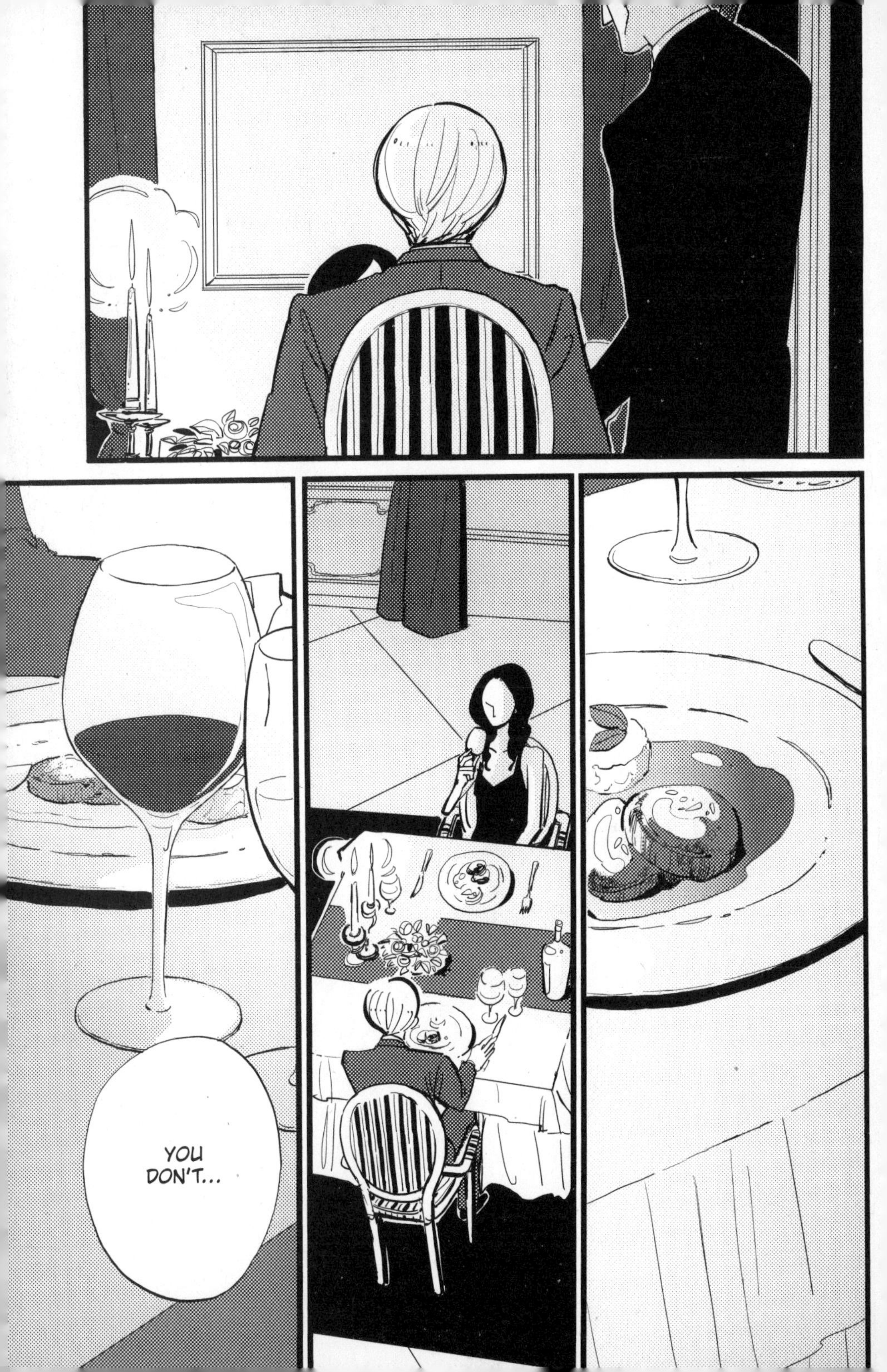
YOU DON'T...

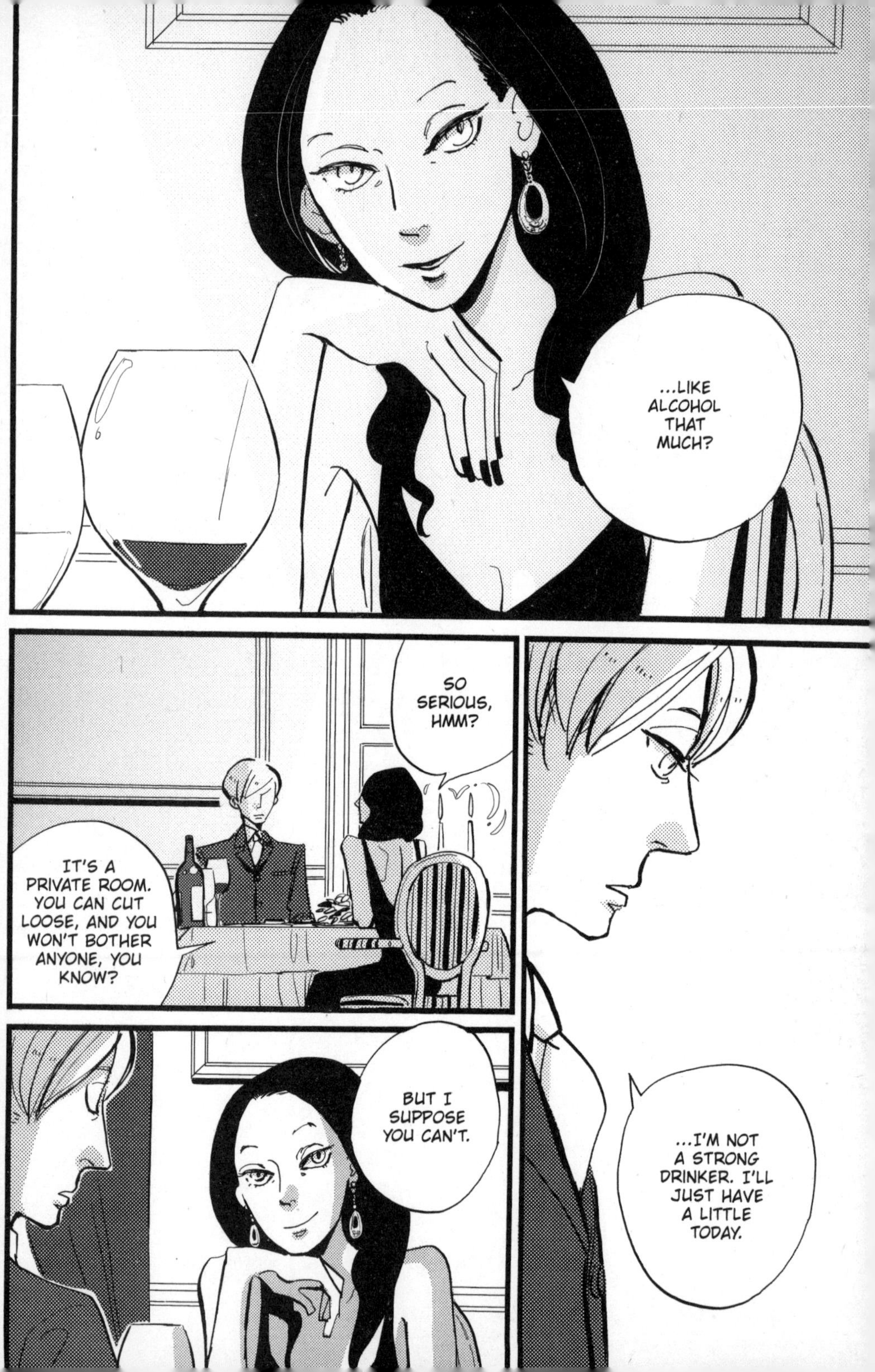
...LIKE ALCOHOL THAT MUCH?
...I'M NOT A STRONG DRINKER. I'LL JUST HAVE A LITTLE TODAY.
SO SERIOUS, HMM?
IT'S A PRIVATE ROOM. YOU CAN CUT LOOSE, AND YOU WON'T BOTHER ANYONE, YOU KNOW?
BUT I SUPPOSE YOU CAN'T.

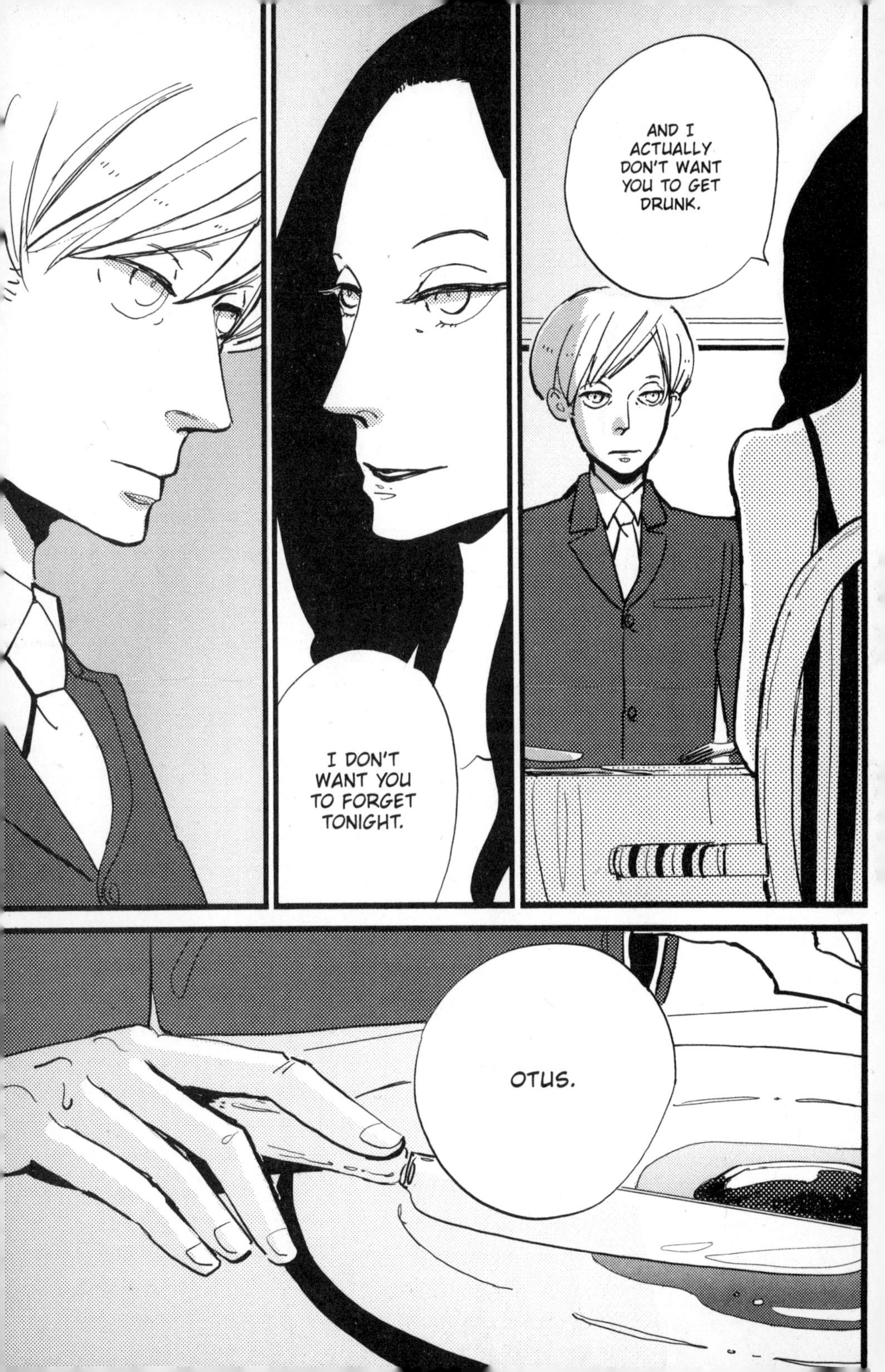
AND I ACTUALLY DON'T WANT YOU TO GET DRUNK.
I DON'T WANT YOU TO FORGET TONIGHT.
OTUS.

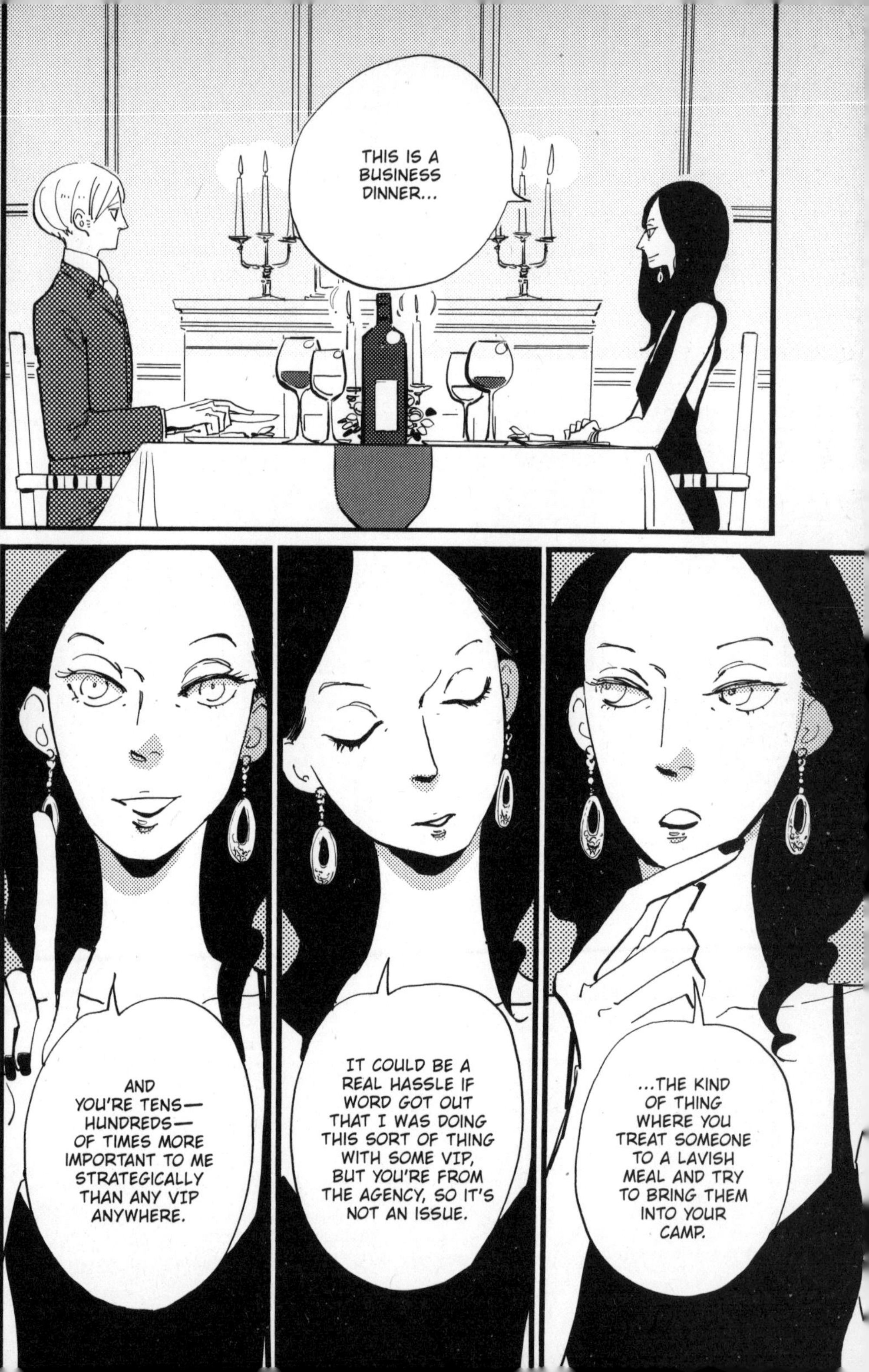
THIS IS A BUSINESS DINNER...
...THE KIND OF THING WHERE YOU TREAT SOMEONE TO A LAVISH MEAL AND TRY TO BRING THEM INTO YOUR CAMP.
IT COULD BE A REAL HASSLE IF WORD GOT OUT THAT I WAS DOING THIS SORT OF THING WITH SOME VIP, BUT YOU'RE FROM THE AGENCY, SO IT'S NOT AN ISSUE.
AND YOU'RE TENS—HUNDREDS—OF TIMES MORE IMPORTANT TO ME STRATEGICALLY THAN ANY VIP ANYWHERE.

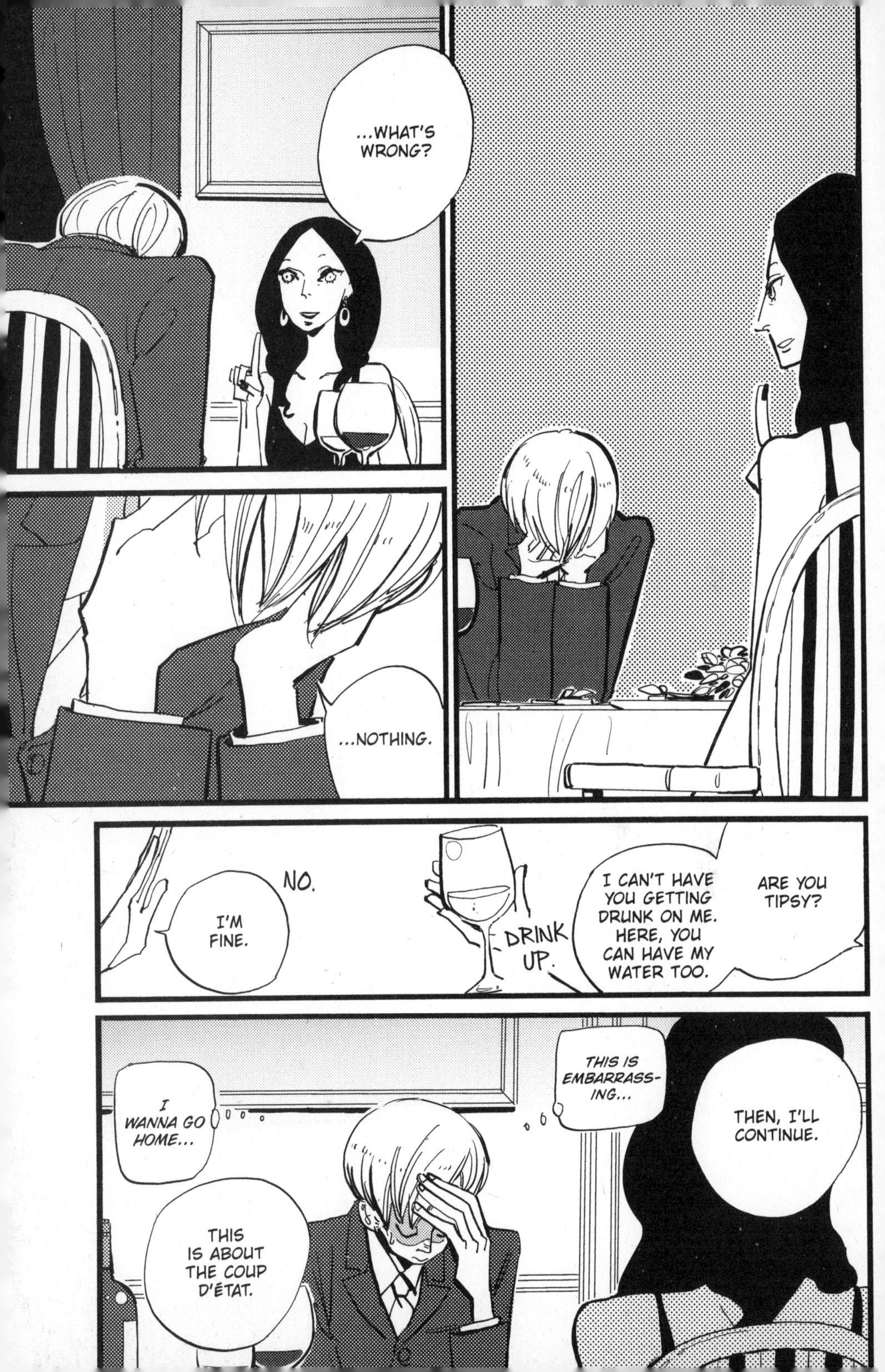
...WHAT'S WRONG?
...NOTHING.
ARE YOU TIPSY?
I CAN'T HAVE YOU GETTING DRUNK ON ME. HERE, YOU CAN HAVE MY WATER TOO.
DRINK UP.
NO.
I'M FINE.
THEN, I'LL CONTINUE.
THIS IS EMBARRASS-ING...
I WANNA GO HOME...
THIS IS ABOUT THE COUP D'ÉTAT.

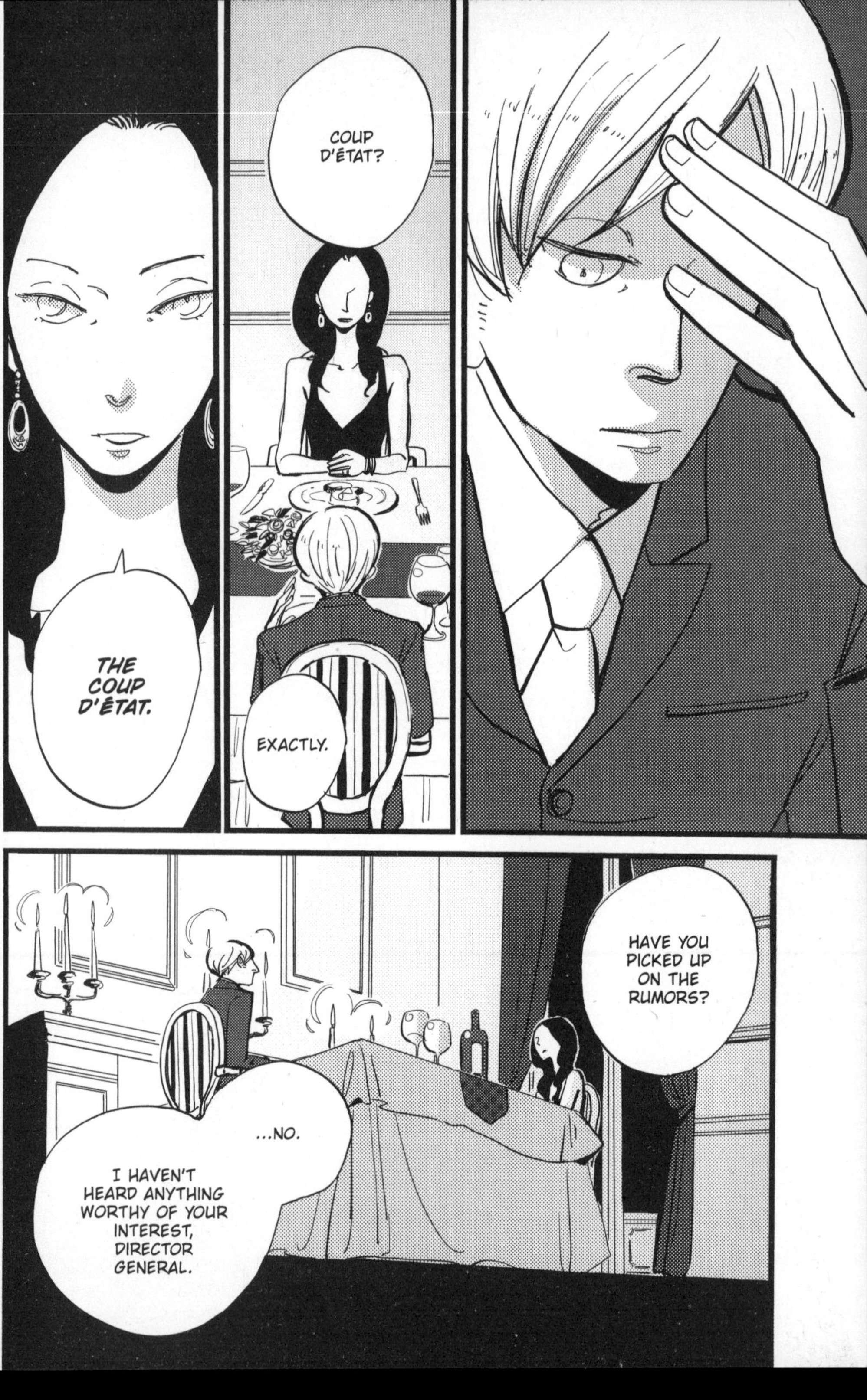
COUP D'ÉTAT?
EXACTLY.
THE COUP D'ÉTAT.
HAVE YOU PICKED UP ON THE RUMORS?
...NO.
I HAVEN'T HEARD ANYTHING WORTHY OF YOUR INTEREST, DIRECTOR GENERAL.

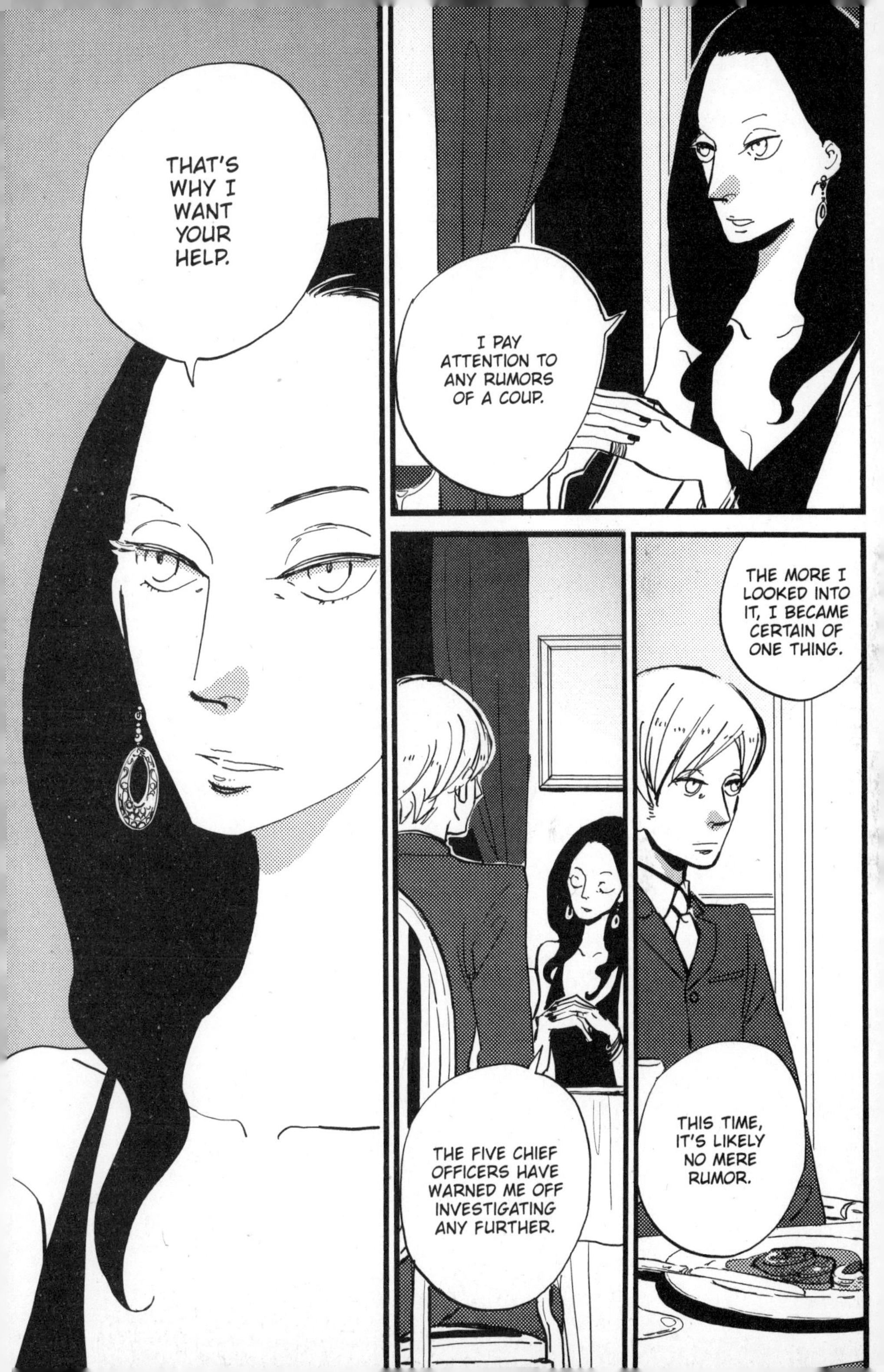
I PAY ATTENTION TO ANY RUMORS OF A COUP.
THE MORE I LOOKED INTO IT, I BECAME CERTAIN OF ONE THING.
THIS TIME, IT'S LIKELY NO MERE RUMOR.
THE FIVE CHIEF OFFICERS HAVE WARNED ME OFF INVESTIGATING ANY FURTHER.
THAT'S WHY I WANT YOUR HELP.

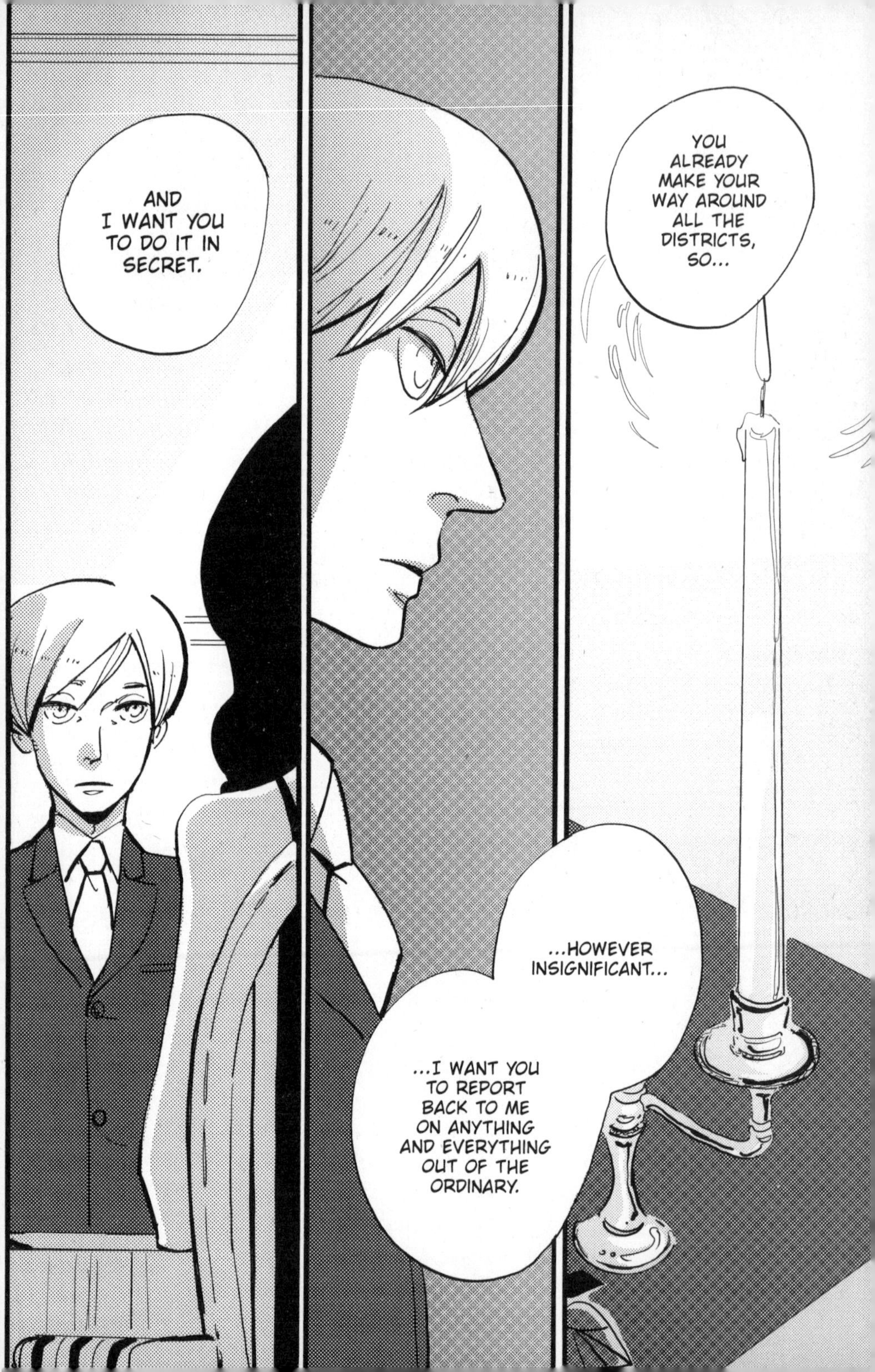
YOU ALREADY MAKE YOUR WAY AROUND ALL THE DISTRICTS, SO...
...HOWEVER INSIGNIFICANT...
...I WANT YOU TO REPORT BACK TO ME ON ANYTHING AND EVERYTHING OUT OF THE ORDINARY.
AND I WANT YOU TO DO IT IN SECRET.

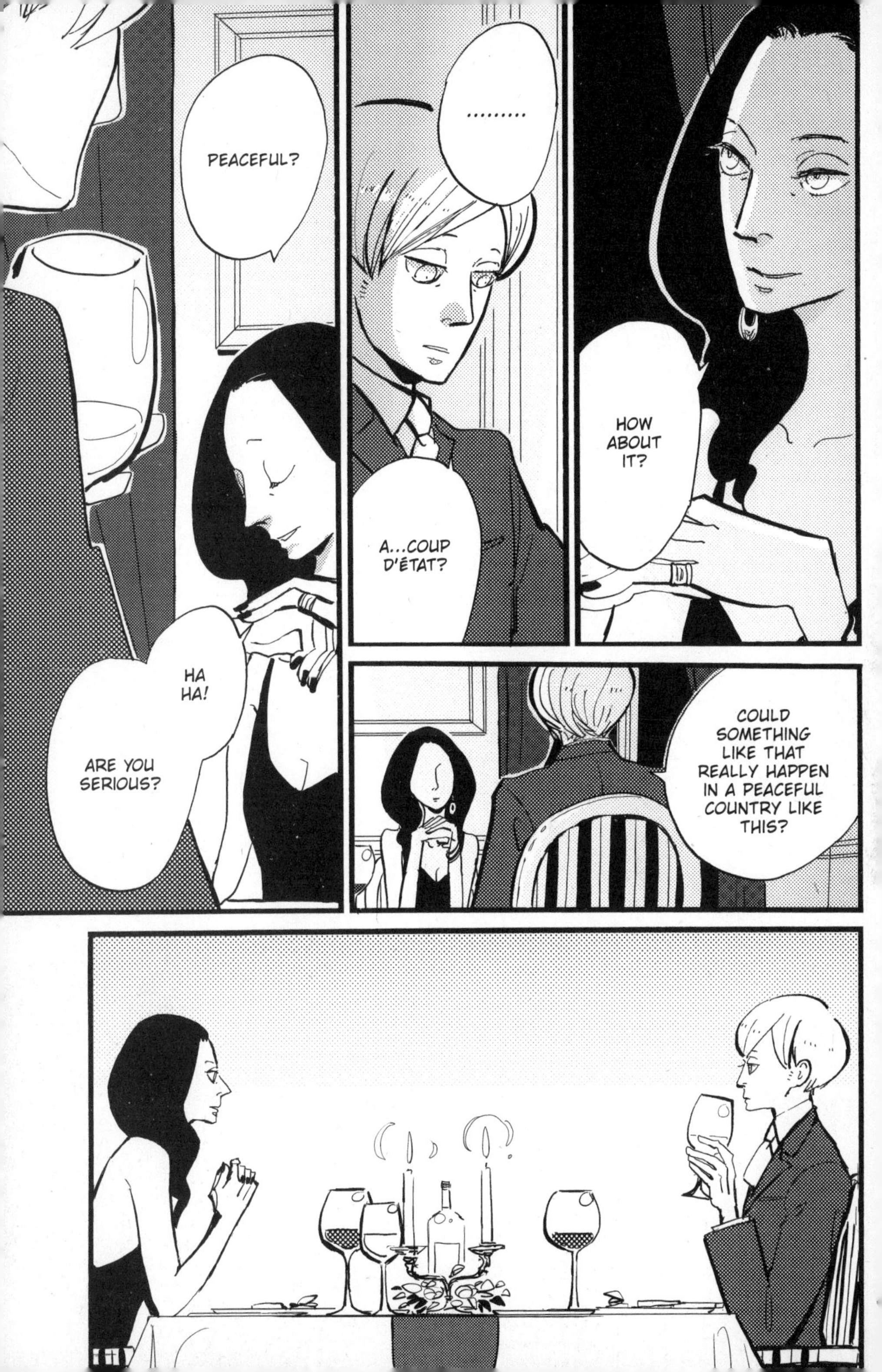
HOW ABOUT IT?
....
A...COUP D'ÉTAT?
COULD SOMETHING LIKE THAT REALLY HAPPEN IN A PEACEFUL COUNTRY LIKE THIS?
PEACEFUL?
HA HA!
ARE YOU SERIOUS?

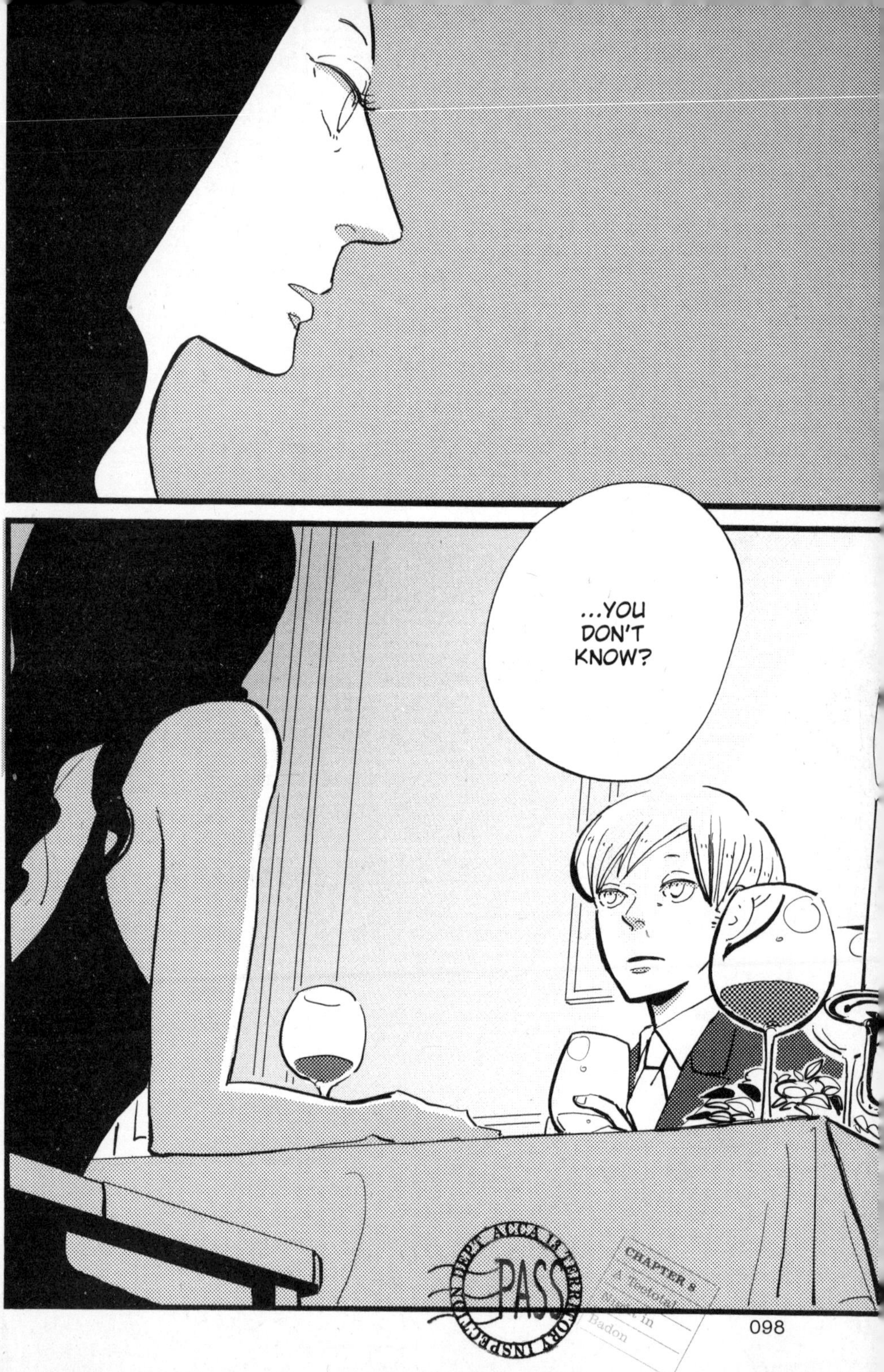
...YOU DON'T KNOW?
ACCA 13 TERRITORY INSPECTION DEPT.
PASS
CHAPTER 8
A Teetotal
in
Badon

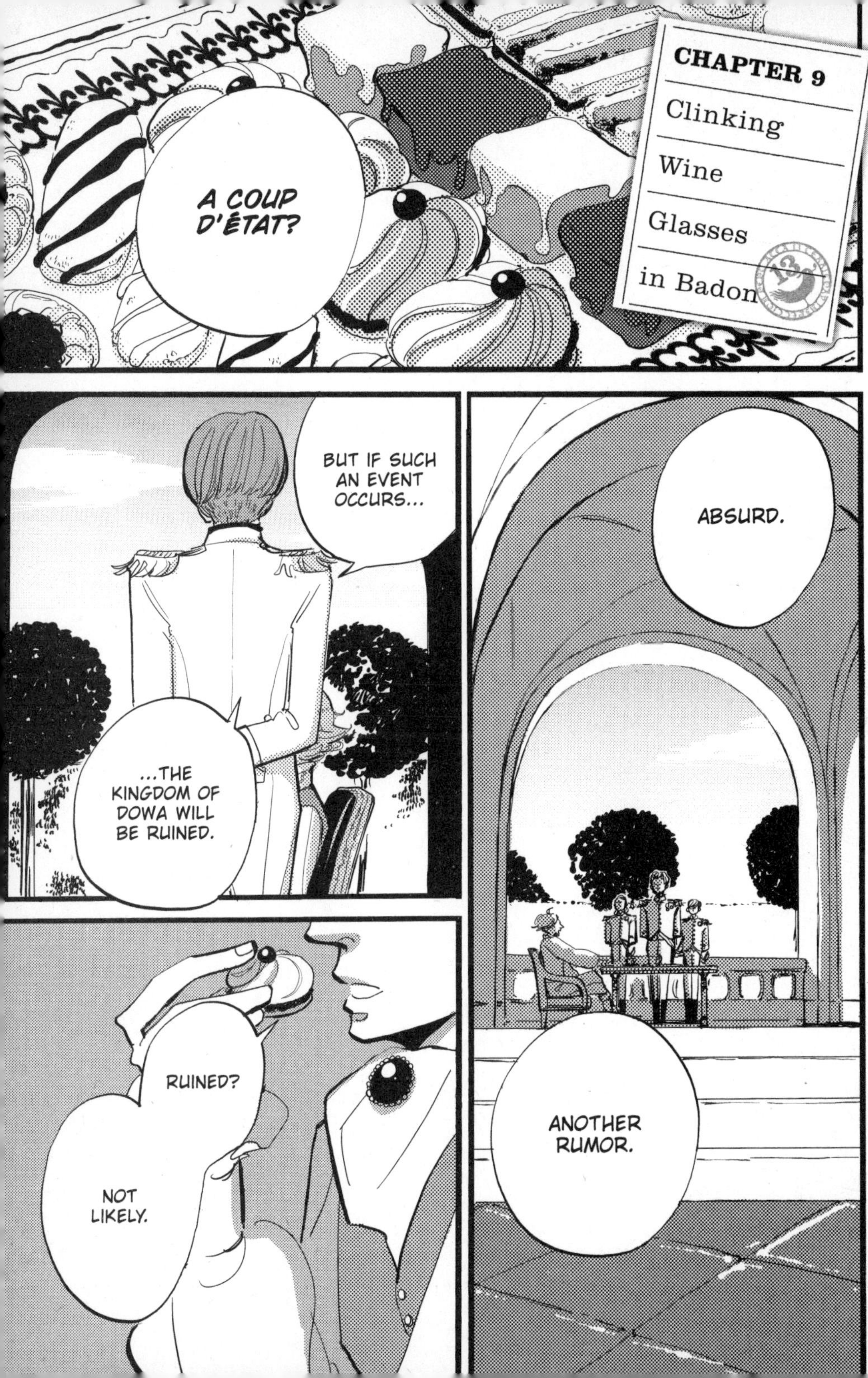
CHAPTER 9
Clinking Wine Glasses in Badon
A COUP D'ÉTAT?
ABSURD.
ANOTHER RUMOR.
BUT IF SUCH AN EVENT OCCURS...
...THE KINGDOM OF DOWA WILL BE RUINED.
RUINED?
NOT LIKELY.

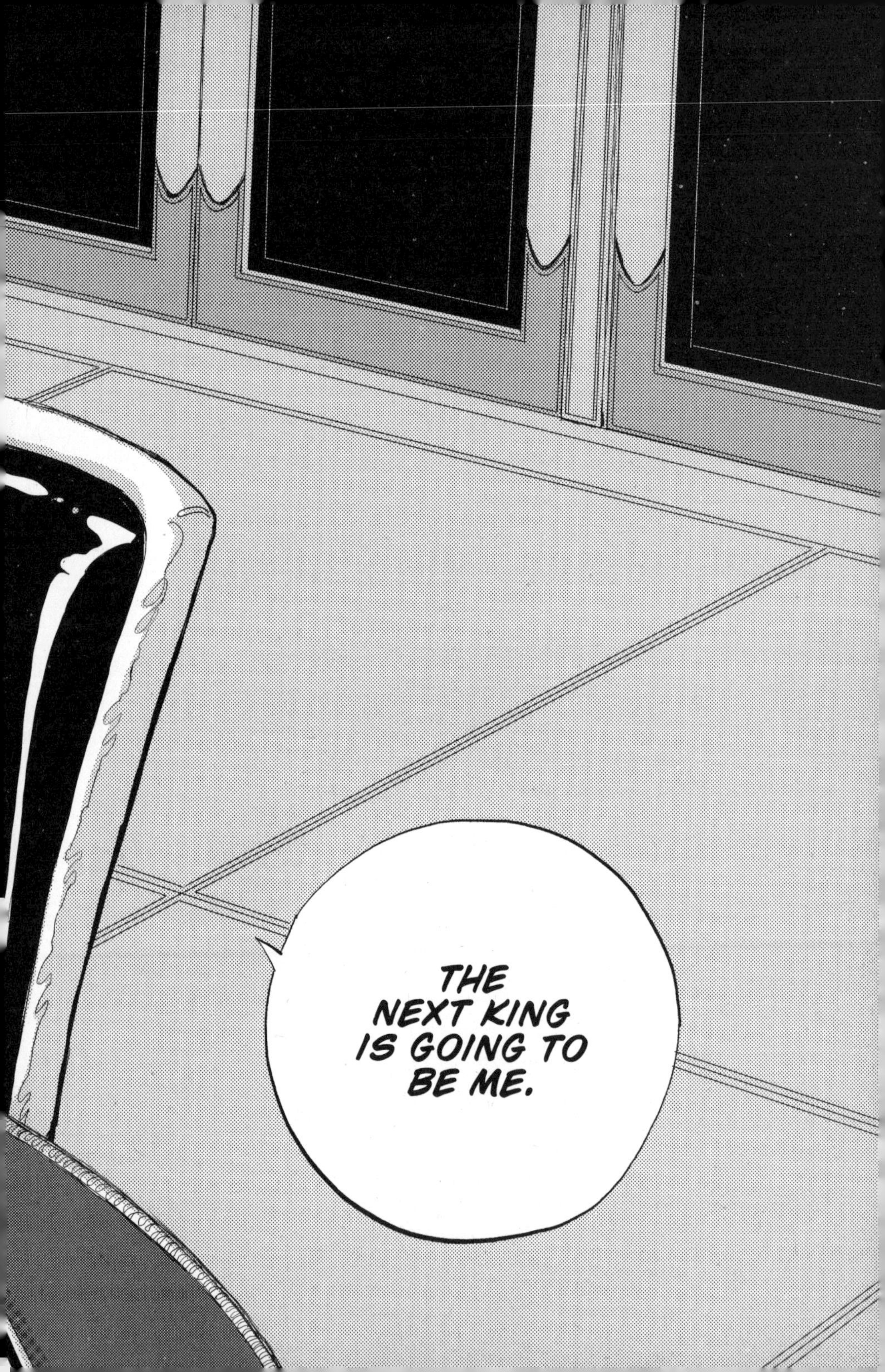
THE NEXT KING IS GOING TO BE ME.

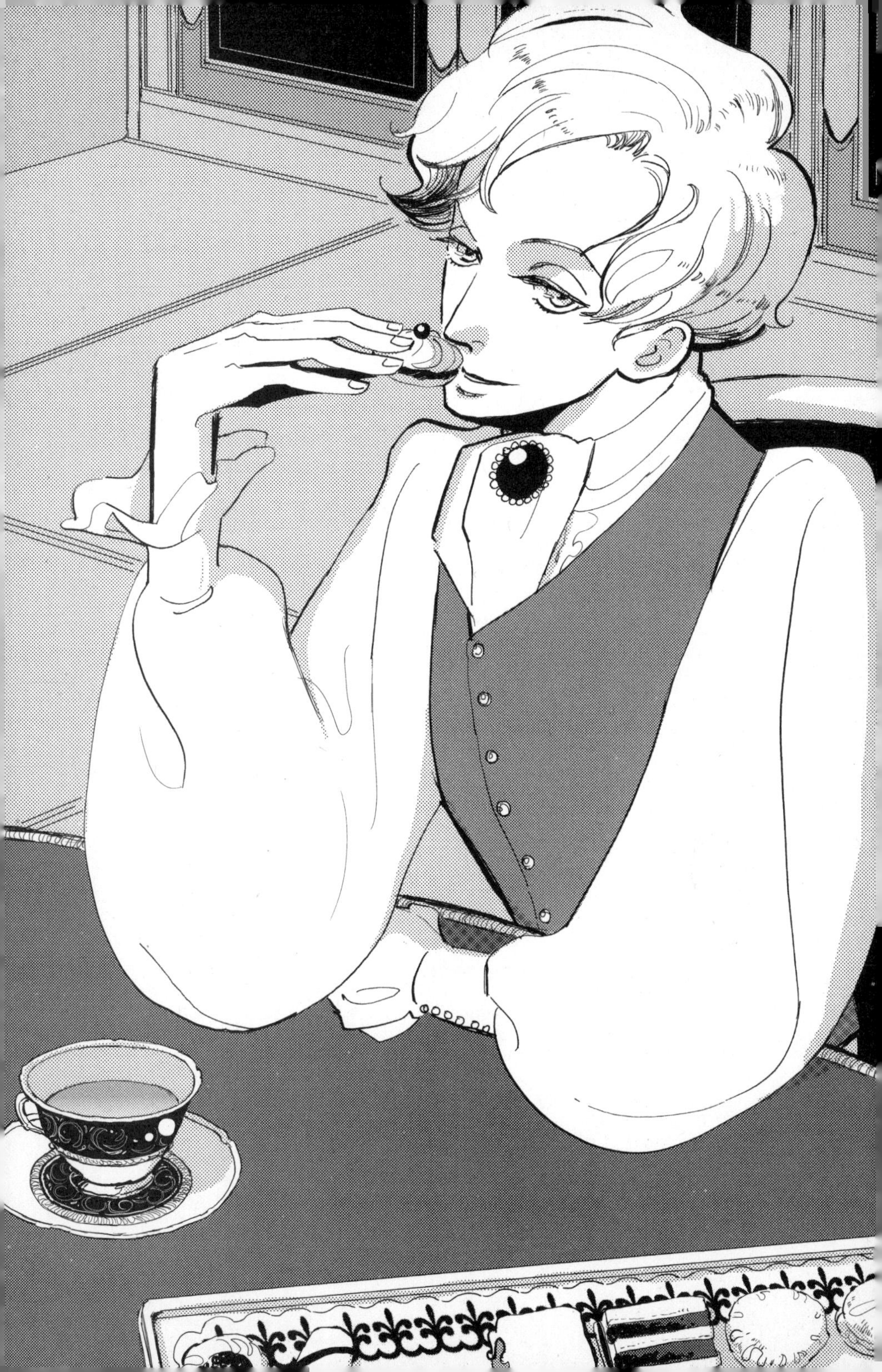

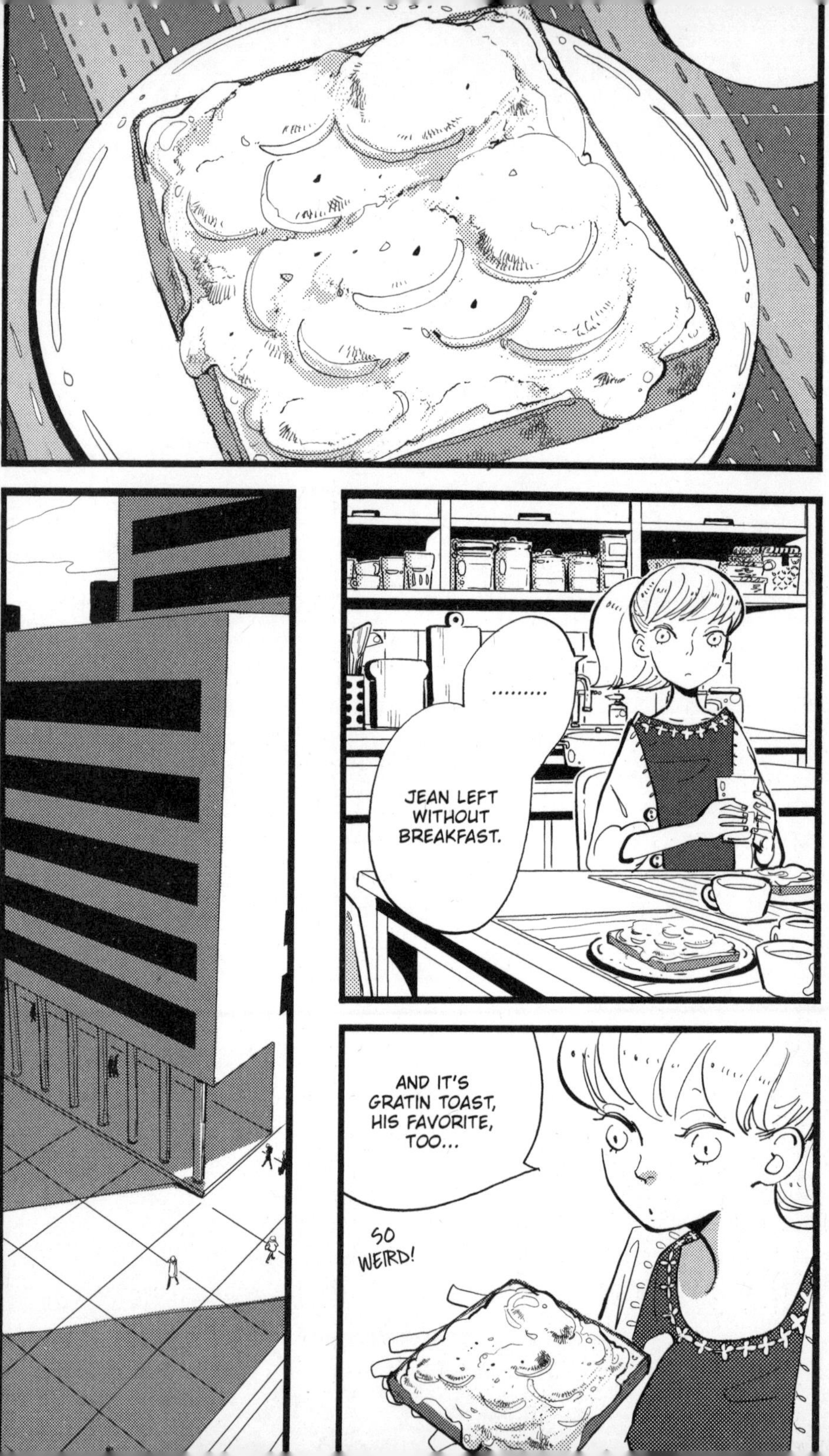
....
JEAN LEFT WITHOUT BREAKFAST.
AND IT'S GRATIN TOAST, HIS FAVORITE, TOO...
SO WEIRD!

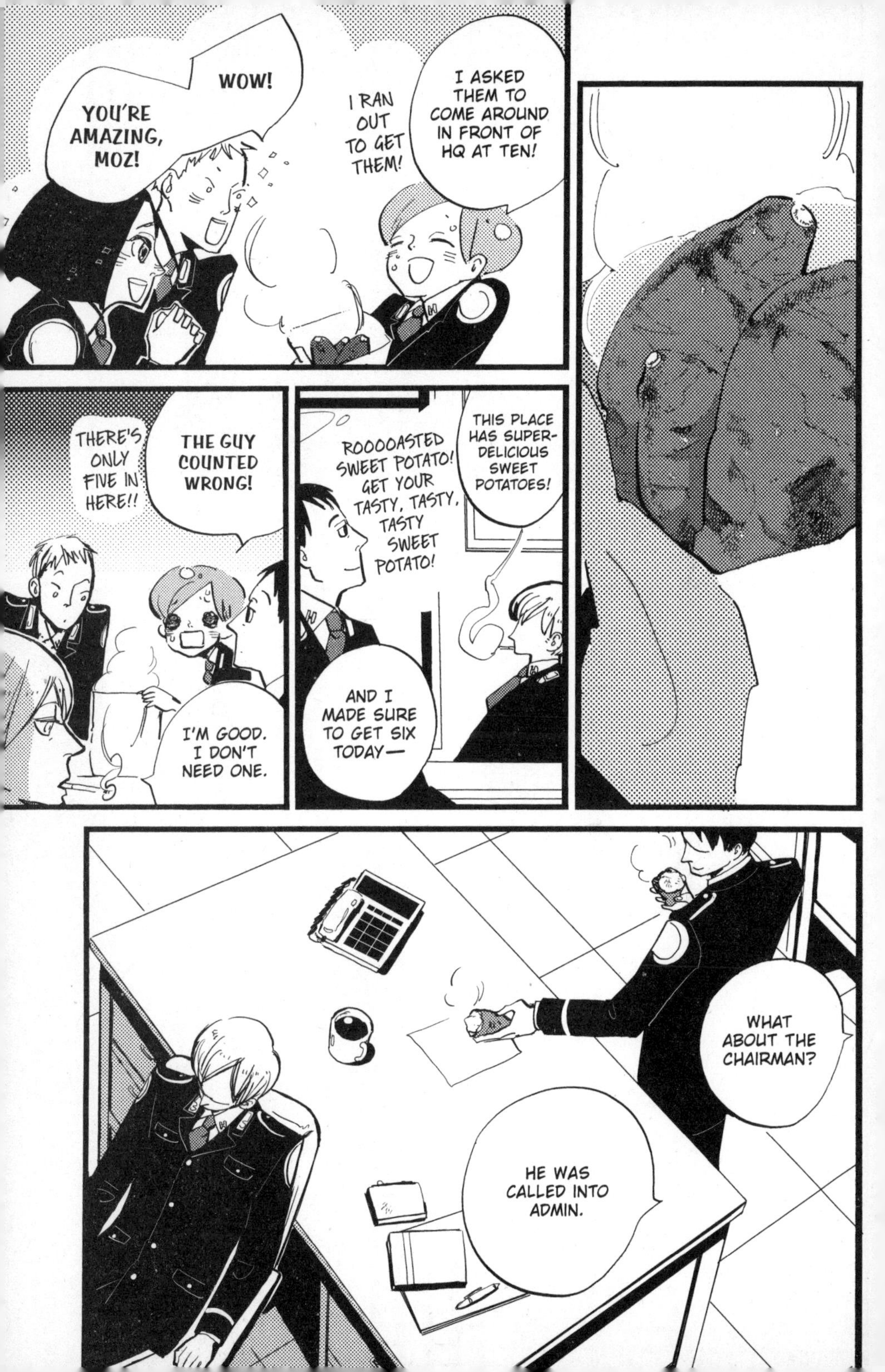
I ASKED THEM TO COME AROUND IN FRONT OF HQ AT TEN!
I RAN OUT TO GET THEM!
WOW!
YOU'RE AMAZING, MOZ!
THIS PLACE HAS SUPER-DELICIOUS SWEET POTATOES!
ROOOOASTED SWEET POTATO! GET YOUR TASTY, TASTY, TASTY SWEET POTATO!
AND I MADE SURE TO GET SIX TODAY—
THE GUY COUNTED WRONG!
THERE'S ONLY FIVE IN HERE!!
I'M GOOD. I DON'T NEED ONE.
WHAT ABOUT THE CHAIRMAN?
HE WAS CALLED INTO ADMIN.

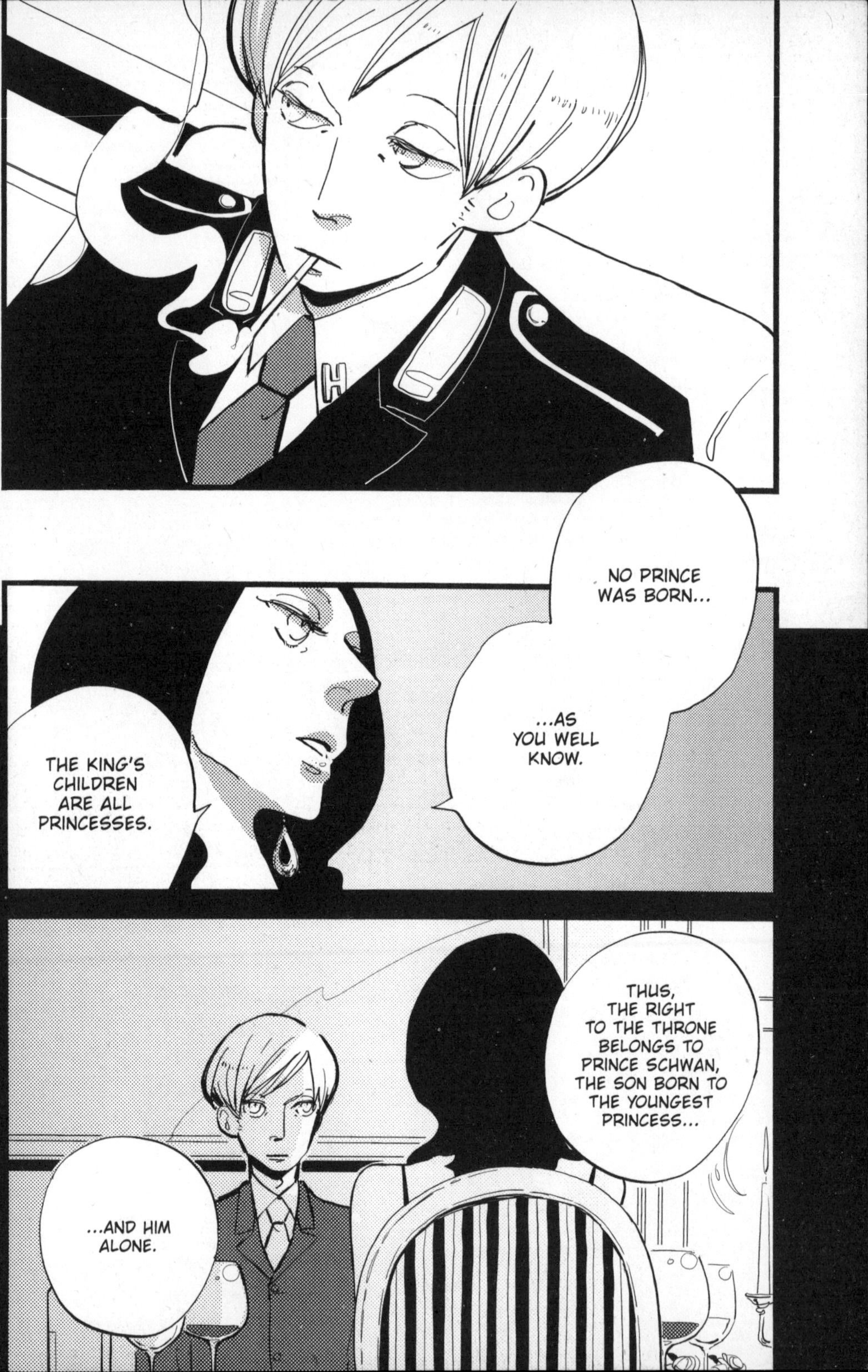
NO PRINCE WAS BORN...
...AS YOU WELL KNOW.
THE KING'S CHILDREN ARE ALL PRINCESSES.
THUS, THE RIGHT TO THE THRONE BELONGS TO PRINCE SCHWAN, THE SON BORN TO THE YOUNGEST PRINCESS...
...AND HIM ALONE.

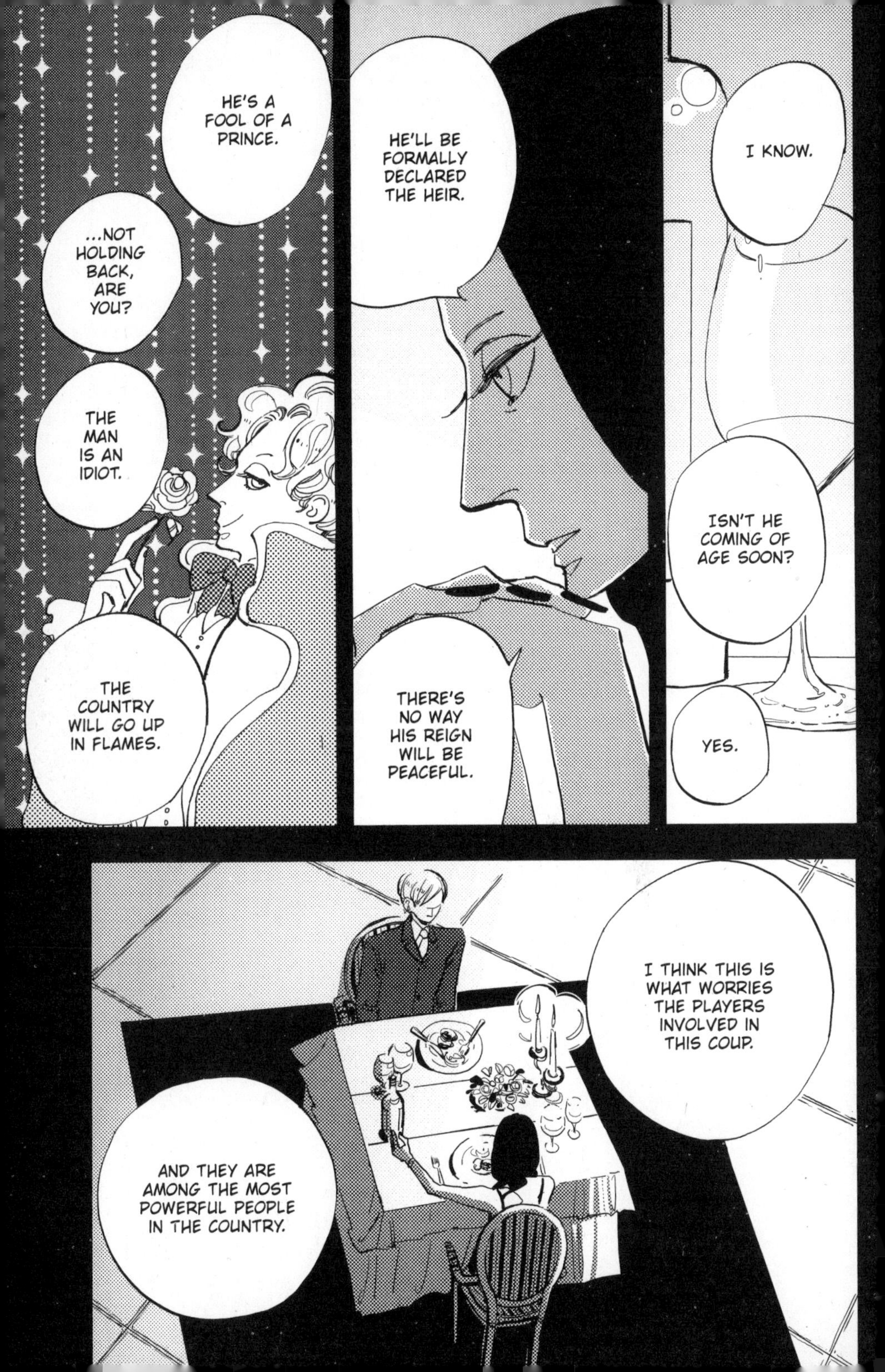
I KNOW.
ISN'T HE COMING OF AGE SOON?
YES.
HE'LL BE FORMALLY DECLARED THE HEIR.
THERE'S NO WAY HIS REIGN WILL BE PEACEFUL.
HE'S A FOOL OF A PRINCE.
...NOT HOLDING BACK, ARE YOU?
THE MAN IS AN IDIOT.
THE COUNTRY WILL GO UP IN FLAMES.
I THINK THIS IS WHAT WORRIES THE PLAYERS INVOLVED IN THIS COUP.
AND THEY ARE AMONG THE MOST POWERFUL PEOPLE IN THE COUNTRY.

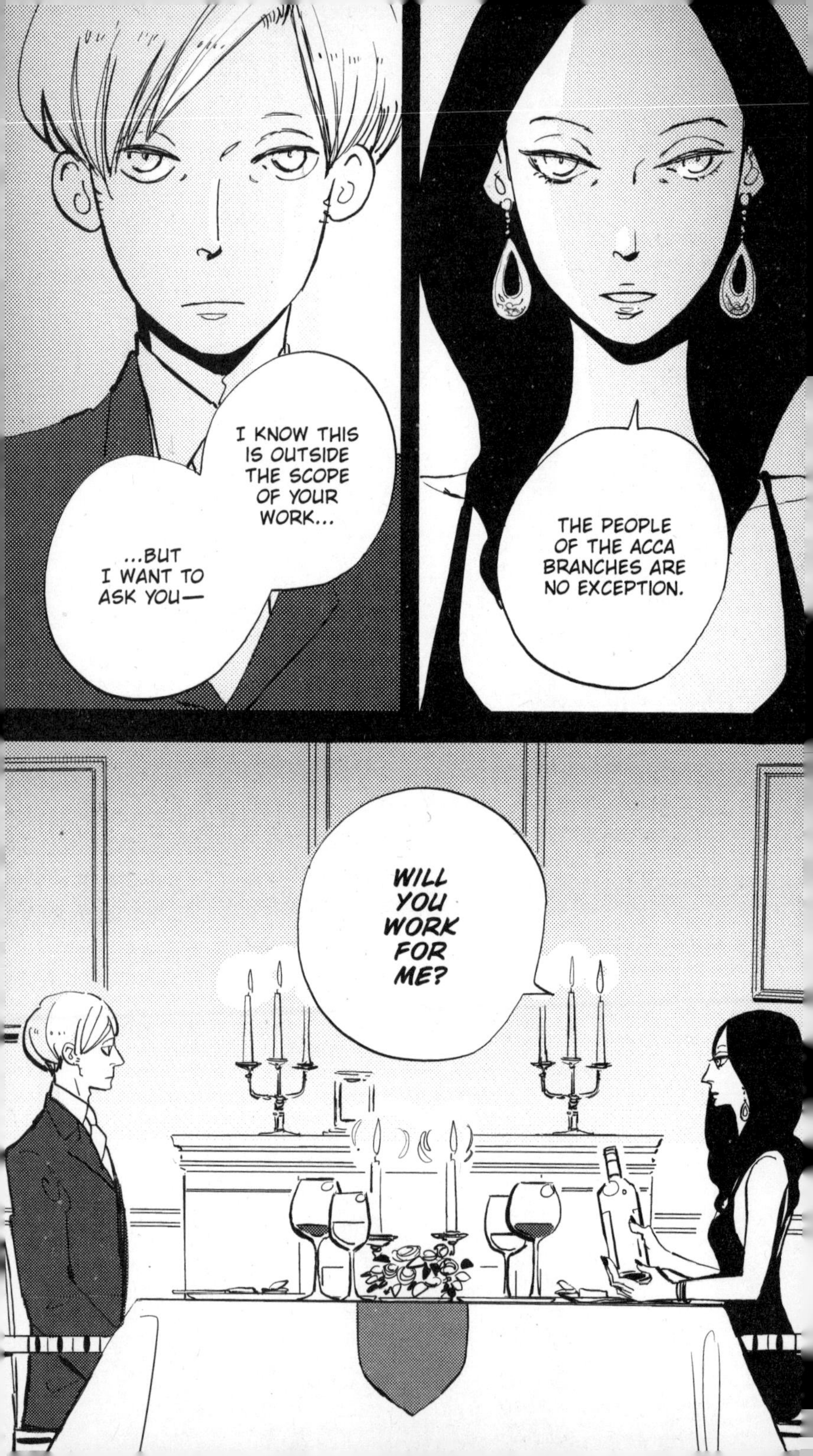
THE PEOPLE OF THE ACCA BRANCHES ARE NO EXCEPTION.
I KNOW THIS IS OUTSIDE THE SCOPE OF YOUR WORK...
...BUT I WANT TO ASK YOU—
WILL YOU WORK FOR ME?

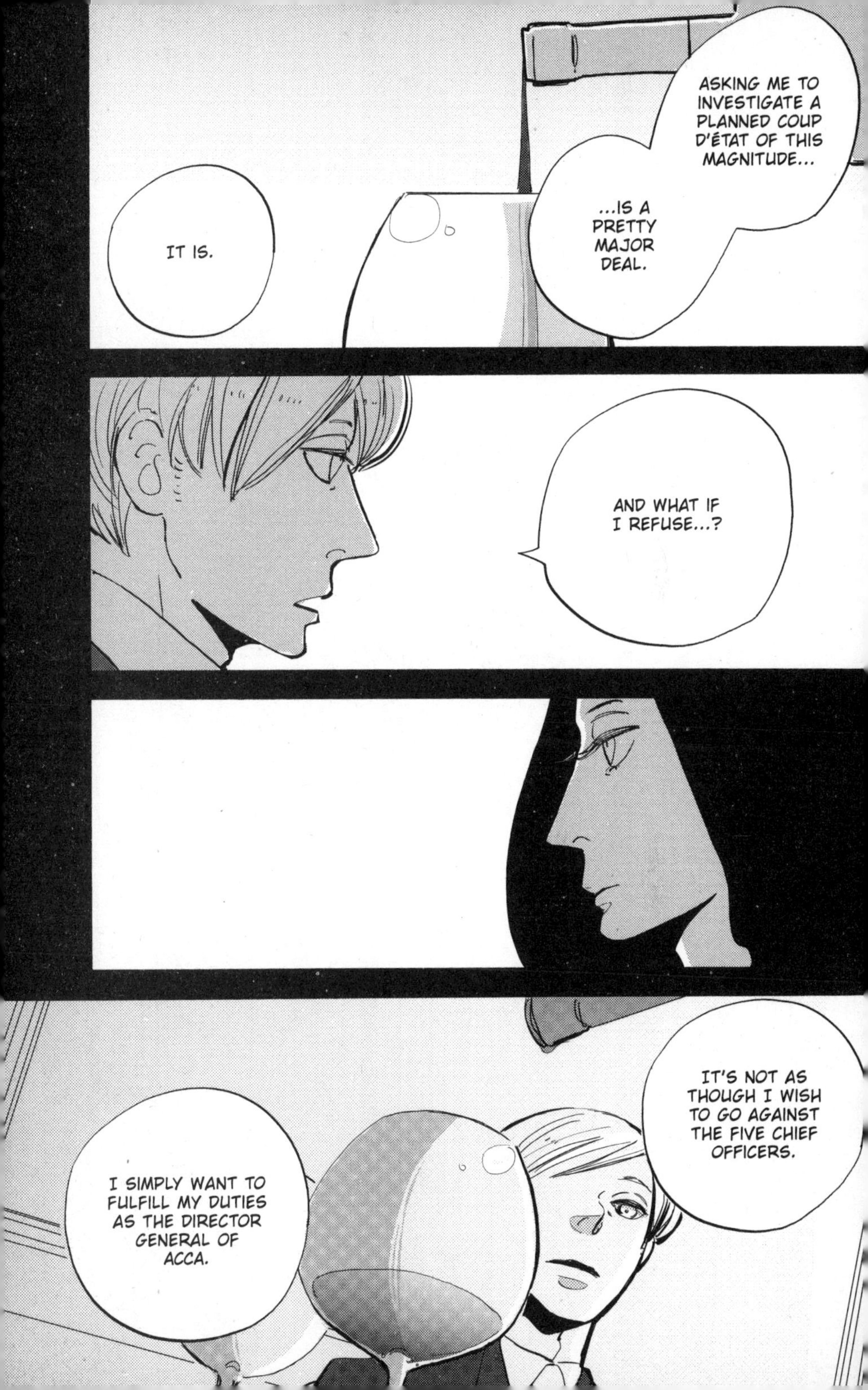
ASKING ME TO INVESTIGATE A PLANNED COUP D'ÉTAT OF THIS MAGNITUDE...
...IS A PRETTY MAJOR DEAL.
IT IS.
AND WHAT IF I REFUSE...?
IT'S NOT AS THOUGH I WISH TO GO AGAINST THE FIVE CHIEF OFFICERS.
I SIMPLY WANT TO FULFILL MY DUTIES AS THE DIRECTOR GENERAL OF ACCA.

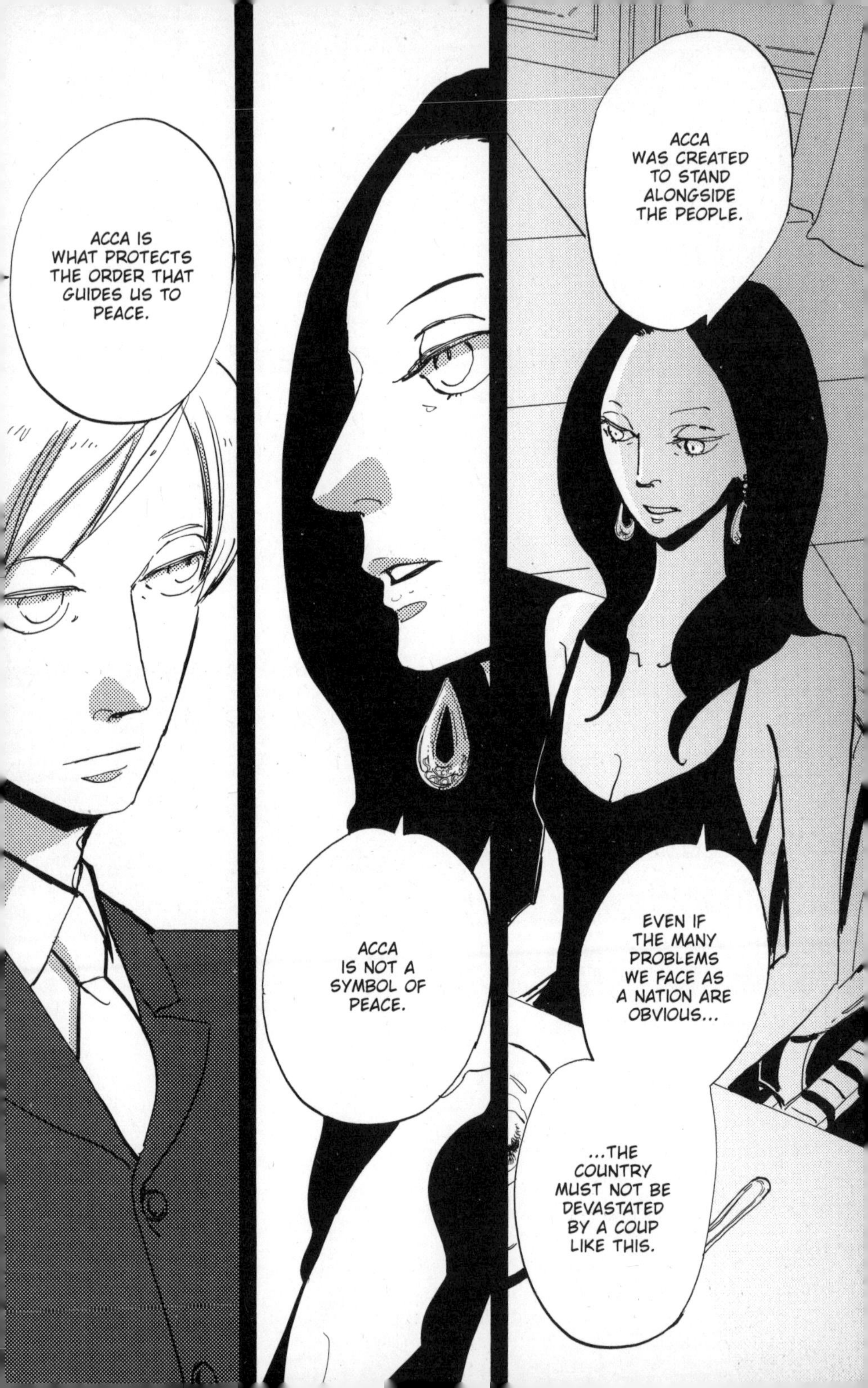
ACCA WAS CREATED TO STAND ALONGSIDE THE PEOPLE.
EVEN IF THE MANY PROBLEMS WE FACE AS A NATION ARE OBVIOUS...
...THE COUNTRY MUST NOT BE DEVASTATED BY A COUP LIKE THIS.
ACCA IS NOT A SYMBOL OF PEACE.
ACCA IS WHAT PROTECTS THE ORDER THAT GUIDES US TO PEACE.

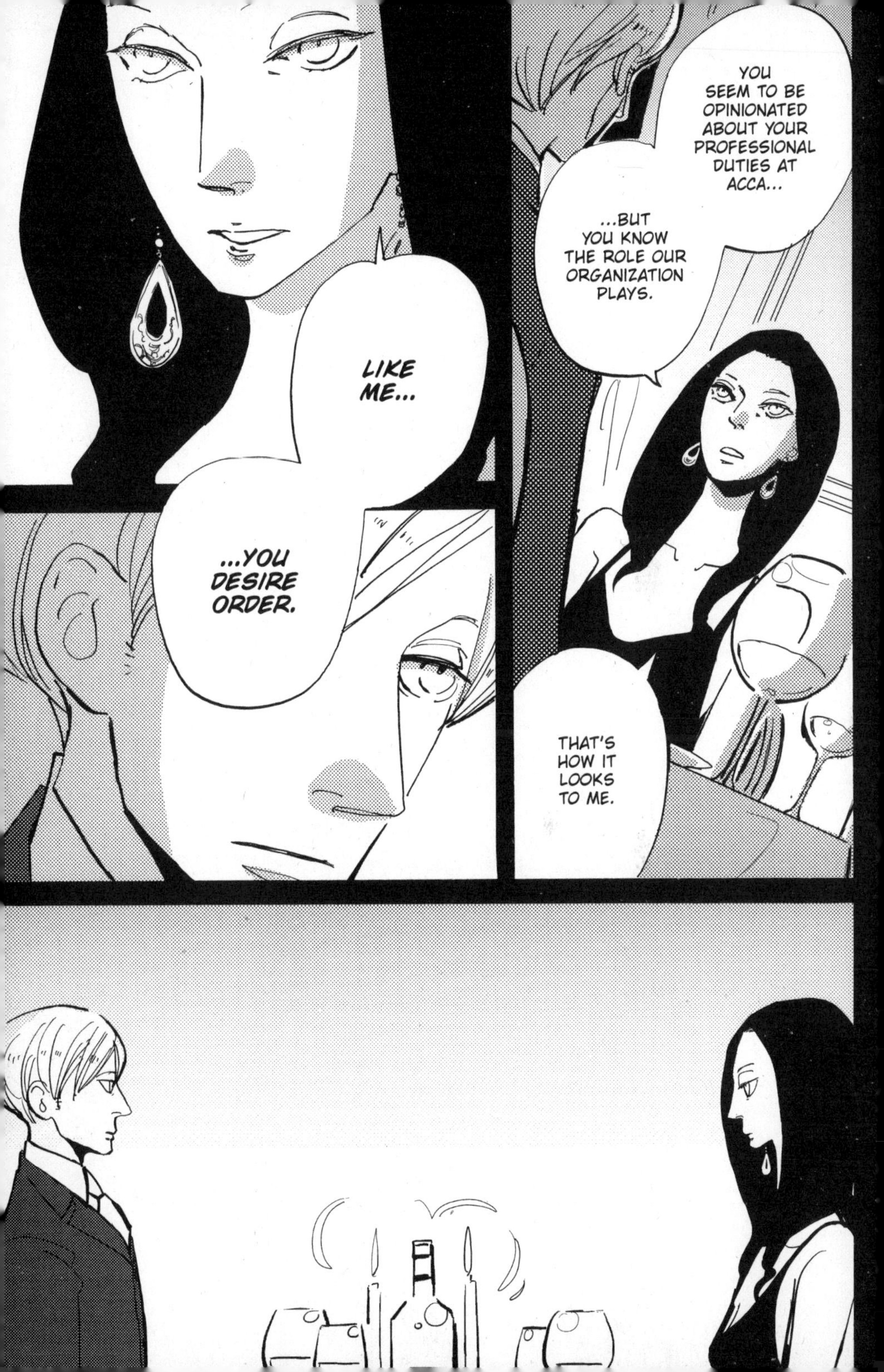
YOU SEEM TO BE OPINIONATED ABOUT YOUR PROFESSIONAL DUTIES AT ACCA...
...BUT YOU KNOW THE ROLE OUR ORGANIZATION PLAYS.
THAT'S HOW IT LOOKS TO ME.
LIKE ME...
...YOU DESIRE ORDER.

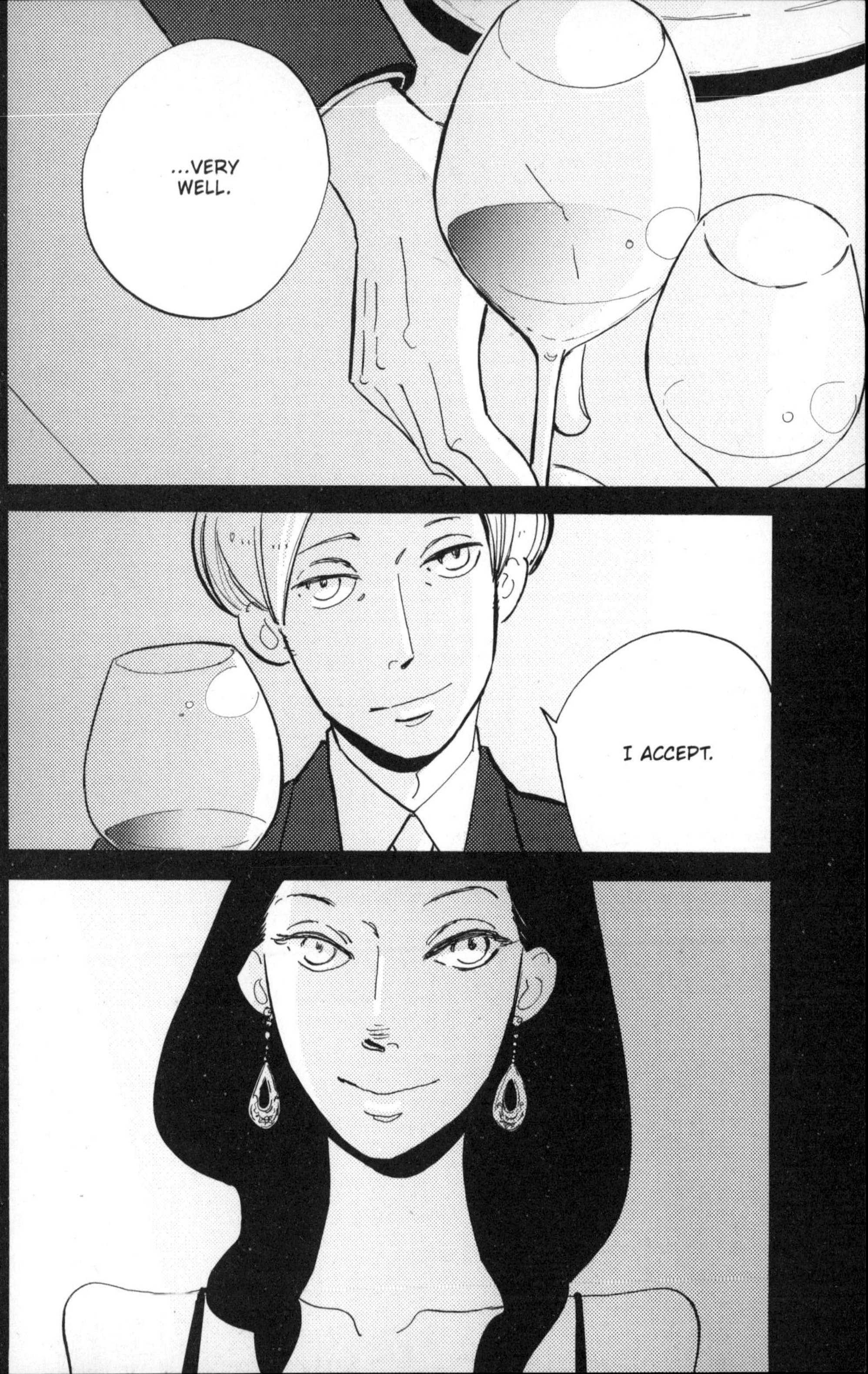
...VERY WELL.
I ACCEPT.

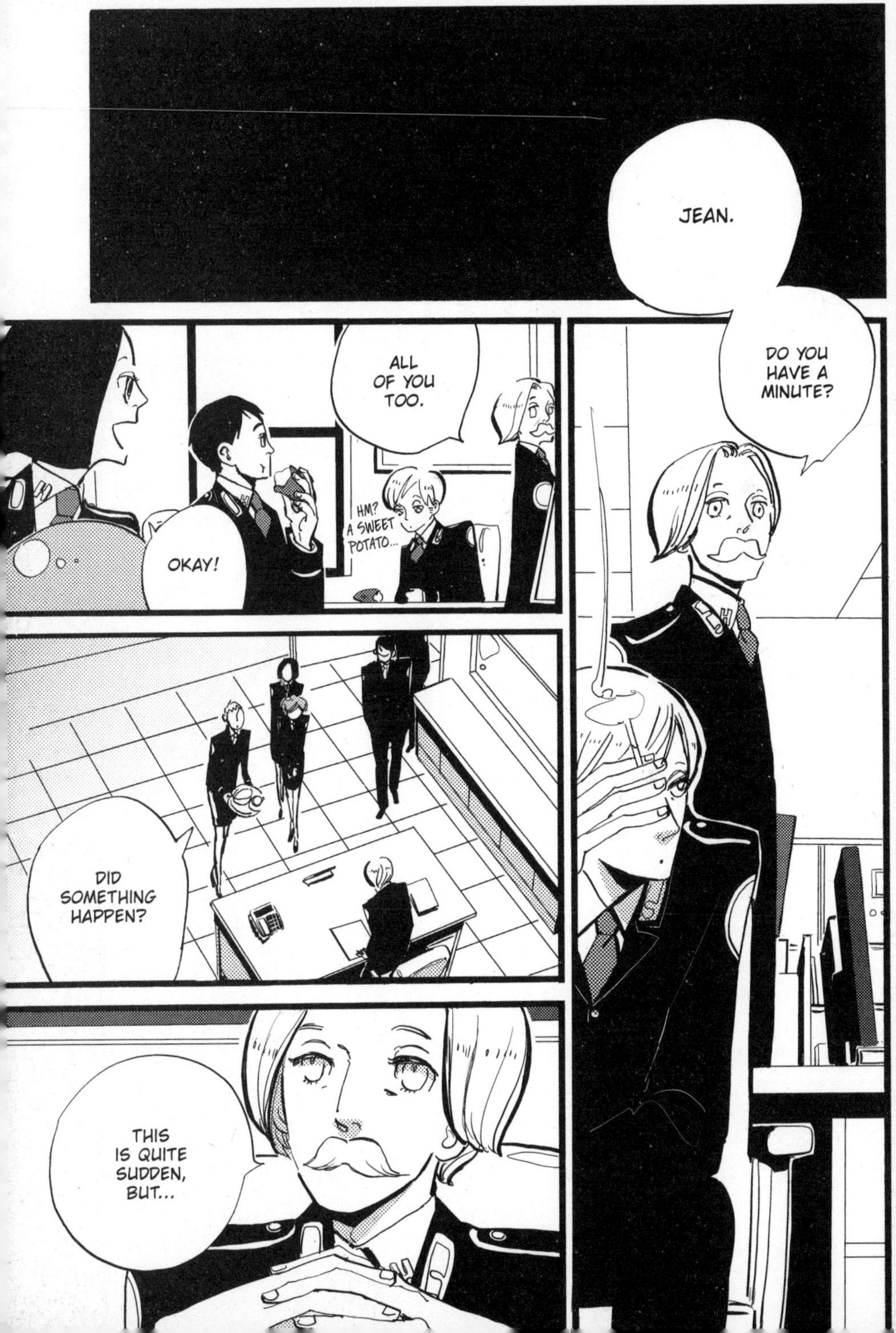
JEAN.
DO YOU HAVE A MINUTE?
ALL OF YOU TOO.
HM? A SWEET POTATO...
OKAY!
DID SOMETHING HAPPEN?
THIS IS QUITE SUDDEN, BUT...

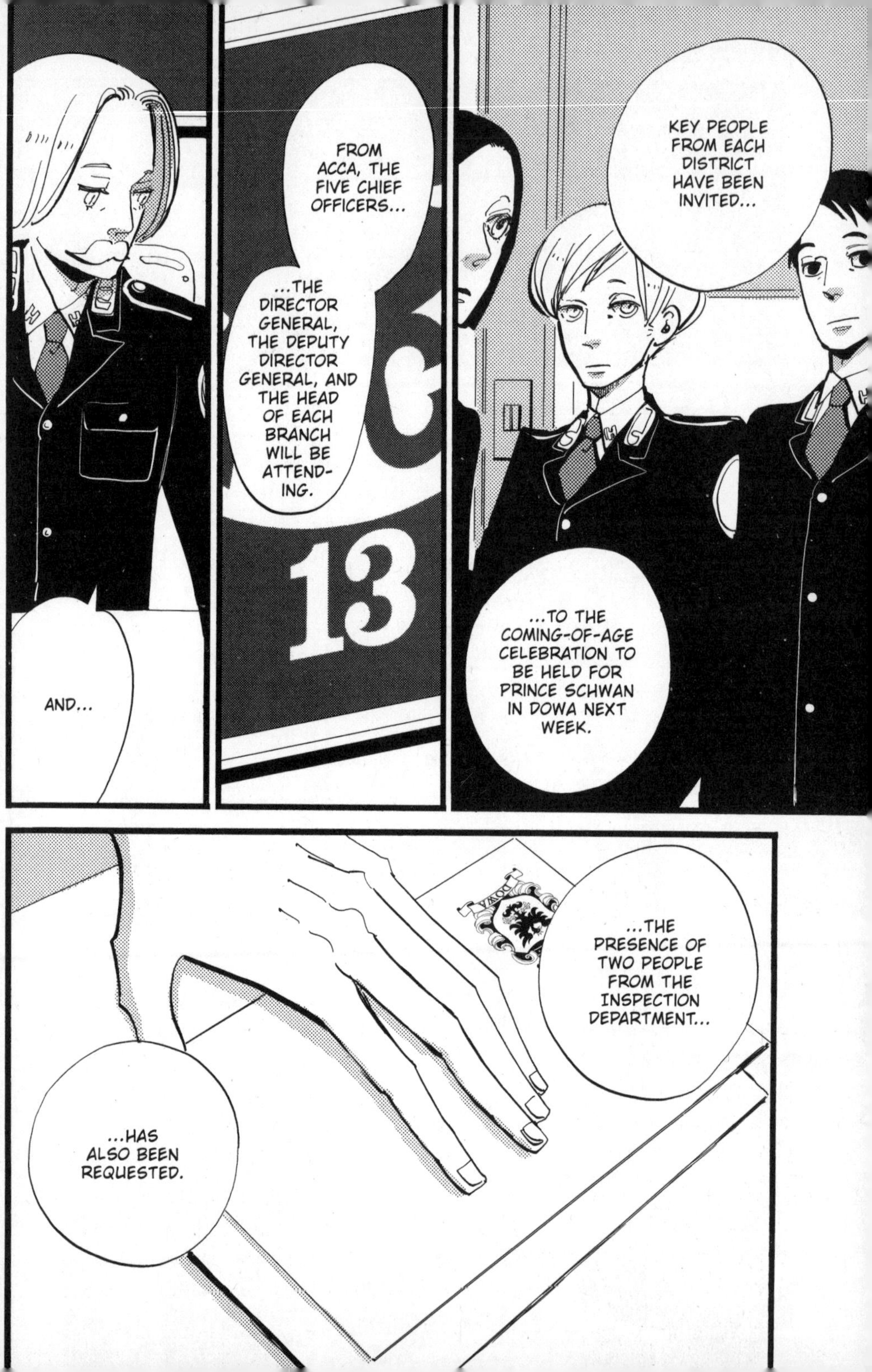
KEY PEOPLE FROM EACH DISTRICT HAVE BEEN INVITED...
...TO THE COMING-OF-AGE CELEBRATION TO BE HELD FOR PRINCE SCHWAN IN DOWA NEXT WEEK.
FROM ACCA, THE FIVE CHIEF OFFICERS...
...THE DIRECTOR GENERAL, THE DEPUTY DIRECTOR GENERAL, AND THE HEAD OF EACH BRANCH WILL BE ATTEND-ING.
13
AND...
...THE PRESENCE OF TWO PEOPLE FROM THE INSPECTION DEPARTMENT...
...HAS ALSO BEEN REQUESTED.

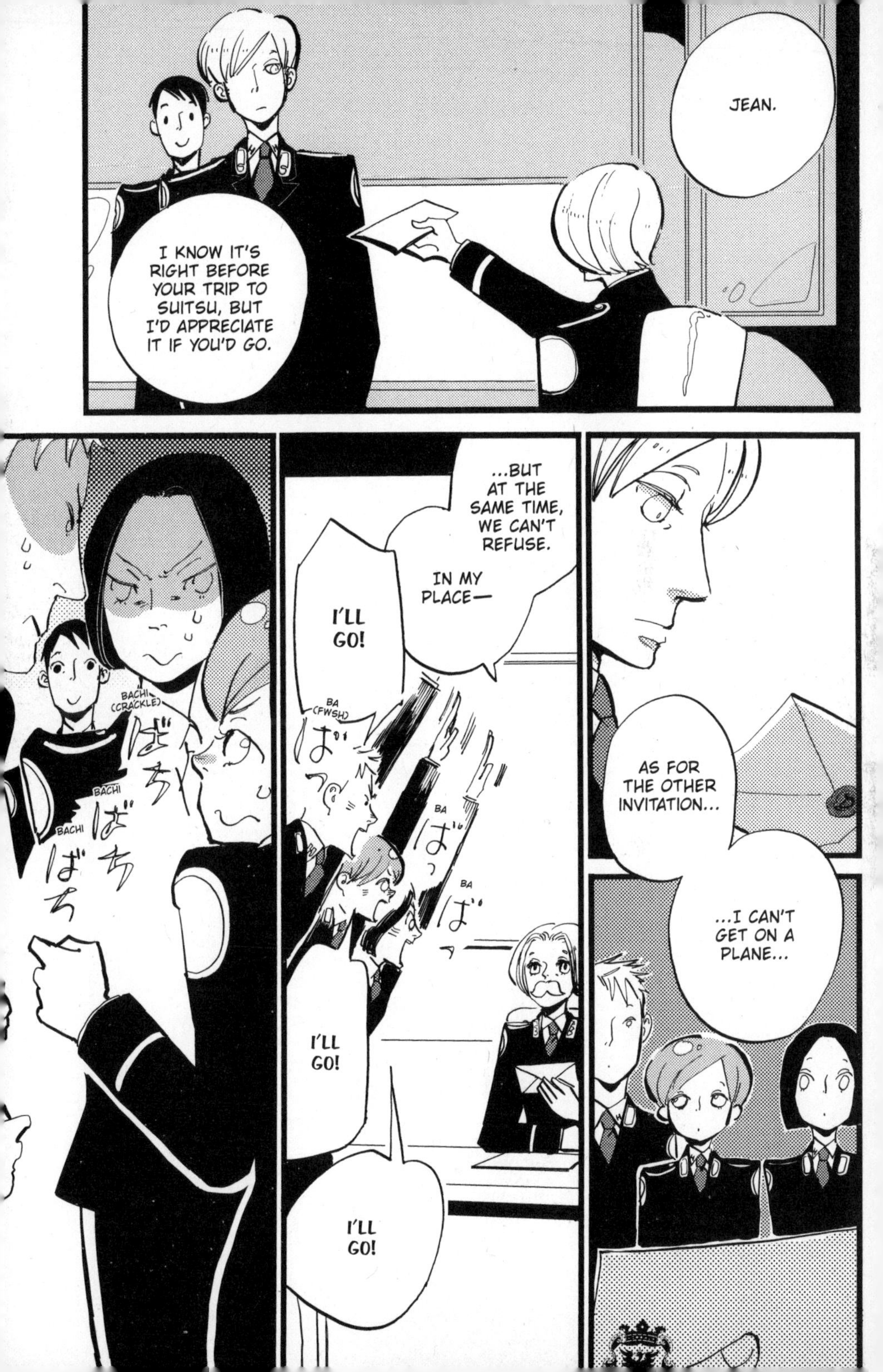
JEAN.
I KNOW IT'S RIGHT BEFORE YOUR TRIP TO SUITSU, BUT I'D APPRECIATE IT IF YOU'D GO.
AS FOR THE OTHER INVITATION...
...I CAN'T GET ON A PLANE...
...BUT AT THE SAME TIME, WE CAN'T REFUSE.
IN MY PLACE—
I'LL GO!
BA (FWSH)
ばっ
BA
ばっ
BA
ばっ
I'LL GO!
I'LL GO!
BACHI (CRACKLE)
ばち
BACHI
ばち
BACHI
ばち

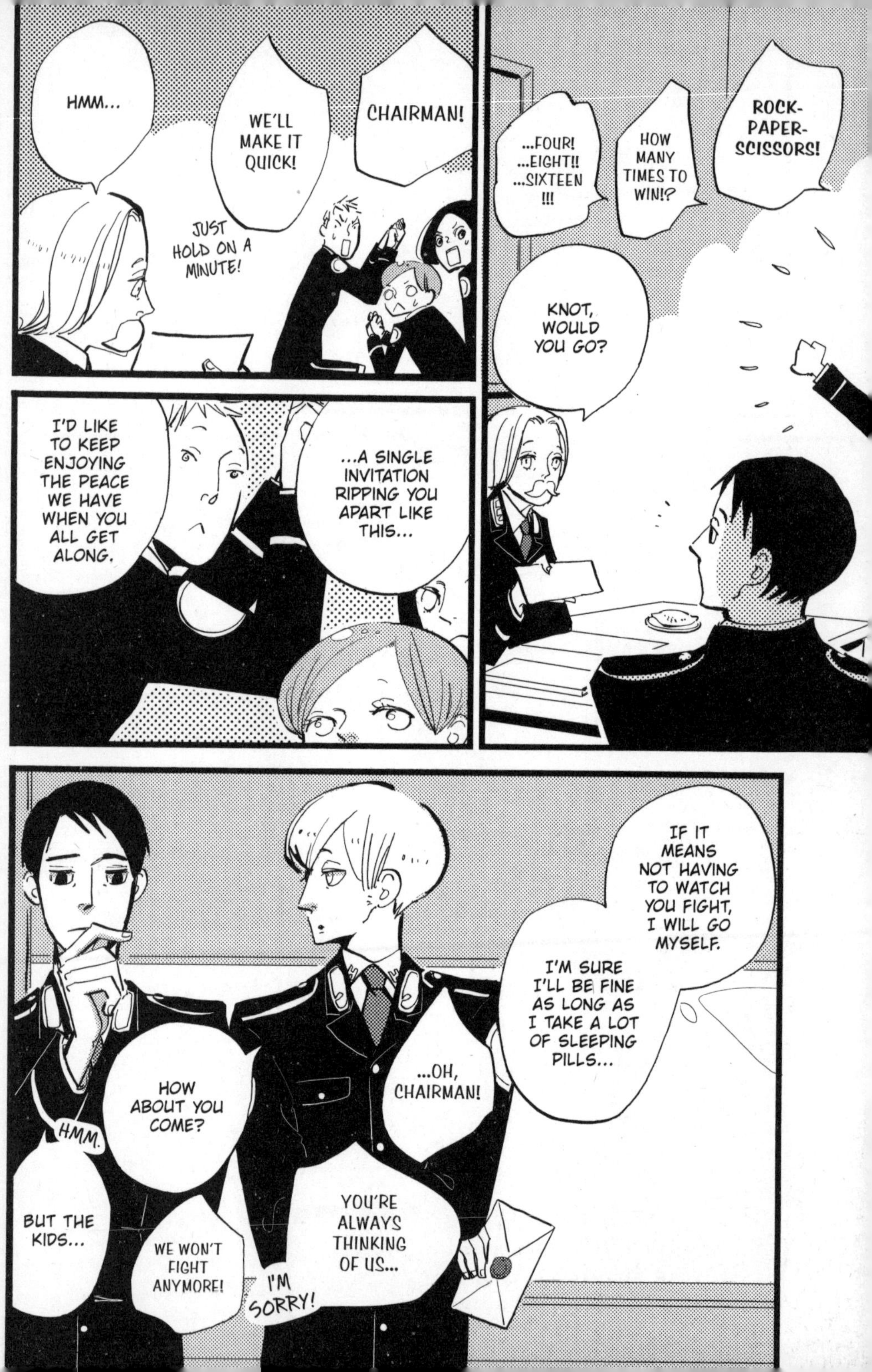
ROCK-PAPER-SCISSORS!
HOW MANY TIMES TO WIN!?
...FOUR! ...EIGHT!! ...SIXTEEN !!!
CHAIRMAN!
WE'LL MAKE IT QUICK!
JUST HOLD ON A MINUTE!
HMM...
KNOT, WOULD YOU GO?
...A SINGLE INVITATION RIPPING YOU APART LIKE THIS...
I'D LIKE TO KEEP ENJOYING THE PEACE WE HAVE WHEN YOU ALL GET ALONG.
IF IT MEANS NOT HAVING TO WATCH YOU FIGHT, I WILL GO MYSELF.
I'M SURE I'LL BE FINE AS LONG AS I TAKE A LOT OF SLEEPING PILLS...
...OH, CHAIRMAN!
HOW ABOUT YOU COME?
HMM.
YOU'RE ALWAYS THINKING OF US...
I'M SORRY!
WE WON'T FIGHT ANYMORE!
BUT THE KIDS...

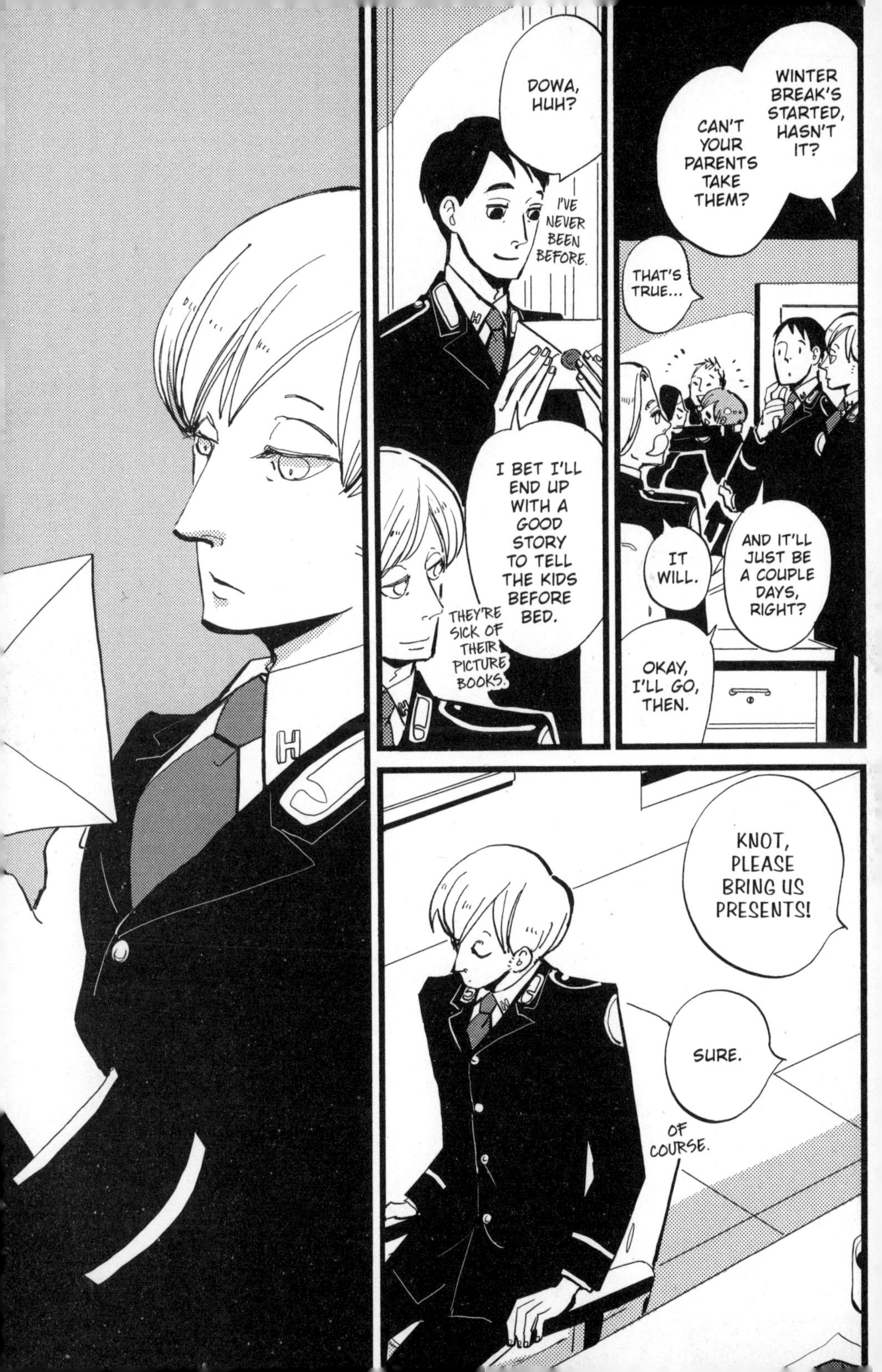
WINTER BREAK'S STARTED, HASN'T IT?
CAN'T YOUR PARENTS TAKE THEM?
THAT'S TRUE...
AND IT'LL JUST BE A COUPLE DAYS, RIGHT?
IT WILL.
OKAY, I'LL GO, THEN.
DOWA, HUH?
I'VE NEVER BEEN BEFORE.
I BET I'LL END UP WITH A GOOD STORY TO TELL THE KIDS BEFORE BED.
THEY'RE SICK OF THEIR PICTURE BOOKS.
KNOT, PLEASE BRING US PRESENTS!
SURE.
OF COURSE.

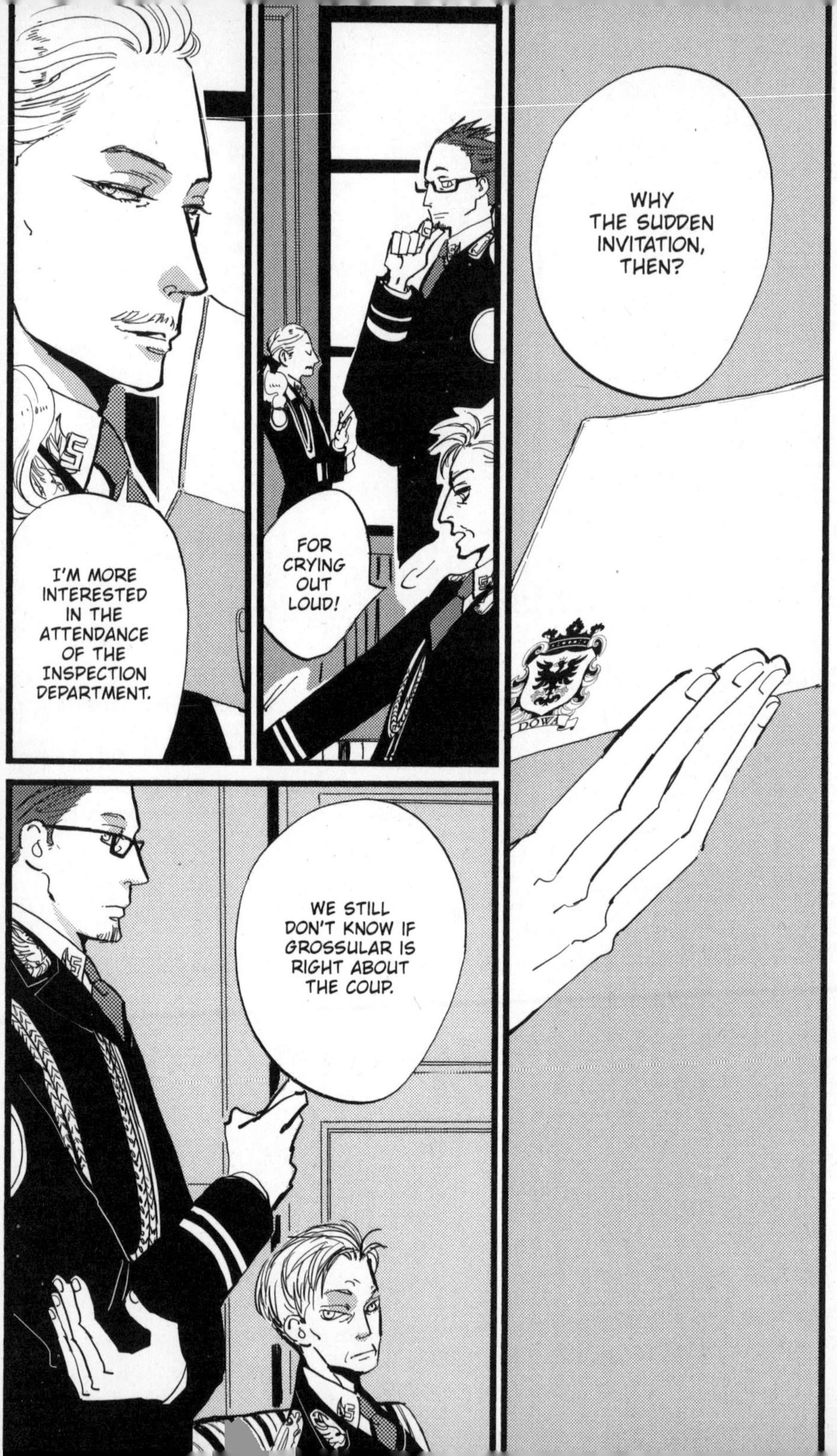
WHY THE SUDDEN INVITATION, THEN?
FOR CRYING OUT LOUD!
I'M MORE INTERESTED IN THE ATTENDANCE OF THE INSPECTION DEPARTMENT.
WE STILL DON'T KNOW IF GROSSULAR IS RIGHT ABOUT THE COUP.

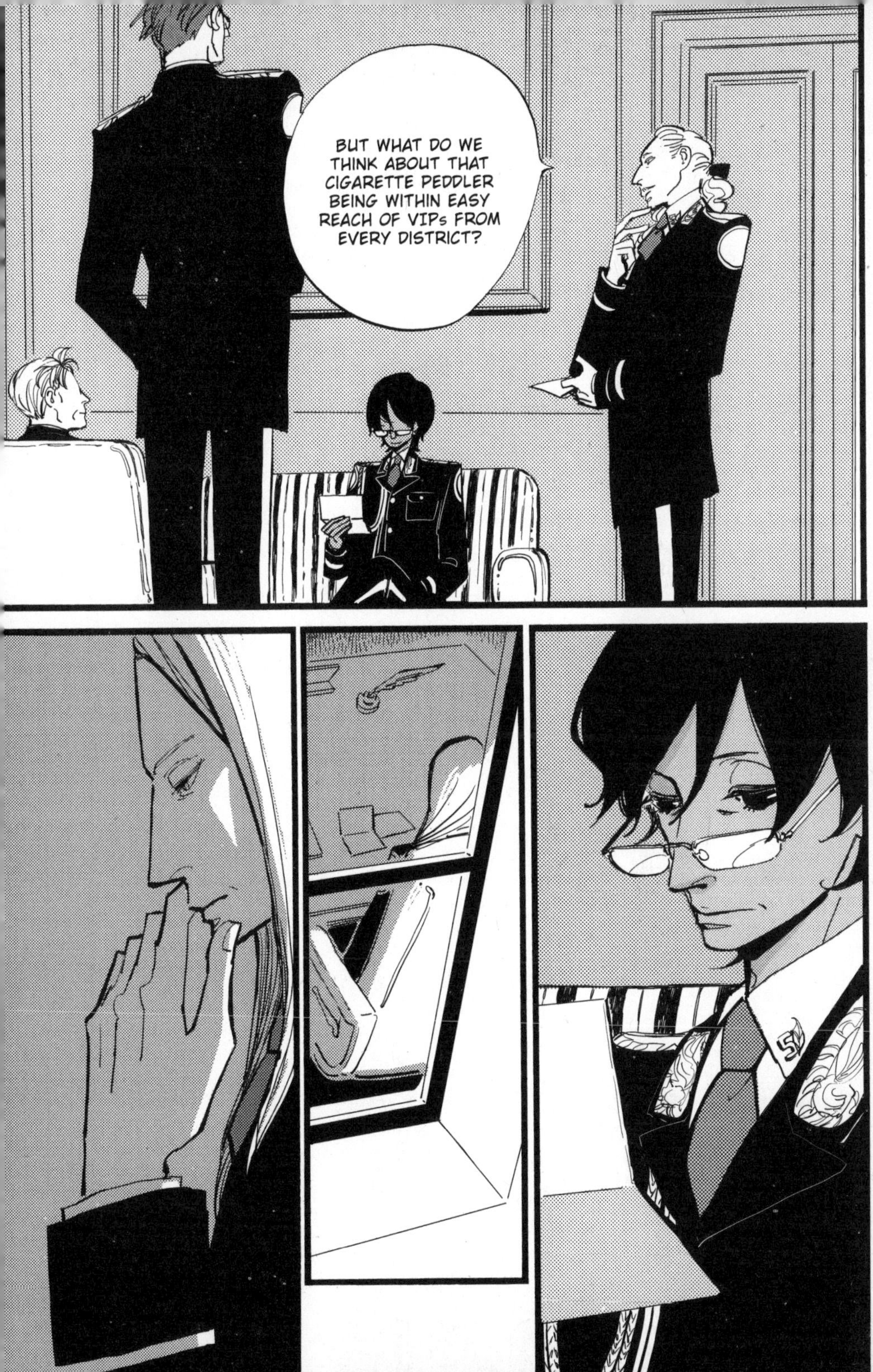
BUT WHAT DO WE THINK ABOUT THAT CIGARETTE PEDDLER BEING WITHIN EASY REACH OF VIPs FROM EVERY DISTRICT?

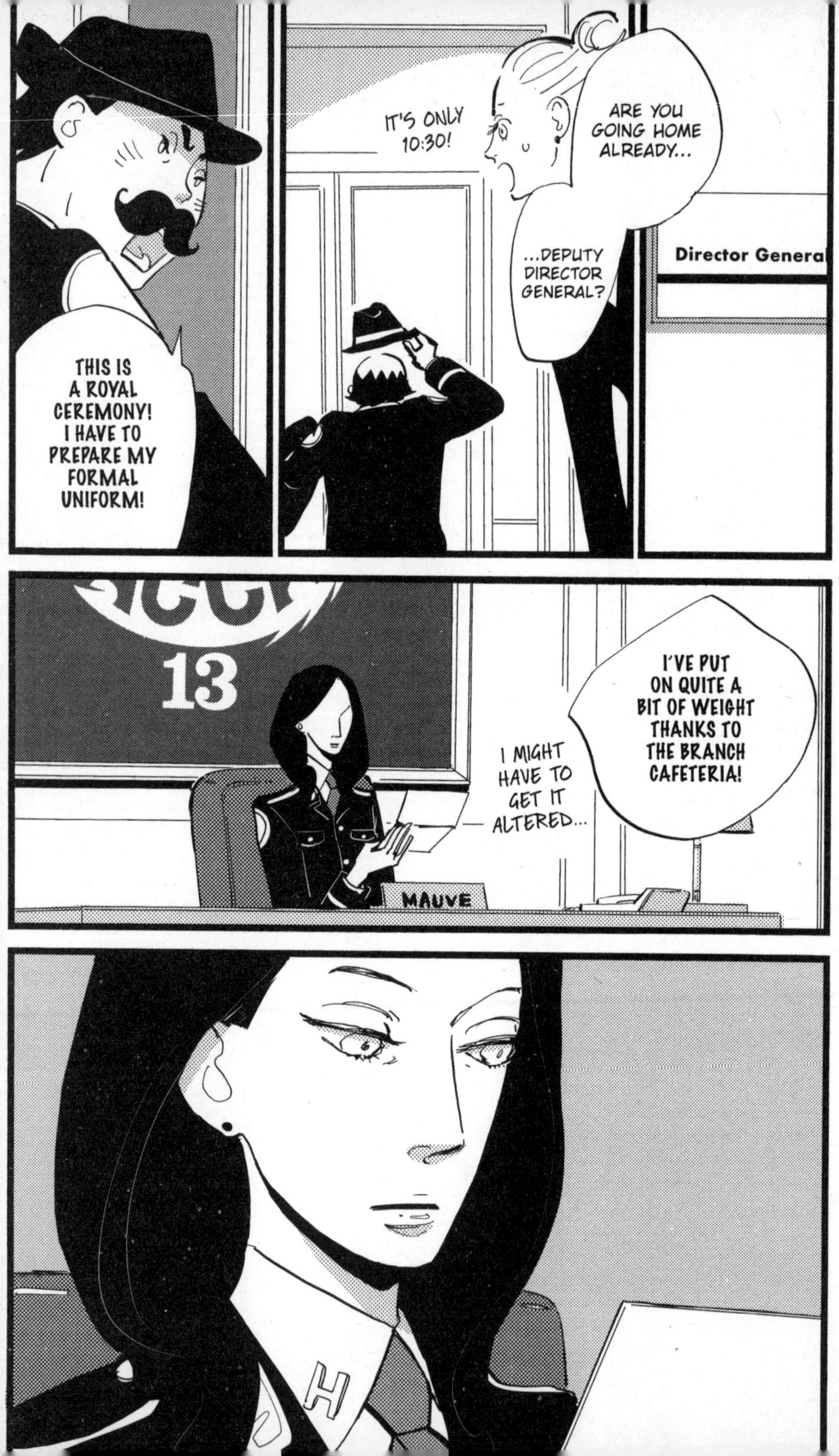
Director General
ARE YOU GOING HOME ALREADY...
...DEPUTY DIRECTOR GENERAL?
IT'S ONLY 10:30!
THIS IS A ROYAL CEREMONY! I HAVE TO PREPARE MY FORMAL UNIFORM!
I'VE PUT ON QUITE A BIT OF WEIGHT THANKS TO THE BRANCH CAFETERIA!
I MIGHT HAVE TO GET IT ALTERED...
13
MAUVE

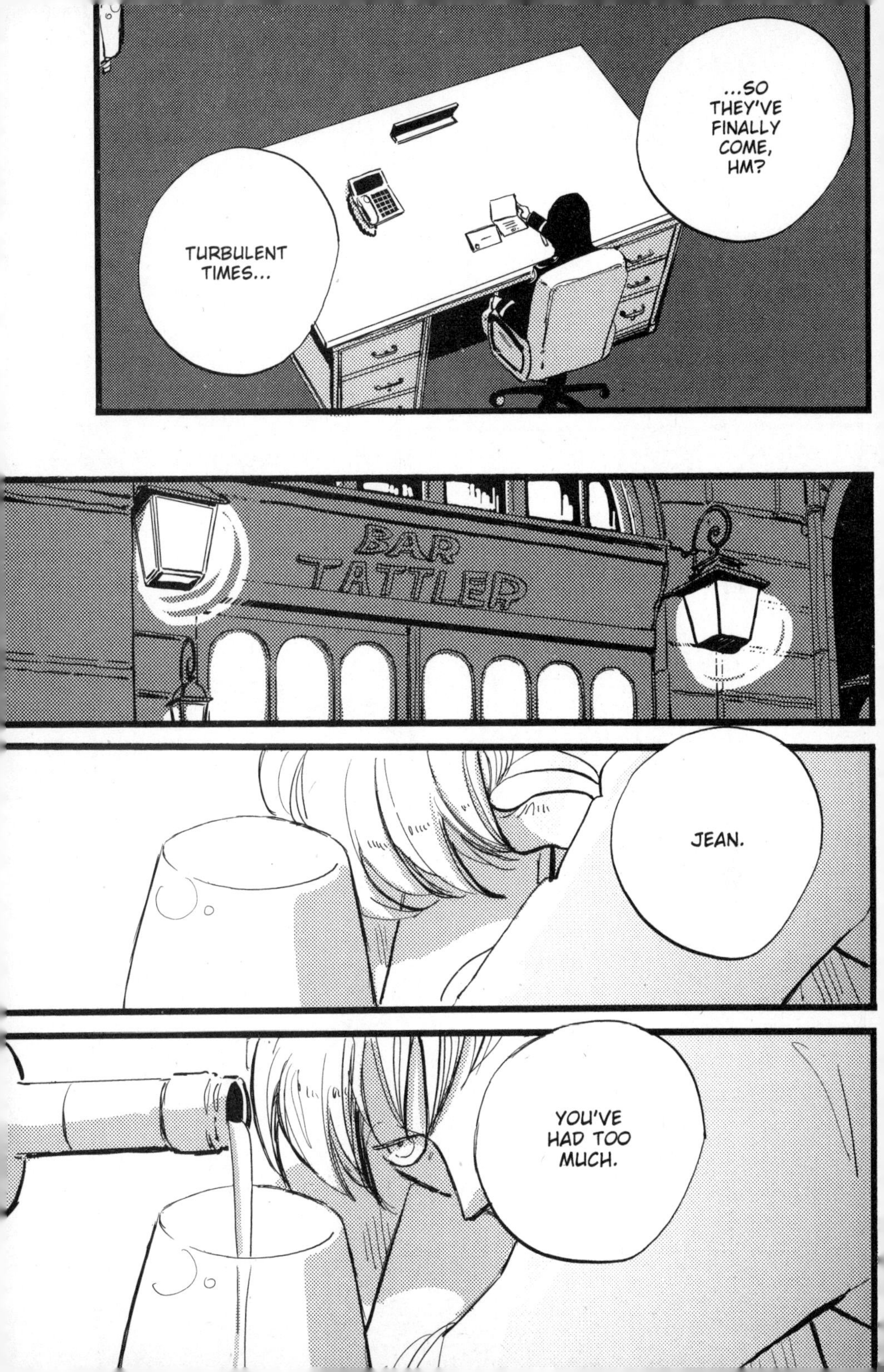
...SO THEY'VE FINALLY COME, HM?
TURBULENT TIMES...
BAR TATTLER
JEAN.
YOU'VE HAD TOO MUCH.

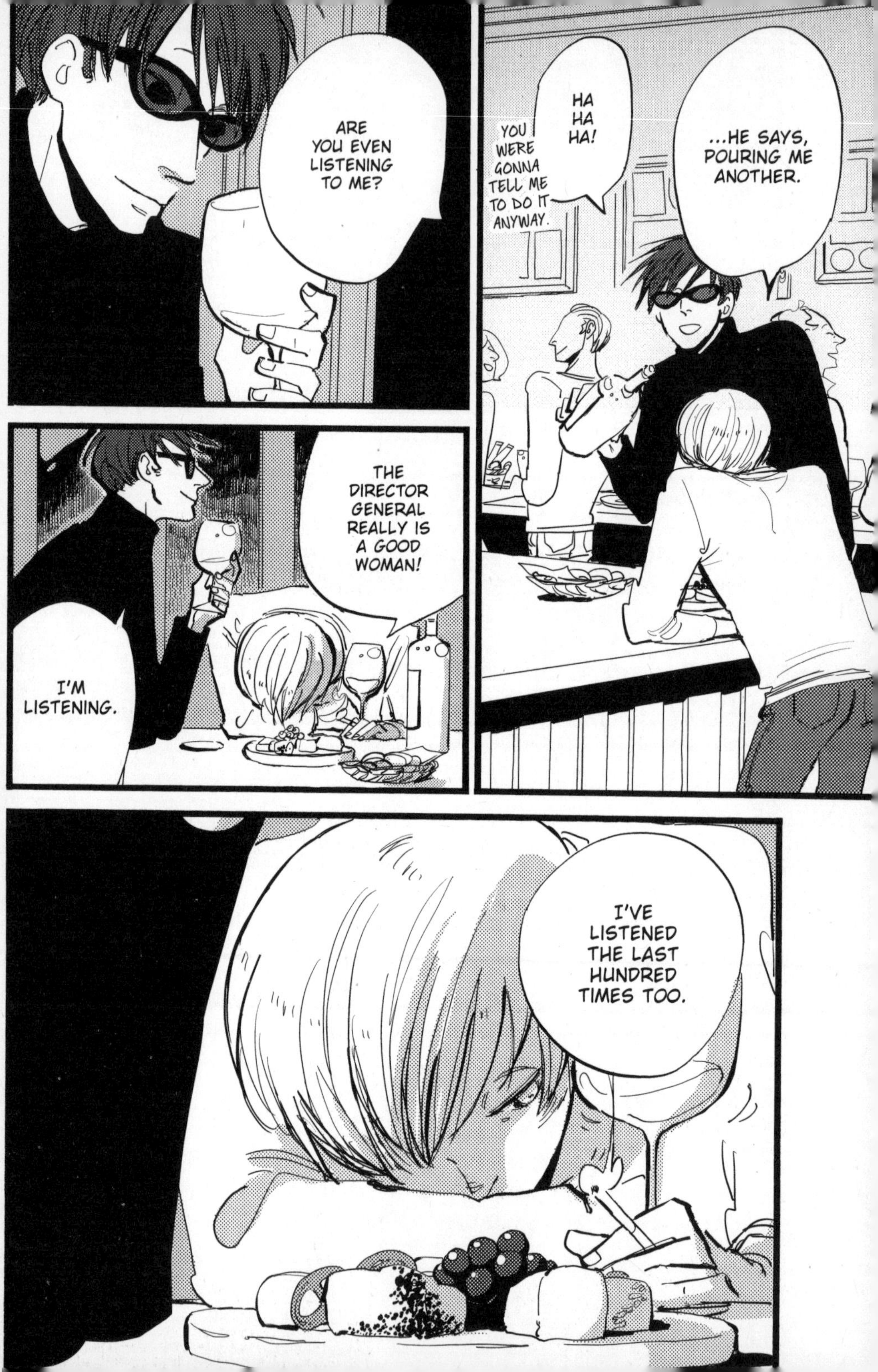
...HE SAYS, POURING ME ANOTHER.
HA HA HA!
YOU WERE GONNA TELL ME TO DO IT ANYWAY.
ARE YOU EVEN LISTENING TO ME?
THE DIRECTOR GENERAL REALLY IS A GOOD WOMAN!
I'M LISTENING.
I'VE LISTENED THE LAST HUNDRED TIMES TOO.

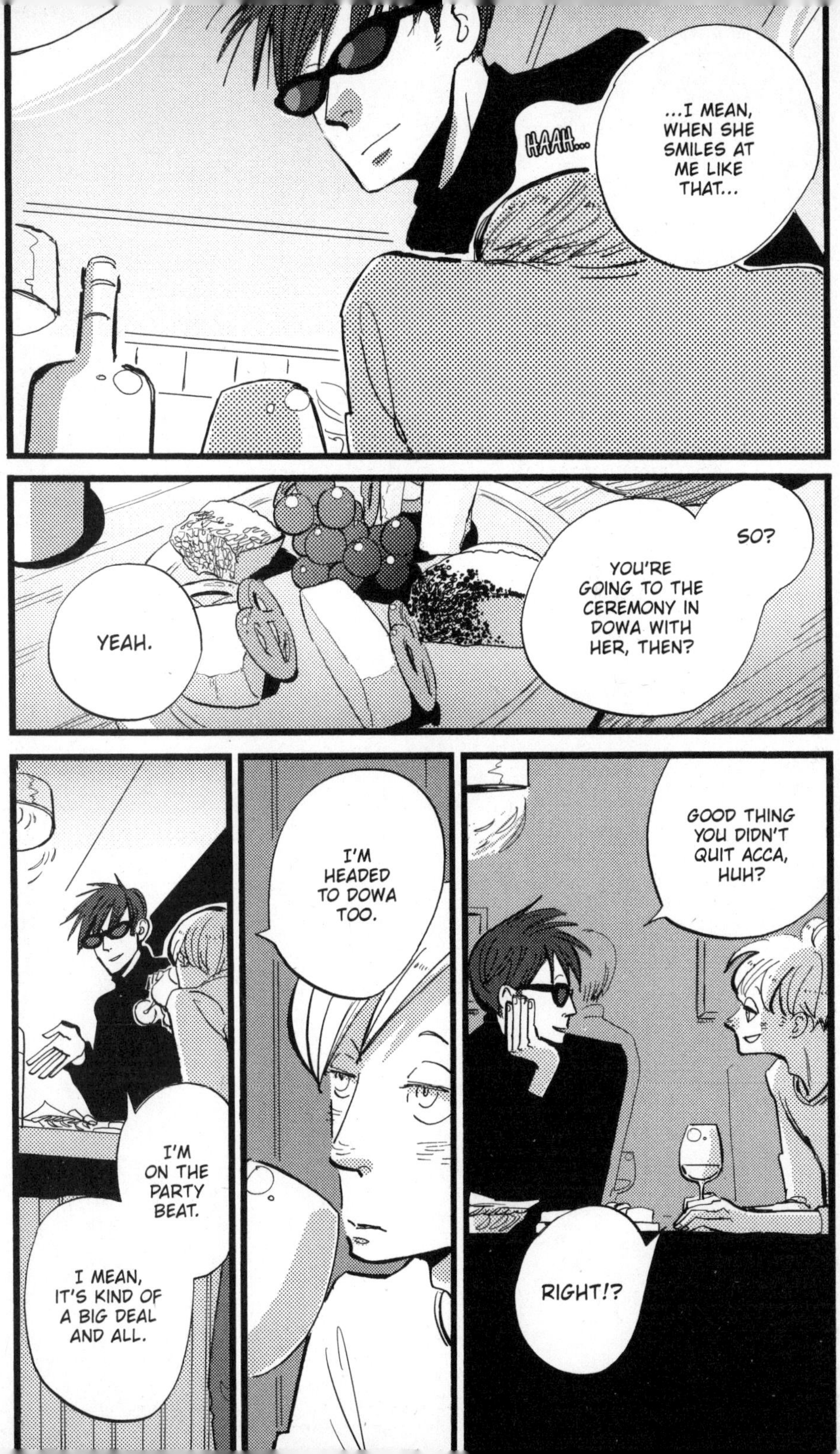
...I MEAN, WHEN SHE SMILES AT ME LIKE THAT...
HAAH...
SO?
YOU'RE GOING TO THE CEREMONY IN DOWA WITH HER, THEN?
YEAH.
GOOD THING YOU DIDN'T QUIT ACCA, HUH?
RIGHT!?
I'M HEADED TO DOWA TOO.
I'M ON THE PARTY BEAT.
I MEAN, IT'S KIND OF A BIG DEAL AND ALL.

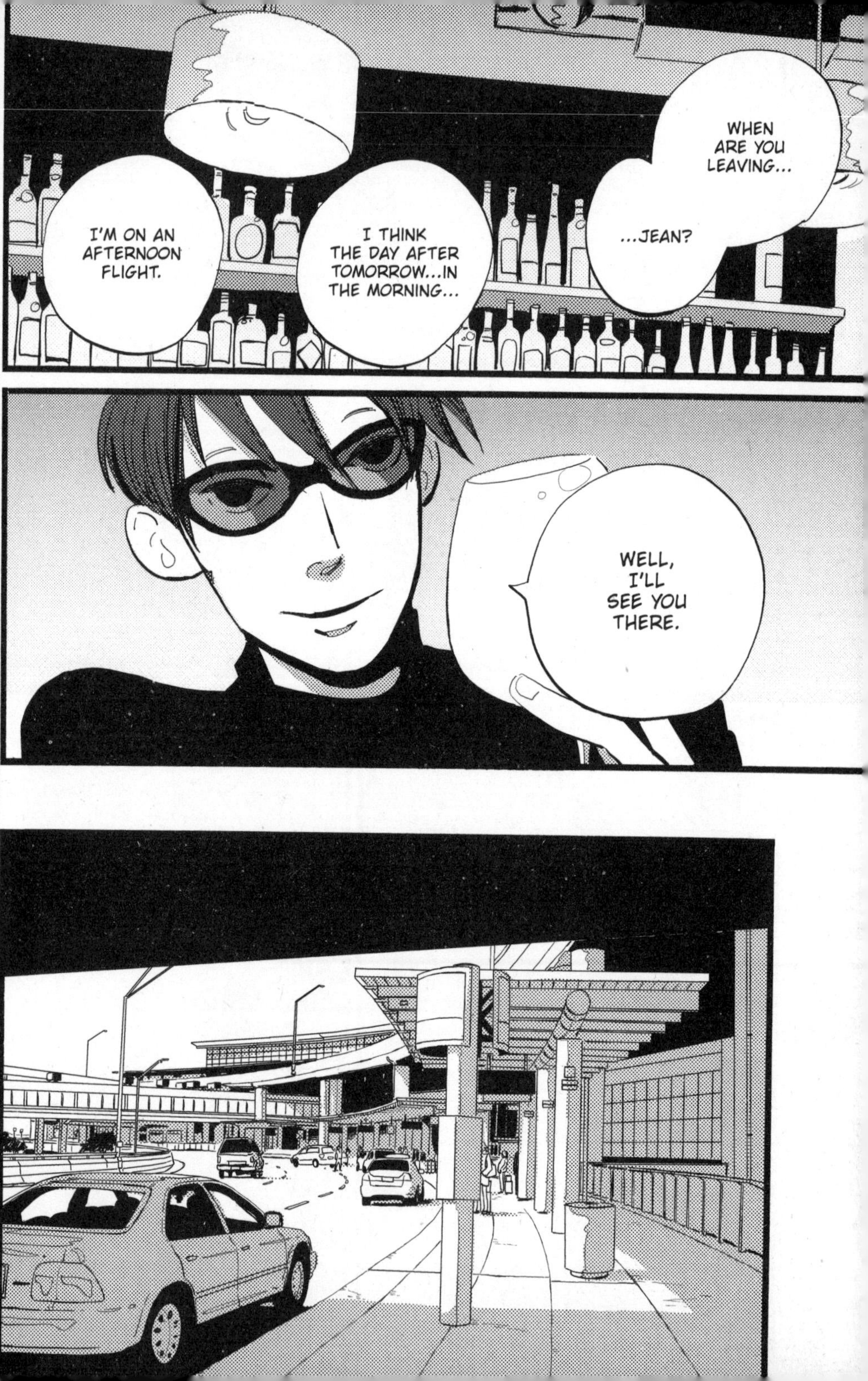
WHEN ARE YOU LEAVING...
...JEAN?
I THINK THE DAY AFTER TOMORROW...IN THE MORNING...
I'M ON AN AFTERNOON FLIGHT.
WELL, I'LL SEE YOU THERE.

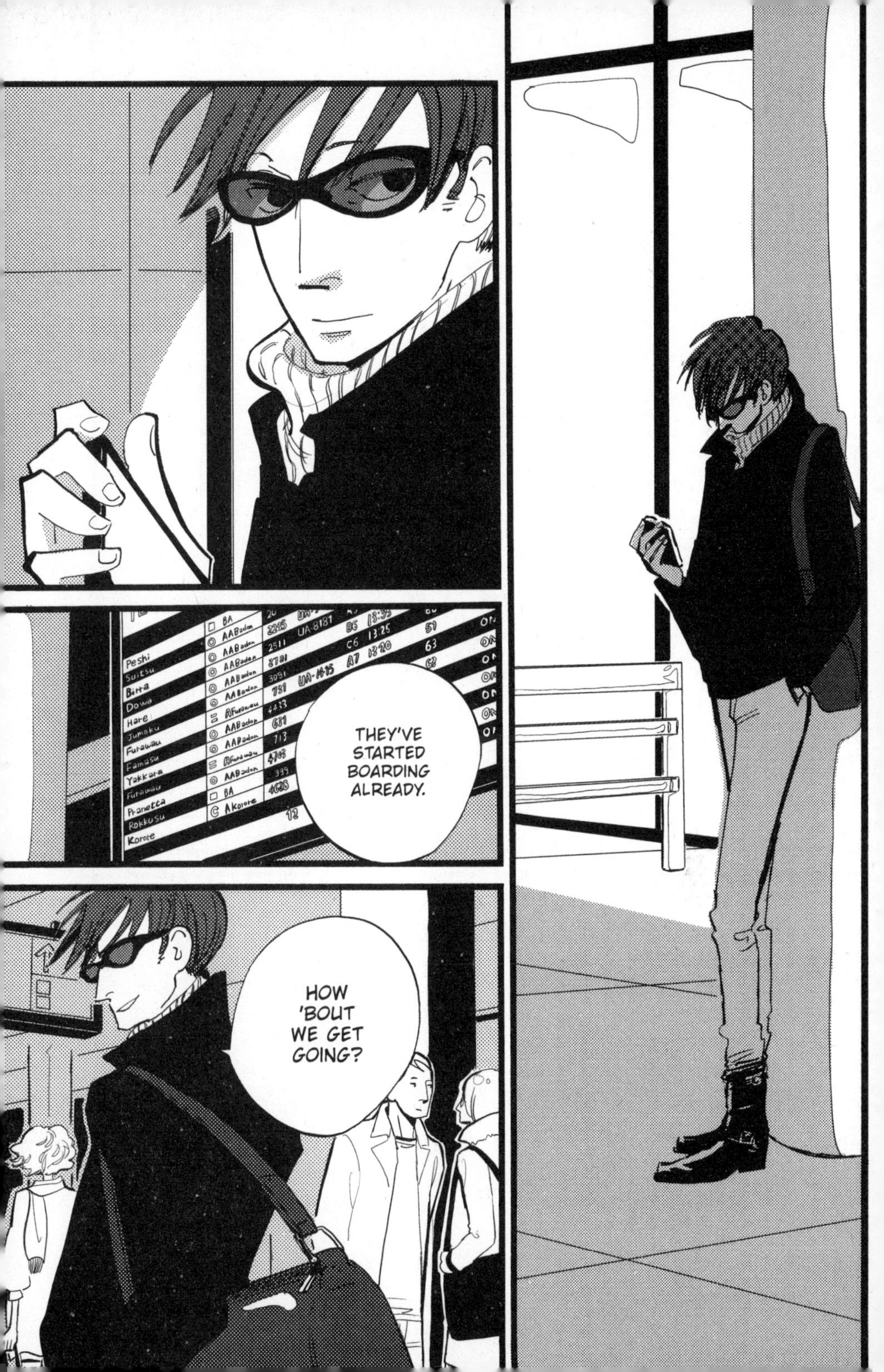
THEY'VE STARTED BOARDING ALREADY.
HOW 'BOUT WE GET GOING?

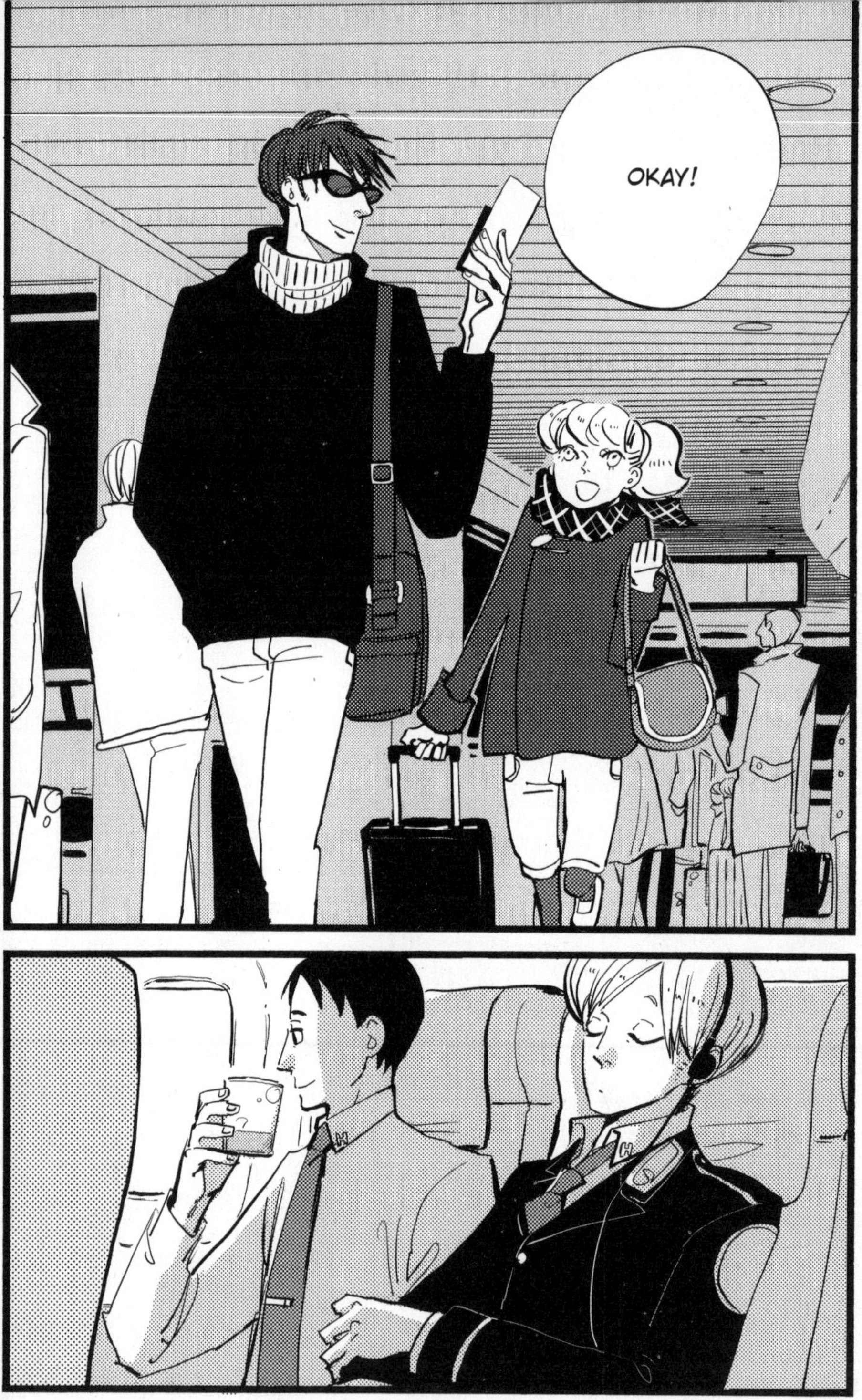
OKAY!

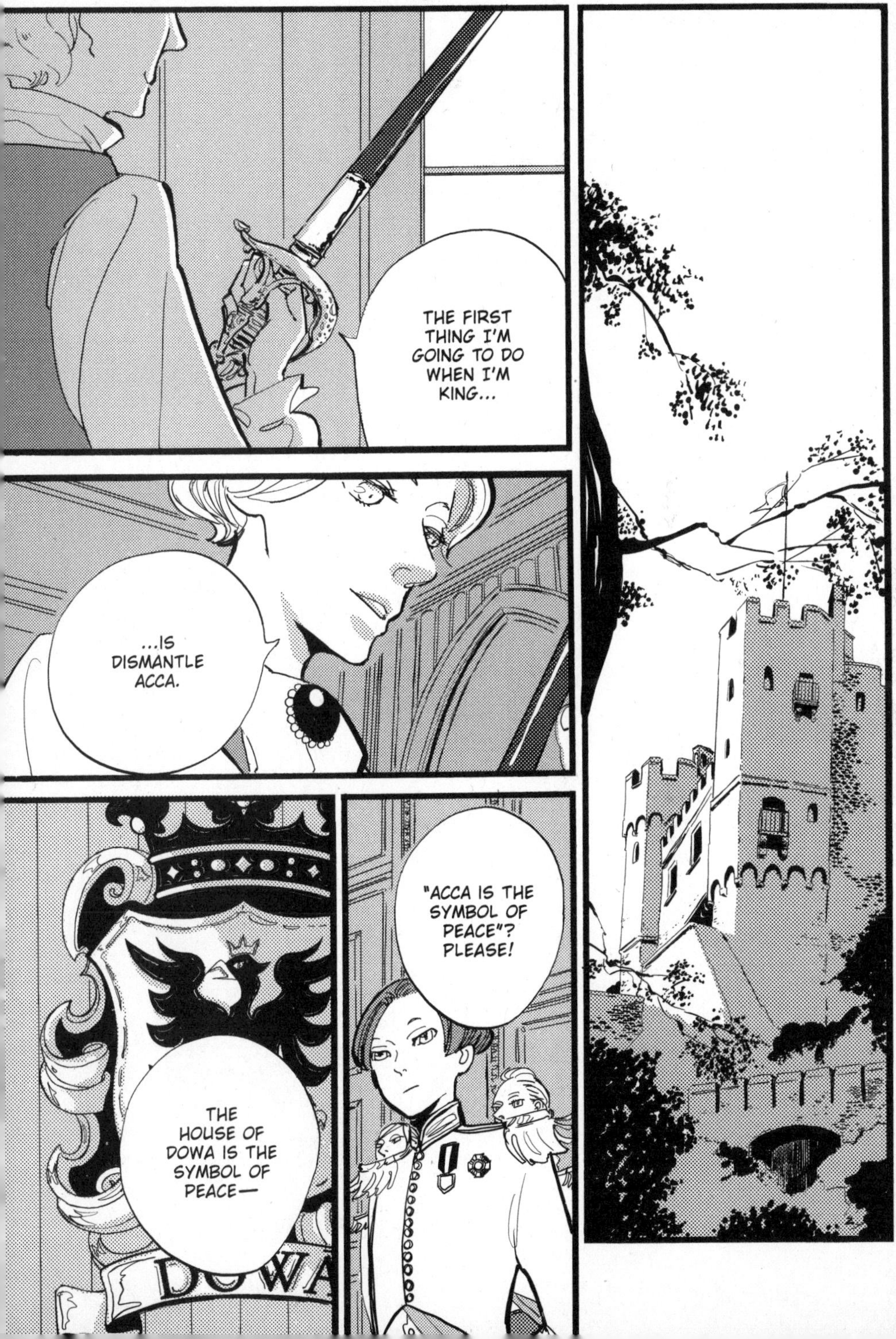
THE FIRST THING I'M GOING TO DO WHEN I'M KING...
...IS DISMANTLE ACCA.
"ACCA IS THE SYMBOL OF PEACE"? PLEASE!
THE HOUSE OF DOWA IS THE SYMBOL OF PEACE—
DOWA

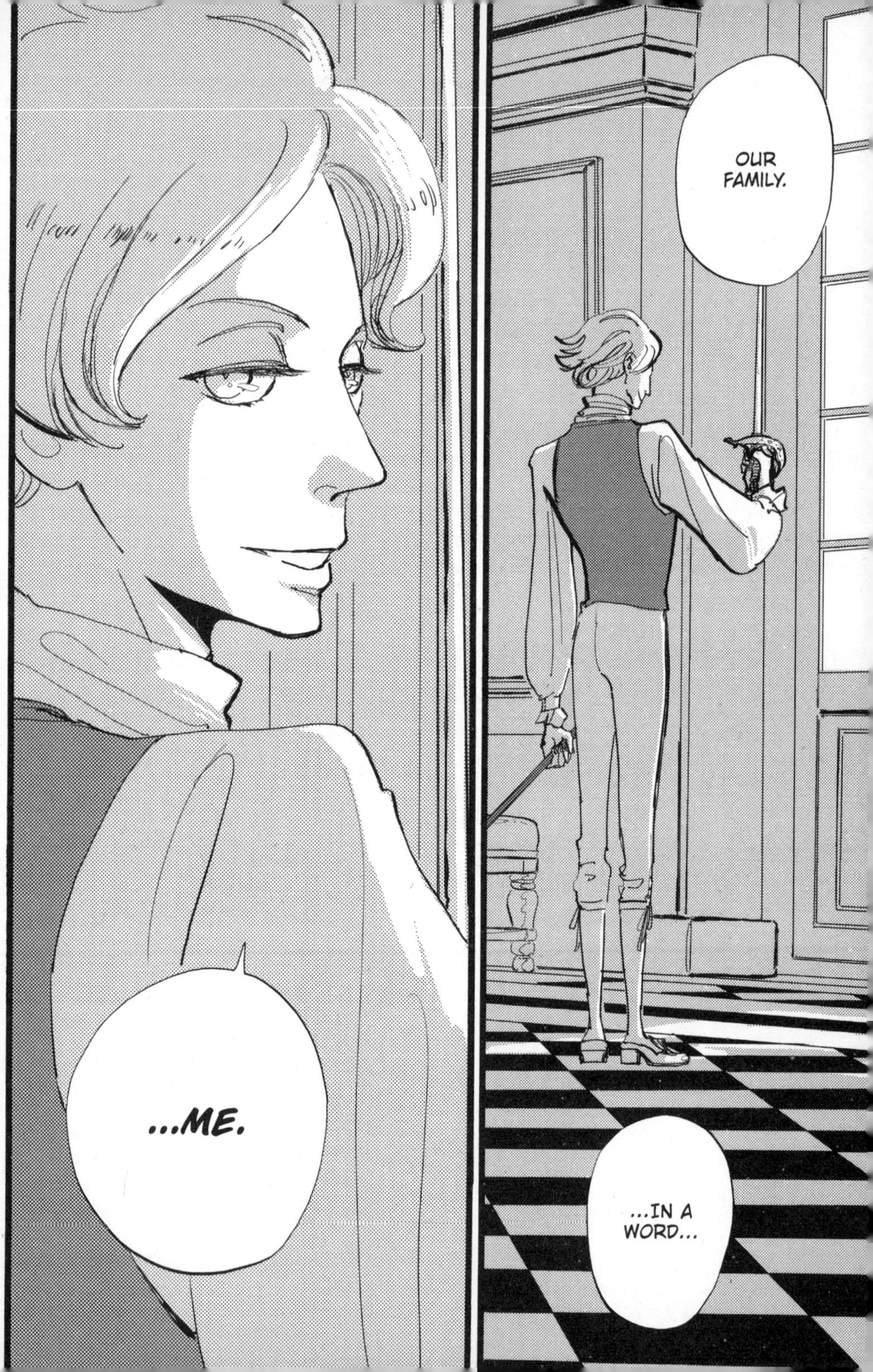
OUR FAMILY.
...IN A WORD...
...ME.

Royal Uniforms

House of Dowa Royal Guard

The Royal Guard is attached to the royal family of the Kingdom of Dowa. Younger soldiers tend to be in the prince's retinue. The decorations on the chest are medals. Magie, attached to the prince, is young but known to be quite talented.

CHAPTER 9

Clinking Wine Glasses in Bad

ACCA 13 TERRITORY INSPECTION DEPT.

PASS

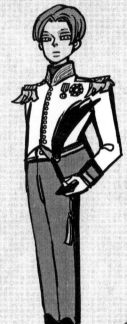

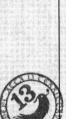

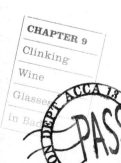

CHAPTER 10
Observing the Smoke Trail in Dowa

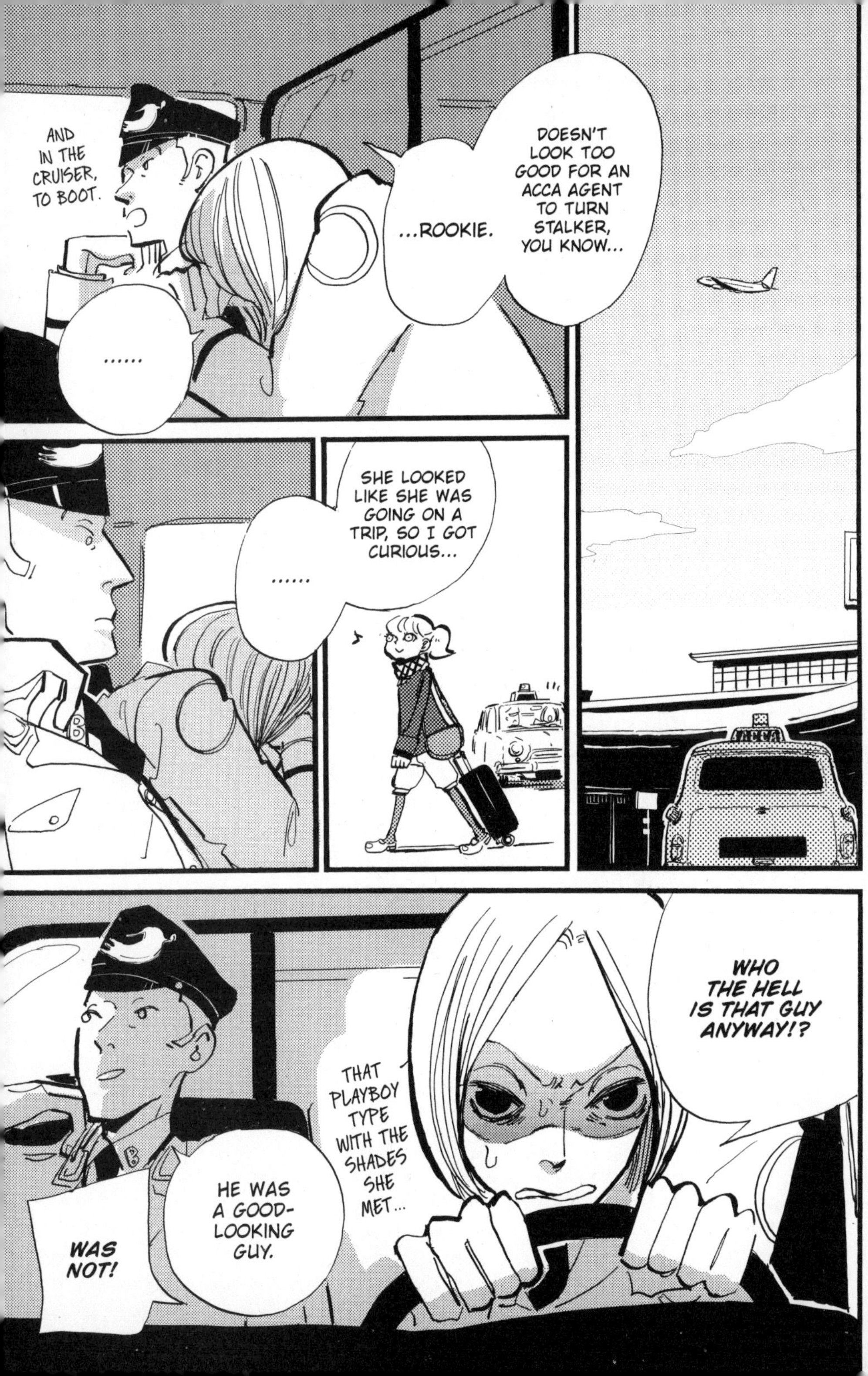
DOESN'T LOOK TOO GOOD FOR AN ACCA AGENT TO TURN STALKER, YOU KNOW...
...ROOKIE.
AND IN THE CRUISER, TO BOOT.
......
SHE LOOKED LIKE SHE WAS GOING ON A TRIP, SO I GOT CURIOUS...
......
WHO THE HELL IS THAT GUY ANYWAY!?
THAT PLAYBOY TYPE WITH THE SHADES SHE MET...
HE WAS A GOOD-LOOKING GUY.
WAS NOT!

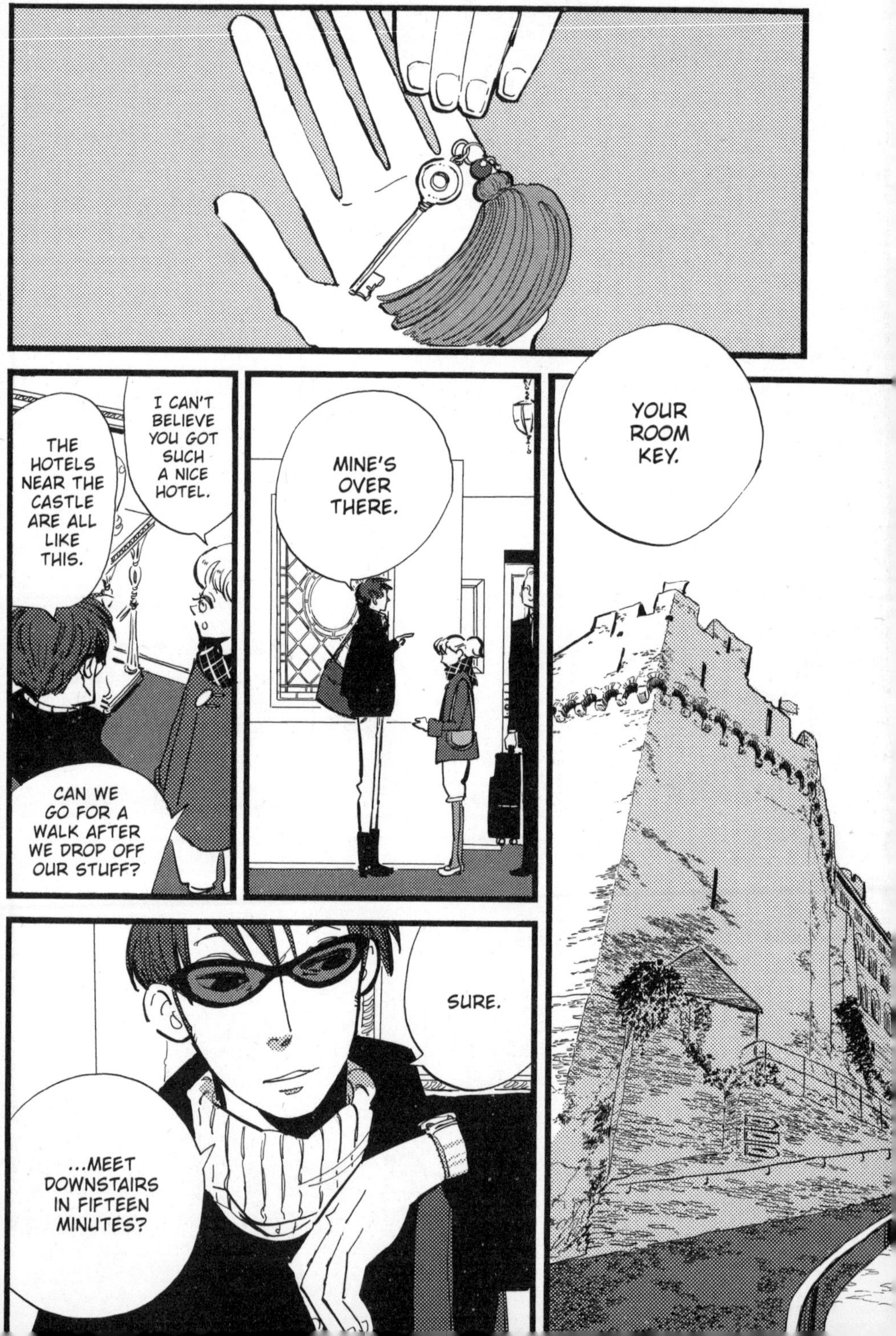
YOUR ROOM KEY.
MINE'S OVER THERE.
I CAN'T BELIEVE YOU GOT SUCH A NICE HOTEL.
THE HOTELS NEAR THE CASTLE ARE ALL LIKE THIS.
CAN WE GO FOR A WALK AFTER WE DROP OFF OUR STUFF?
SURE.
...MEET DOWNSTAIRS IN FIFTEEN MINUTES?

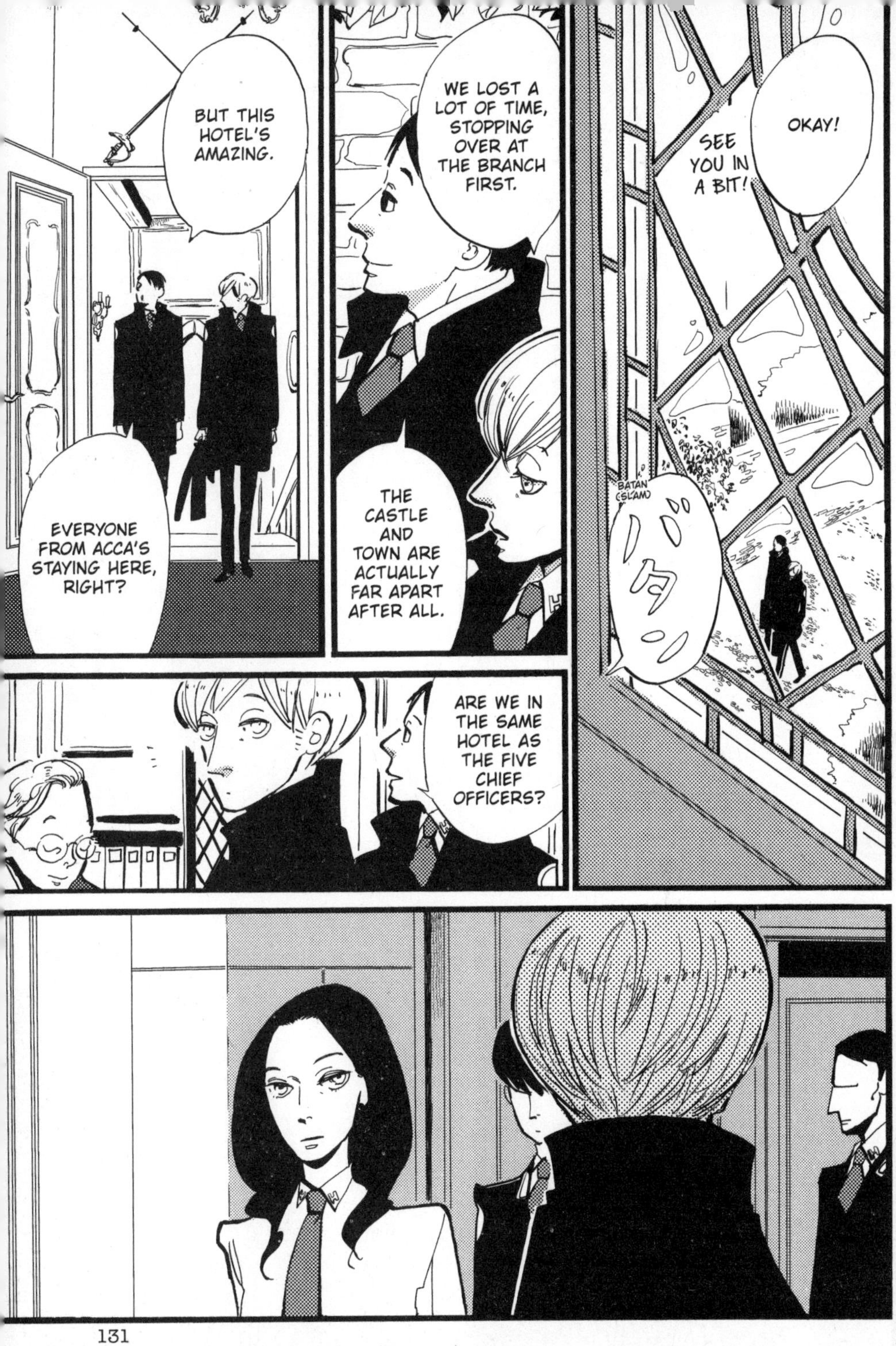
OKAY!
SEE YOU IN A BIT!
BATAN (SLAM)
WE LOST A LOT OF TIME, STOPPING OVER AT THE BRANCH FIRST.
THE CASTLE AND TOWN ARE ACTUALLY FAR APART AFTER ALL.
BUT THIS HOTEL'S AMAZING.
EVERYONE FROM ACCA'S STAYING HERE, RIGHT?
ARE WE IN THE SAME HOTEL AS THE FIVE CHIEF OFFICERS?

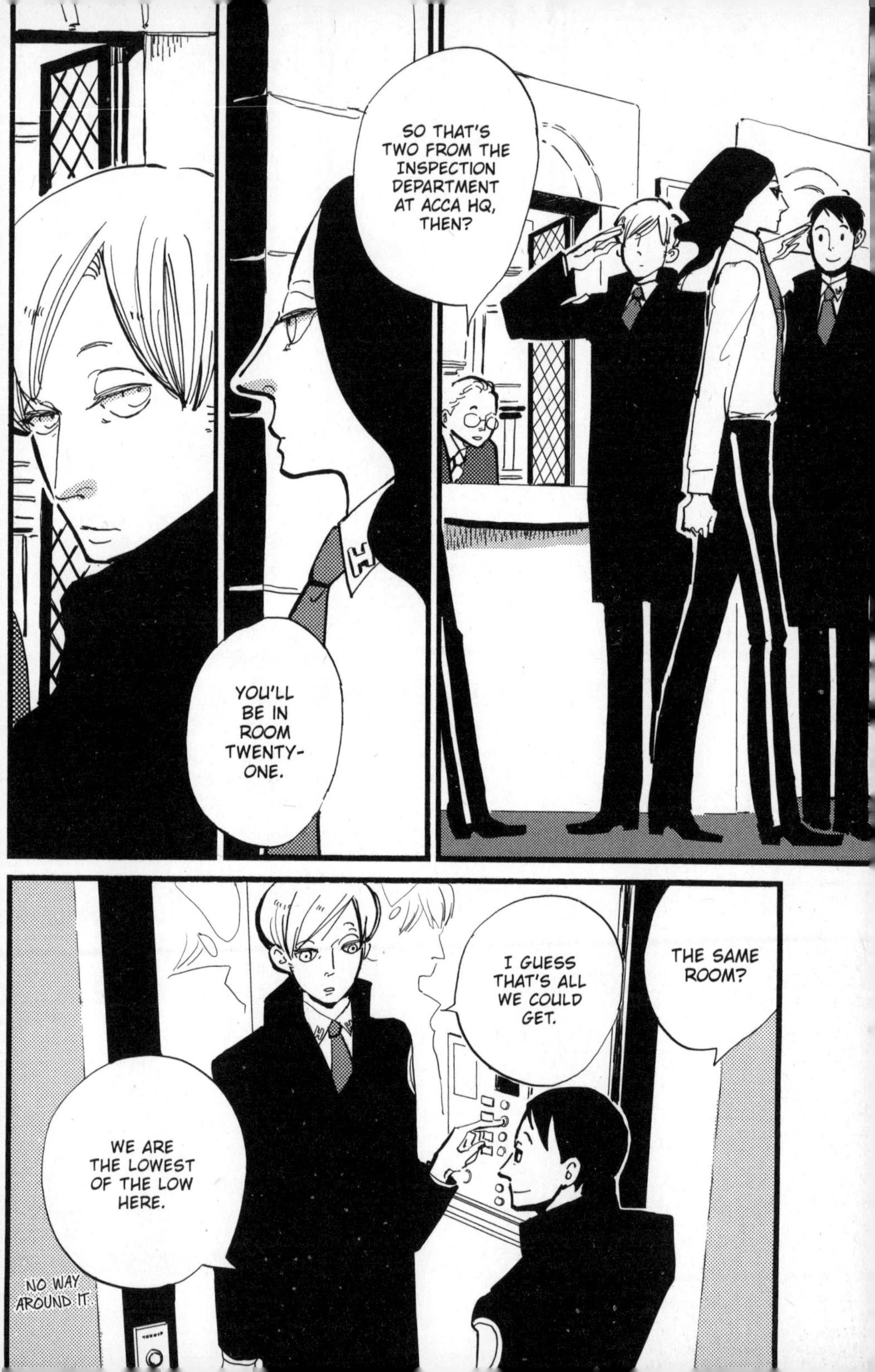
SO THAT'S TWO FROM THE INSPECTION DEPARTMENT AT ACCA HQ, THEN?
YOU'LL BE IN ROOM TWENTY-ONE.
THE SAME ROOM?
I GUESS THAT'S ALL WE COULD GET.
WE ARE THE LOWEST OF THE LOW HERE.
NO WAY AROUND IT.

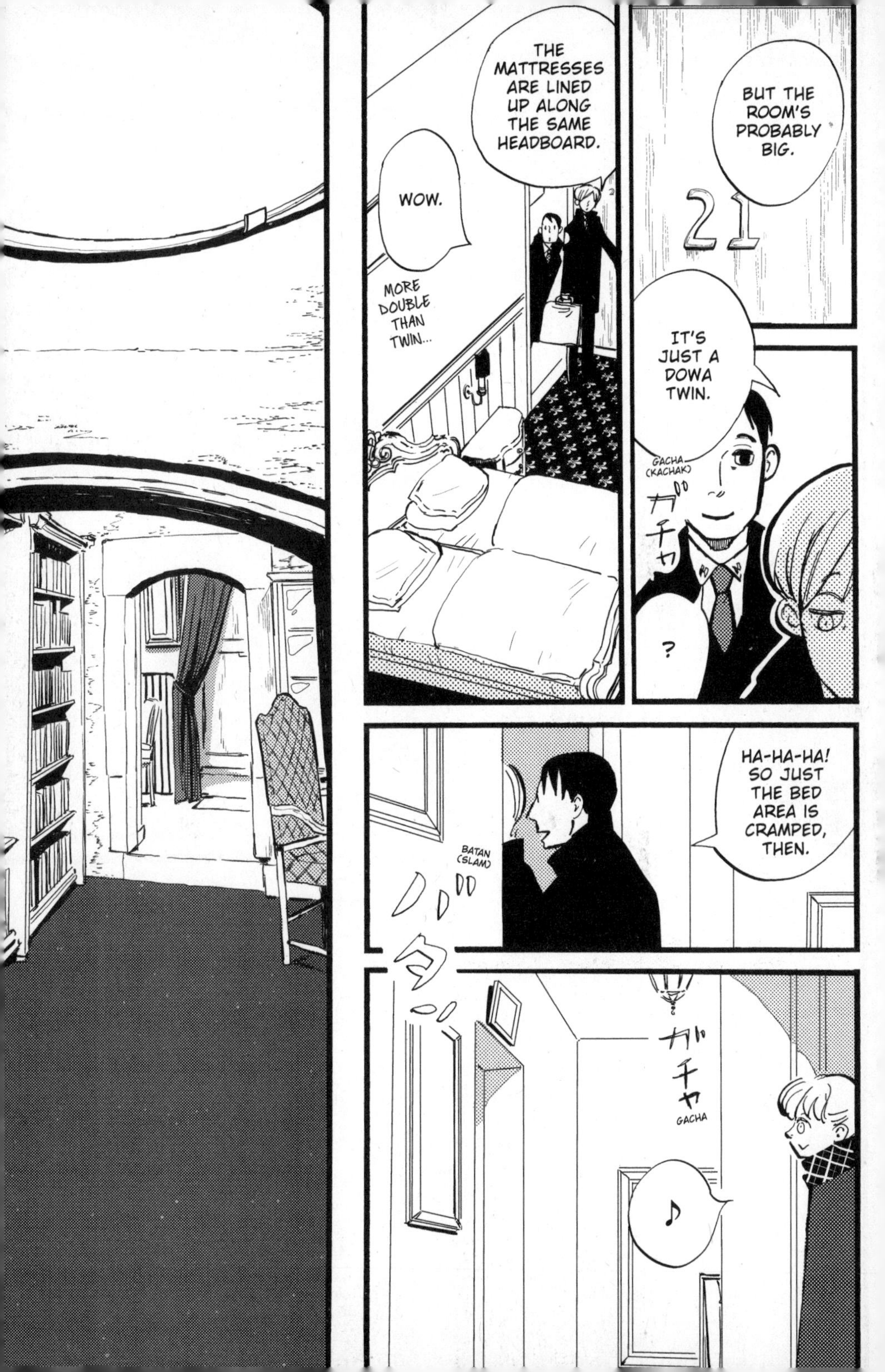
BUT THE ROOM'S PROBABLY BIG.
IT'S JUST A DOWA TWIN.
GACHA (KACHAK)
?
THE MATTRESSES ARE LINED UP ALONG THE SAME HEADBOARD.
WOW.
MORE DOUBLE THAN TWIN...
HA-HA-HA! SO JUST THE BED AREA IS CRAMPED, THEN.
BATAN (SLAM)
GACHA
♪

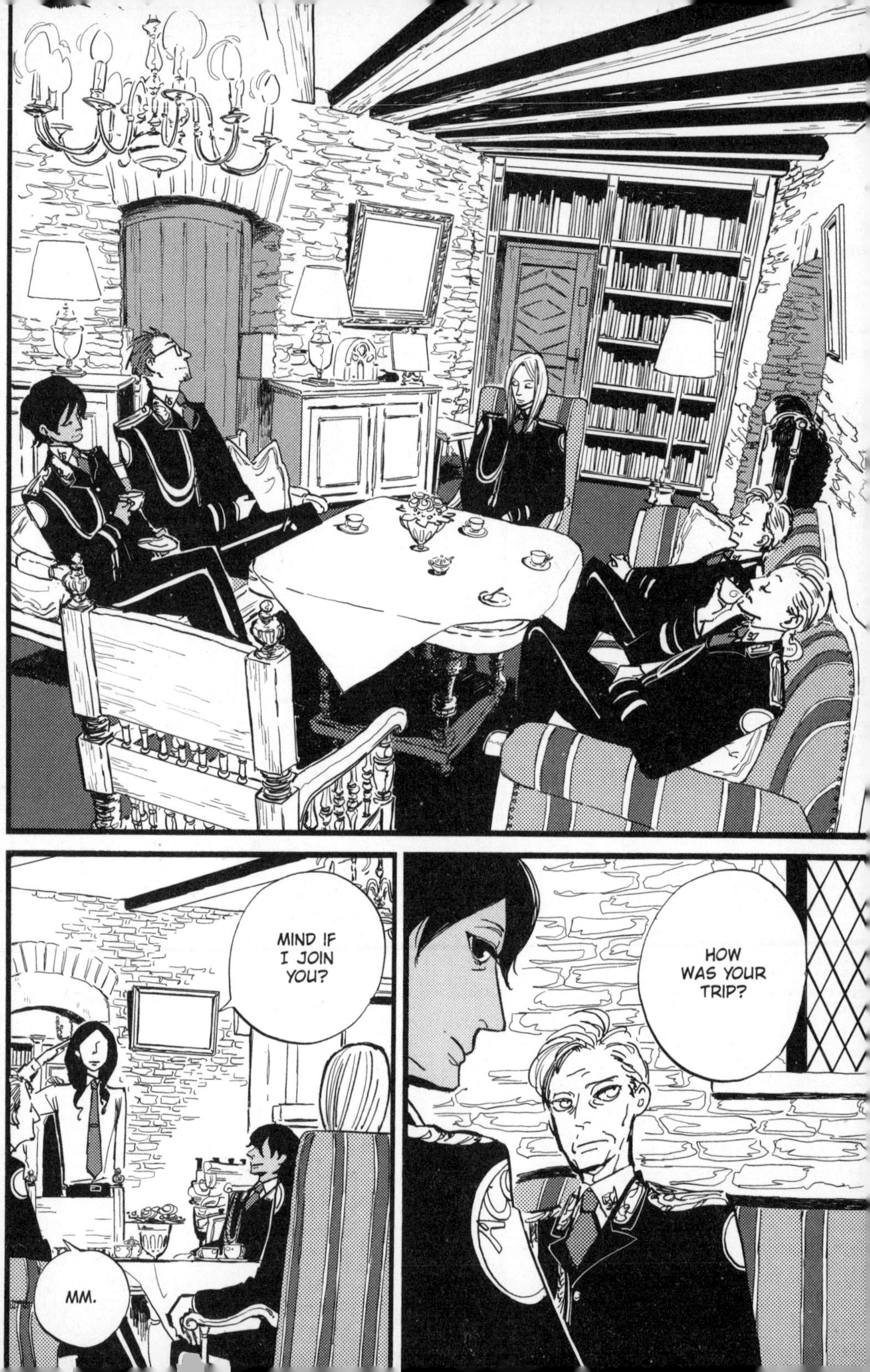
HOW WAS YOUR TRIP?
MIND IF I JOIN YOU?
MM.

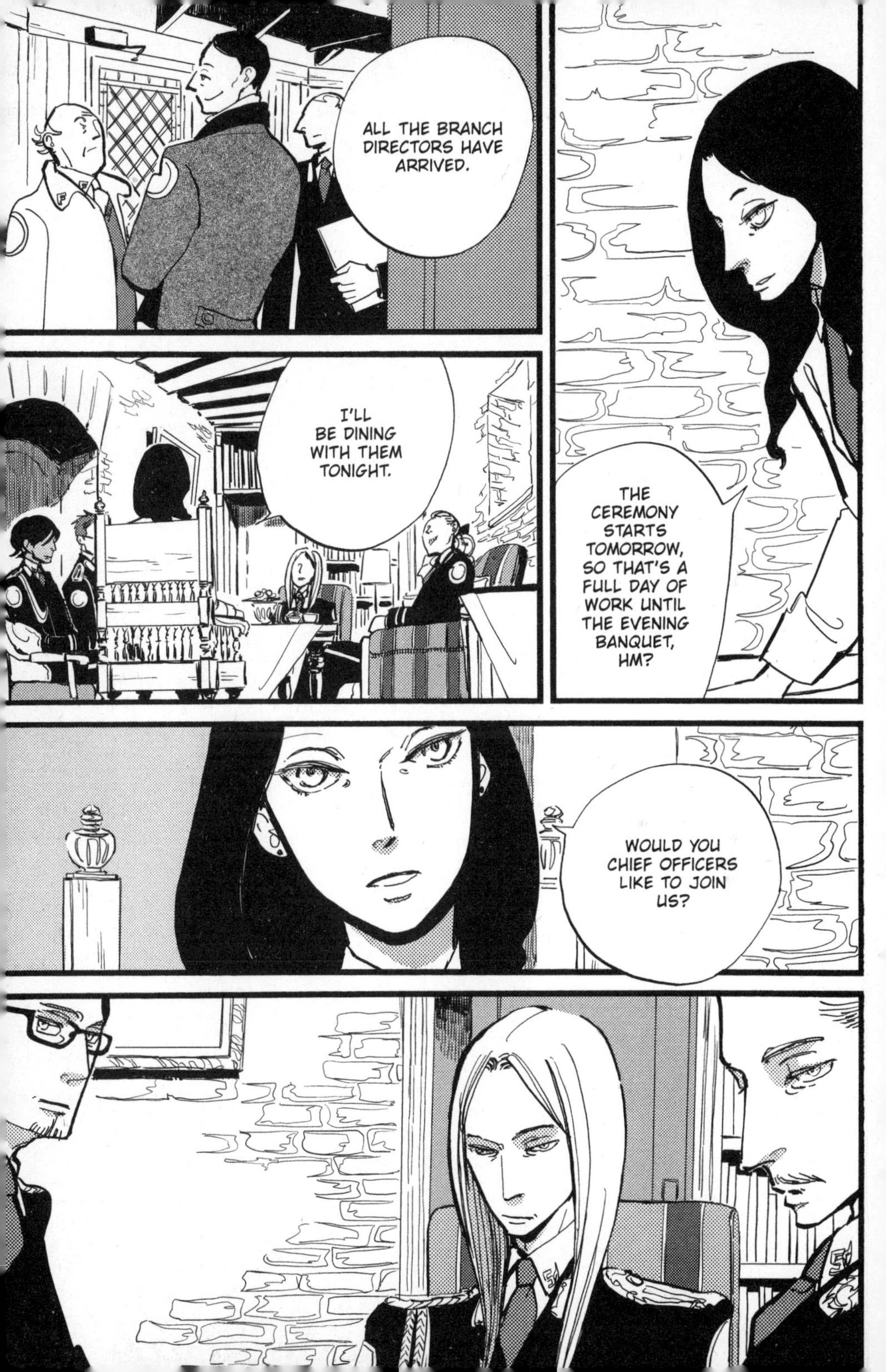
ALL THE BRANCH DIRECTORS HAVE ARRIVED.
I'LL BE DINING WITH THEM TONIGHT.
THE CEREMONY STARTS TOMORROW, SO THAT'S A FULL DAY OF WORK UNTIL THE EVENING BANQUET, HM?
WOULD YOU CHIEF OFFICERS LIKE TO JOIN US?

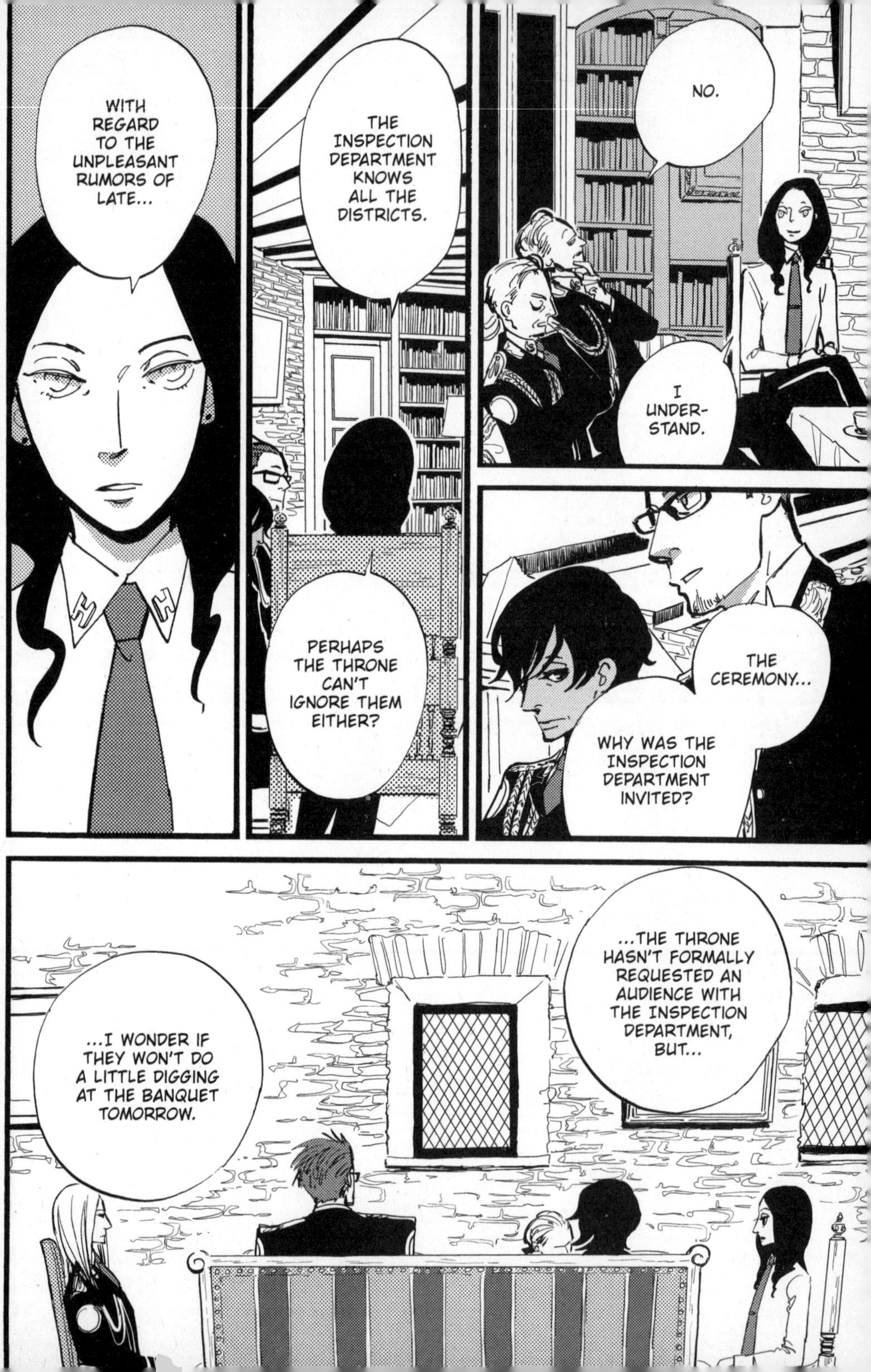
NO.
I UNDERSTAND.
THE CEREMONY...
WHY WAS THE INSPECTION DEPARTMENT INVITED?
THE INSPECTION DEPARTMENT KNOWS ALL THE DISTRICTS.
PERHAPS THE THRONE CAN'T IGNORE THEM EITHER?
WITH REGARD TO THE UNPLEASANT RUMORS OF LATE...
...THE THRONE HASN'T FORMALLY REQUESTED AN AUDIENCE WITH THE INSPECTION DEPARTMENT, BUT...
...I WONDER IF THEY WON'T DO A LITTLE DIGGING AT THE BANQUET TOMORROW.

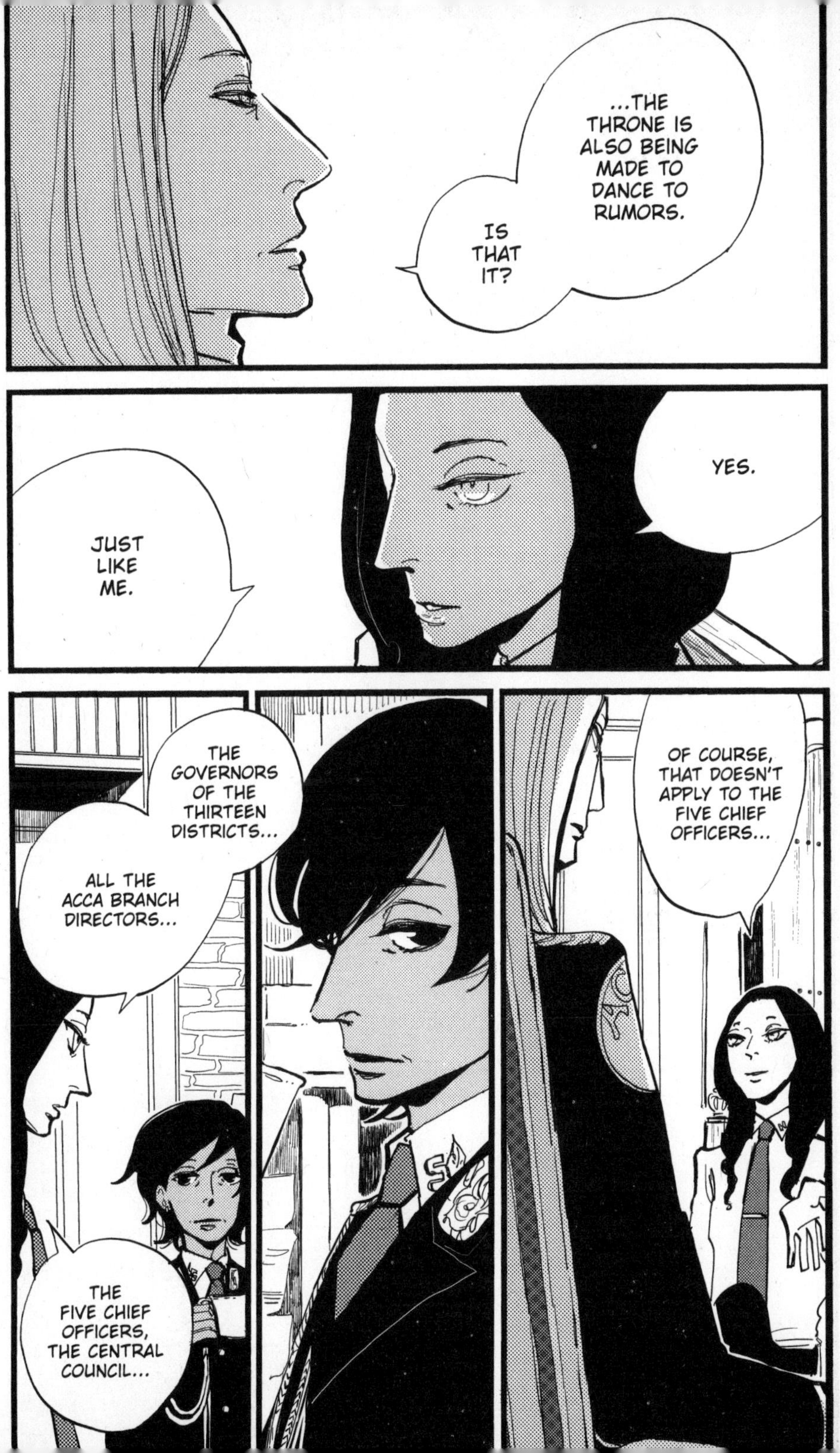
...THE THRONE IS ALSO BEING MADE TO DANCE TO RUMORS.
IS THAT IT?
YES.
JUST LIKE ME.
OF COURSE, THAT DOESN'T APPLY TO THE FIVE CHIEF OFFICERS...
THE GOVERNORS OF THE THIRTEEN DISTRICTS...
ALL THE ACCA BRANCH DIRECTORS...
THE FIVE CHIEF OFFICERS, THE CENTRAL COUNCIL...

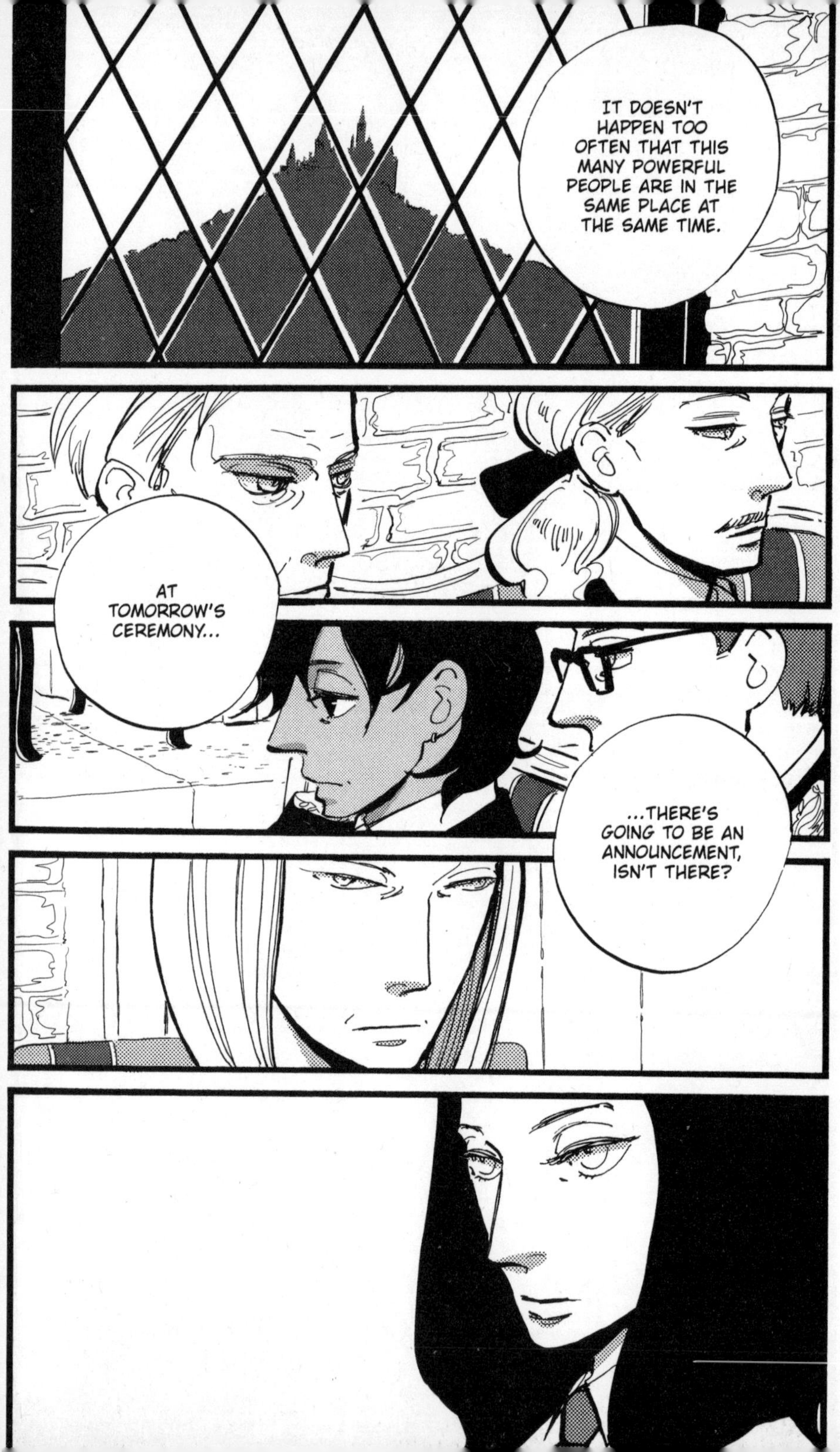
IT DOESN'T HAPPEN TOO OFTEN THAT THIS MANY POWERFUL PEOPLE ARE IN THE SAME PLACE AT THE SAME TIME.
AT TOMORROW'S CEREMONY...
...THERE'S GOING TO BE AN ANNOUNCEMENT, ISN'T THERE?

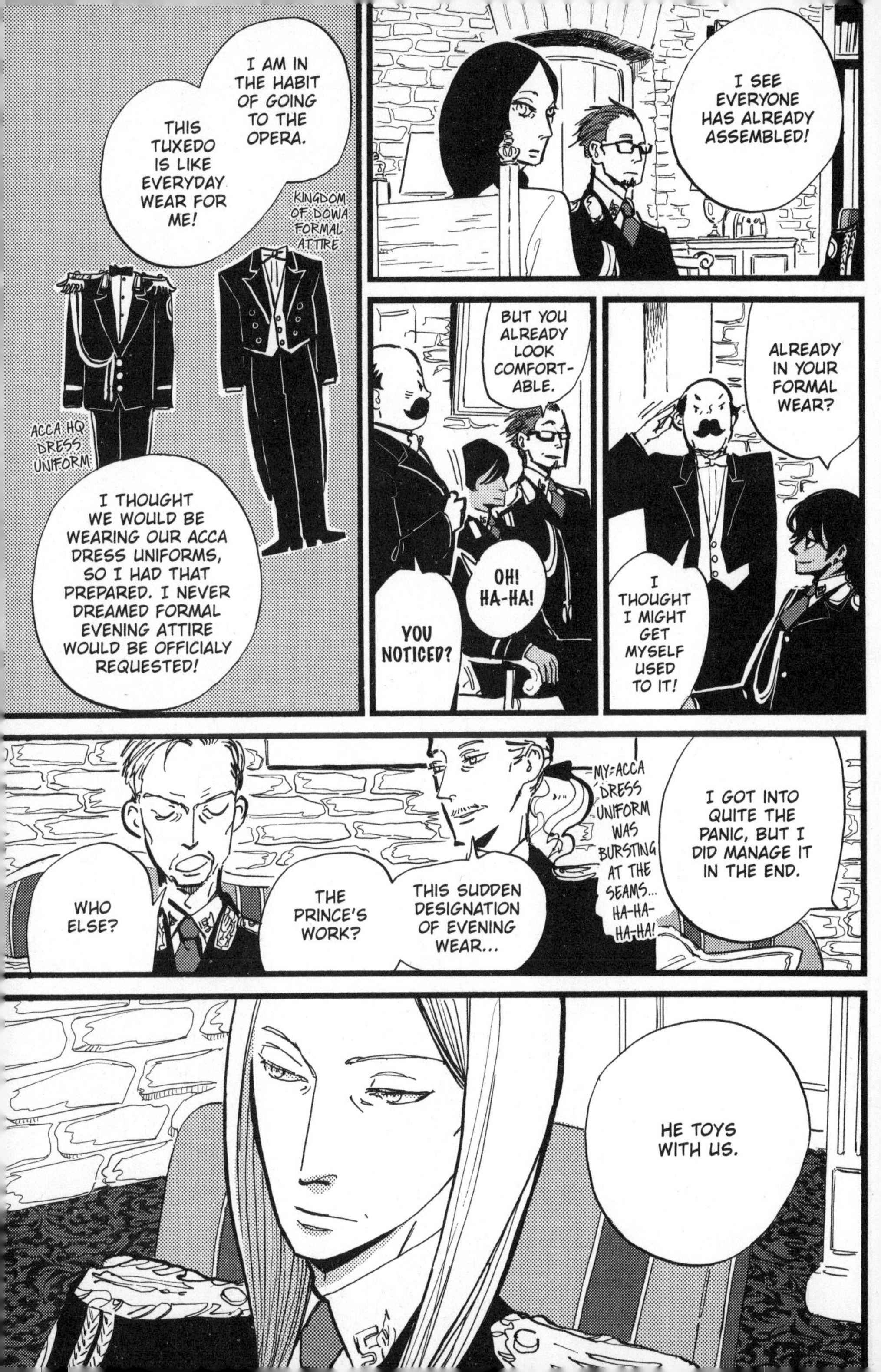
I SEE EVERYONE HAS ALREADY ASSEMBLED!
ALREADY IN YOUR FORMAL WEAR?
I THOUGHT I MIGHT GET MYSELF USED TO IT!
BUT YOU ALREADY LOOK COMFORTABLE.
OH! HA-HA!
YOU NOTICED?
I AM IN THE HABIT OF GOING TO THE OPERA.
THIS TUXEDO IS LIKE EVERYDAY WEAR FOR ME!
KINGDOM OF DOWA FORMAL ATTIRE
ACCA HQ DRESS UNIFORM
I THOUGHT WE WOULD BE WEARING OUR ACCA DRESS UNIFORMS, SO I HAD THAT PREPARED. I NEVER DREAMED FORMAL EVENING ATTIRE WOULD BE OFFICIALY REQUESTED!
I GOT INTO QUITE THE PANIC, BUT I DID MANAGE IT IN THE END.
MY ACCA DRESS UNIFORM WAS BURSTING AT THE SEAMS... HA-HA-HA-HA!
THIS SUDDEN DESIGNATION OF EVENING WEAR...
THE PRINCE'S WORK?
WHO ELSE?
HE TOYS WITH US.

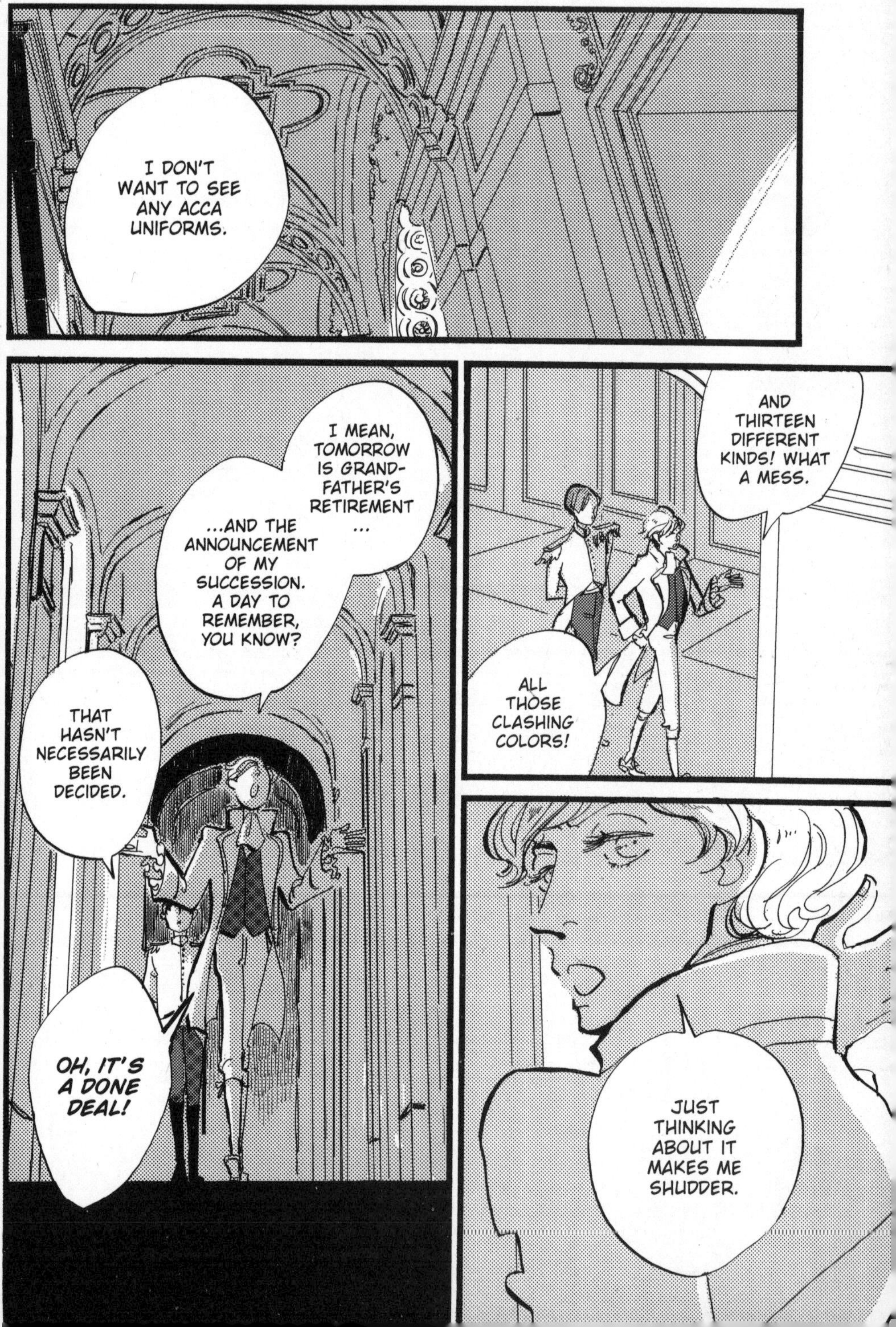
I DON'T WANT TO SEE ANY ACCA UNIFORMS.
AND THIRTEEN DIFFERENT KINDS! WHAT A MESS.
ALL THOSE CLASHING COLORS!
JUST THINKING ABOUT IT MAKES ME SHUDDER.
I MEAN, TOMORROW IS GRAND-FATHER'S RETIREMENT ...
...AND THE ANNOUNCEMENT OF MY SUCCESSION. A DAY TO REMEMBER, YOU KNOW?
THAT HASN'T NECESSARILY BEEN DECIDED.
OH, IT'S A DONE DEAL!

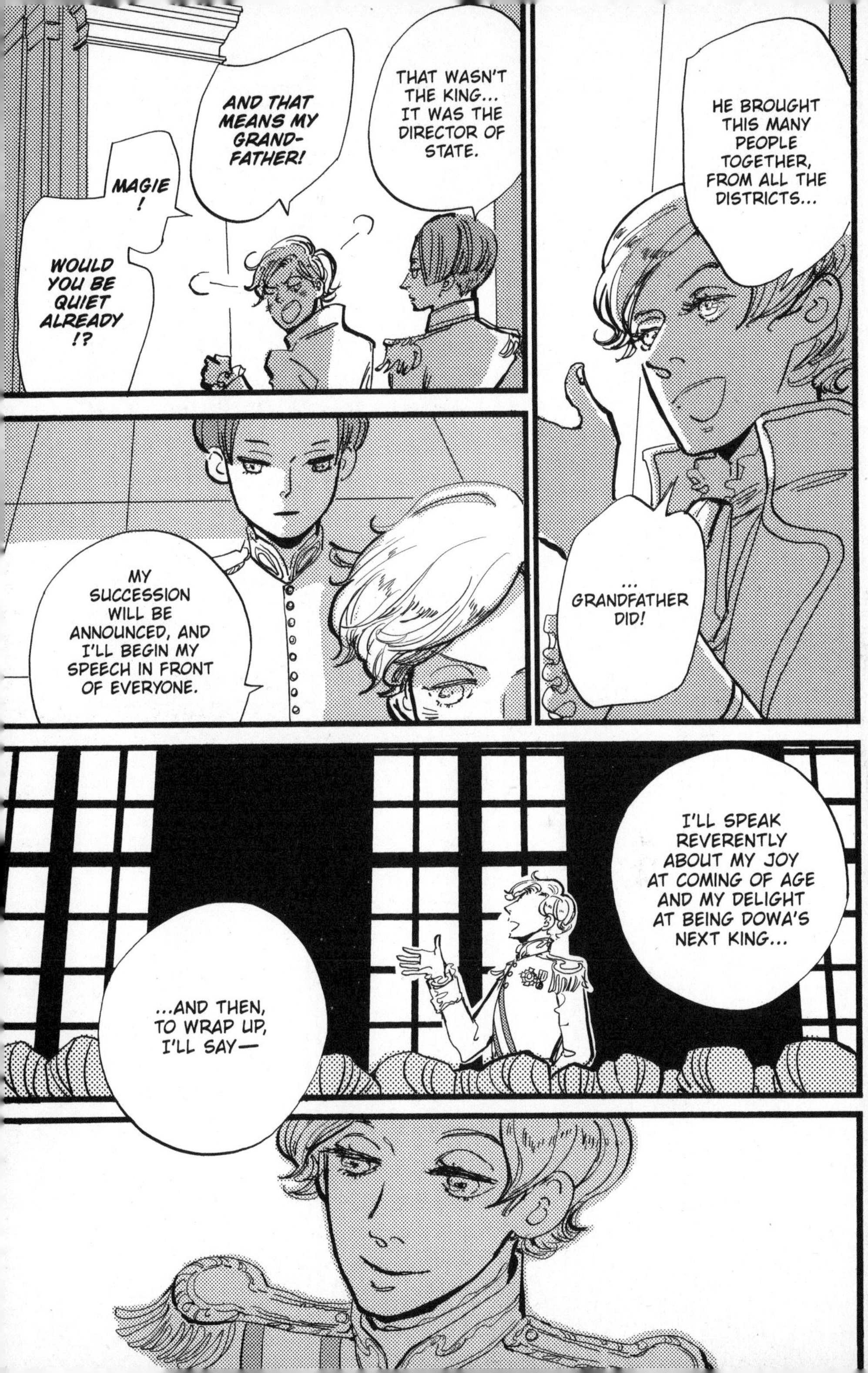
HE BROUGHT THIS MANY PEOPLE TOGETHER, FROM ALL THE DISTRICTS...
...GRANDFATHER DID!
THAT WASN'T THE KING... IT WAS THE DIRECTOR OF STATE.
AND THAT MEANS MY GRANDFATHER!
MAGIE!
WOULD YOU BE QUIET ALREADY!?
MY SUCCESSION WILL BE ANNOUNCED, AND I'LL BEGIN MY SPEECH IN FRONT OF EVERYONE.
I'LL SPEAK REVERENTLY ABOUT MY JOY AT COMING OF AGE AND MY DELIGHT AT BEING DOWA'S NEXT KING...
...AND THEN, TO WRAP UP, I'LL SAY—

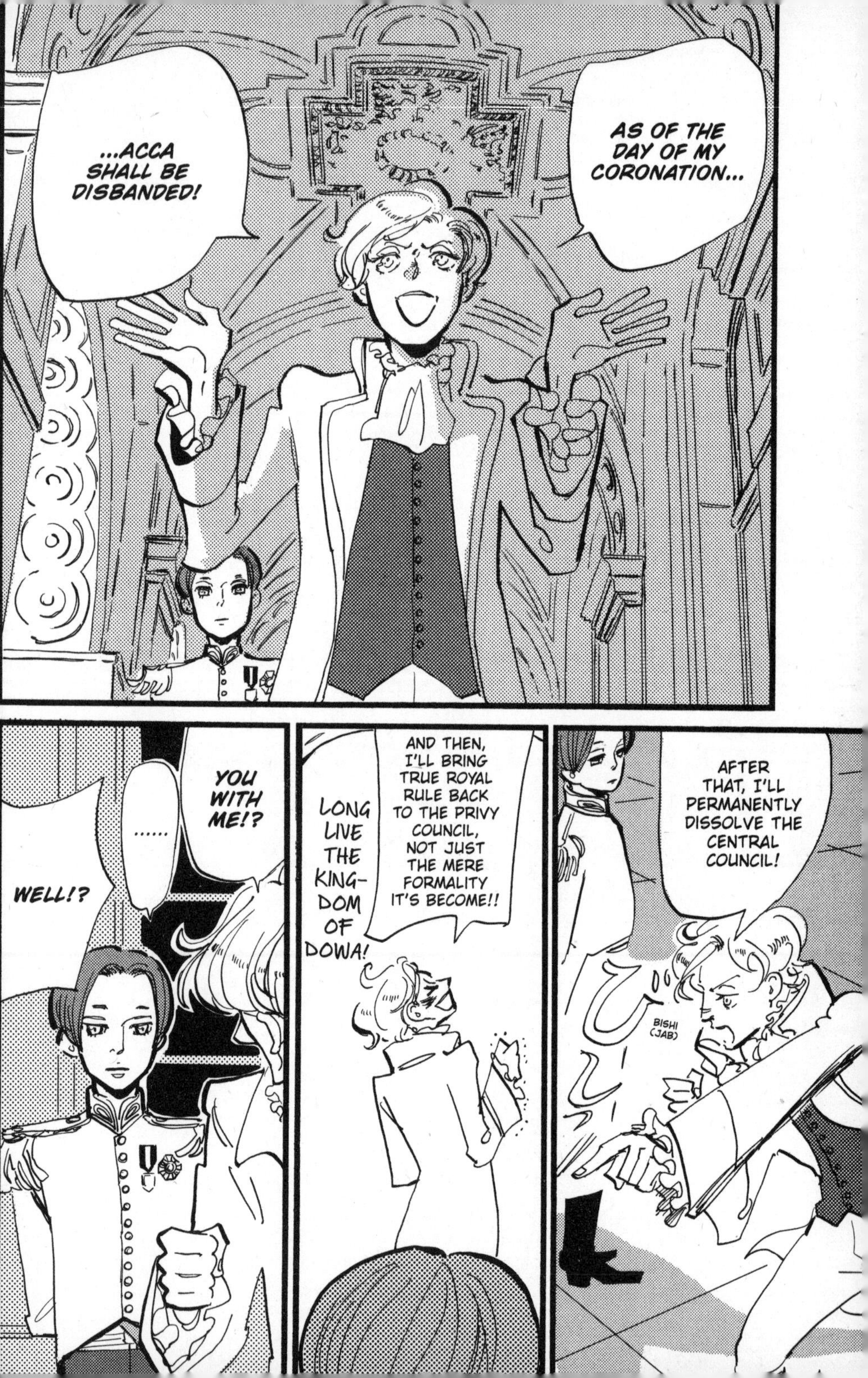
AS OF THE DAY OF MY CORONATION...
...ACCA SHALL BE DISBANDED!
AFTER THAT, I'LL PERMANENTLY DISSOLVE THE CENTRAL COUNCIL!
BISHI (JAB)
AND THEN, I'LL BRING TRUE ROYAL RULE BACK TO THE PRIVY COUNCIL, NOT JUST THE MERE FORMALITY IT'S BECOME!!
LONG LIVE THE KINGDOM OF DOWA!
YOU WITH ME!?
......
WELL!?

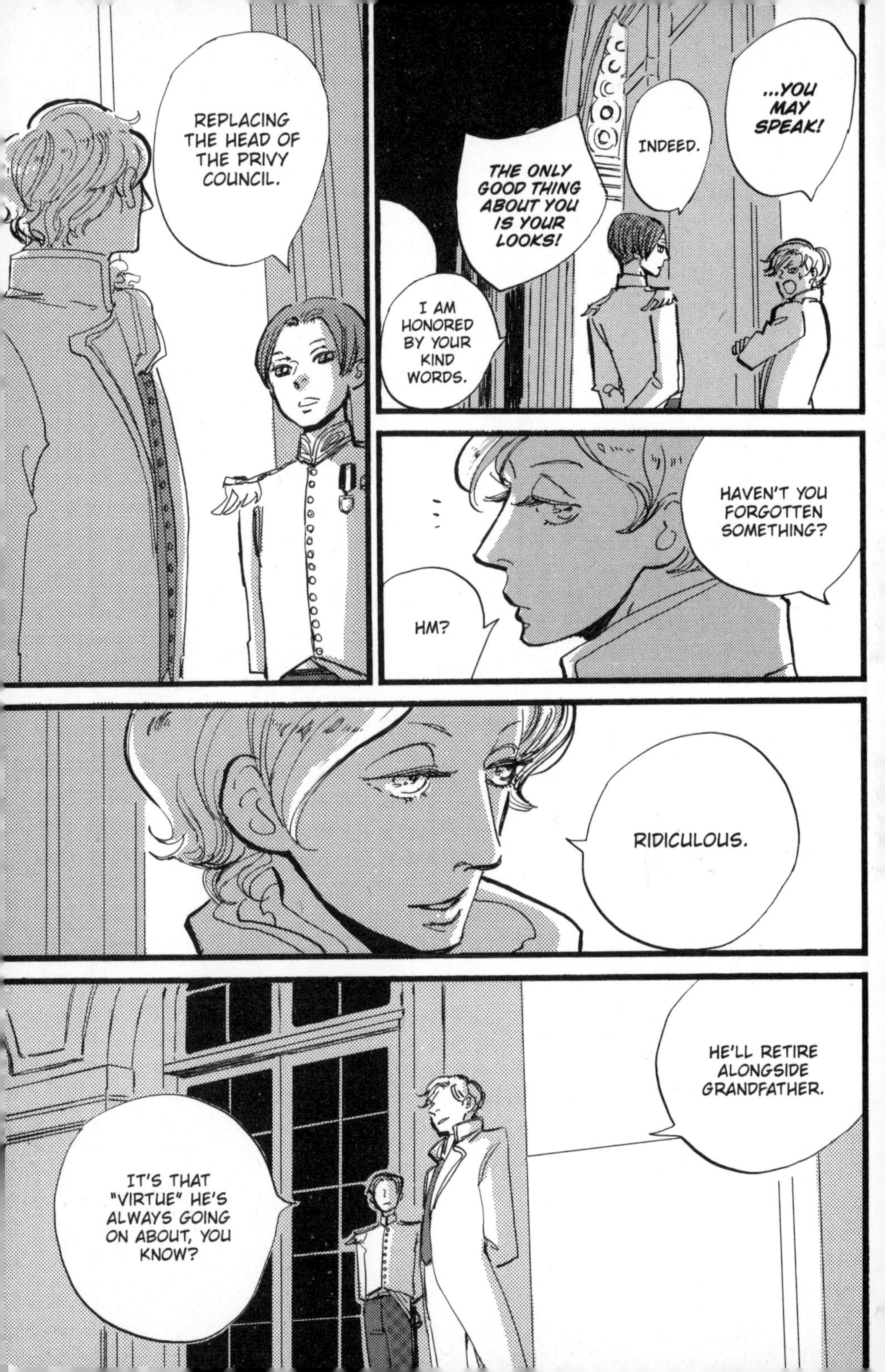
...YOU MAY SPEAK!
INDEED.
THE ONLY GOOD THING ABOUT YOU IS YOUR LOOKS!
I AM HONORED BY YOUR KIND WORDS.
HAVEN'T YOU FORGOTTEN SOMETHING?
HM?
REPLACING THE HEAD OF THE PRIVY COUNCIL.
RIDICULOUS.
HE'LL RETIRE ALONGSIDE GRANDFATHER.
IT'S THAT "VIRTUE" HE'S ALWAYS GOING ON ABOUT, YOU KNOW?

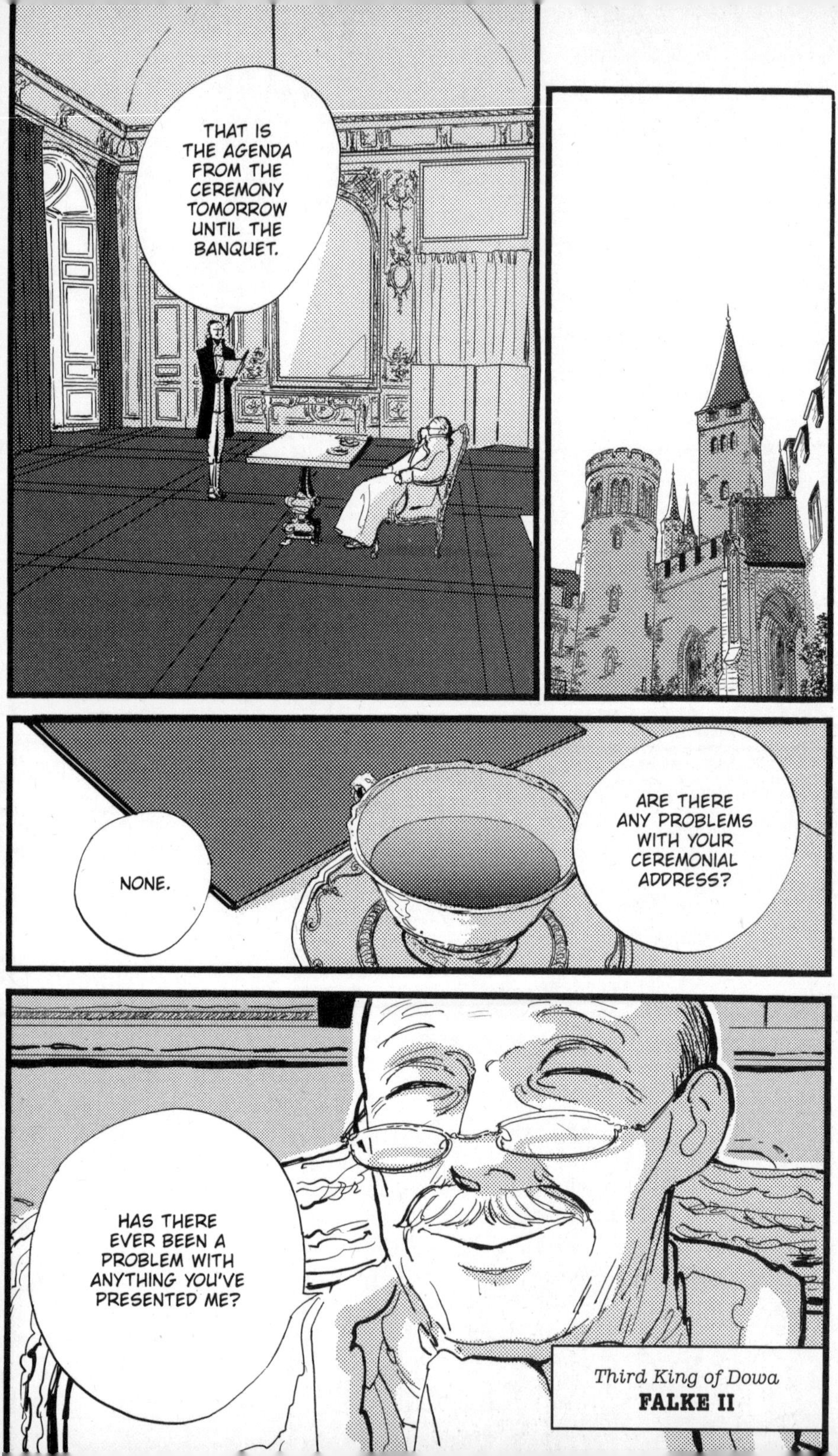
THAT IS THE AGENDA FROM THE CEREMONY TOMORROW UNTIL THE BANQUET.
ARE THERE ANY PROBLEMS WITH YOUR CEREMONIAL ADDRESS?
NONE.
HAS THERE EVER BEEN A PROBLEM WITH ANYTHING YOU'VE PRESENTED ME?
Third King of Dowa
FALKE II

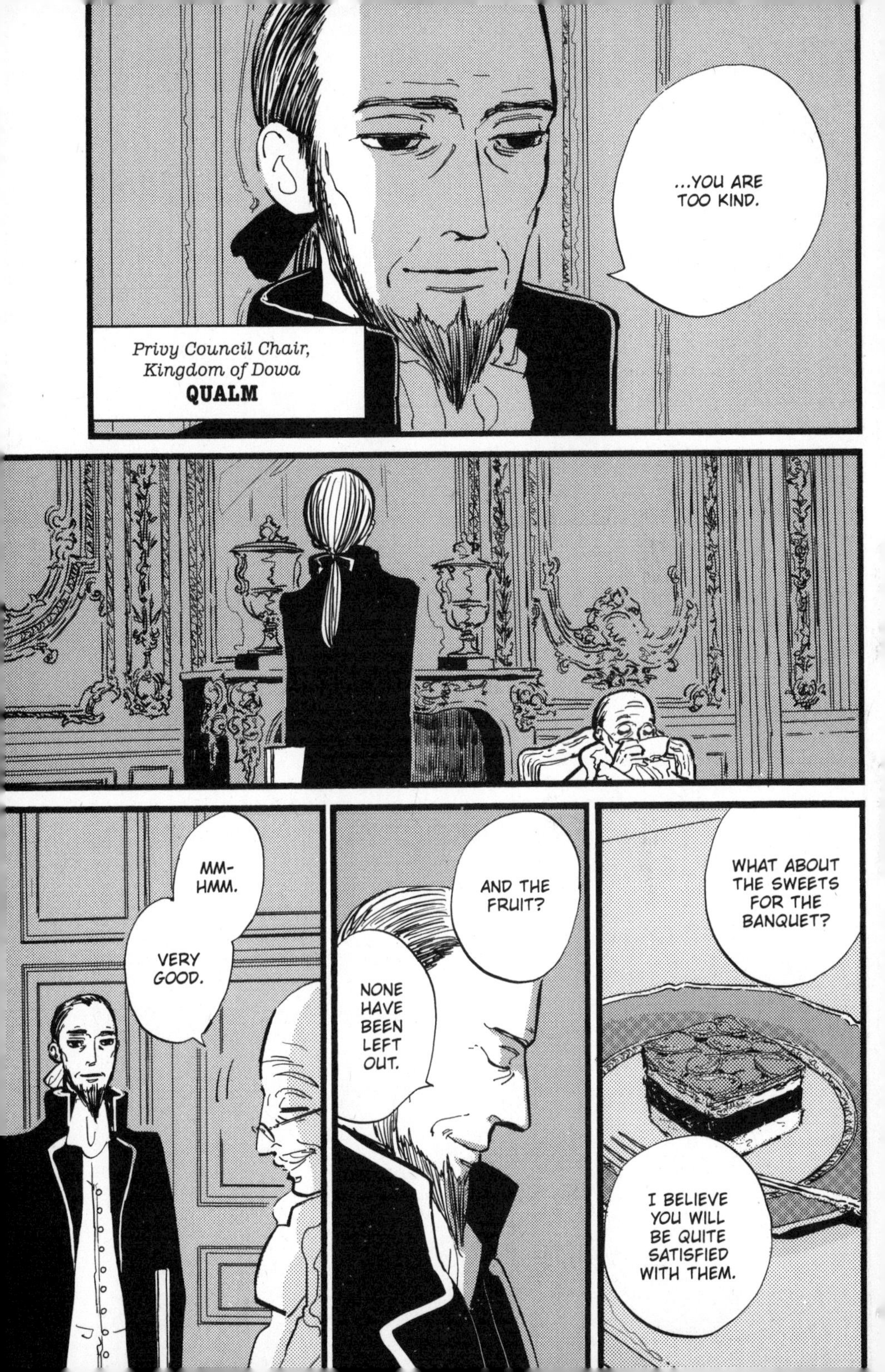
...YOU ARE TOO KIND.
Privy Council Chair, Kingdom of Dowa
QUALM
WHAT ABOUT THE SWEETS FOR THE BANQUET?
I BELIEVE YOU WILL BE QUITE SATISFIED WITH THEM.
AND THE FRUIT?
NONE HAVE BEEN LEFT OUT.
MM-HMM.
VERY GOOD.

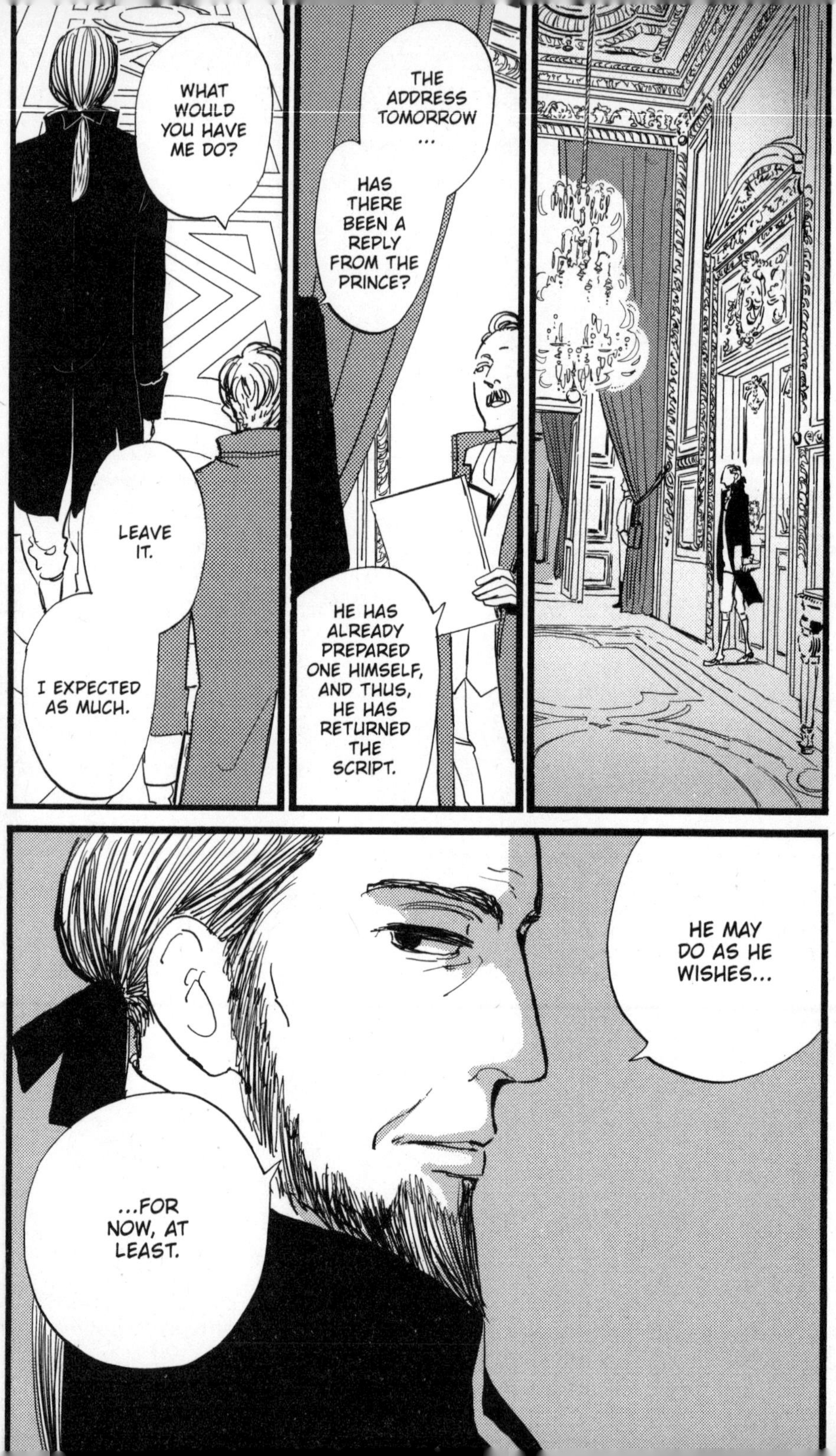
THE ADDRESS TOMORROW ...
HAS THERE BEEN A REPLY FROM THE PRINCE?
HE HAS ALREADY PREPARED ONE HIMSELF, AND THUS, HE HAS RETURNED THE SCRIPT.
WHAT WOULD YOU HAVE ME DO?
LEAVE IT.
I EXPECTED AS MUCH.
HE MAY DO AS HE WISHES...
...FOR NOW, AT LEAST.

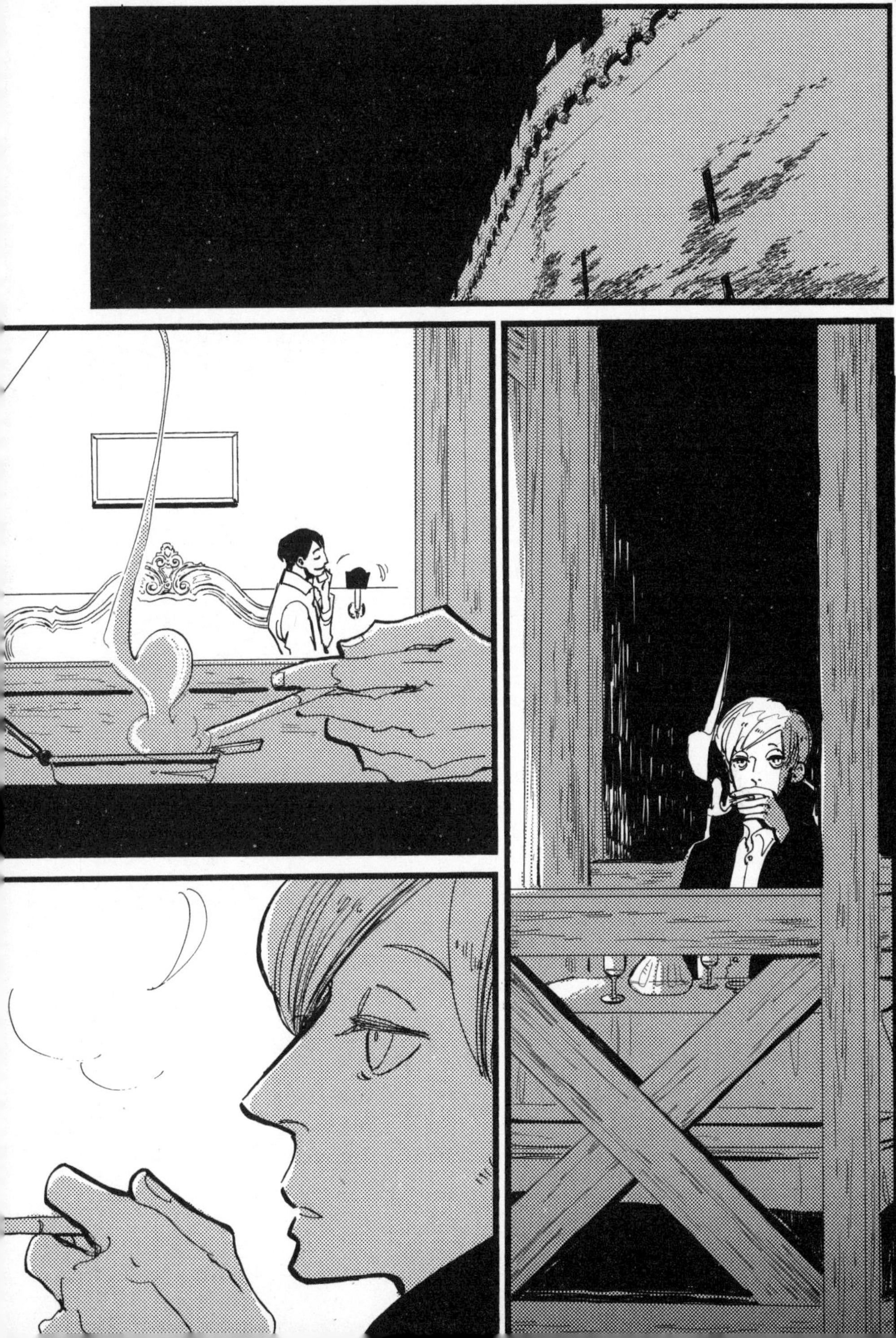

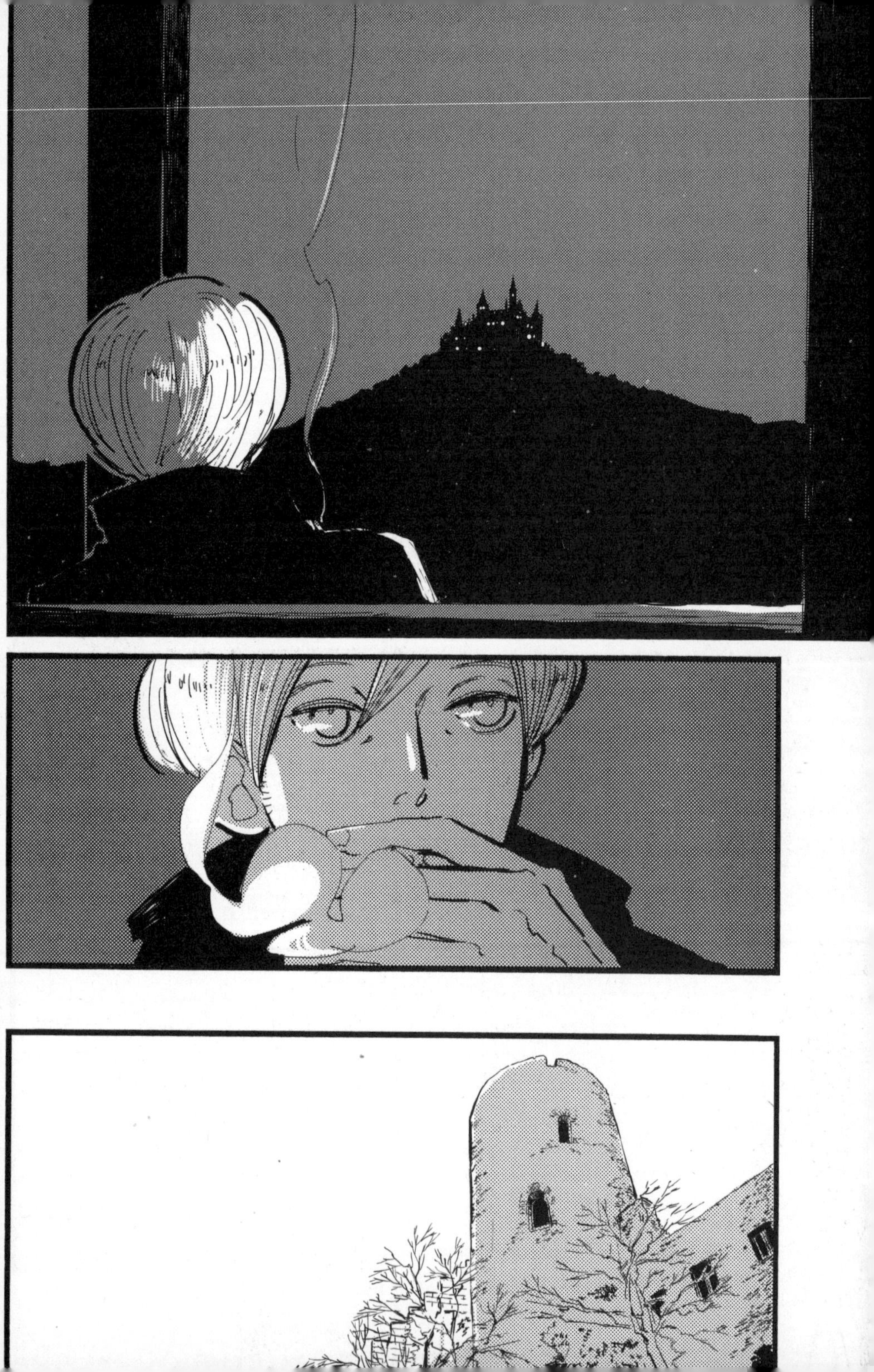

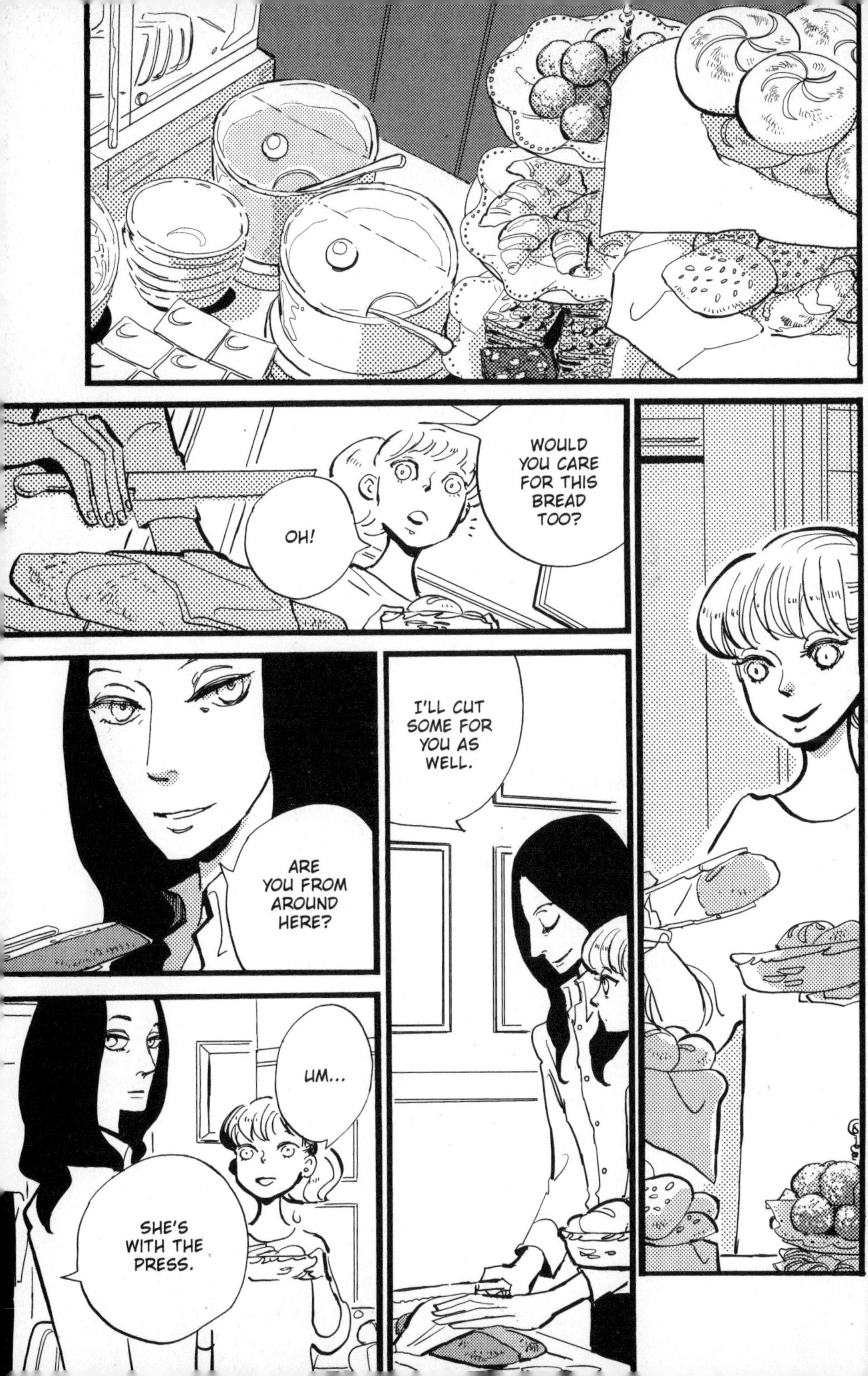
WOULD YOU CARE FOR THIS BREAD TOO?
OH!
I'LL CUT SOME FOR YOU AS WELL.
ARE YOU FROM AROUND HERE?
UM...
SHE'S WITH THE PRESS.

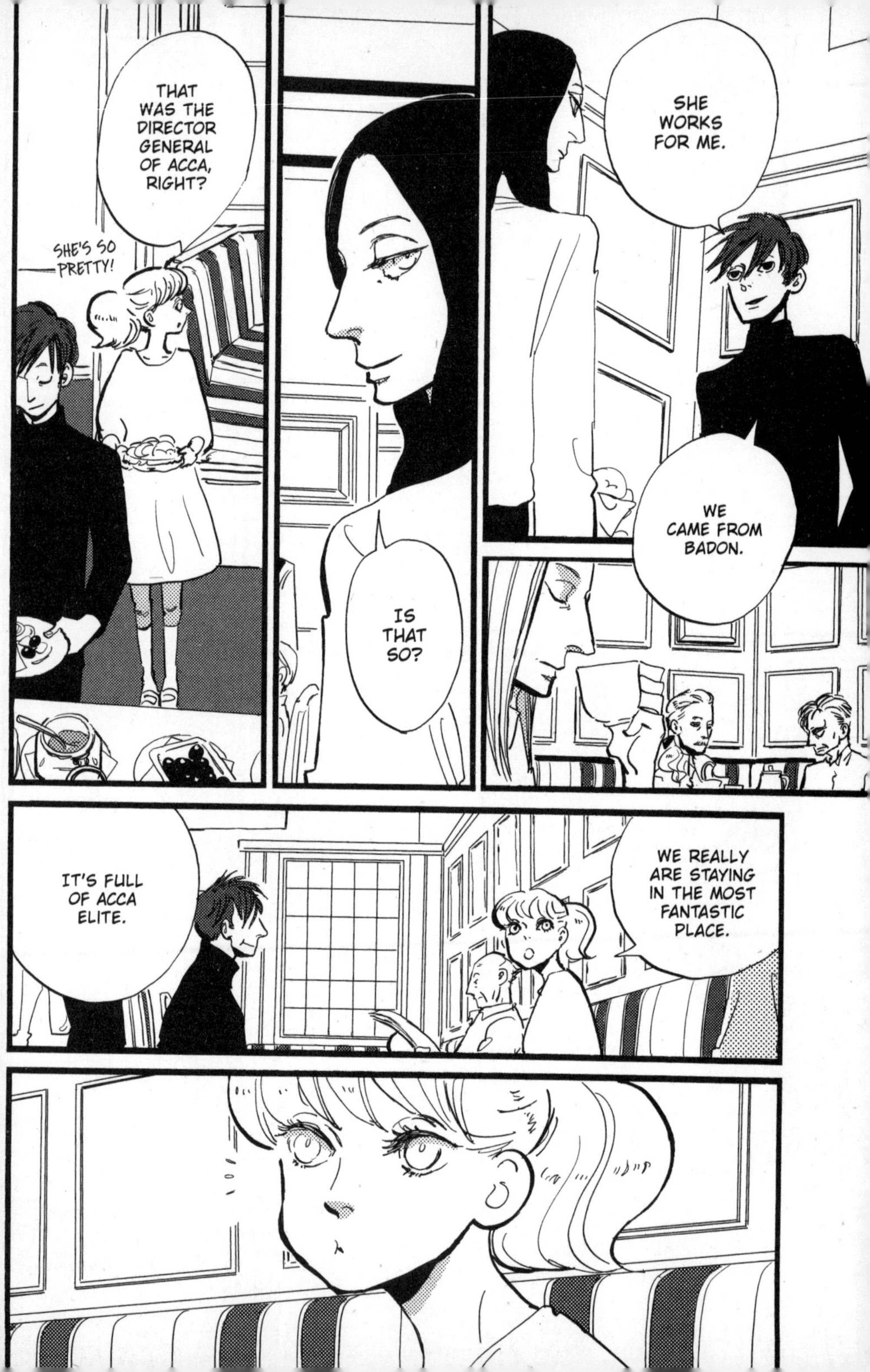
SHE WORKS FOR ME.
WE CAME FROM BADON.
IS THAT SO?
THAT WAS THE DIRECTOR GENERAL OF ACCA, RIGHT?
SHE'S SO PRETTY!
WE REALLY ARE STAYING IN THE MOST FANTASTIC PLACE.
IT'S FULL OF ACCA ELITE.

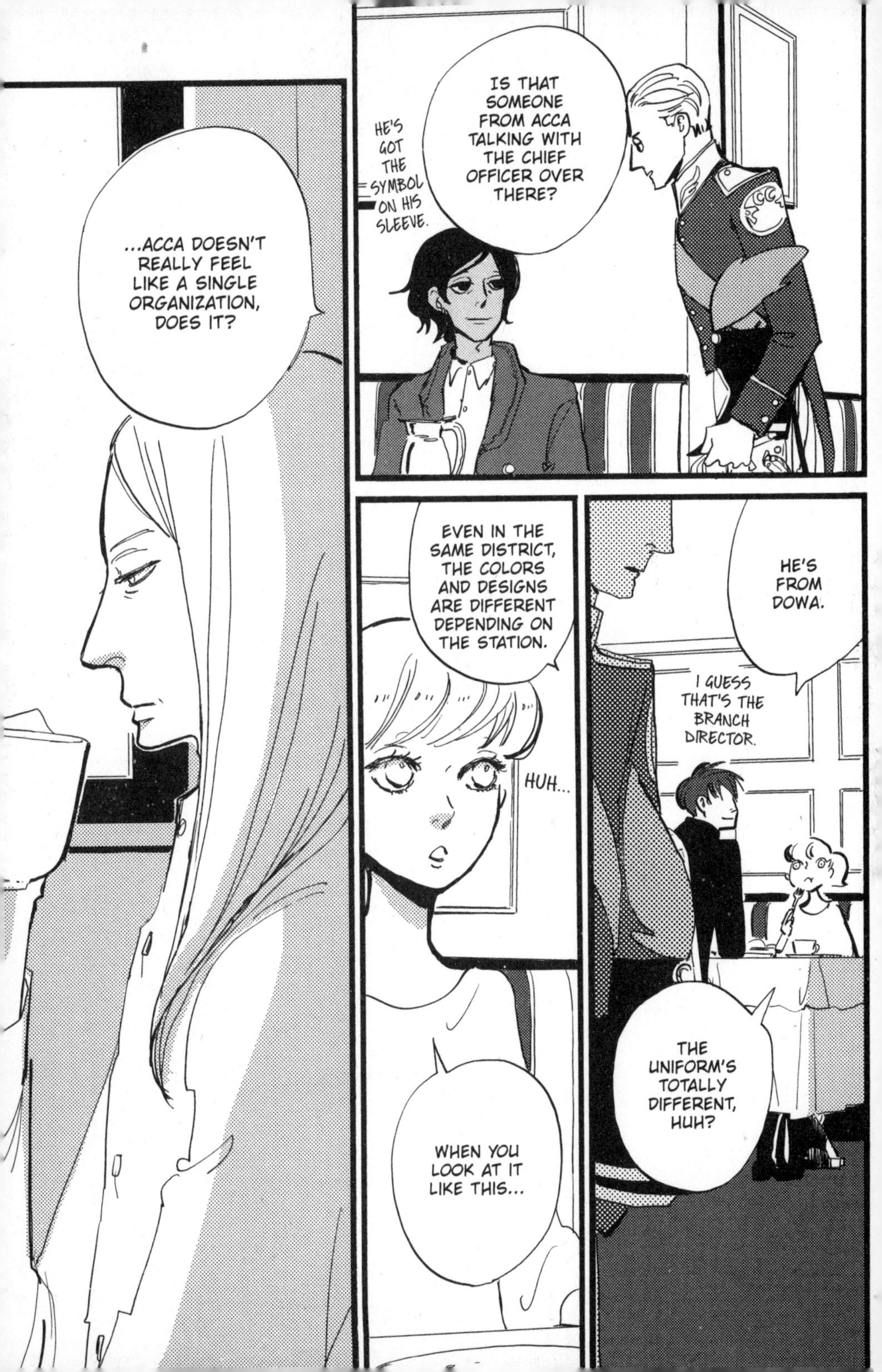
IS THAT SOMEONE FROM ACCA TALKING WITH THE CHIEF OFFICER OVER THERE?
HE'S GOT THE SYMBOL ON HIS SLEEVE.
HE'S FROM DOWA.
I GUESS THAT'S THE BRANCH DIRECTOR.
THE UNIFORM'S TOTALLY DIFFERENT, HUH?
HUH...
WHEN YOU LOOK AT IT LIKE THIS...
EVEN IN THE SAME DISTRICT, THE COLORS AND DESIGNS ARE DIFFERENT DEPENDING ON THE STATION.
...ACCA DOESN'T REALLY FEEL LIKE A SINGLE ORGANIZATION, DOES IT?

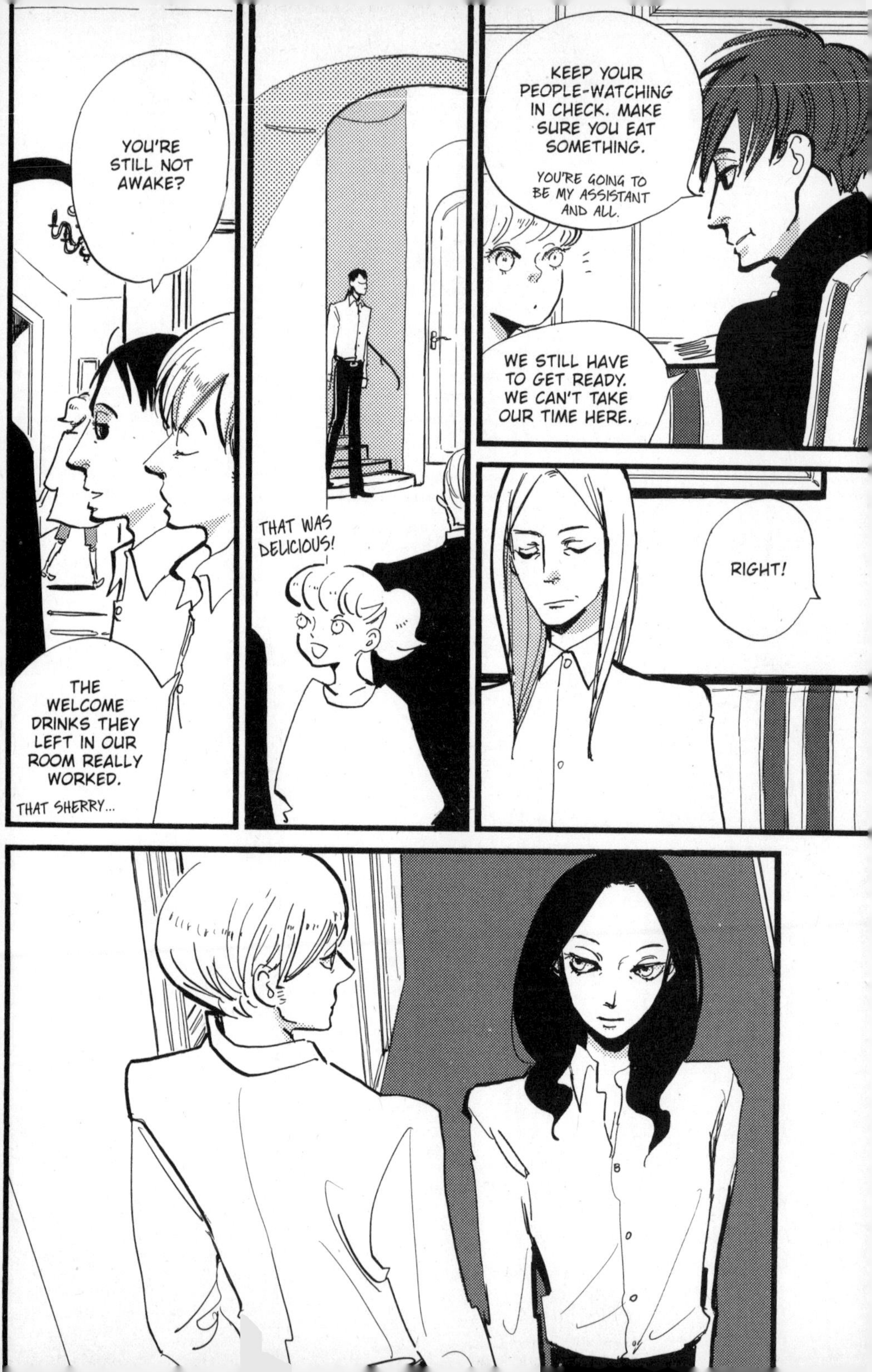
KEEP YOUR PEOPLE-WATCHING IN CHECK. MAKE SURE YOU EAT SOMETHING.
YOU'RE GOING TO BE MY ASSISTANT AND ALL.
WE STILL HAVE TO GET READY. WE CAN'T TAKE OUR TIME HERE.
RIGHT!
THAT WAS DELICIOUS!
YOU'RE STILL NOT AWAKE?
THE WELCOME DRINKS THEY LEFT IN OUR ROOM REALLY WORKED.
THAT SHERRY...

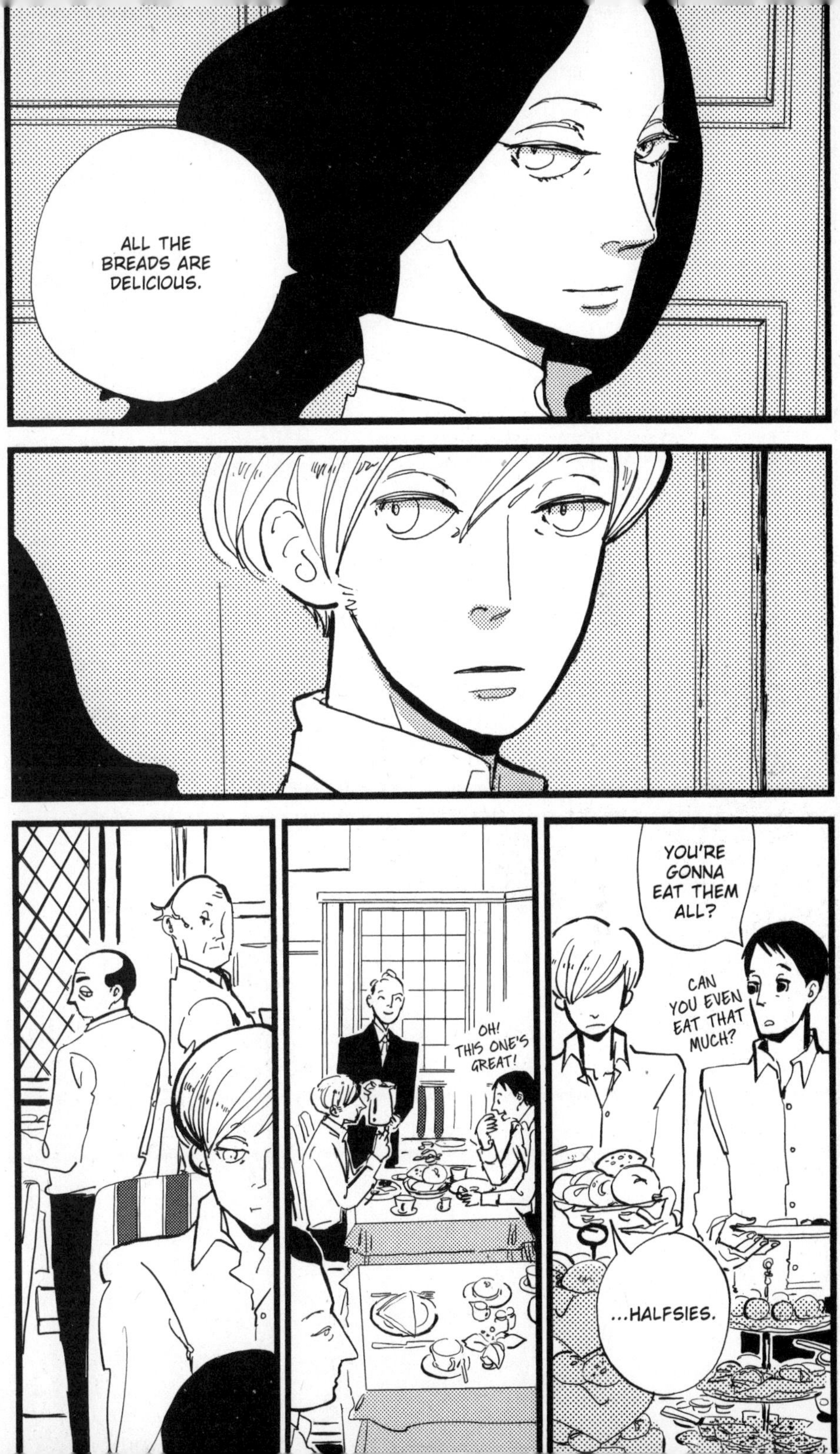
ALL THE BREADS ARE DELICIOUS.
YOU'RE GONNA EAT THEM ALL?
CAN YOU EVEN EAT THAT MUCH?
...HALFSIES.
OH! THIS ONE'S GREAT!

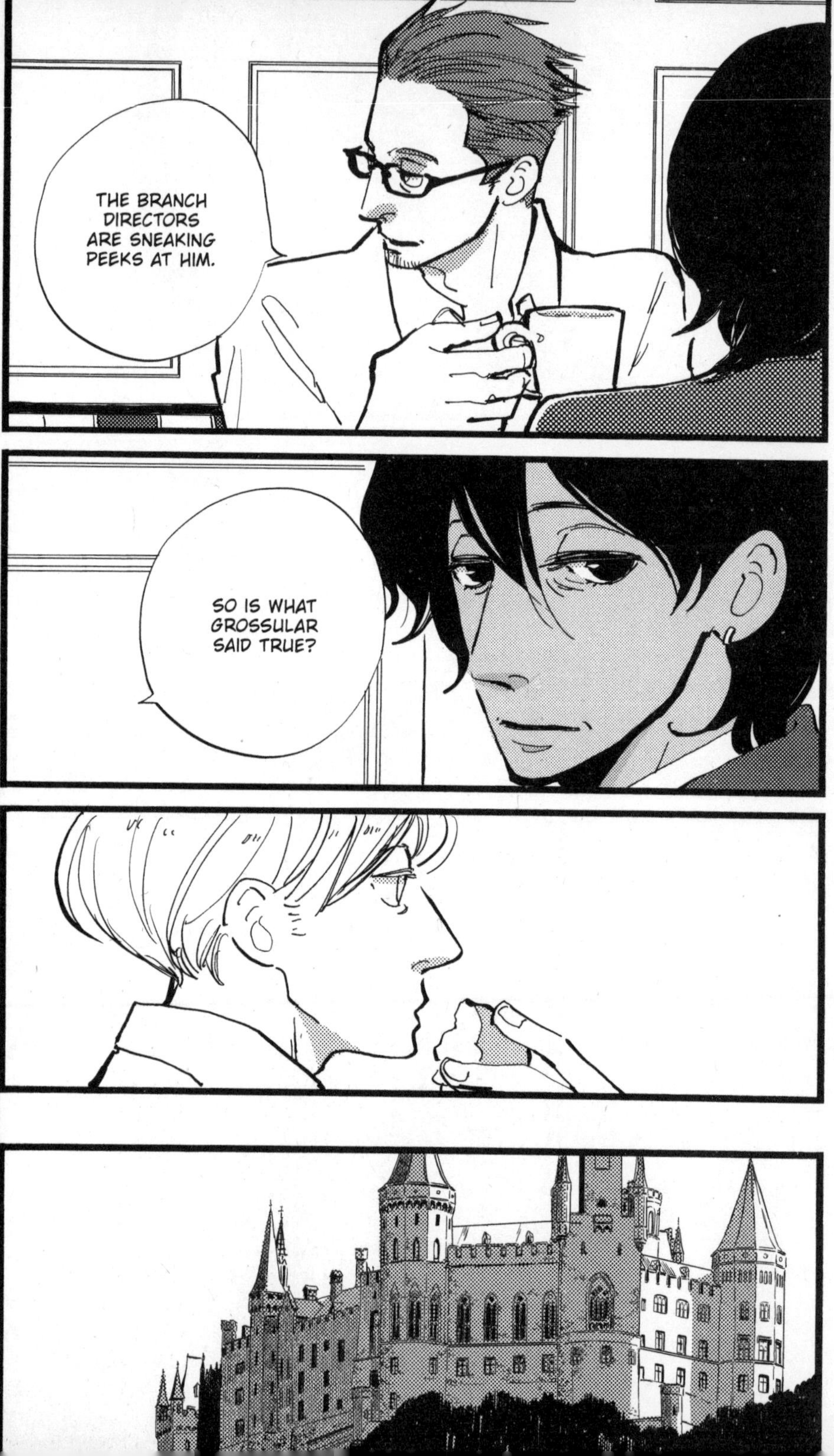
THE BRANCH DIRECTORS ARE SNEAKING PEEKS AT HIM.
SO IS WHAT GROSSULAR SAID TRUE?

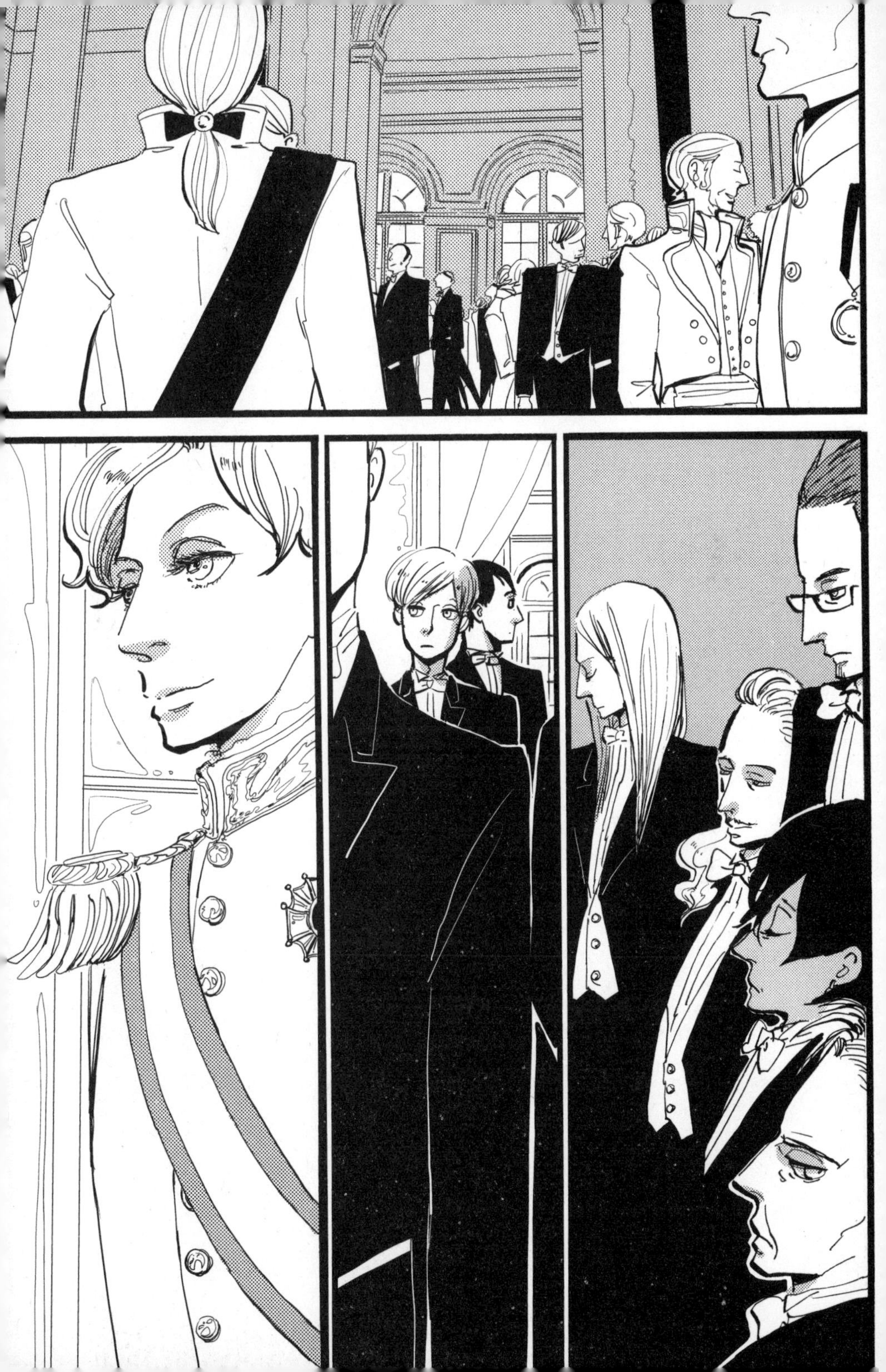

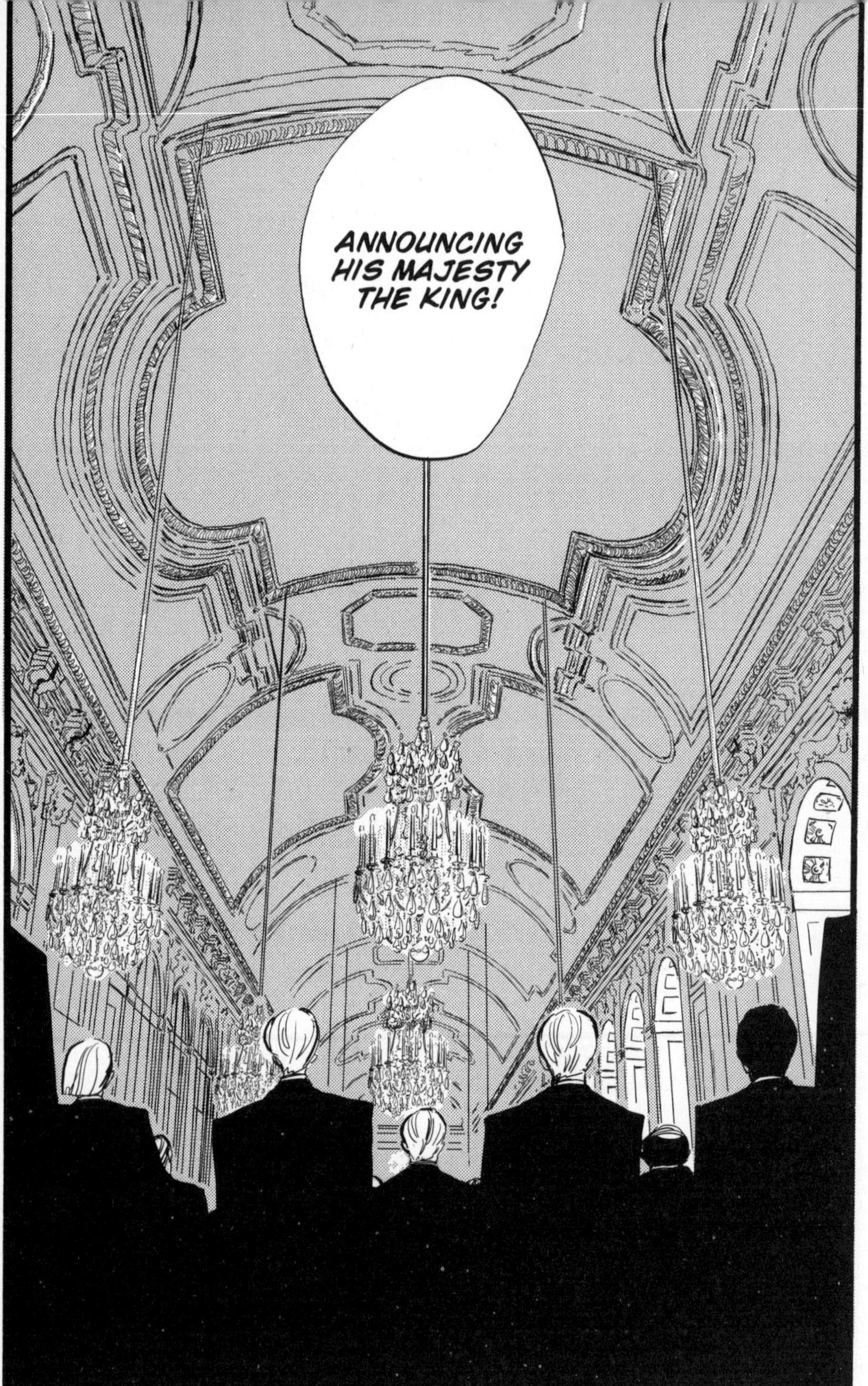
ANNOUNCING HIS MAJESTY THE KING!

ACCA Branch Uniforms 4

With its sabers and sashes, this uniform has a style approaching that of the Royal Guard, in consideration of the royal family, given that the agents are assigned to work in the royal capital.

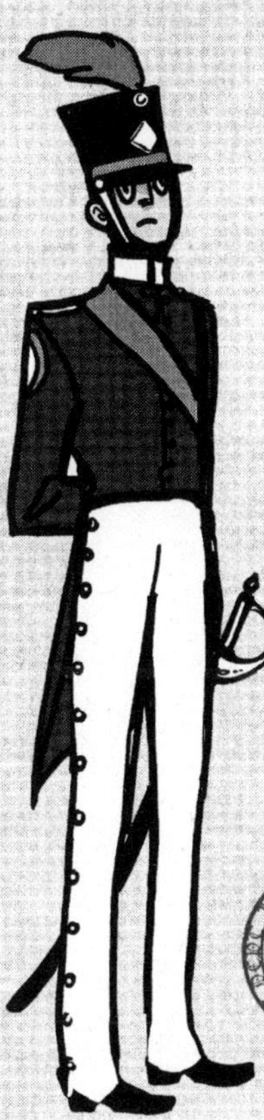

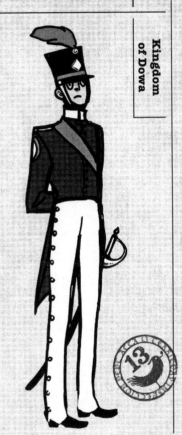

Kingdom of Dowa

CHAPTER 10

Observing the Smoke Trail in Dowa

PASS

INSPECTION DEPT ACCA 13 TERRITORY

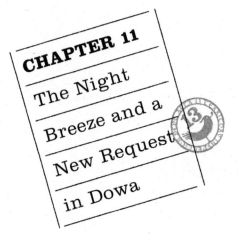

CHAPTER 11

The Night Breeze and a New Request in Dowa

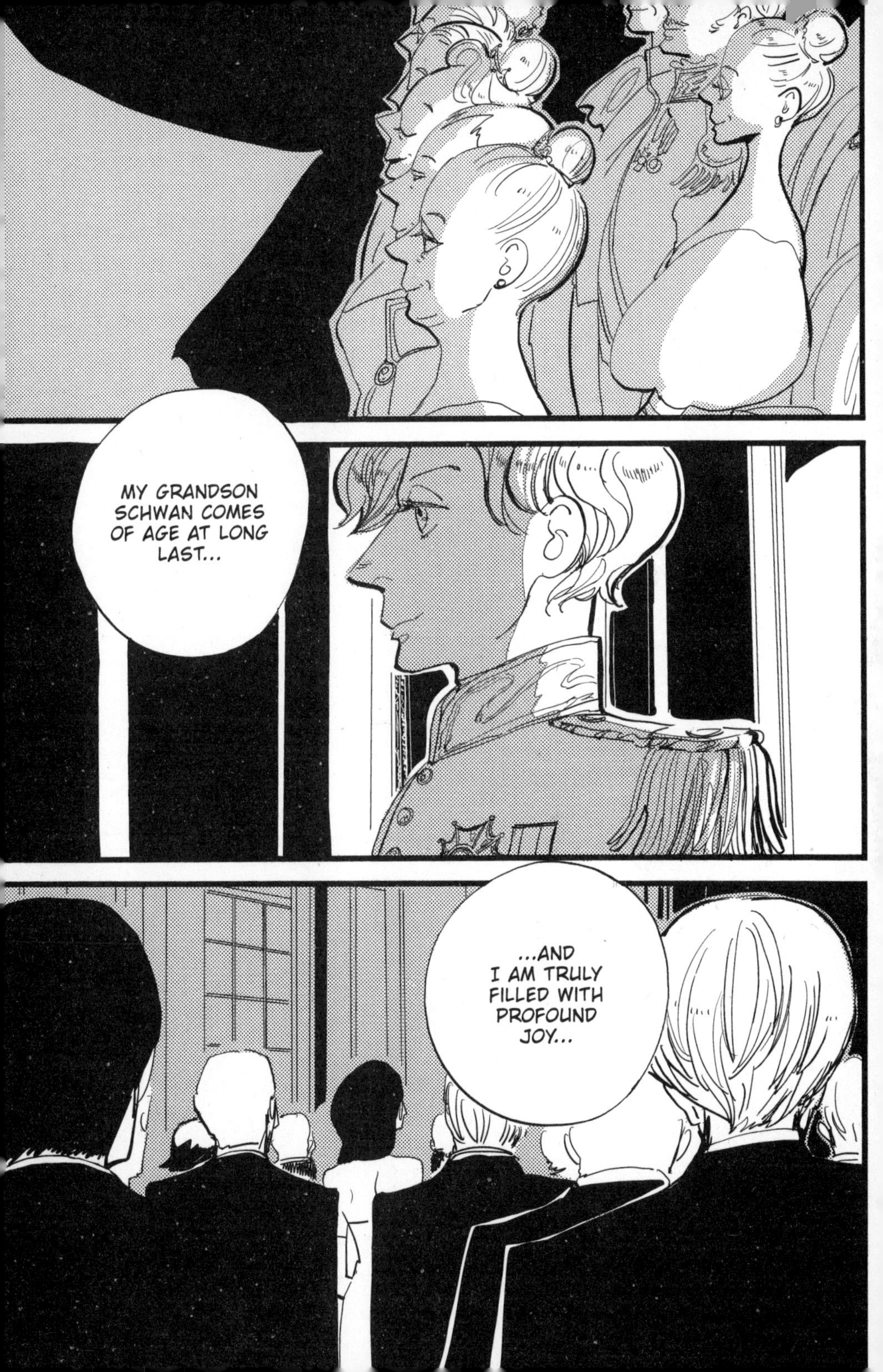
MY GRANDSON SCHWAN COMES OF AGE AT LONG LAST...
...AND I AM TRULY FILLED WITH PROFOUND JOY...

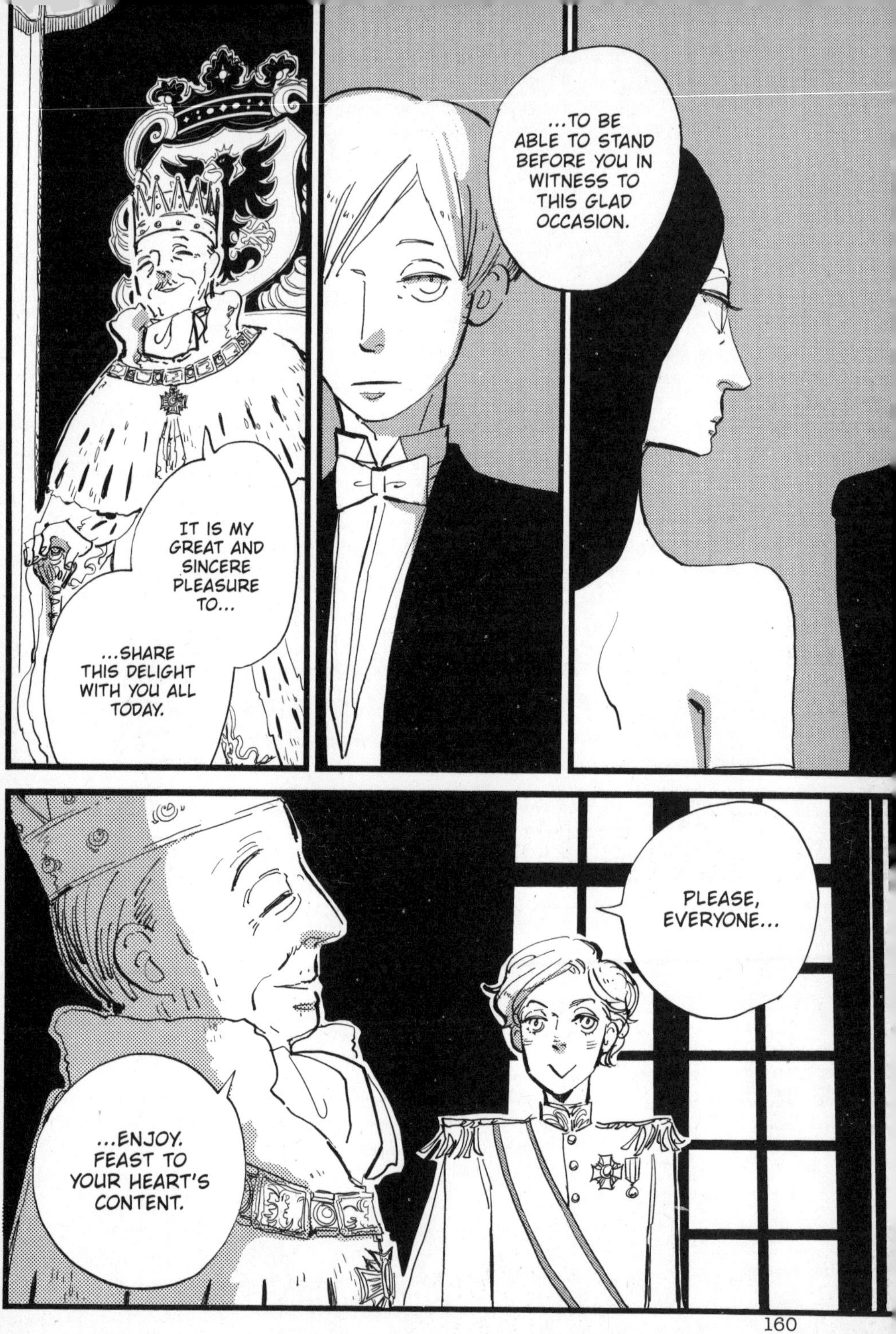
...TO BE ABLE TO STAND BEFORE YOU IN WITNESS TO THIS GLAD OCCASION.
IT IS MY GREAT AND SINCERE PLEASURE TO...
...SHARE THIS DELIGHT WITH YOU ALL TODAY.
PLEASE, EVERYONE...
...ENJOY. FEAST TO YOUR HEART'S CONTENT.

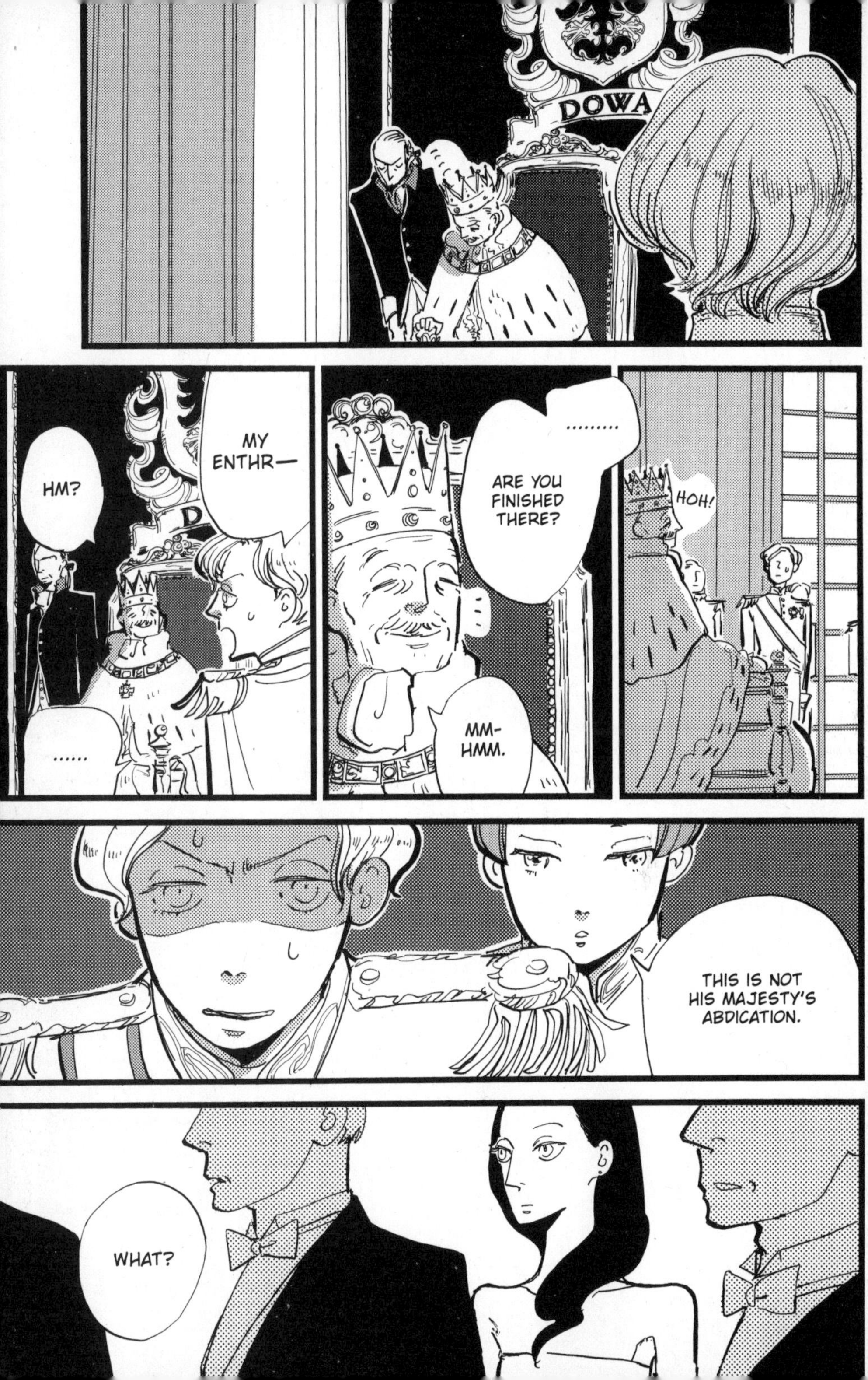
DOWA
HOH!
....
ARE YOU FINISHED THERE?
MM-HMM.
MY ENTHR—
HM?
......
THIS IS NOT HIS MAJESTY'S ABDICATION.
WHAT?

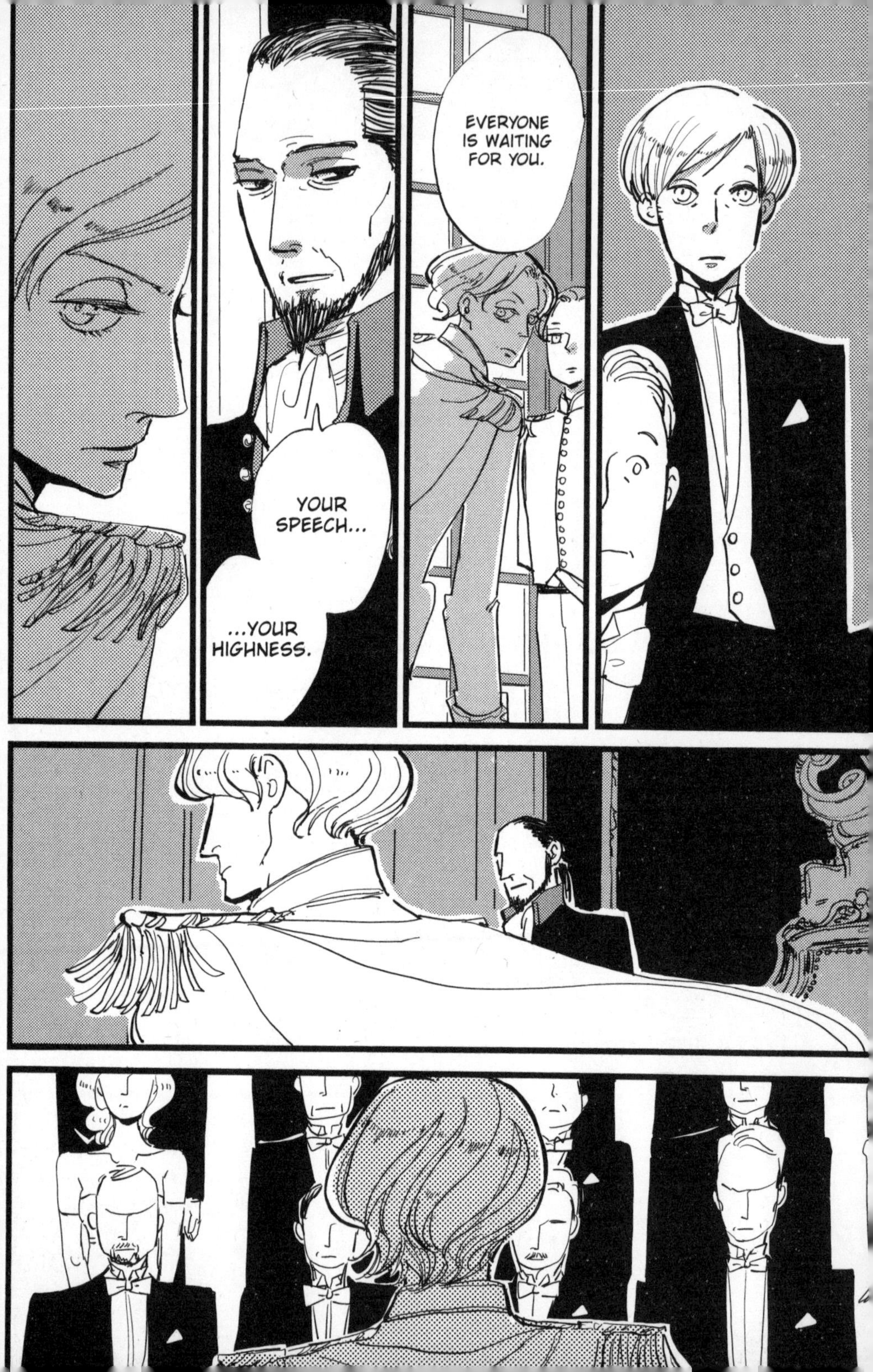
EVERYONE IS WAITING FOR YOU.
YOUR SPEECH...
...YOUR HIGHNESS.

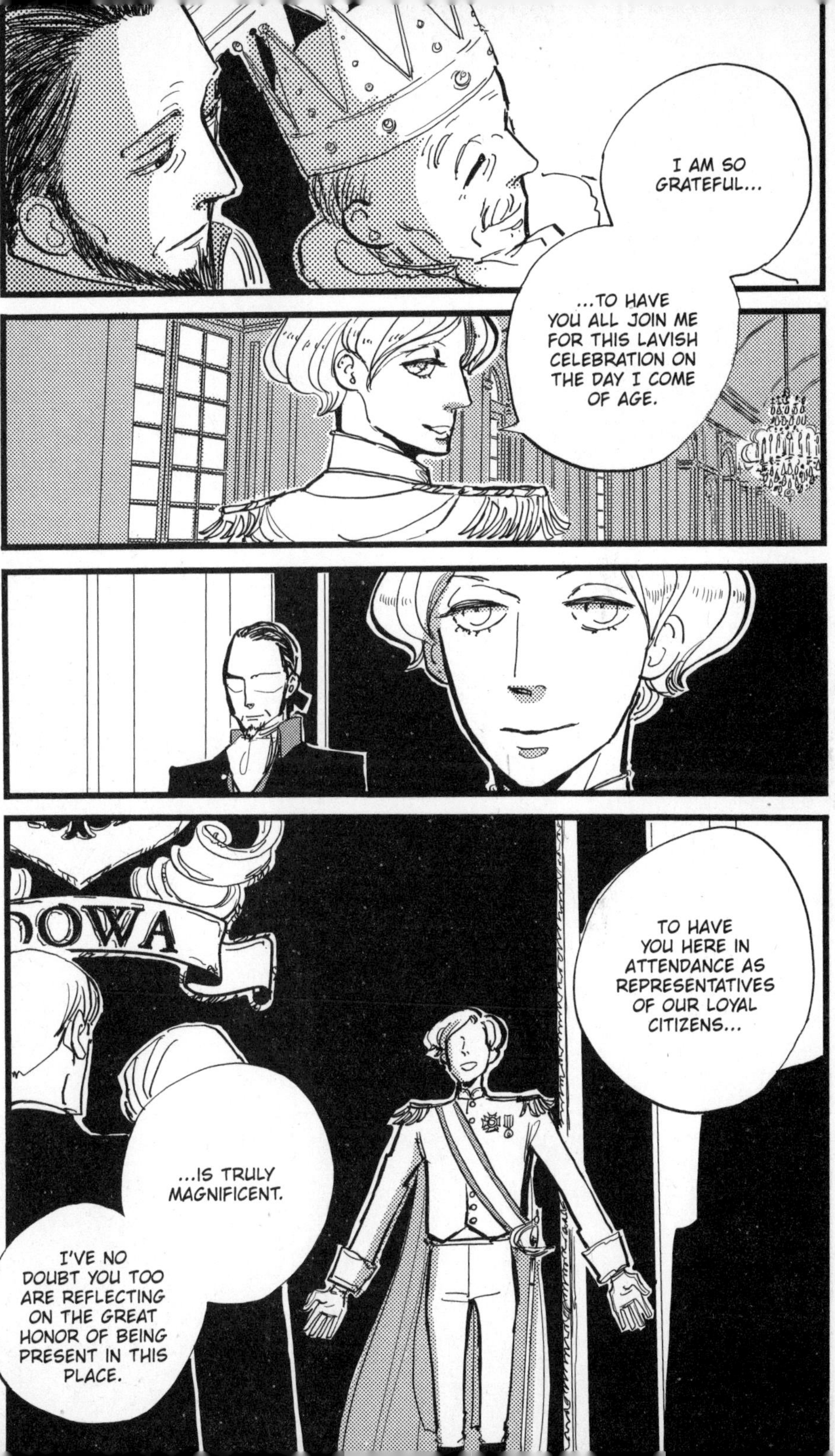
I AM SO GRATEFUL...
...TO HAVE YOU ALL JOIN ME FOR THIS LAVISH CELEBRATION ON THE DAY I COME OF AGE.
TO HAVE YOU HERE IN ATTENDANCE AS REPRESENTATIVES OF OUR LOYAL CITIZENS...
...IS TRULY MAGNIFICENT.
I'VE NO DOUBT YOU TOO ARE REFLECTING ON THE GREAT HONOR OF BEING PRESENT IN THIS PLACE.

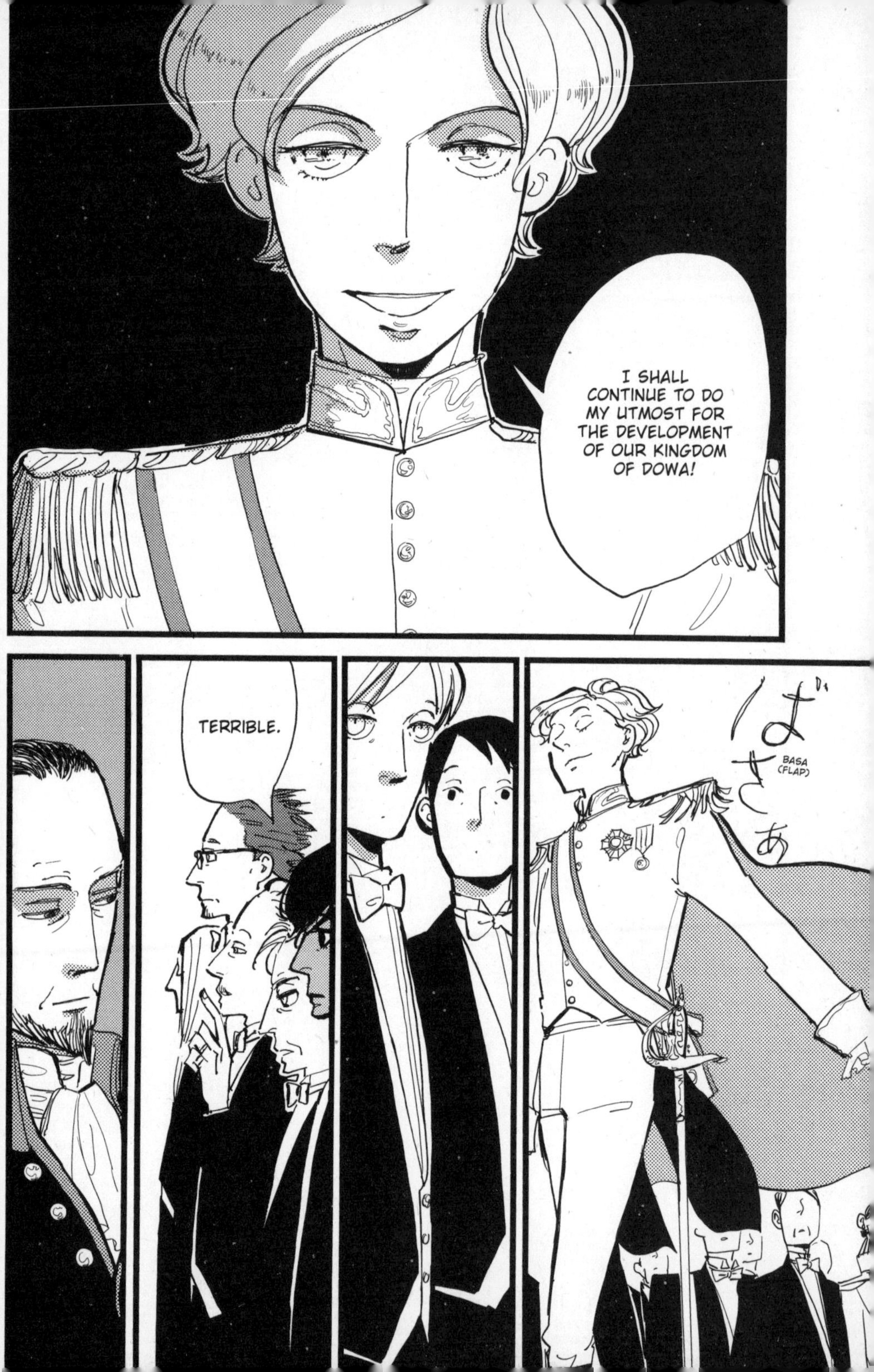
I SHALL CONTINUE TO DO MY UTMOST FOR THE DEVELOPMENT OF OUR KINGDOM OF DOWA!
ばさ
BASA (FLAP)
あ
TERRIBLE.

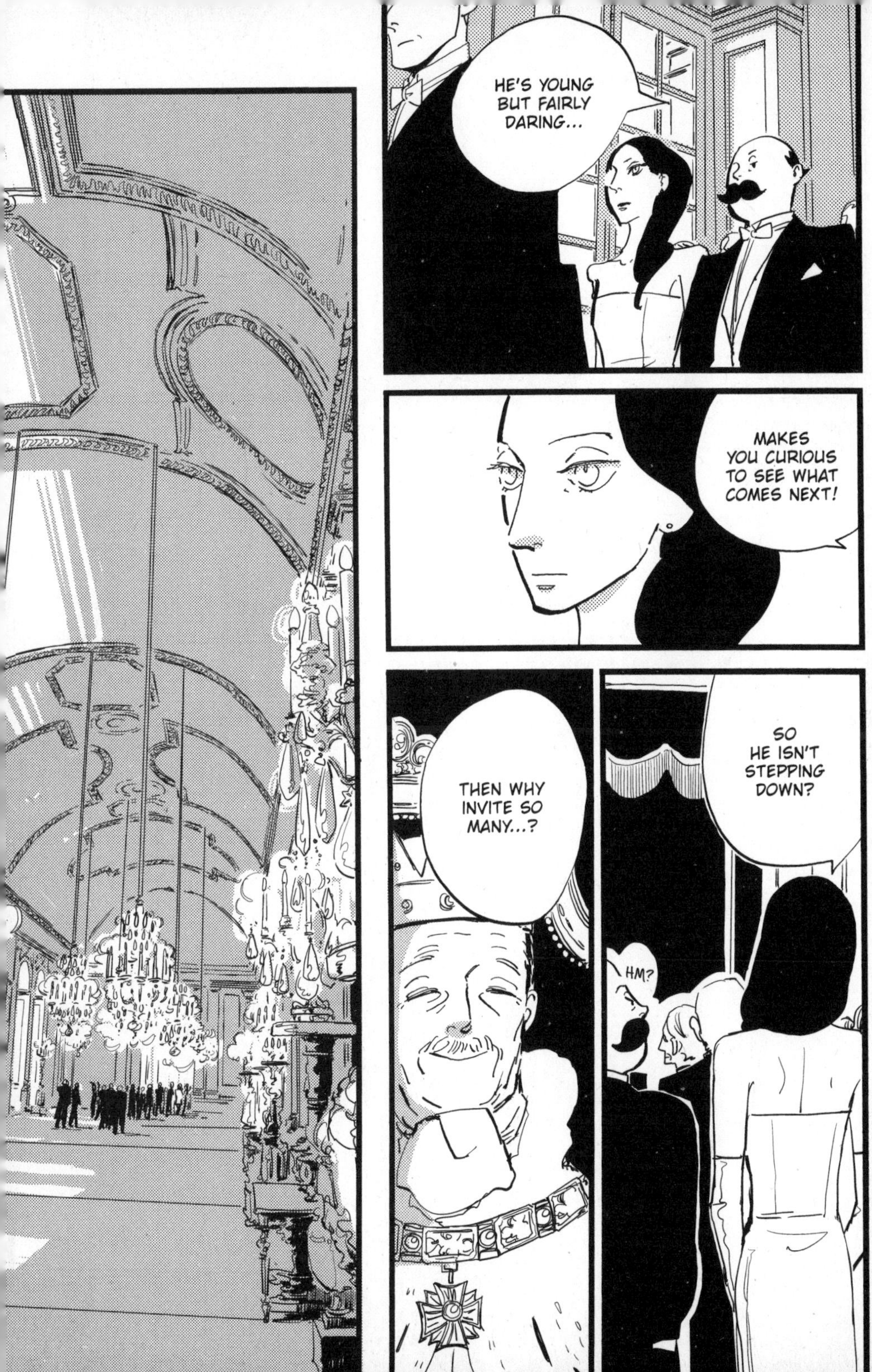
HE'S YOUNG BUT FAIRLY DARING...
MAKES YOU CURIOUS TO SEE WHAT COMES NEXT!
SO HE ISN'T STEPPING DOWN?
HM?
THEN WHY INVITE SO MANY...?

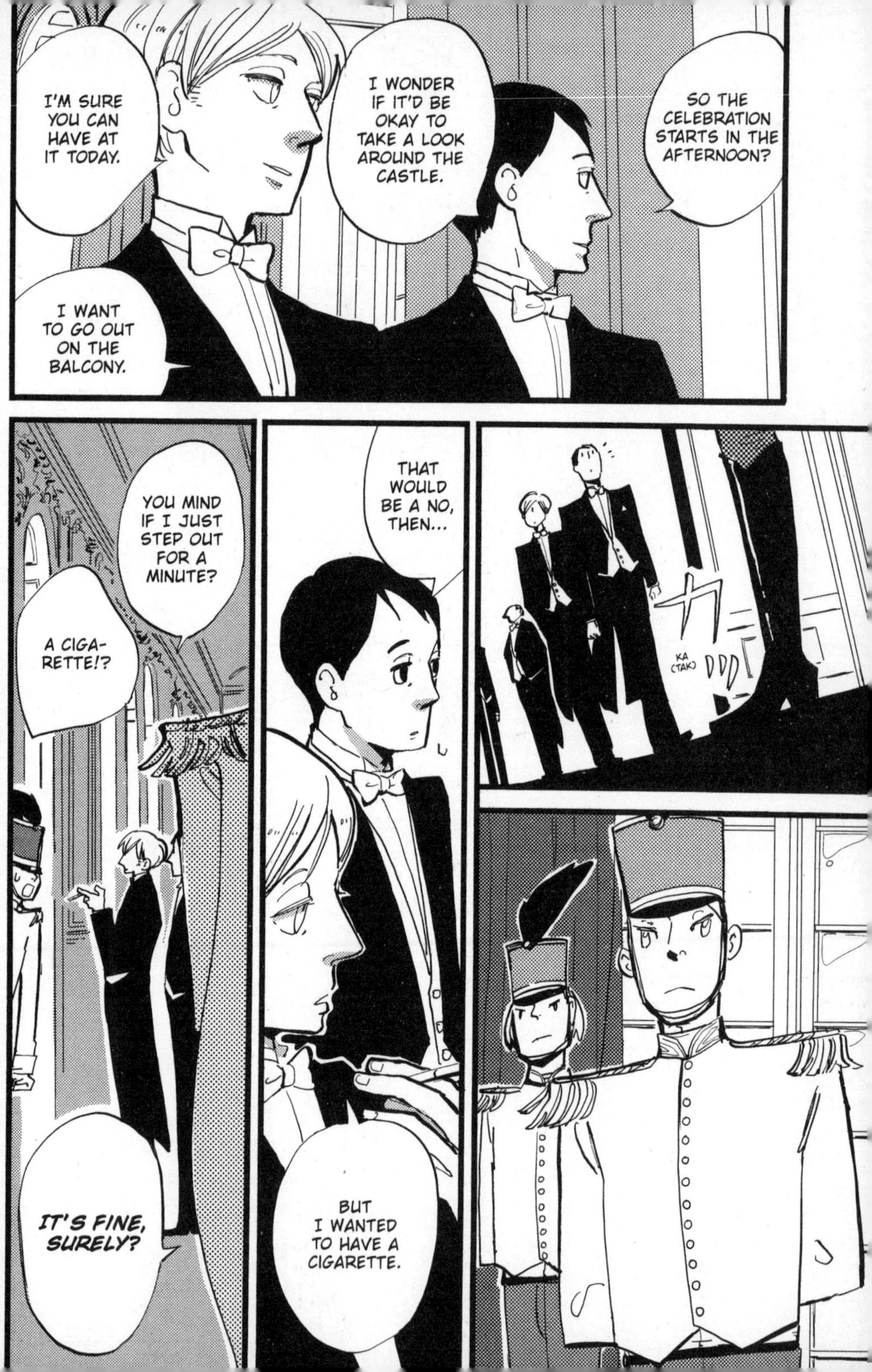
SO THE CELEBRATION STARTS IN THE AFTERNOON?
I WONDER IF IT'D BE OKAY TO TAKE A LOOK AROUND THE CASTLE.
I'M SURE YOU CAN HAVE AT IT TODAY.
I WANT TO GO OUT ON THE BALCONY.
カ
KA (TAK)
THAT WOULD BE A NO, THEN...
BUT I WANTED TO HAVE A CIGARETTE.
YOU MIND IF I JUST STEP OUT FOR A MINUTE?
A CIGARETTE!?
IT'S FINE, SURELY?

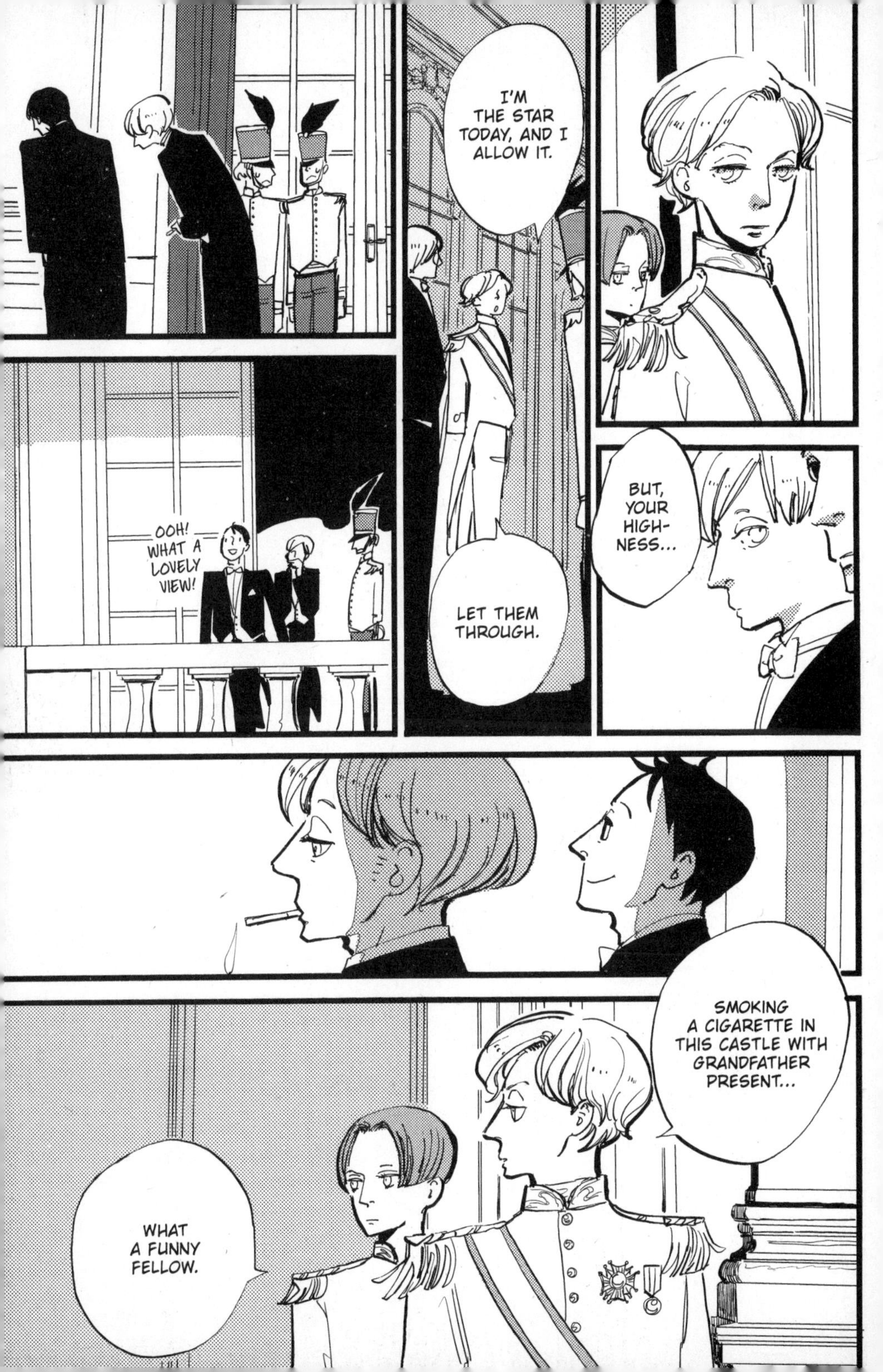
BUT, YOUR HIGHNESS...
I'M THE STAR TODAY, AND I ALLOW IT.
LET THEM THROUGH.
OOH! WHAT A LOVELY VIEW!
SMOKING A CIGARETTE IN THIS CASTLE WITH GRANDFATHER PRESENT...
WHAT A FUNNY FELLOW.

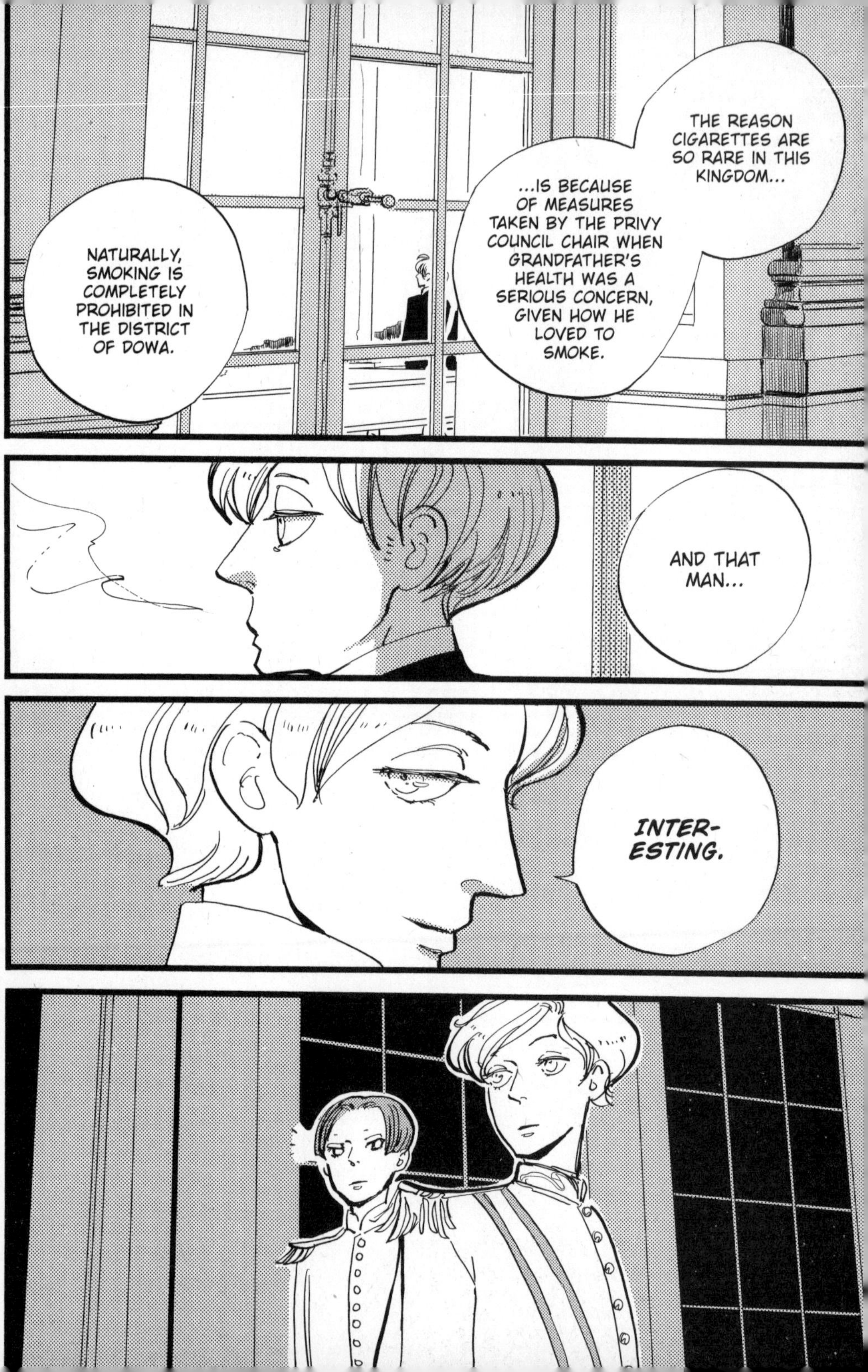
THE REASON CIGARETTES ARE SO RARE IN THIS KINGDOM...
...IS BECAUSE OF MEASURES TAKEN BY THE PRIVY COUNCIL CHAIR WHEN GRANDFATHER'S HEALTH WAS A SERIOUS CONCERN, GIVEN HOW HE LOVED TO SMOKE.
NATURALLY, SMOKING IS COMPLETELY PROHIBITED IN THE DISTRICT OF DOWA.
AND THAT MAN...
INTER- ESTING.

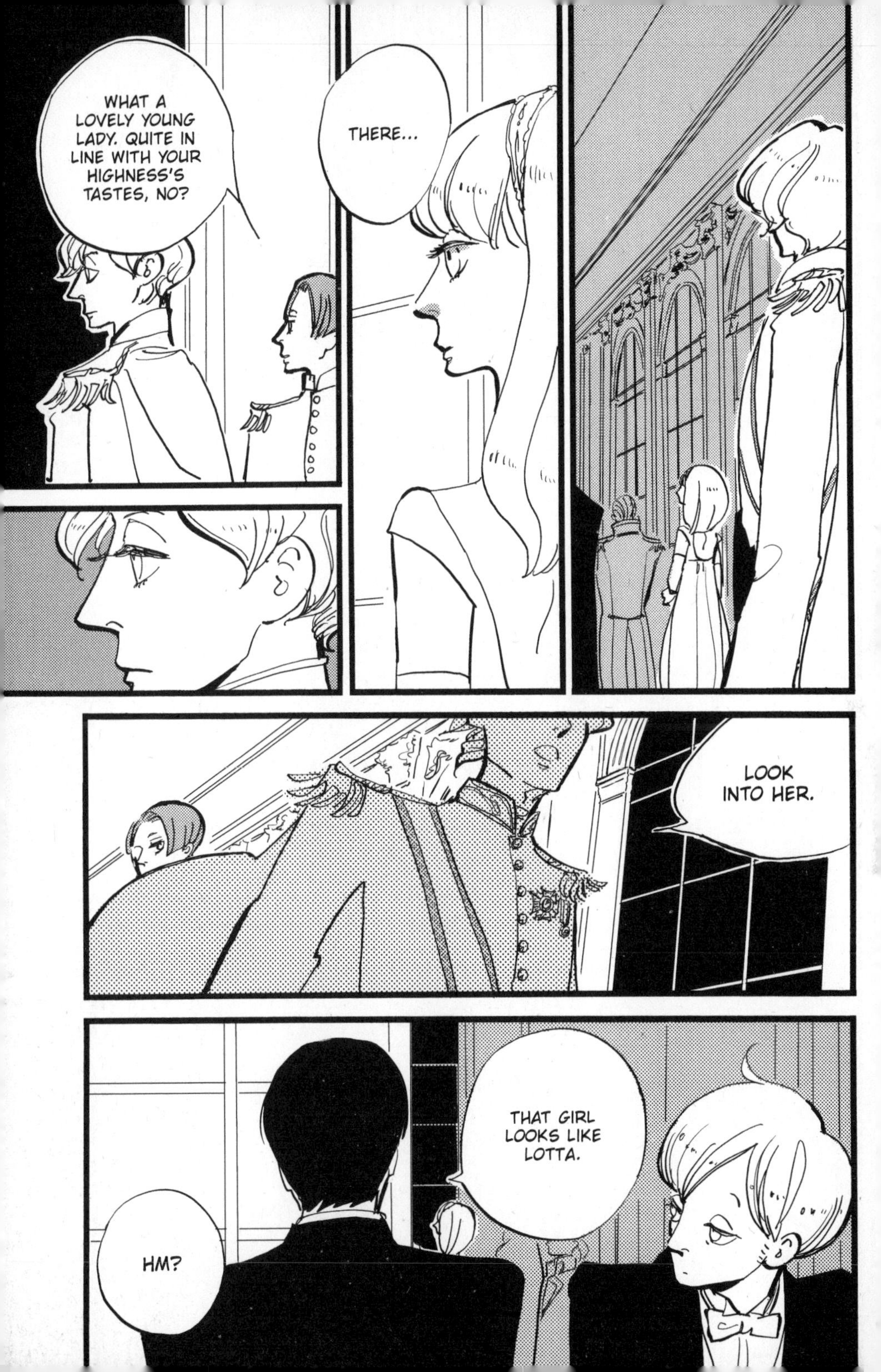
THERE...
WHAT A LOVELY YOUNG LADY. QUITE IN LINE WITH YOUR HIGHNESS'S TASTES, NO?
LOOK INTO HER.
THAT GIRL LOOKS LIKE LOTTA.
HM?

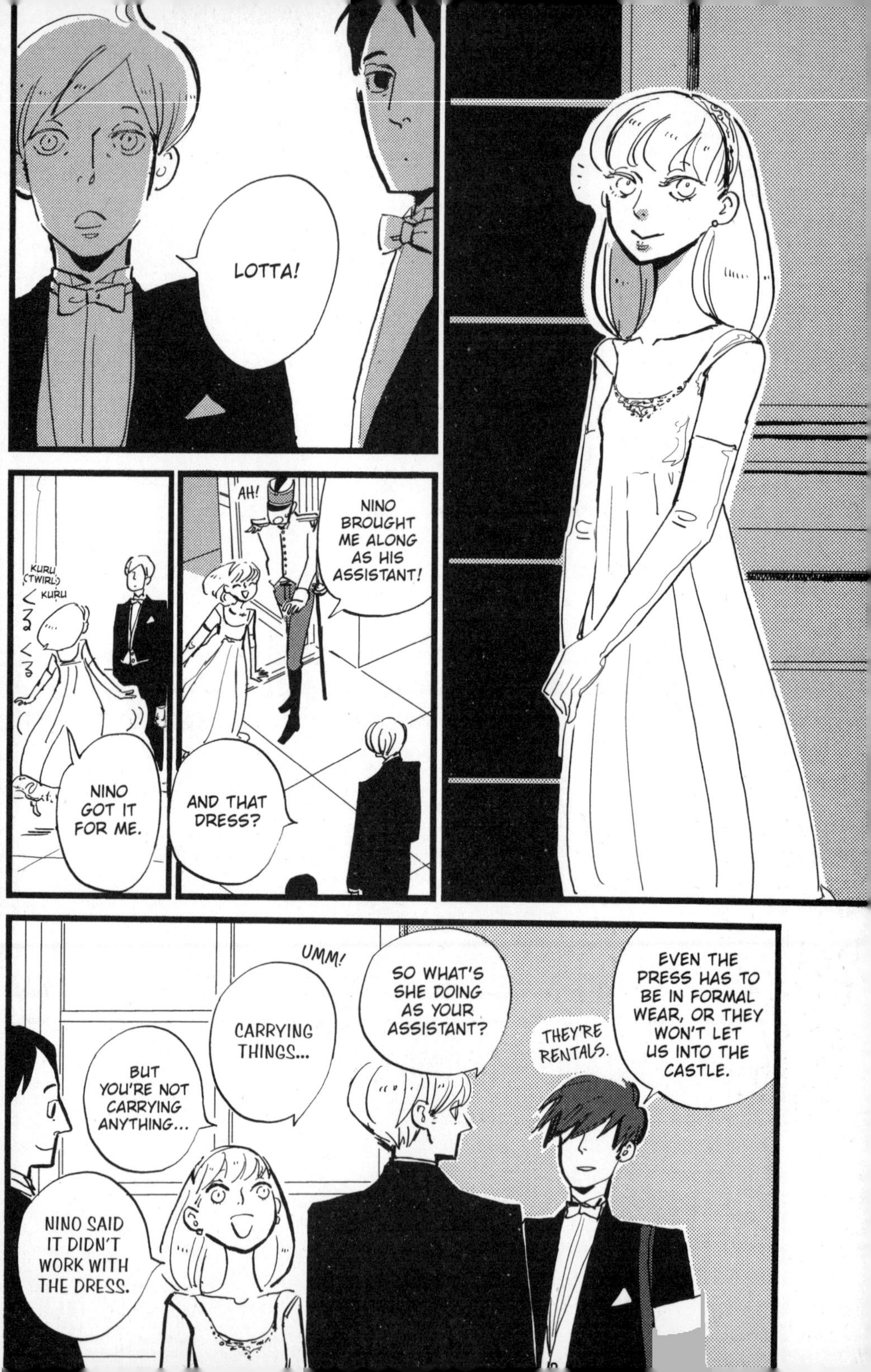
LOTTA!
AH!
NINO BROUGHT ME ALONG AS HIS ASSISTANT!
AND THAT DRESS?
KURU (TWIRL) KURU
くるくる
NINO GOT IT FOR ME.
EVEN THE PRESS HAS TO BE IN FORMAL WEAR, OR THEY WON'T LET US INTO THE CASTLE.
THEY'RE RENTALS.
SO WHAT'S SHE DOING AS YOUR ASSISTANT?
UMM!
CARRYING THINGS...
BUT YOU'RE NOT CARRYING ANYTHING...
NINO SAID IT DIDN'T WORK WITH THE DRESS.

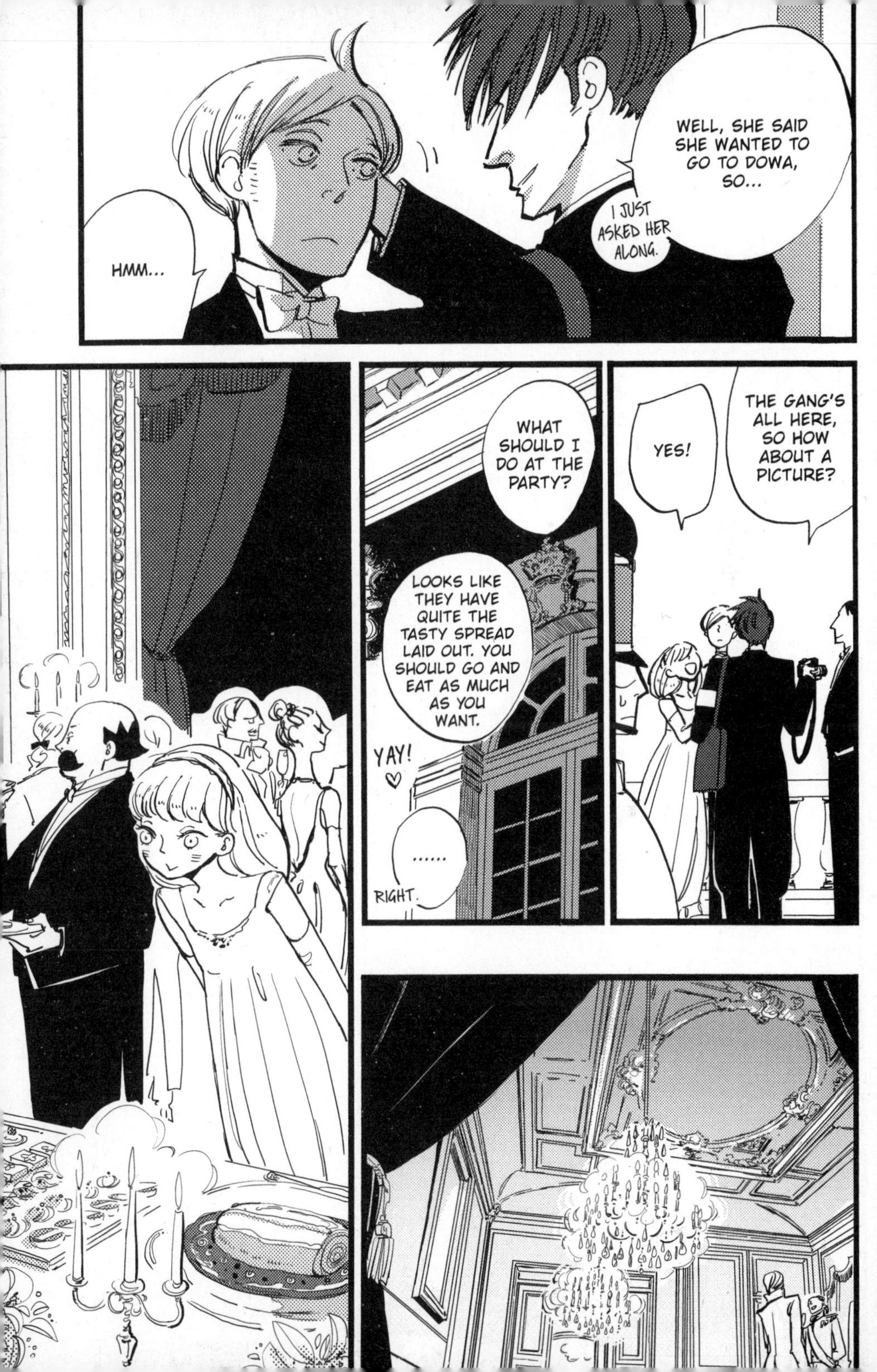
WELL, SHE SAID SHE WANTED TO GO TO DOWA, SO...
I JUST ASKED HER ALONG.
HMM...
THE GANG'S ALL HERE, SO HOW ABOUT A PICTURE?
YES!
WHAT SHOULD I DO AT THE PARTY?
LOOKS LIKE THEY HAVE QUITE THE TASTY SPREAD LAID OUT. YOU SHOULD GO AND EAT AS MUCH AS YOU WANT.
YAY! ♥
......
RIGHT.

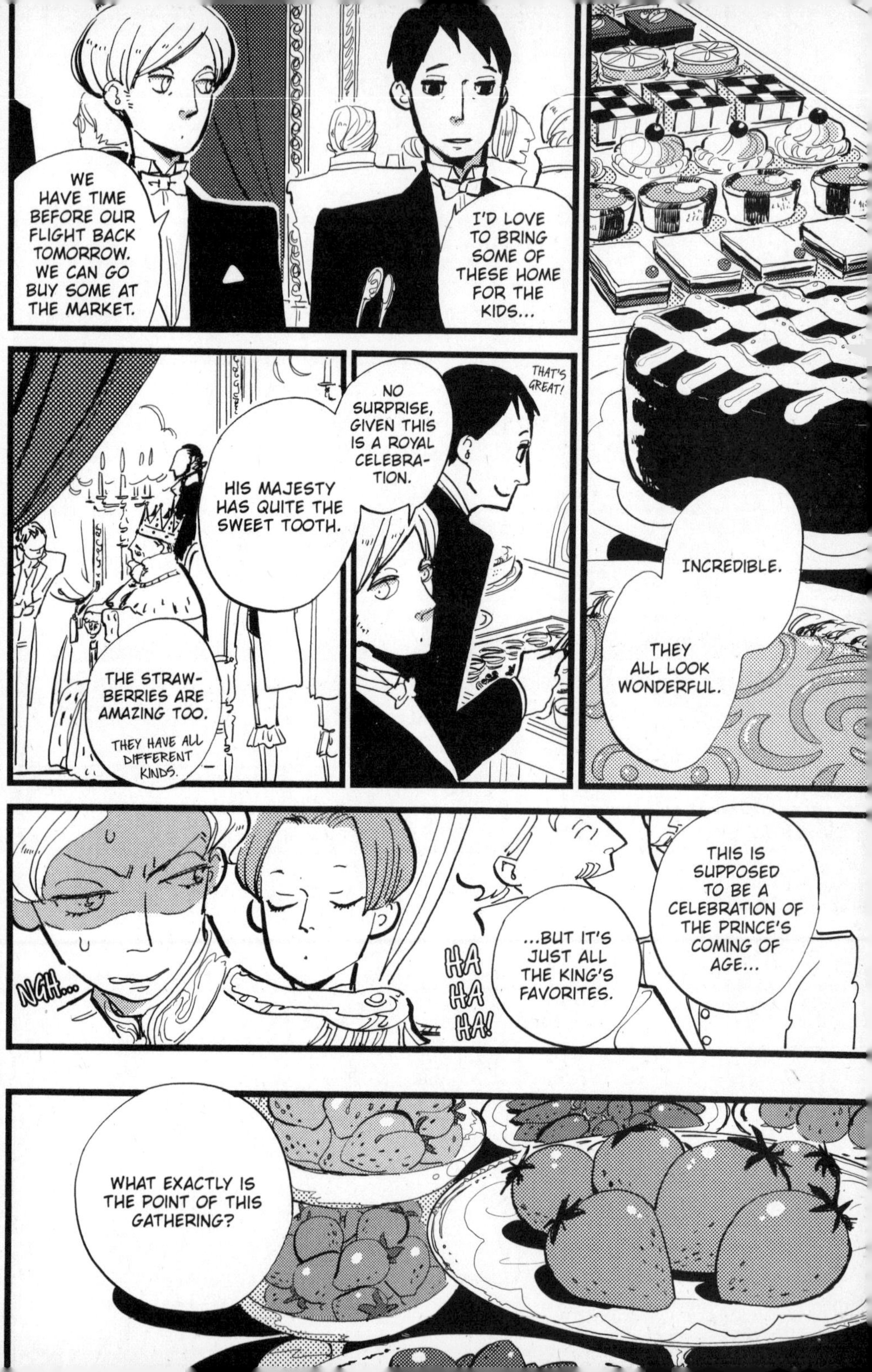
INCREDIBLE.
THEY ALL LOOK WONDERFUL.
I'D LOVE TO BRING SOME OF THESE HOME FOR THE KIDS...
WE HAVE TIME BEFORE OUR FLIGHT BACK TOMORROW. WE CAN GO BUY SOME AT THE MARKET.
THAT'S GREAT!
NO SURPRISE, GIVEN THIS IS A ROYAL CELEBRATION.
HIS MAJESTY HAS QUITE THE SWEET TOOTH.
THE STRAWBERRIES ARE AMAZING TOO.
THEY HAVE ALL DIFFERENT KINDS.
THIS IS SUPPOSED TO BE A CELEBRATION OF THE PRINCE'S COMING OF AGE...
...BUT IT'S JUST ALL THE KING'S FAVORITES.
HA HA HA!
NGH...
WHAT EXACTLY IS THE POINT OF THIS GATHERING?

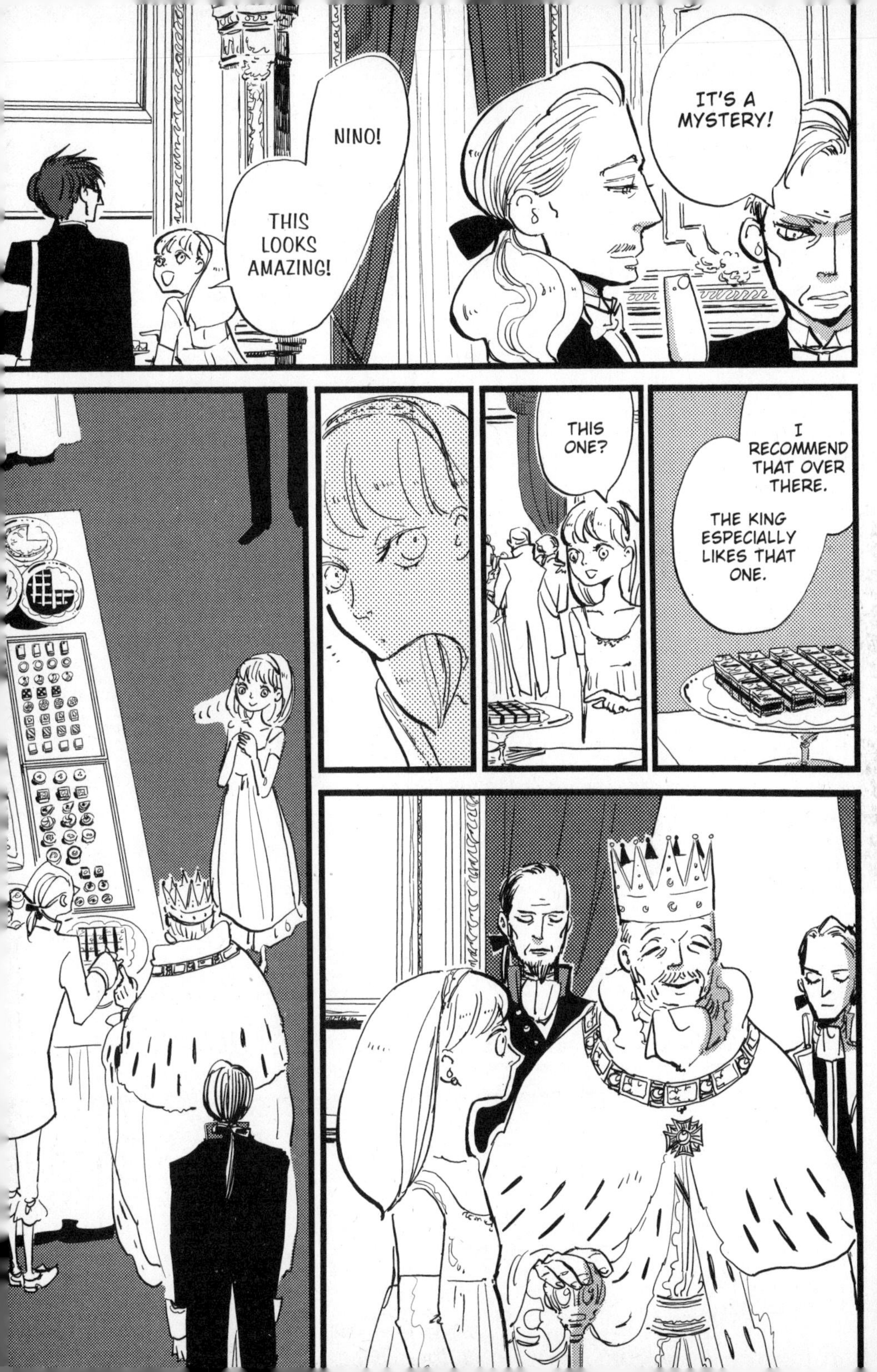
IT'S A MYSTERY!
NINO!
THIS LOOKS AMAZING!
I RECOMMEND THAT OVER THERE.
THE KING ESPECIALLY LIKES THAT ONE.
THIS ONE?

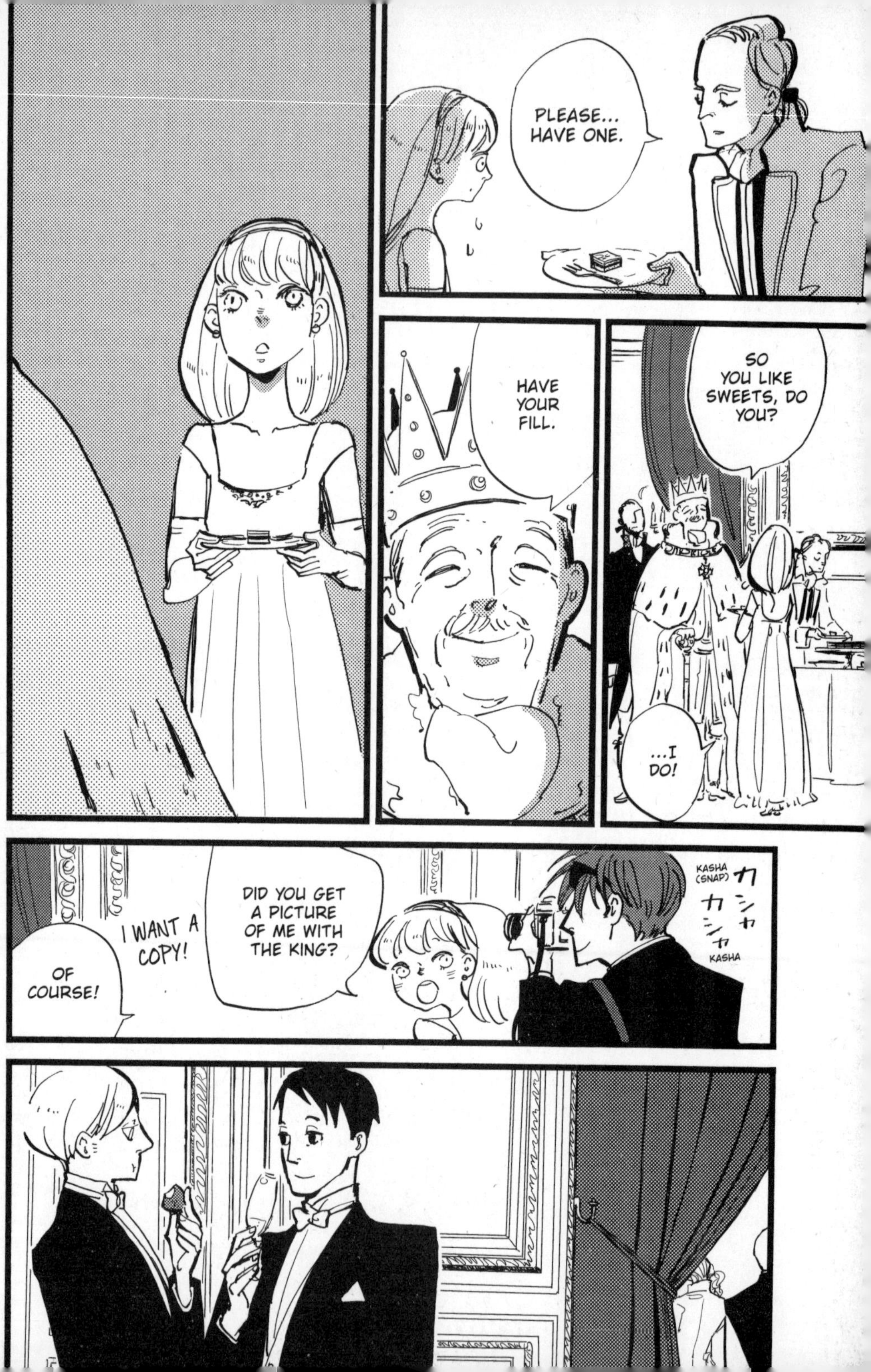
PLEASE... HAVE ONE.
SO YOU LIKE SWEETS, DO YOU?
...I DO!
HAVE YOUR FILL.
KASHA (SNAP)
カシャ
カシャ
KASHA
DID YOU GET A PICTURE OF ME WITH THE KING?
I WANT A COPY!
OF COURSE!

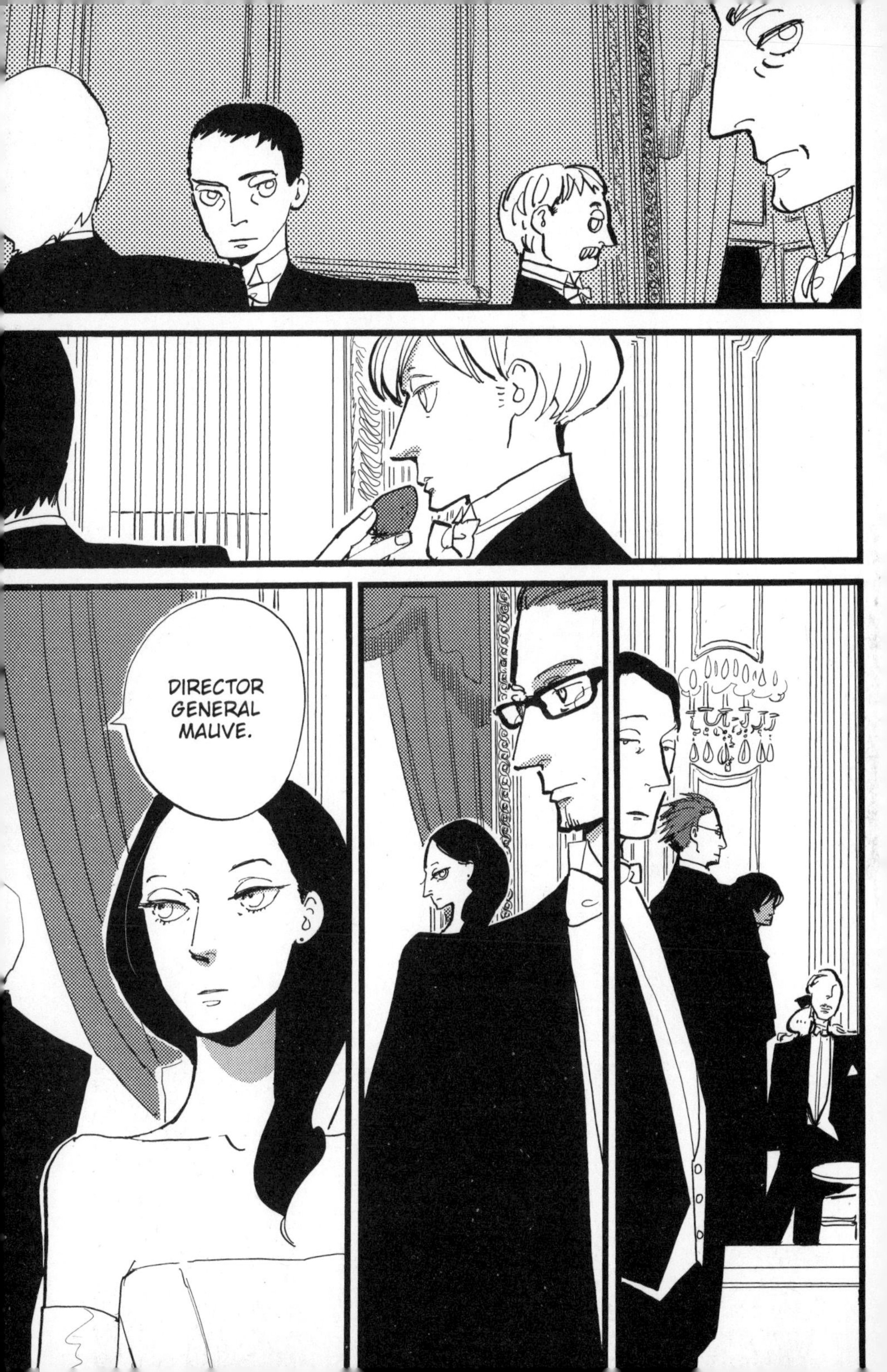
DIRECTOR GENERAL MAUVE.

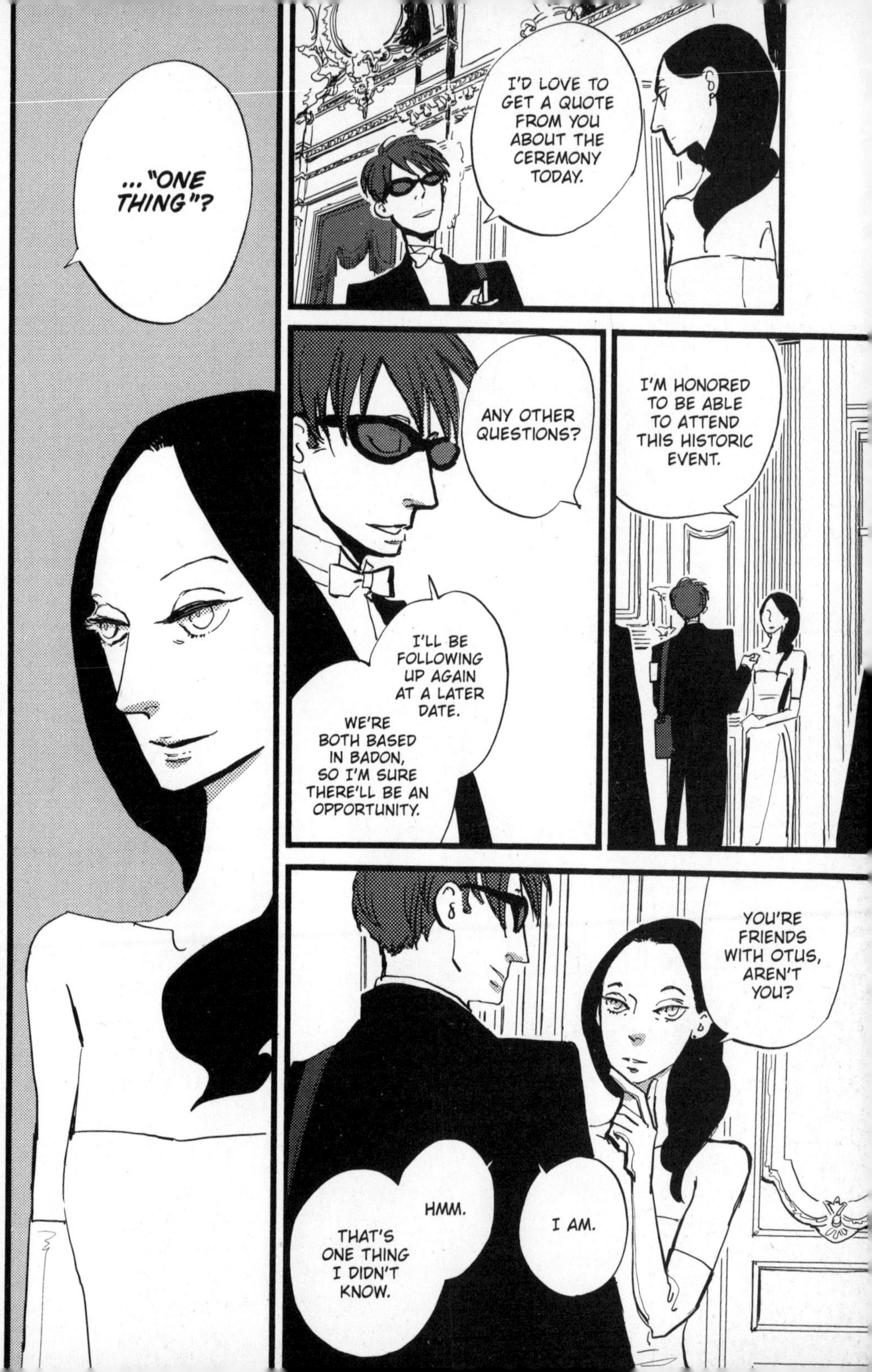
I'D LOVE TO GET A QUOTE FROM YOU ABOUT THE CEREMONY TODAY.
I'M HONORED TO BE ABLE TO ATTEND THIS HISTORIC EVENT.
ANY OTHER QUESTIONS?
I'LL BE FOLLOWING UP AGAIN AT A LATER DATE.
WE'RE BOTH BASED IN BADON, SO I'M SURE THERE'LL BE AN OPPORTUNITY.
YOU'RE FRIENDS WITH OTUS, AREN'T YOU?
I AM.
HMM.
THAT'S ONE THING I DIDN'T KNOW.
..."ONE THING"?

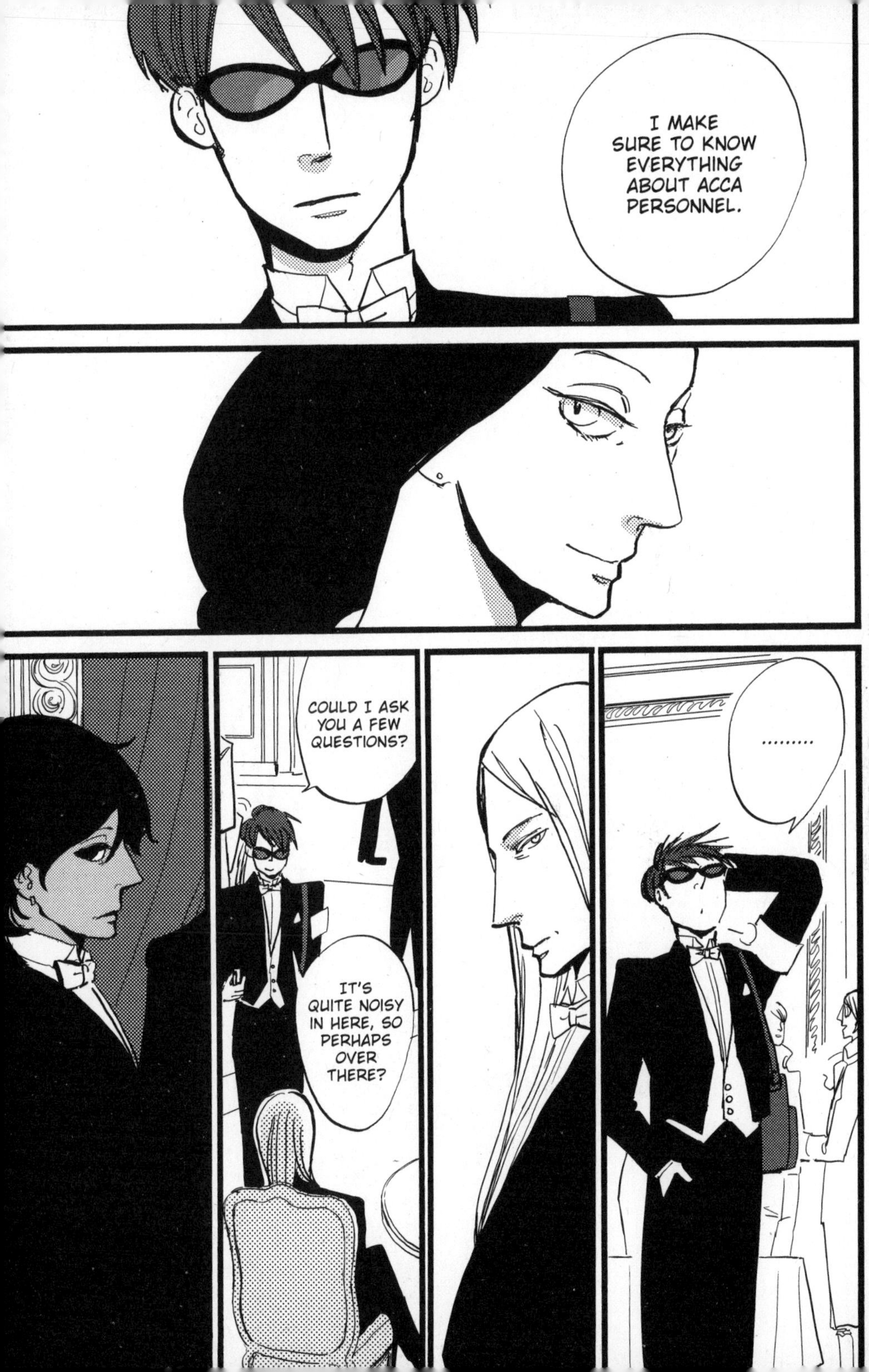
I MAKE SURE TO KNOW EVERYTHING ABOUT ACCA PERSONNEL.
....
COULD I ASK YOU A FEW QUESTIONS?
IT'S QUITE NOISY IN HERE, SO PERHAPS OVER THERE?

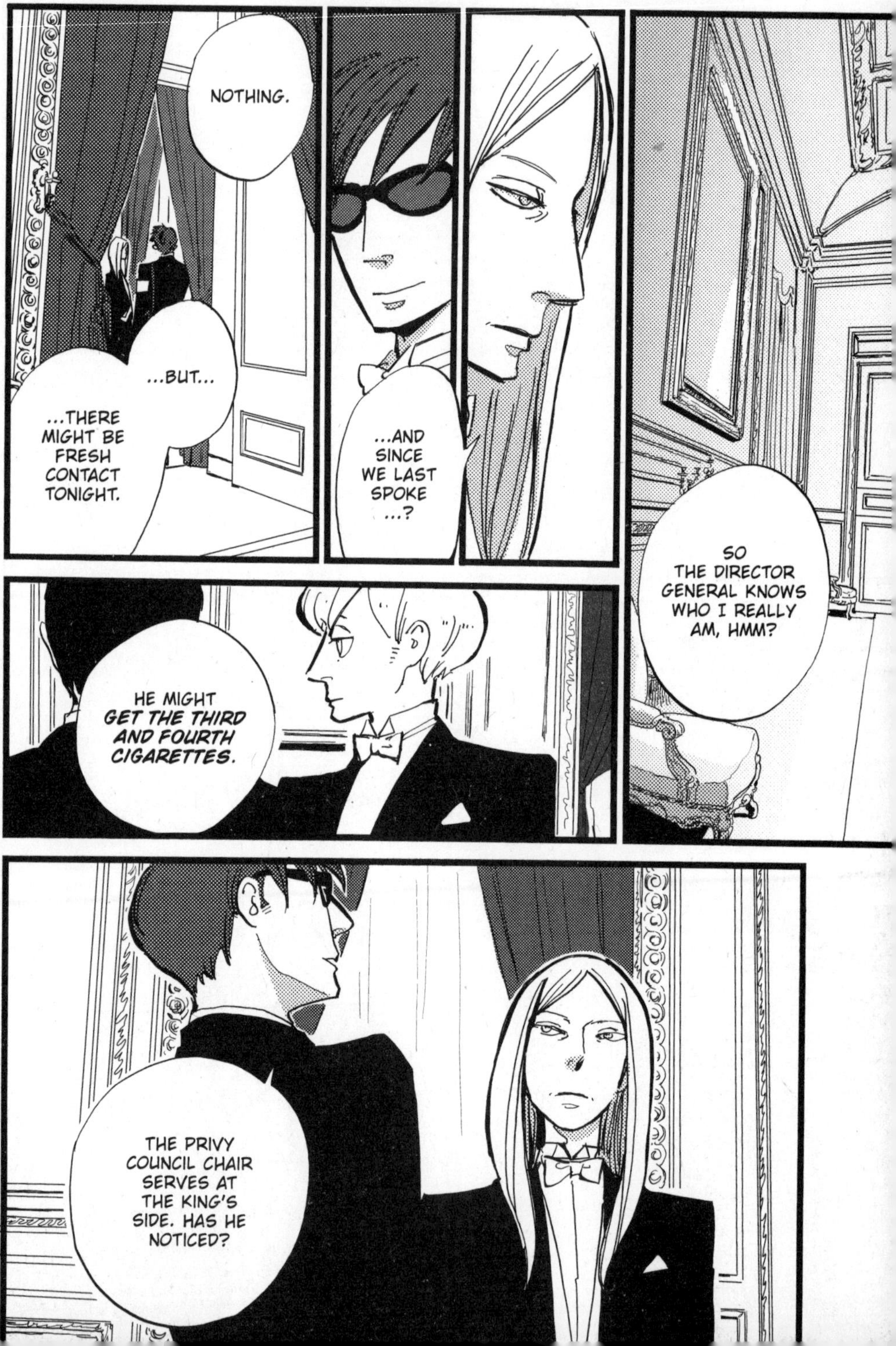

SO THE DIRECTOR GENERAL KNOWS WHO I REALLY AM, HMM?
...AND SINCE WE LAST SPOKE ...?
NOTHING.
...BUT...
...THERE MIGHT BE FRESH CONTACT TONIGHT.
HE MIGHT ***GET THE THIRD AND FOURTH CIGARETTES.***
THE PRIVY COUNCIL CHAIR SERVES AT THE KING'S SIDE. HAS HE NOTICED?

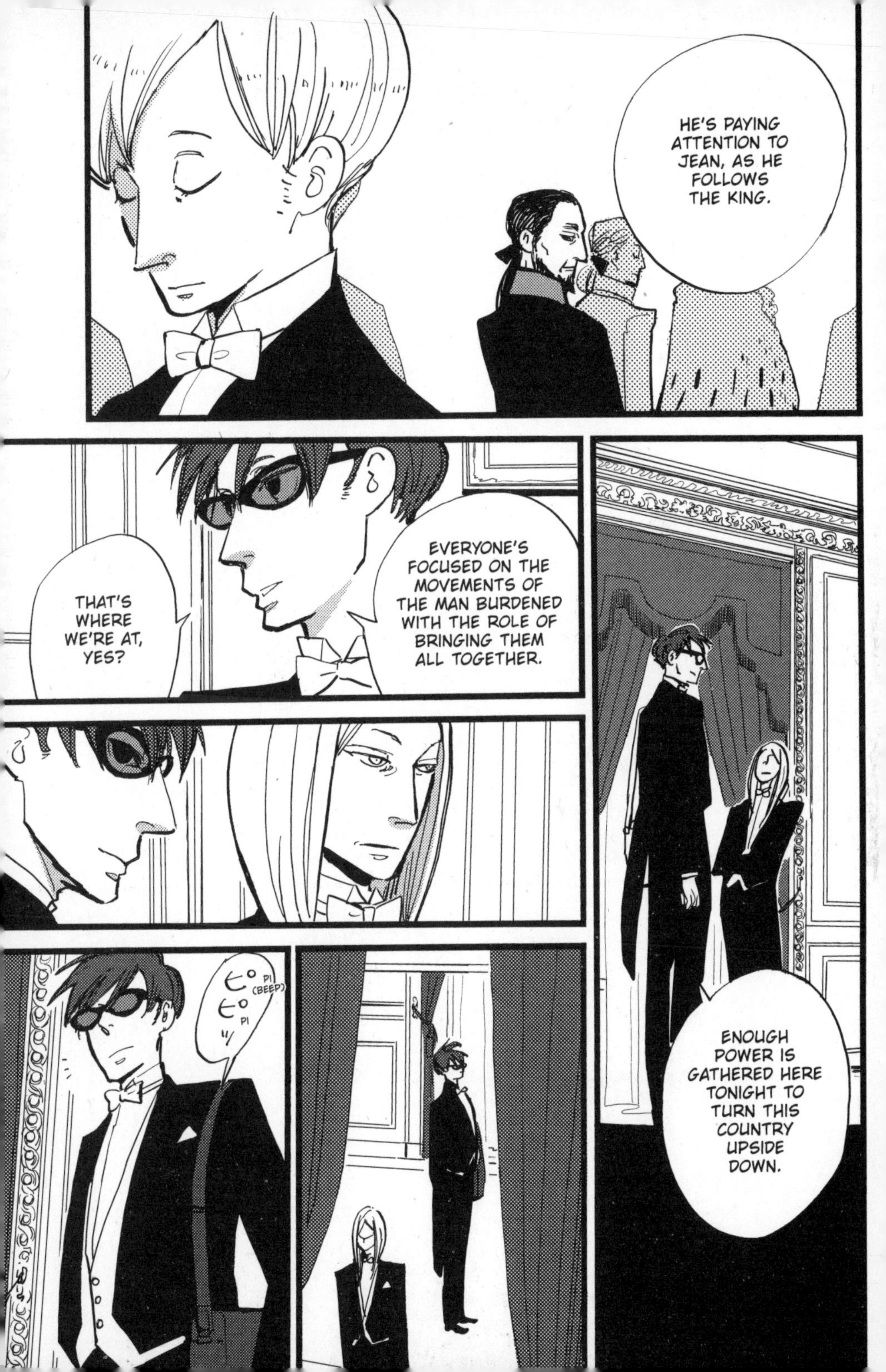
HE'S PAYING ATTENTION TO JEAN, AS HE FOLLOWS THE KING.
ENOUGH POWER IS GATHERED HERE TONIGHT TO TURN THIS COUNTRY UPSIDE DOWN.
EVERYONE'S FOCUSED ON THE MOVEMENTS OF THE MAN BURDENED WITH THE ROLE OF BRINGING THEM ALL TOGETHER.
THAT'S WHERE WE'RE AT, YES?
ピ PI (BEEP)
ピ PI

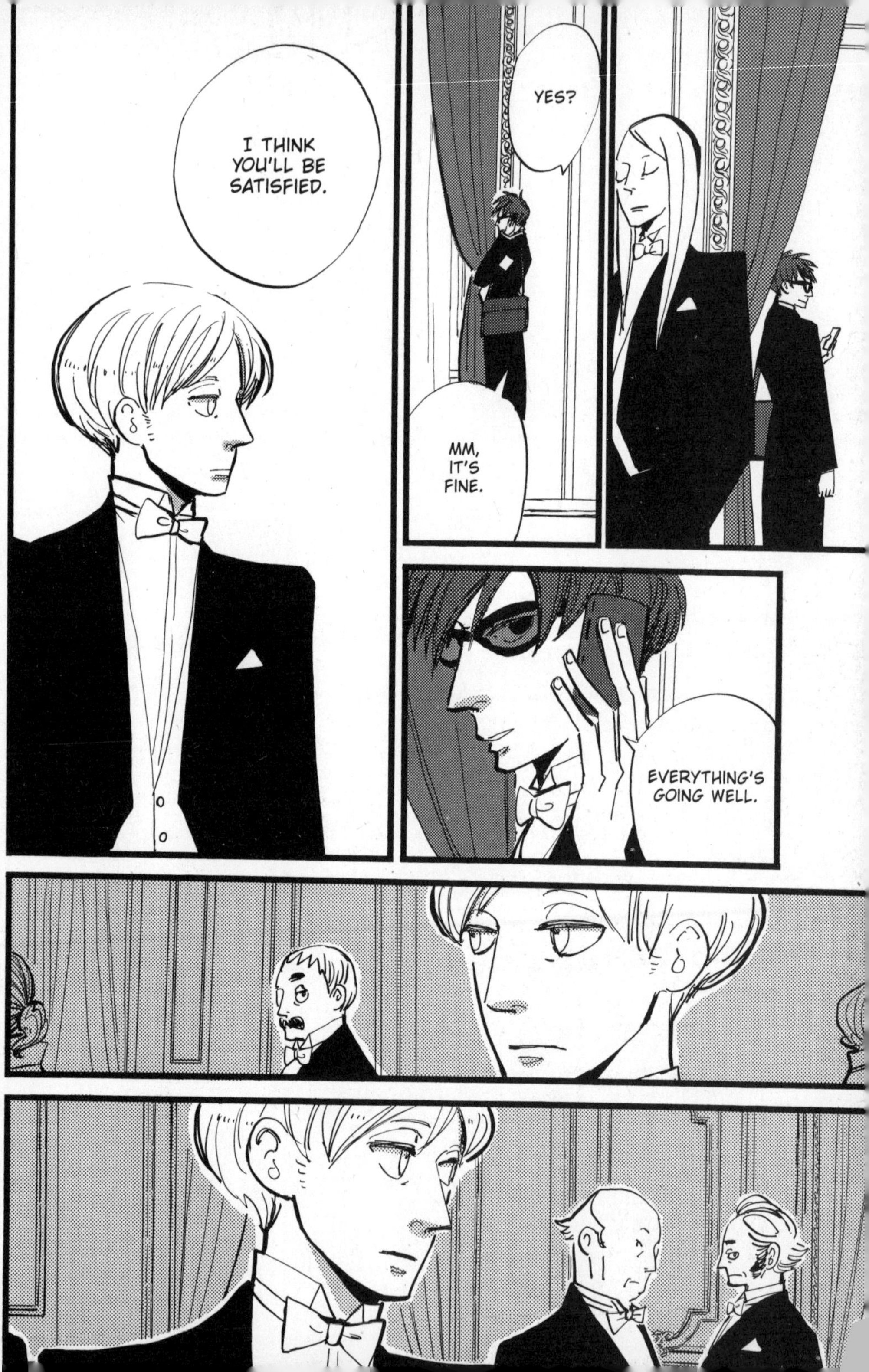
YES?
MM, IT'S FINE.
EVERYTHING'S GOING WELL.
I THINK YOU'LL BE SATISFIED.

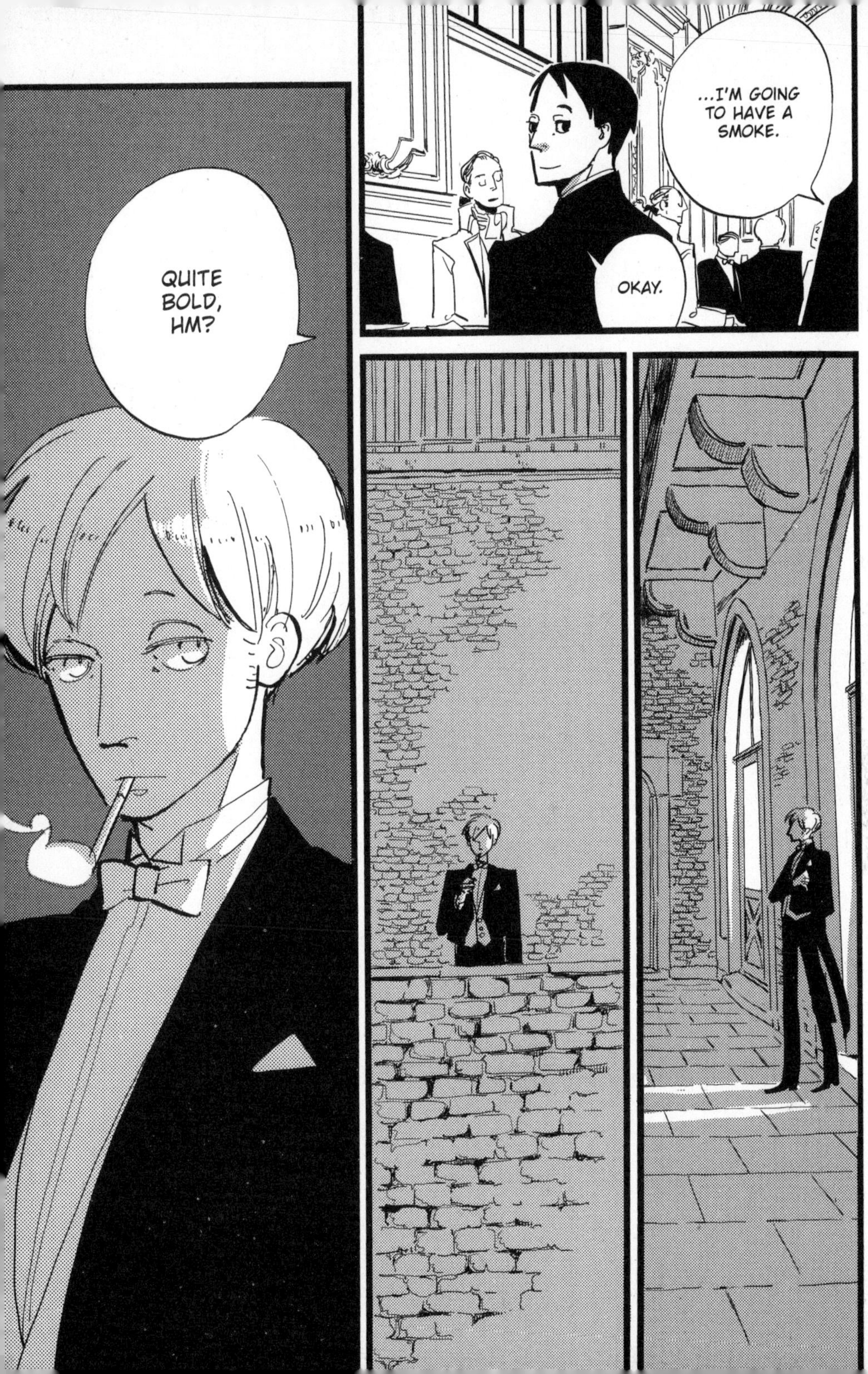
...I'M GOING TO HAVE A SMOKE.
OKAY.
QUITE BOLD, HM?

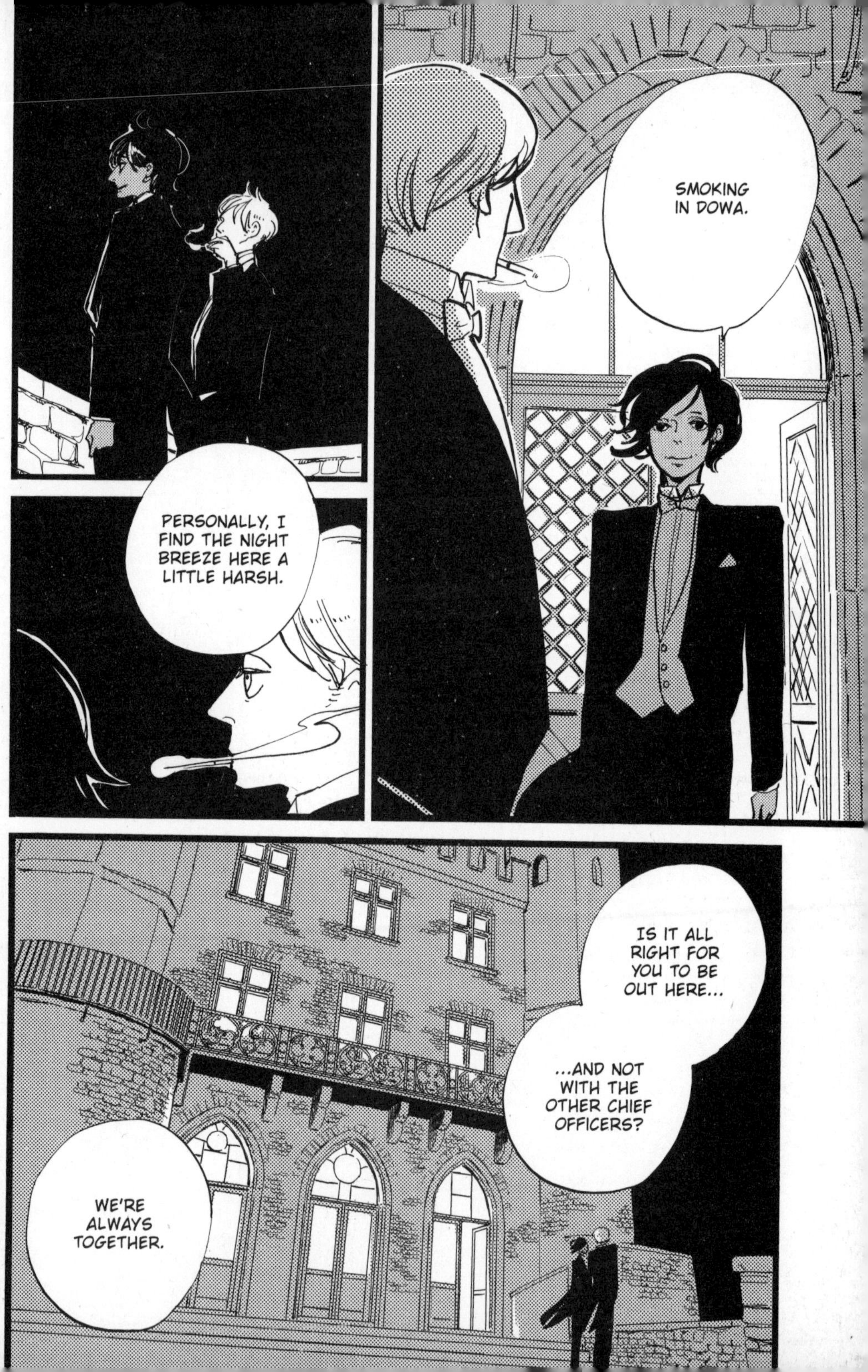
SMOKING IN DOWA.
PERSONALLY, I FIND THE NIGHT BREEZE HERE A LITTLE HARSH.
IS IT ALL RIGHT FOR YOU TO BE OUT HERE...
...AND NOT WITH THE OTHER CHIEF OFFICERS?
WE'RE ALWAYS TOGETHER.

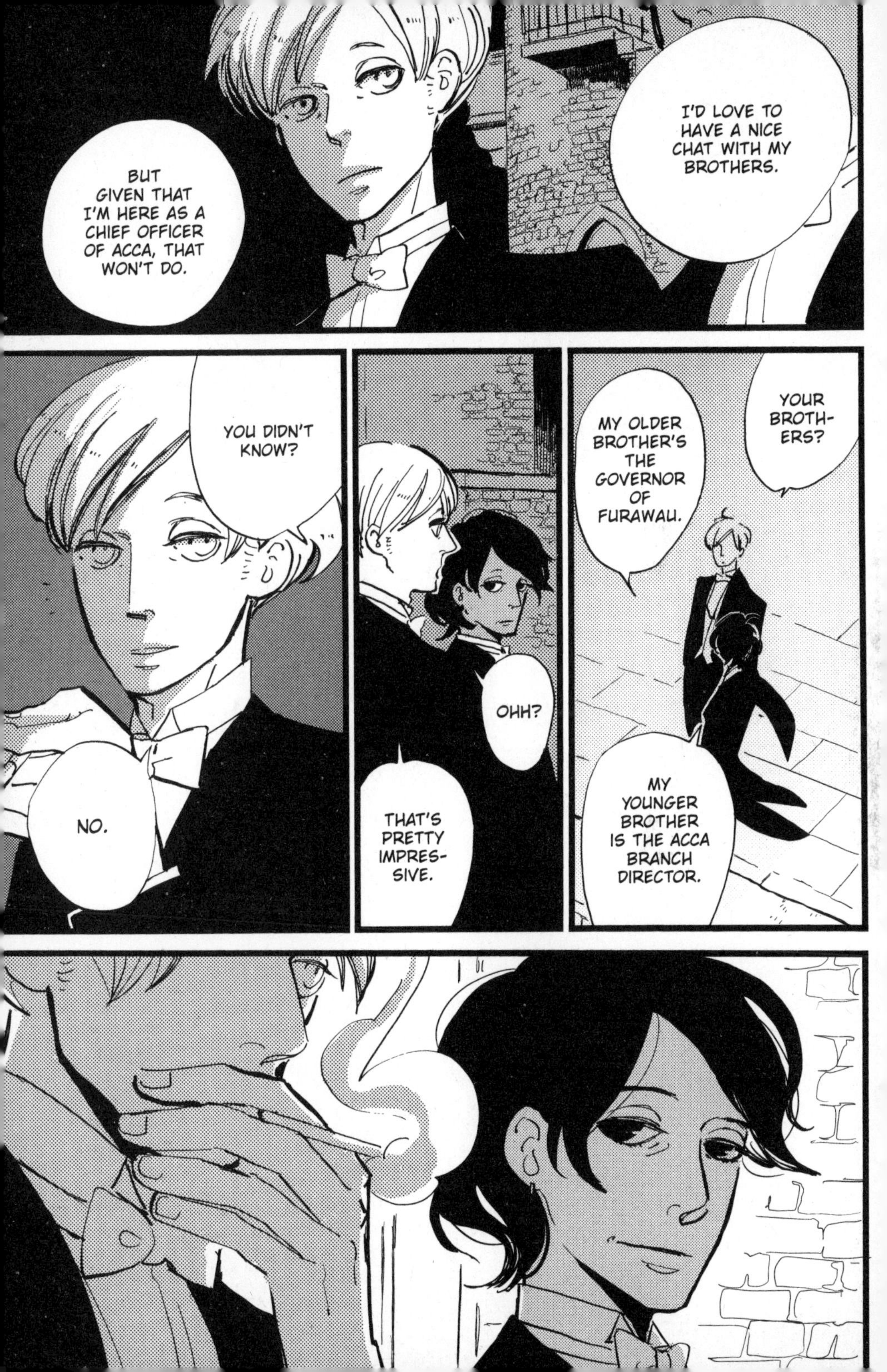
I'D LOVE TO HAVE A NICE CHAT WITH MY BROTHERS.
BUT GIVEN THAT I'M HERE AS A CHIEF OFFICER OF ACCA, THAT WON'T DO.
YOUR BROTHERS?
MY OLDER BROTHER'S THE GOVERNOR OF FURAWAU.
MY YOUNGER BROTHER IS THE ACCA BRANCH DIRECTOR.
OHH?
THAT'S PRETTY IMPRES-SIVE.
YOU DIDN'T KNOW?
NO.

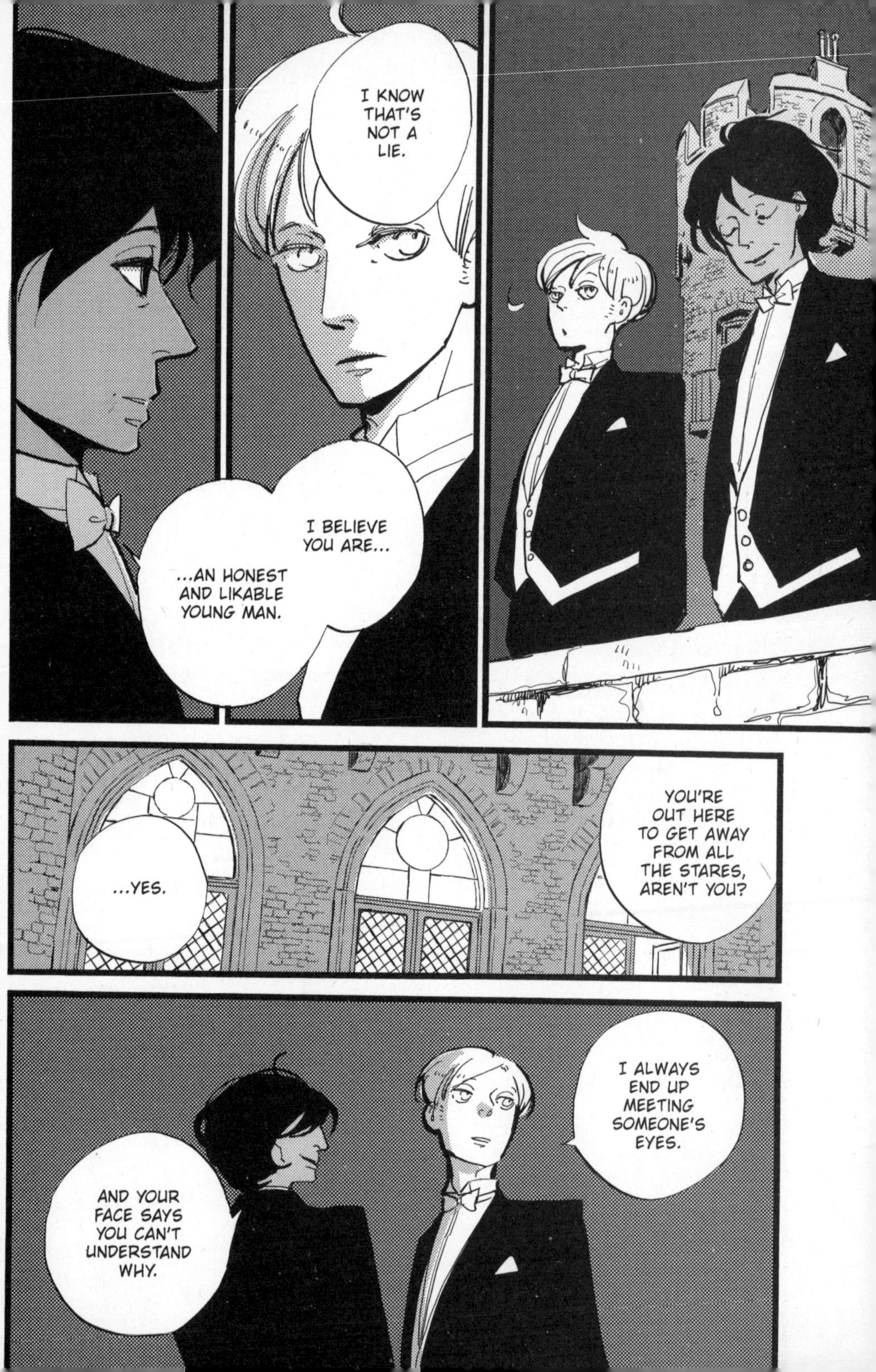
I KNOW THAT'S NOT A LIE.
I BELIEVE YOU ARE...
...AN HONEST AND LIKABLE YOUNG MAN.
YOU'RE OUT HERE TO GET AWAY FROM ALL THE STARES, AREN'T YOU?
...YES.
I ALWAYS END UP MEETING SOMEONE'S EYES.
AND YOUR FACE SAYS YOU CAN'T UNDERSTAND WHY.

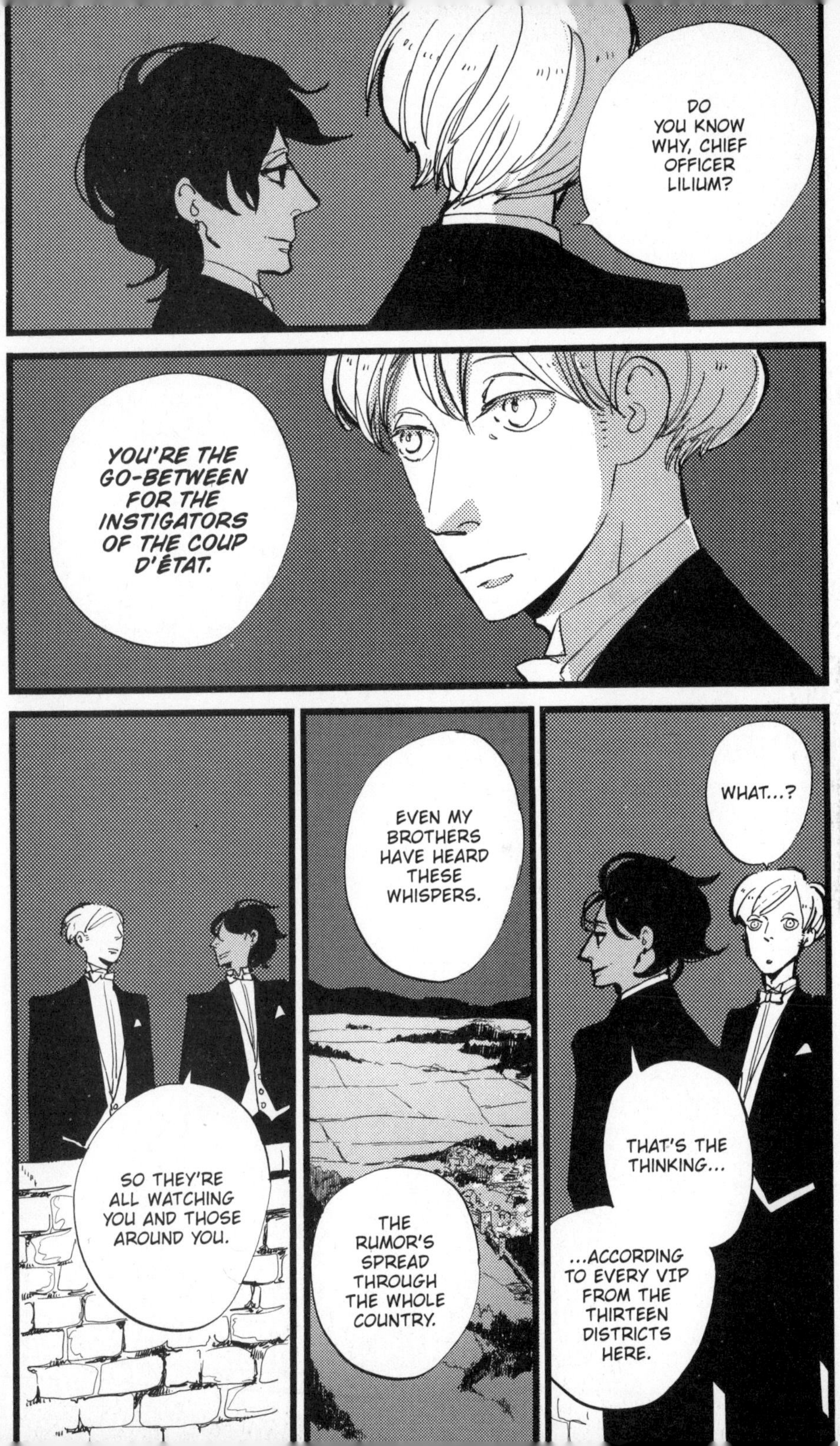
DO YOU KNOW WHY, CHIEF OFFICER LILIUM?
YOU'RE THE GO-BETWEEN FOR THE INSTIGATORS OF THE COUP D'ÉTAT.
WHAT...?
THAT'S THE THINKING...
...ACCORDING TO EVERY VIP FROM THE THIRTEEN DISTRICTS HERE.
EVEN MY BROTHERS HAVE HEARD THESE WHISPERS.
THE RUMOR'S SPREAD THROUGH THE WHOLE COUNTRY.
SO THEY'RE ALL WATCHING YOU AND THOSE AROUND YOU.

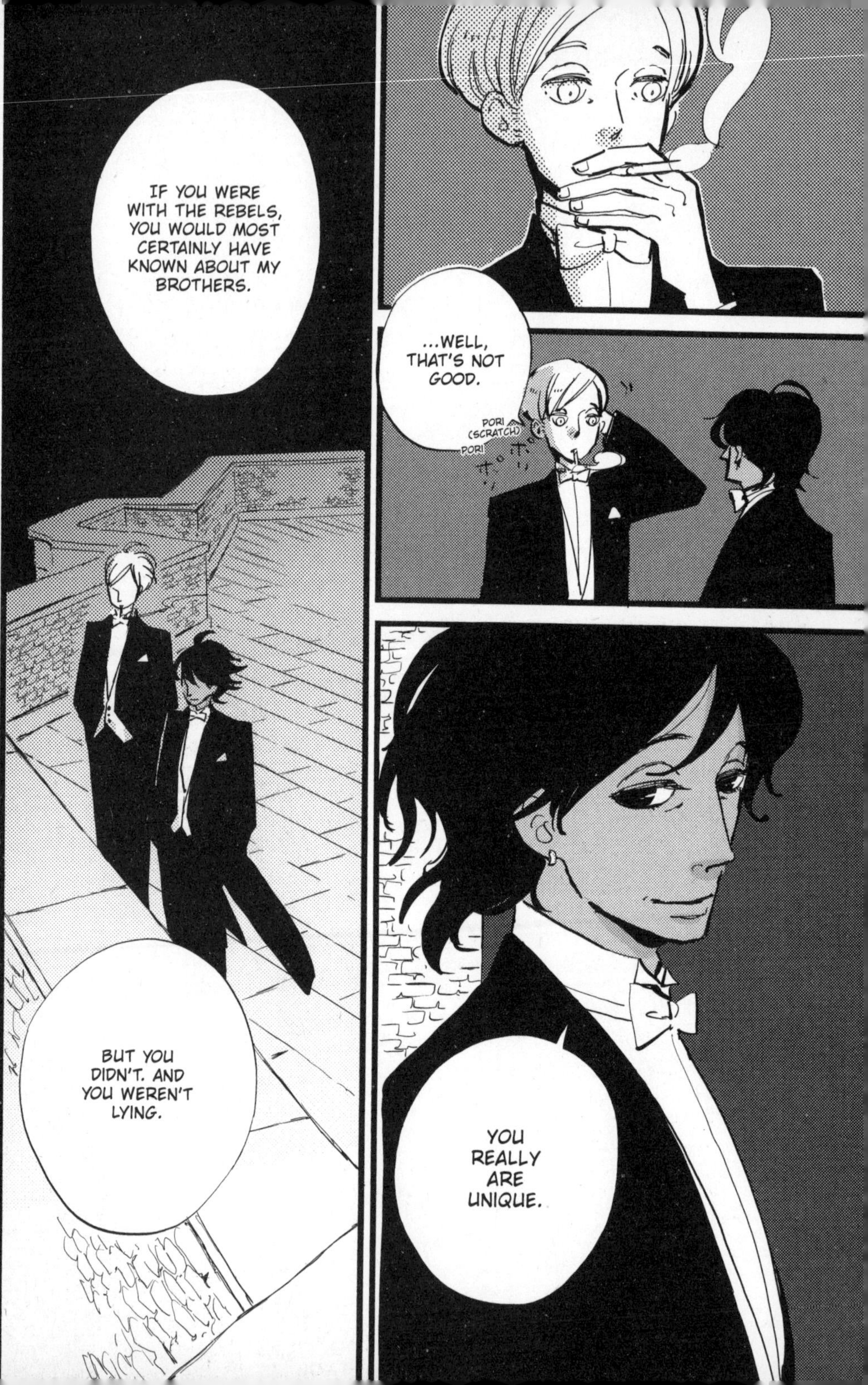
...WELL, THAT'S NOT GOOD.
PORI (SCRATCH) PORI
YOU REALLY ARE UNIQUE.
IF YOU WERE WITH THE REBELS, YOU WOULD MOST CERTAINLY HAVE KNOWN ABOUT MY BROTHERS.
BUT YOU DIDN'T. AND YOU WEREN'T LYING.

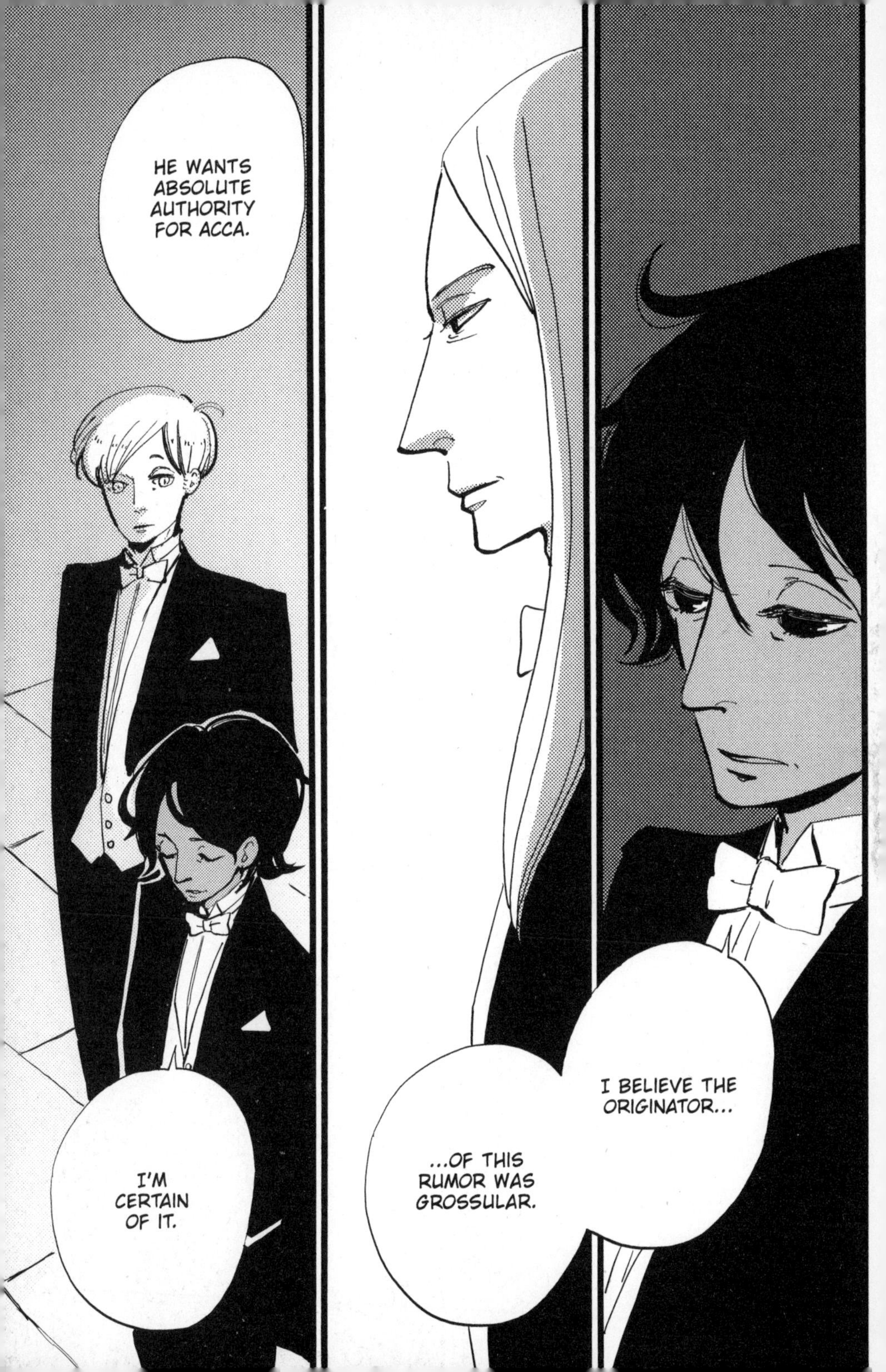
I BELIEVE THE ORIGINATOR...
...OF THIS RUMOR WAS GROSSULAR.
HE WANTS ABSOLUTE AUTHORITY FOR ACCA.
I'M CERTAIN OF IT.

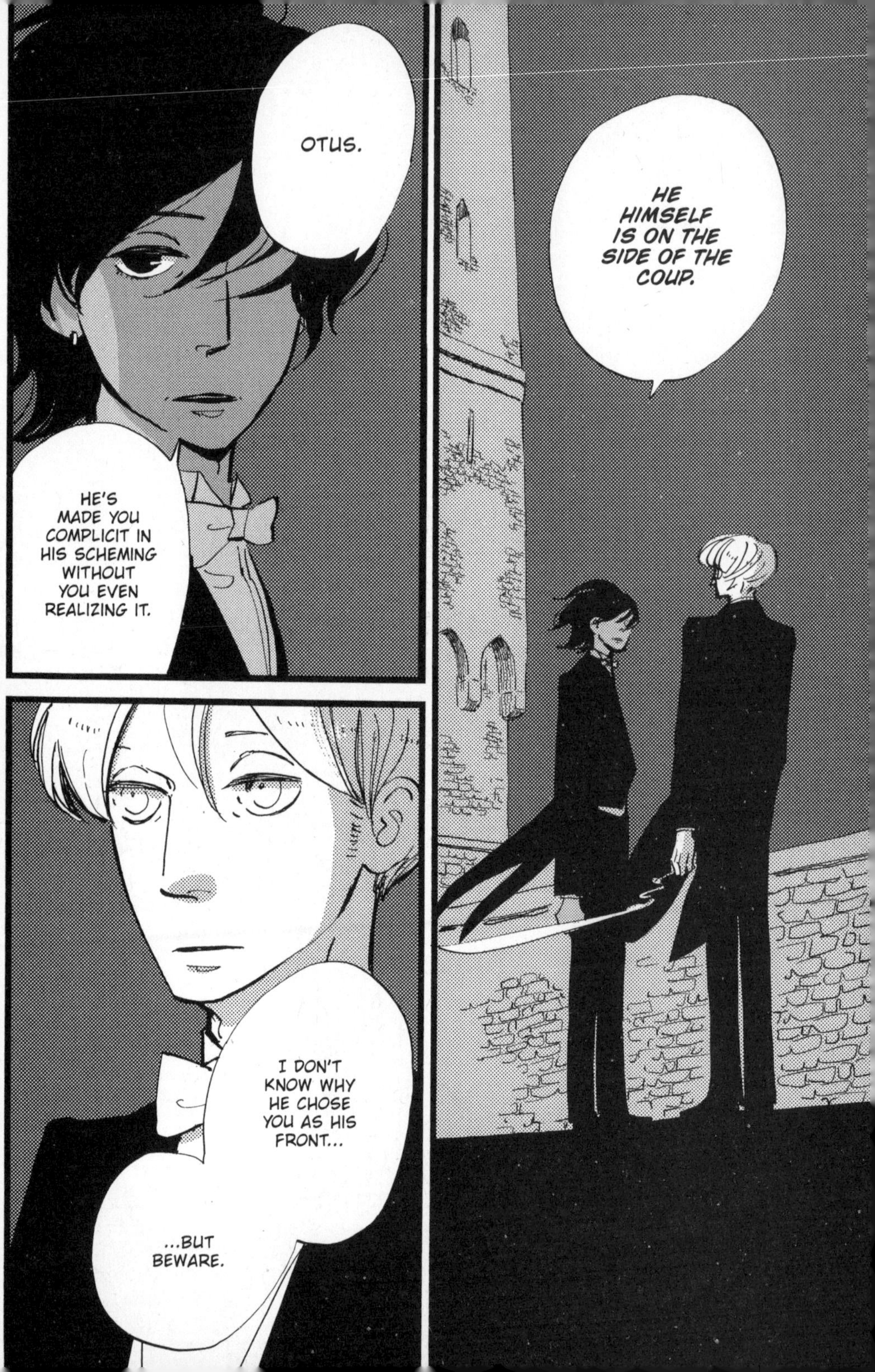
HE HIMSELF IS ON THE SIDE OF THE COUP.
OTUS.
HE'S MADE YOU COMPLICIT IN HIS SCHEMING WITHOUT YOU EVEN REALIZING IT.
I DON'T KNOW WHY HE CHOSE YOU AS HIS FRONT...
...BUT BEWARE.

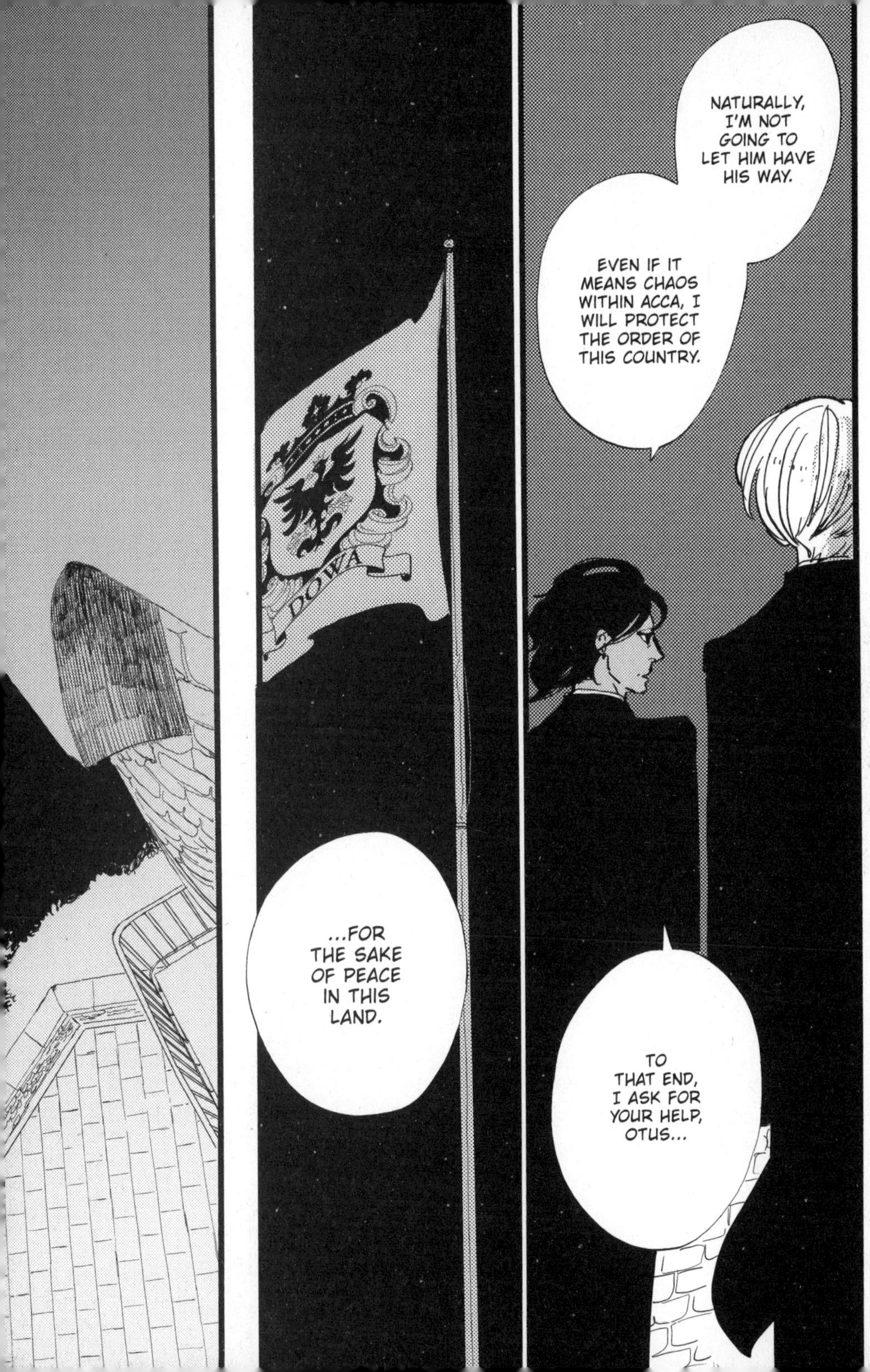
NATURALLY, I'M NOT GOING TO LET HIM HAVE HIS WAY.
EVEN IF IT MEANS CHAOS WITHIN ACCA, I WILL PROTECT THE ORDER OF THIS COUNTRY.
TO THAT END, I ASK FOR YOUR HELP, OTUS...
DOWA
...FOR THE SAKE OF PEACE IN THIS LAND.

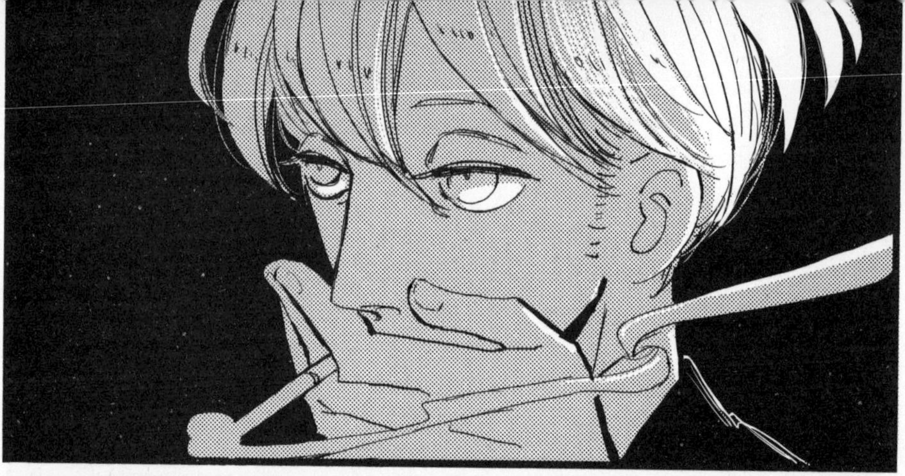

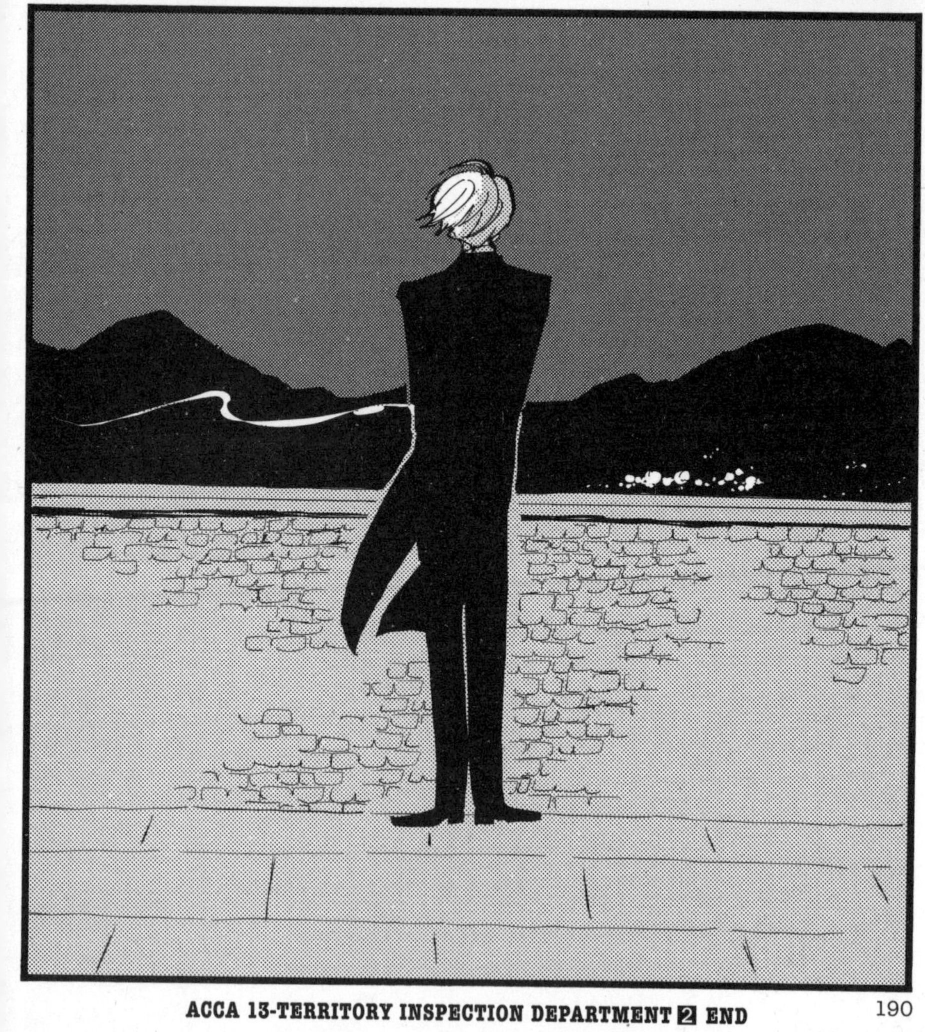

ACCA 13-TERRITORY INSPECTION DEPARTMENT 2 END

Kingdom of Dowa

Dowa, a kingdom with regional self-government, is divided into thirteen districts, with each district having its own unique culture.

ACCA is a massive unified organization, encompassing the police department, the fire department, and medical services, among others. The organization is managed by the branches in each district, with Headquarters in the capital performing the role of uniting the thirteen ACCA branches. The Inspection Department Jean belongs to has Headquarters agents stationed at each branch and also sends a supervisor to audit at irregular intervals in order to monitor the daily operations of the branches.

Birra
Badon
Korore
Dowa
Peshi
Suitsu
Rokkusu
Yakkara
Jumoku
Pranetta
Famasu
Furawau
N
Hare

※ Darker areas on the map are districts where the audit has been completed.

Kingdom of Dowa

DEPT. ACCA 13 TERRITORY INSPECTION

PASS

CHAPTER 11

The Night Breeze and a New Request

Dowa

EXTRA STORY
Papa Knot's Business Trip
FOUR EACH OF THESE AND THESE...
...AND FOUR OF THESE.
SO YOU ALWAYS GET FOUR EACH, HUH?
THREE FOR THE KIDS, ONE FOR YOU?
YUP.
I COULD DO WITHOUT ONE FOR ME, BUT IF I GO HOME WITH THREE...
...MY OLDEST WILL GIVE ME HALF OF HIS.
HERE!
CUPCAKES
AND THEN, THE YOUNGER ONES COPY HIM AND TRY TO GIVE ME HALF OF THEIRS.
SO I HAVE TO GET FOUR.
I WONDER WHY HIS WIFE LEFT...

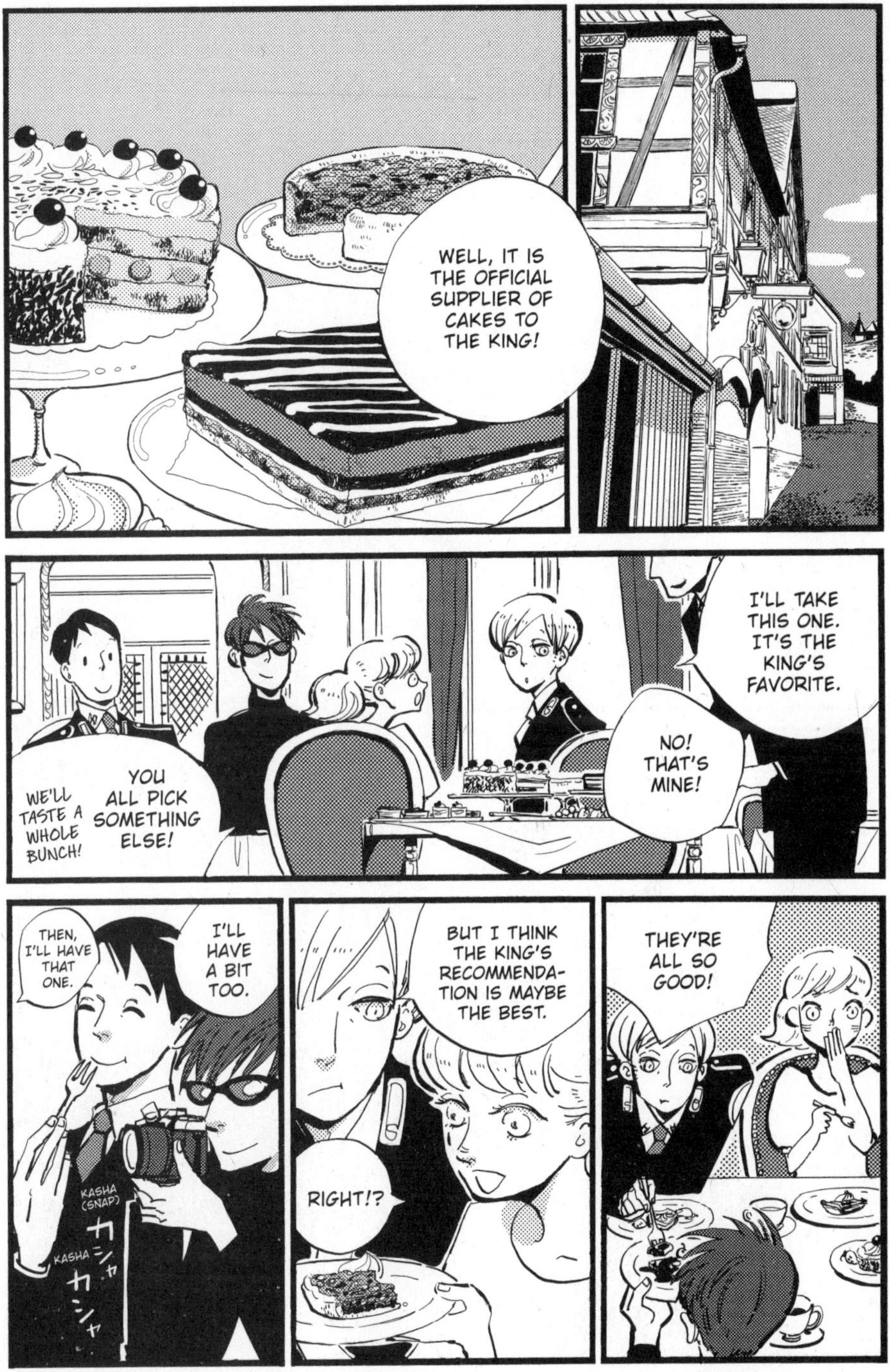
WELL, IT IS THE OFFICIAL SUPPLIER OF CAKES TO THE KING!
I'LL TAKE THIS ONE. IT'S THE KING'S FAVORITE.
NO! THAT'S MINE!
YOU ALL PICK SOMETHING ELSE!
WE'LL TASTE A WHOLE BUNCH!
THEY'RE ALL SO GOOD!
BUT I THINK THE KING'S RECOMMENDA-TION IS MAYBE THE BEST.
RIGHT!?
I'LL HAVE A BIT TOO.
THEN, I'LL HAVE THAT ONE.
KASHA (SNAP)
カシャ
KASHA
カシャ

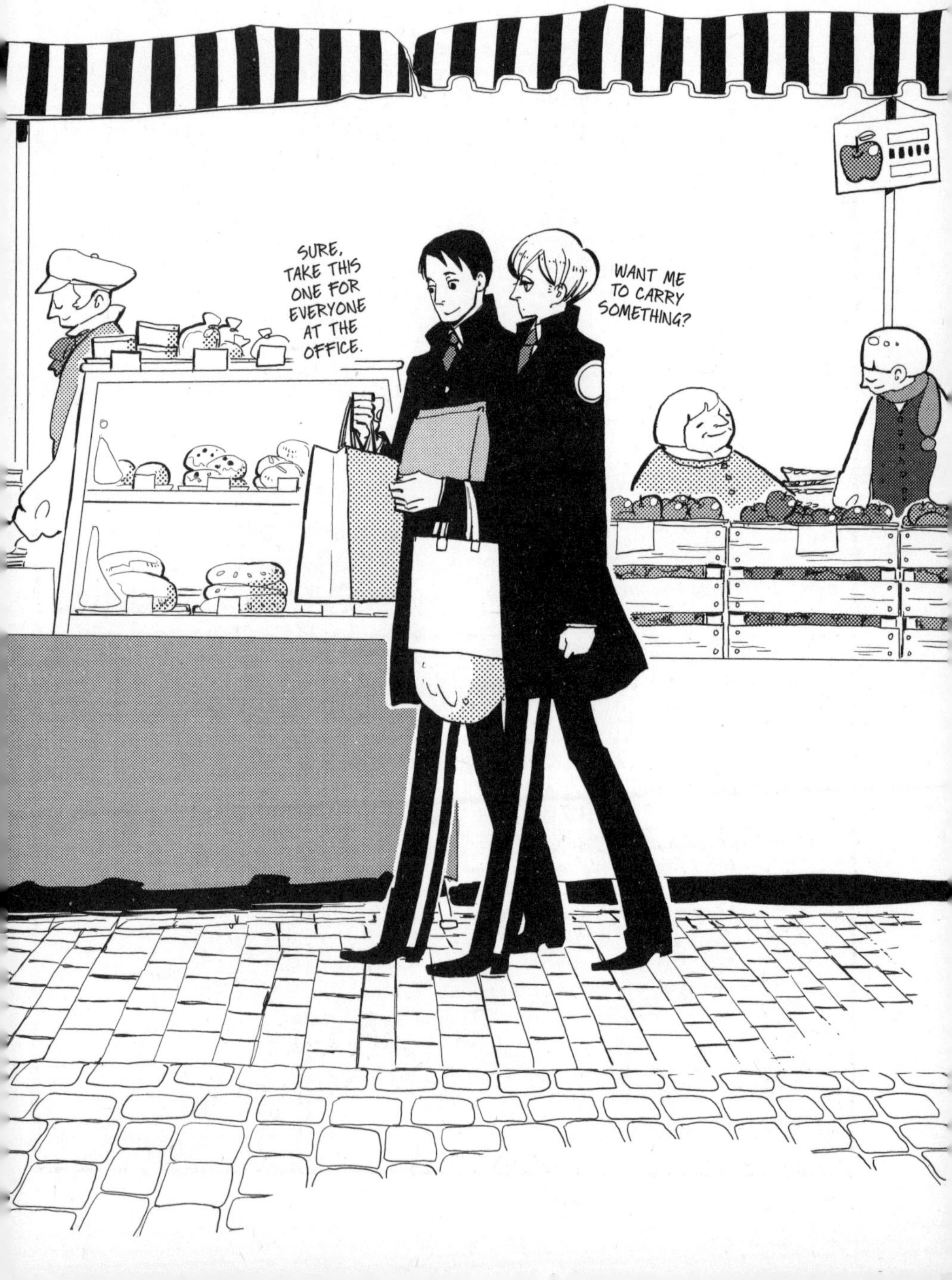
WANT ME TO CARRY SOMETHING?
SURE, TAKE THIS ONE FOR EVERYONE AT THE OFFICE.

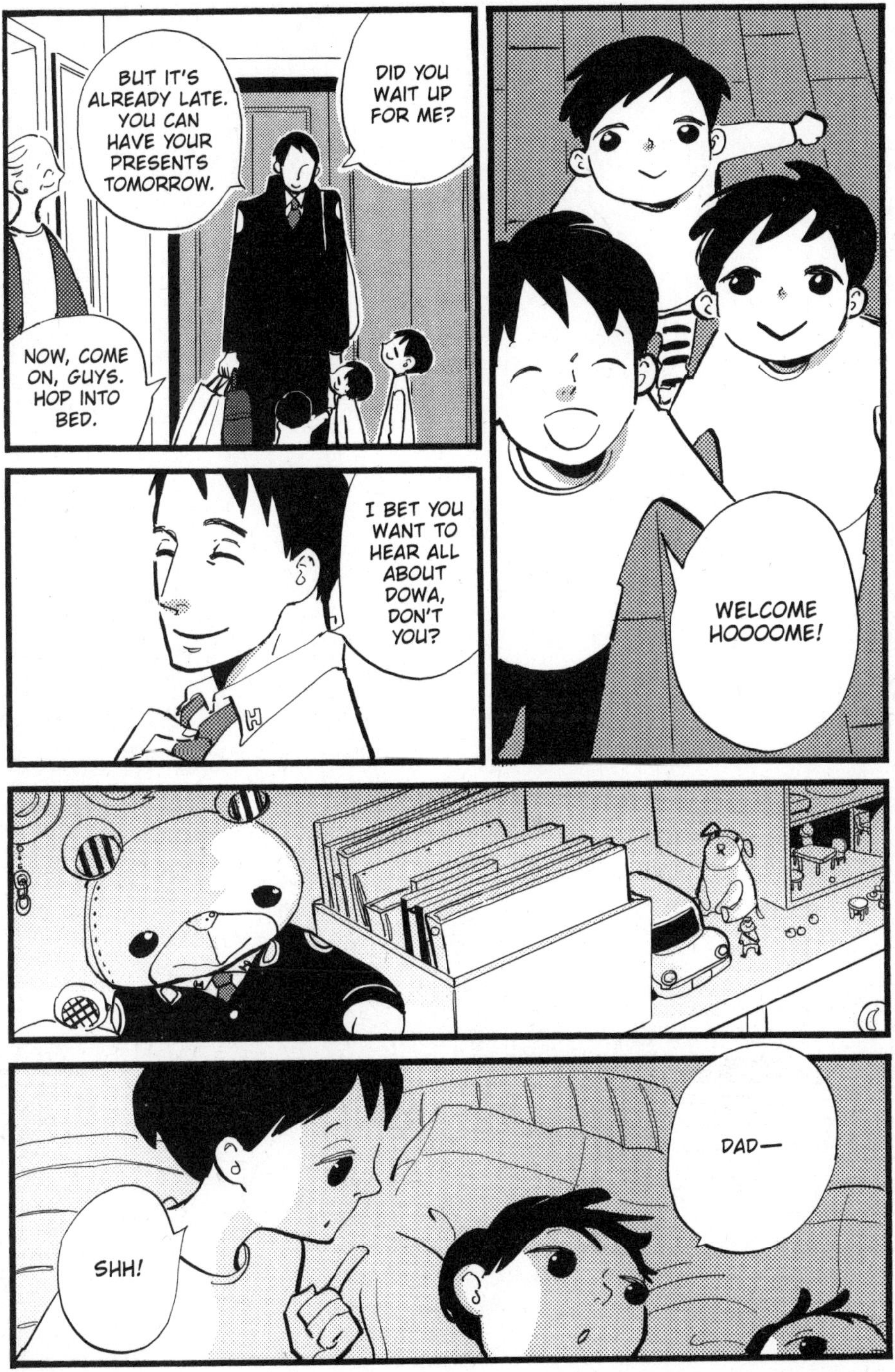
WELCOME HOOOOME!
DID YOU WAIT UP FOR ME?
BUT IT'S ALREADY LATE. YOU CAN HAVE YOUR PRESENTS TOMORROW.
NOW, COME ON, GUYS. HOP INTO BED.
I BET YOU WANT TO HEAR ALL ABOUT DOWA, DON'T YOU?
DAD—
SHH!

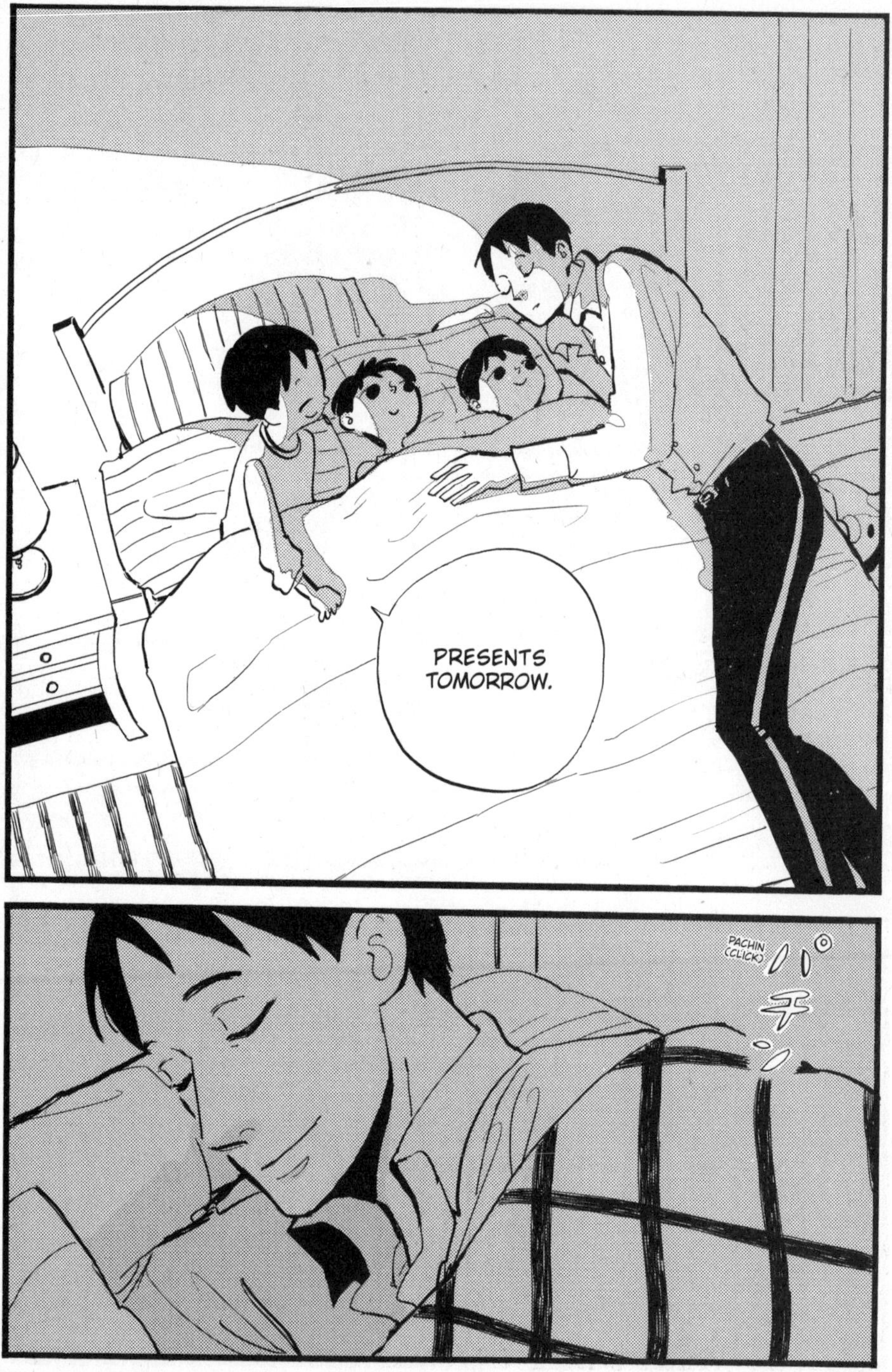
PRESENTS TOMORROW.
PACHIN (CLICK)
パチン

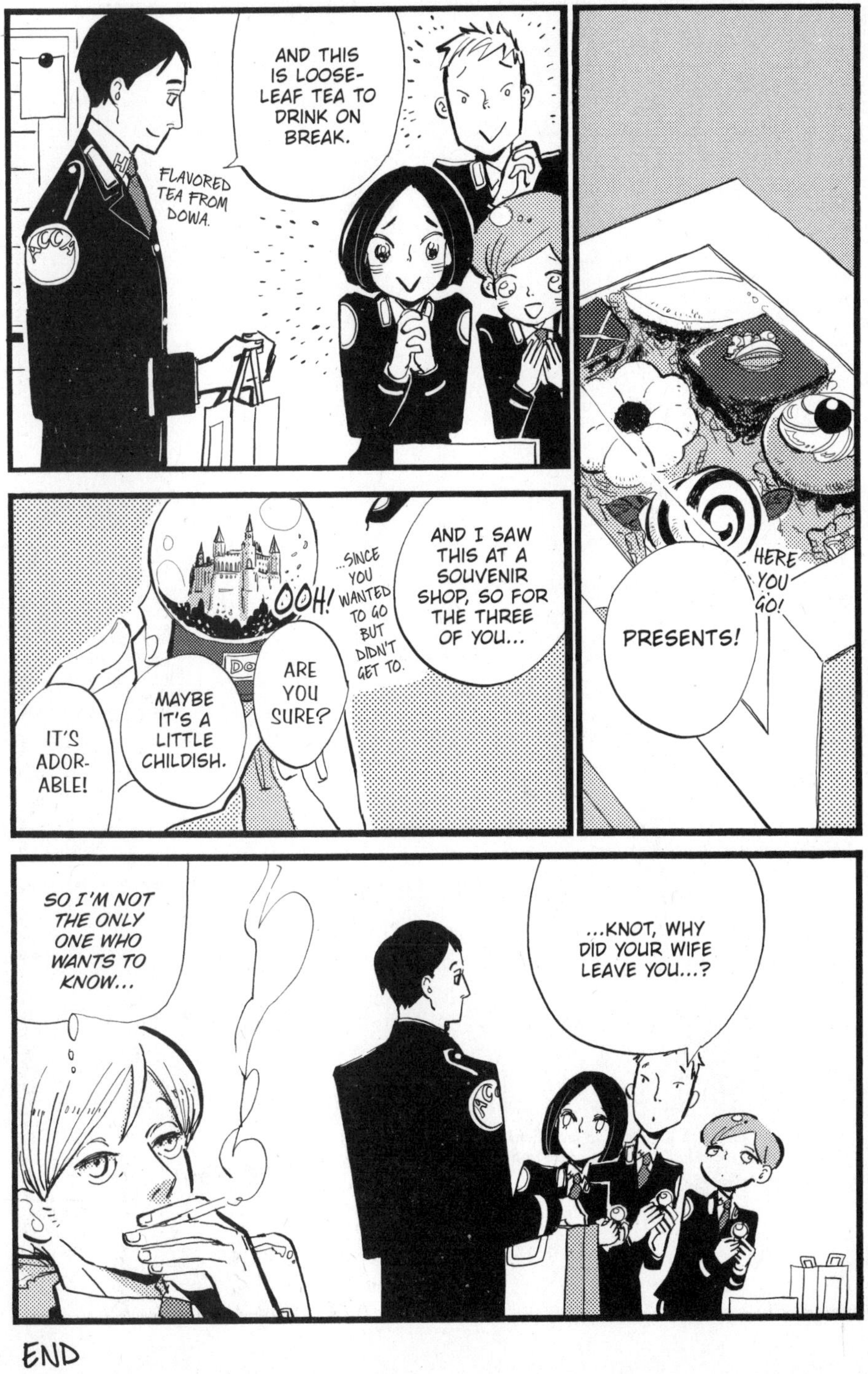
HERE YOU GO!
PRESENTS!
AND THIS IS LOOSE-LEAF TEA TO DRINK ON BREAK.
FLAVORED TEA FROM DOWA.
AND I SAW THIS AT A SOUVENIR SHOP, SO FOR THE THREE OF YOU...
...SINCE YOU WANTED TO GO BUT DIDN'T GET TO.
OOH!
ARE YOU SURE?
MAYBE IT'S A LITTLE CHILDISH.
IT'S ADORABLE!
...KNOT, WHY DID YOUR WIFE LEAVE YOU...?
SO I'M NOT THE ONLY ONE WHO WANTS TO KNOW...

END

ACCA
13 TERRITORY INSPECTION DEPARTMENT

NATSUME ONO

2

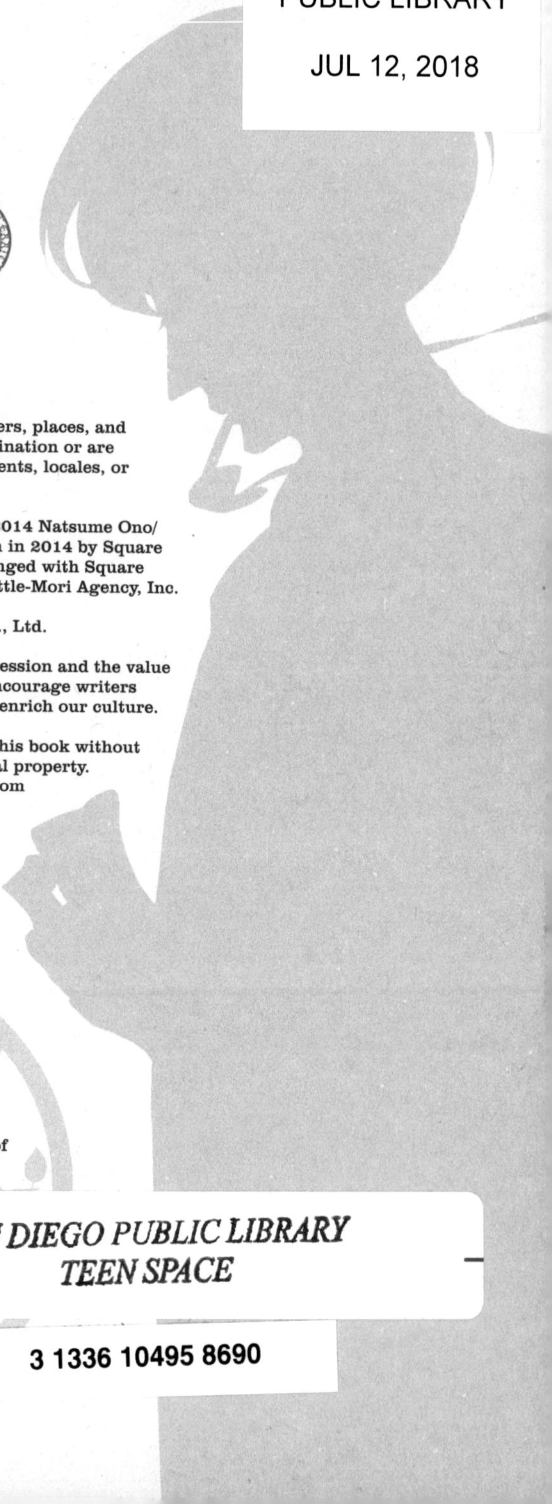

Translation:
Jocelyne Allen

Lettering:
Lys Blakeslee

This book is a work of fiction. Names, characters, places, and incidents are the product of the author's imagination or are used fictitiously. Any resemblance to actual events, locales, or persons, living or dead, is coincidental.

ACCA JUSAN-KU KANSATSU-KA Volume 2 ©2014 Natsume Ono/ Square Enix Co., Ltd. First published in Japan in 2014 by Square Enix Co., Ltd. English translation rights arranged with Square Enix Co., Ltd. and Yen Press, LLC through Tuttle-Mori Agency, Inc.

English translation ©2018 by Square Enix Co., Ltd.

Yen Press
1290 Avenue of the Americas
New York, NY 10104

Visit us at yenpress.com
facebook.com/yenpress
twitter.com/yenpress
yenpress.tumblr.com
instagram.com/yenpress

First Yen Press Edition: March 2018

Yen Press is an imprint of Yen Press, LLC.
The Yen Press name and logo are trademarks of Yen Press, LLC.

The publisher is not respons
content) that are not owned

Library of Congress Control

ISBNs: 978-0-316-41596-5 (p
978-0-316-44677-8 (ebook)

10 9 8 7 6 5 4 3 2 1

WOR

Printed in the United States of America